T

P

2 'ERFORMANCE,

2 TECHNOLOGY,

& SCIENCE

Performance, Technology, & Science

Johannes Birringer

New York, New York

Performance, Technology, & Science is published by PAJ Publications, P.O. Box 532, Village Station, New York, NY 10014.

PAJ Publications is distributed to the trade by Consortium Book Sales and Distribution: www.cbsd.com

Publisher of PAJ Publications: Bonnie Marranca

Cover and book design by Susan Quasha

Library of Congress Cataloging-in-Publication Data

Birringer, Johannes H.
 Performance, technology, and science / Johannes Birringer.
    p. cm.
 Includes bibliographical references and index.
 ISBN-13: 978-1-55554-079-1 (alk. paper)
 ISBN-10: 1-55554-079-1 (alk. paper)
 1. Performing arts—Technique. 2. Performing arts—Technological innovations.
 3. Performance art. 4. Digital media. I. Title.
 PN1590.T43B57 2008
 790.20285—dc22

                     2008020980

                 First Edition, 2008
          Printed in the United States of America

For M.D.

▲▼

I dance, therefore I sense.

—Indian proverb

... and I say this
as I know how to say this
immediately
you will see my present body
burst into fragments
and remake itself
under ten thousand notorious aspects
a new image
undressed
you will
never forget me
when you wear me

—Antonin Artaud remix

Contents

Acknowledgments

Many artists, galleries, performance venues, organizations, and research institutions have helped to make this book a reality, and I owe thanks to everyone who contributed to the creative practices and pioneered the pathways described here. I am grateful to all those who kindly provided the images and illustrations or generously shared their technical expertise during the workshops and performances which are depicted. Most of all, my gratitude extends to all those friends and practitioners who worked with me in many laboratories and artistic productions over the past decade, who invited me to different parts of the world where we could exchange our artistic and research interests in digital performance, or who visited my labs in Columbus, Houston, Göttelborn, Nottingham, and London. The foundation for the practices of artistic production and research were laid in Houston in the 1980s, and I am particularly grateful to all those who supported my work in Texas and participated in the performances and installations of AlienNation Co. (<http://www.aliennationcompany.com>), which became an independent arts organization in 1997. I now divide my time between working with the company and directing the research labs in Germany (<http://interaktionslabor.de>) and at Brunel University (<http://www.brunel.ac.uk/dap>). I therefore must acknowledge the formidable support I received from individuals and government agencies who let me plant an interactive media workshop in an abandoned coal mine, and from my colleagues at the Brunel University School of Arts who shared my research interests in performance technologies and welcomed the introduction of new courses in electronic arts and digital performance into the curriculum. The first testing ground for the introduction of a new MFA in dance and technology presented itself at The Ohio State University from 1999–2003, and without the skepticism and enthusiasm of the dance scholars and students at OSU many lessons would not have been learnt. Introducing the digital into our creative lives is a long and ongoing process, and if the computer presents an anthropological challenge, I am grateful to those who taught me protocols and shared open sources and their stories with me.

I particularly want to thank all the artists and researchers who participated in the Digital Cultures Laboratory and Festival which I organized in
Nottingham (2005) and for which I received funding support from Arts
Council England. In addition, the responses of artists and audience mem-
bers at various venues where I presented versions of my performances and
ideas have been extremely helpful. These venues include the following: Di-
verseWorks, Houston; Aurora Picture Show, Houston; Nordic Solo Forum,
Copenhagen; Performance Studies International Conference, Tempe, Ari-
zona; Real-Time and Presence: Composing Virtual Environments Project,
Trans-Media Akademie and CYNETart, Festspielhaus Hellerau, Dresden;
Dancing with the Mouse NDA Conference, Texas Christian University, Fort
Worth; Cross Fair Symposium, Choreographic Center, PACT Zollverein,
Essen; Intermediale Festival, Mainz; Vogelfrei Biennial, Darmstadt; CORD
Conference, New York University, New York; Wissen schaffen über Tanz,
Gesellschaft für Tanzforschung, Akademie der Künste, Berlin; DanceThe-
Net telepresence forum, Vincent Dance Theatre, Sheffield; Second Interna-
tional Congress on Art and Technology, University of Brasilia; University
of Brasilia Art Gallery; Media Center, Graduate School of Semiotics and
Communication-PUC-University, São Paulo; Subtle Technologies Confer-
ence, Toronto; DEAF/V2 Festival, Rotterdam; Graphite Conference, SIG-
GRAPH, Melbourne; Association of Internet Researchers Conference,
Toronto; ScreenPlay Festival, Nottingham; RePerCute: Reflexiones sobre
Performance, Cultura y Tecnología, Hypermedia Studio, UCLA, Los Angeles; DAMP Lab, V2_Institute of the Unstable Media, Rotterdam; Flesh
Made Text Conference, Aristotle University, Thessaloniki; TransNet Performance and Science Laboratory, Simon Fraser University, Vancouver;
Beijing Dance Academy, Beijing; Real-time, Light, Video and Sound Space
workshop series, Monaco Dance Forum, Monaco; Tanz Anders Wo, Gesellschaft für Tanzforschung, Tanzquartier, Vienna; Synaesthesie und Mul-
timedien Workshop, Universität Erfurt; MotionBound to Virtual Skeleton,
Dance Technology Workshop, Essexdance, Guildford; gage05 conference
on interactive media, Hull Time Based Art Festival, Hull; PARIP, University
of Leeds; SCUDD conference, University of Northampton; Çaty Dance Studio and TECHNE Platform, Istanbul; Wearable Futures: Hybrid Culture
in the Design and Development of Soft Technology, University of Wales,
Newport; Architectures of Interaction Laboratory, Chisenhale Dance Space,

London; In-Between Time Festival, Arnolfini Gallery, Bristol; Performance Space, Sydney; University of New South Wales, Film & Theatre Seminar Series, Sydney; IN TRANSIT Festival, Haus der Kulturen der Welt, Berlin; Performance Studies International Conference, Queen Mary, University of London; Digital Resources in the Humanities and Arts, Dartington College of Arts; Reconfigurations: Points of View on Dance and Technology, Wesleyan University, Middletown; 15th Annual Conference of the Society of Contemporary Theatre and Drama in English, Augsburg; Imagined Landscapes Conference, Cumbria Institute of the Arts, Carlisle; Anthropology Department, Rice University, Houston; Digital Dance workshop, Monaco Dance Festival; Movement, Sound, and Network Project, SARC, Queen's University, Belfast; Boston Cyberarts Festival, Boston; 3rd Annual Moves Festival of Screen Choreography, Manchester; Prague Quadrennial, Prague.

It will become clear throughout the book where personal relationships to artists have been particularly inspiring to me. I obviously owe much to the continuous explorations carried out with members of the Design and Performance Lab in London. I also wish to thank for the continuous and trustworthy support I have received from my editor and publisher, Bonnie Marranca, and for the permission to use some of the materials and earlier versions of essays previously published in *PAJ: A Journal of Performance and Art*, and in other journals, anthologies, and magazines. Finally, I am moved to thank my closest creative partners without whose love and passion none of this work would have been possible.

INTRODUCTION

During the last decades of the twentieth century, a growing number of performing artists in many countries of the world began to experiment with computer-assisted work linking live performance and new technologies. Dancers quickly took on a pioneering role in these experimentations with digital media tools, joining forces with electronic musicians, media artists, and programmers to develop a wide spectrum of new practices. Computer music had set the pace for this development, and the marriage of dance and music, which looks back upon a very long historical relationship, expanded into a new framework for innovative audio-visual compositions using digitally augmented human gestures and expressions. For the text-based theatre, the computational developments seemed to harbor fewer points of access, and thus dramaturgical innovation mostly restricted itself to the incorporation of video and cameras on the stage. The postdramatic theatre, on the other hand, has had a much closer historical and aesthetic relationship to dance, film, and the visual arts, and thus the emergence of multimedia performance in the 1970s and 1980s predates the digital art forms foregrounded in this book. The crucial incursion of the visual arts (and visualization technologies) into performance has in fact made older disciplinary separations redundant.

But my goal for this book is broader and more fundamental. Focusing on the significance of the digital for performance, and looking at various manifestations of a digital aesthetic in contemporary art, it will be necessary to view performance experimentation in close relationship to the scientific and technological imagination, which drives and challenges the new compositional frameworks. Rather than approaching innovative technologies from a scientific point of view, I look at the folds and flows of information in performance and the emerging correlations between aesthetics and science, between the human and the technical. Divided into five sections, the fifteen chapters conclude with a biotechnological perspective on creativity, which provides a fascinating yet troubling commentary on earlier investigations of machine culture, engineering and computation. Compared to the late industrial accomplishments of physics and engineering in the age of space travel, our civilization has reached an era of biocybernetic reproduction in which genetic engineering and the life sciences shape the fundamental discourses of the present century.

While digital technologies have permeated most areas of life and cultural production, socio-political organization and economic activity, this book focuses its lens on performance technologies, and the crucial role of embodied performance in the human-machine interface, as a paradigmatic laboratory for a new aesthetics. The writing is not about virtual realities, therefore, but about a present reality of techno-cultural shifts that have taken place and turned the digital into a mainstream phenomenon. This phenomenon, which we could also call the contemporary technosphere, implies that we not only live with the digital but are informed by the scientific knowledge and information processing systems which underlie human-computer interaction.

Before I analyze more closely what such a digital aesthetics might be, it is helpful to recall the wider historical contexts, the modern developments in science and technology, industry and culture. If one were to write a detailed story of *digital performance*—a term I want to use for performances that depend on the use of digital interfaces—a stronger emphasis on the cultural history of science and invention, informatics, computation, and artificial intelligence would yield a broader but also more refined sense of the folding relations between artistic practices and scientific methods. Regarding the latter, one could think of the research into, and applications of, new visualization techniques in the medical field. Looking at socio-economic, political, ideological and cultural contexts that enable certain kinds of scientific investigation, a cultural historian recently argued that the history of electroencephalography, as an example of the evolution of new inventions in brain research (and interventions into life), demonstrates how electrical technology in the early part of the last century became a mediator in neuroscientific study, and how such "epistemological laboratories" of research brought attention to visualization techniques as the interface between knowledge and its objects. In the same vein, Bruno Latour has drawn much attention to the *mediating* role of laboratories.[1]

Epistemological Laboratories

This book, more intensively than my previous writings on performance and media art, investigates mediator technologies and probes their results in the realm of cultural production, both in regard to the knowledge that is generated and in view of the practical consequences for the ways in which we work as performers, designers, programmers, and composers in the visual domain. As to directing and choreographing, I sense that changes have already taken place in the manner of working which put a question mark behind an older notion of "choreography" and its historical root meaning as a *technology of writing dance* (in Arbeau's *Orchesographie*). The link between *writing dance* and programming an interactive design patch for live performance may be a close one, but the crucial differences in designing a *physical interface* (for wearables or machine vision) will become apparent in the following pages. Choreographing a dance, directing a performance, and composing music for a concert, assume different meanings of "writing" when we turn to digital interfaces and, crucially, to real-time computer processing in interactive art.

The notion of "interactive art," on the other hand, is complementary to my focus on digital performance, and it would be tempting to dedicate an entire book on the evolving practices of "interactivity." Since interactivity relates to most human-computer interfaces, the scope would be rather wide. I limit myself here to the performing arts and their paradigmatic relationship to "new" media, which had existed since the beginnings of photography and film. Today, these recording technologies also have a clear mediator role for analysis and description.

For an overview of the "epistemological laboratories" in technological art, throughout the ambivalent stages of convergence and competition between science and art, research methodologies and cultural practices of aesthetic transformation, one could travel to many sources. Each cross-disciplinary venture ought to be able to find fascinating historical meeting places, currents of ideas and material practices that tell us something about experimentation in design, discovery in industrial manufacture, and conceptual movements in science and technology. Scientific discovery was often reflected in the arts or envisioned in creative applications that were perhaps not practical but liberating, poetically fantastic in the sense in which we think of the power of fantasy in music, literature, film, fashion, and architecture; or the kind of fantasy embedded in games, and in many popular-cultural forms that have created their enthusiastic communities of practitioners and consumers. Once mankind could imagine walking on the moon, the idea of aliens landing on planet earth made more sense, and each epistemological laboratory, if we think of ancient cosmologies and modern space science, would necessarily generate its families of believers and its families of skeptics. In the year before writing this introduction, I witnessed some devastating hurricanes which visited devastation upon human settlements and, consequently, upon one's faith in technocracies and organizational management. When New Orleans drowned, and the invisible men and women began to show up on rooftops and in makeshift shelters without recourse to emergency help, a superficial faith in technological solutions was left shattered but also dropped back behind the more obvious political crises and contradictions that the natural catastrophe revealed. Social cohesion and justice became very thin layers that floated on contaminated waters.

In the same year, 2005, a famous electronic arts festival chose "Hybrid: Living in Paradox" for its theme, declaring its intention to examine the implosive tendencies that digital technologies impose on a globalized world, bringing cultures on top of each other and flouting boundaries: national, material, technological, and psychological. For ars electronica, "hybrid creations and creatures, identities and cultures emerge from recombinations of our three basic codes: numeric, genetic and atomic. Digital media art itself is a hybrid born from the connection of art and technology, accumulating diverse modes of expression and demanding a unique crossover of expertise and knowledge."[2]

The hybrid image printed on the cover of the festival catalog shows a "recombined" human-animal or animal-human, an in-between species walking on hands and legs, a quadrupede-satyr, a robot/cyborg, a transgenic artwork. Such chimeras, strange objects, and alien artifacts have a long history in the religious mythologies and iconographies of many cultures. Deeply embedded in the unconscious, they tend to drive people's libidinal energies in today's hyper-event culture of idols and idolatries. The Italian philosopher Giorgio Agamben has suggested that such hybridity is part of a very long history of messianic thought as well as scientific and anthropological taxonomies. In *The Open: Man and Animal*, Agamben argues that the "human" has always been thought of as a mysterious conjunction of a natural living body and a supernatural, social or divine (non-human) element, and therefore it makes sense to think of the human as that which results from practical and political separations of the human and the not-human.[3]

Today, recombination is a primary process of digital manipulation and of the use of databases. The Critical Art Ensemble spoke of a recombinant poetics in regard to the narrative and fantastic potentials, which began to become apparent in the era of information aesthetics. Writers took notice, and there was an upsurge of interest in hypertext and electronic writing toward the end of the last millennium, soon to be dubbed "digital creativity." The novelist Sue Thomas published her memoires under the title *Hello World: travels in virtuality*, and her publisher had previously released *Cyborg Lives: Women's Technobiographies*, a collection of autobiographical essays looking at women's everyday encounters with an assortment of technologies from CD-ROMs and Web pages to science laboratories, ante-natal screening, nuclear power, and appliances in the home. Not surprisingly, these personal narratives seemed inspired by Donna Haraway's cyborg metaphor, much as contemporaneous sci-fi movies since *Blade Runner* had harvested the fictional universes of Philip K. Dick or William Gibson to probe the baroque recombinations of the human and the not-human and the mysterious darker sides (*The X-Files*) of the forensic dramas which now entertain a mass audience with a clinical, scientific attitude toward crime solving.

The philosophical and political aspects of this "openness" (Agamben) were often neglected during the decades of technocentric enthusiasm, when cyberspace, interaction design, pervasive computing, mobile communications, and the Internet were greeted as if the uncanny networks were a new democratic transcendentalism, and information society an inevitable utopian promise. Another cornucopia has now been hailed for fashion design and its future manufacturing of intelligent clothes with embedded soft technologies. Suzanne Lee, in *Fashioning the Future*, claims that new materials and technologies offer exciting creative possibilities for the design of future wearables: not on the runways, but in laboratories a new fashion landscape of electro-textiles and smart fibres emerges at the intersections of materials science, electrical engineering, chemistry, biotechnology, and nanotechnology.[4]

However, ethical and critical debate also entered these utopian weather forecasts, in some regions and cultural sectors more so than in others. Looking at "Hybrid: Living in Paradox," one notes the care and concern for multiple viewpoints that characterize the investigation of ethno-digital cultures, diasporic subjectivities, and hybrid identities. The emphasis is not on a presumed global village but on accentuating policies of difference, and such policies touch upon life, on the code of life but also on intertwined matter, "real life," on bodies and on what is at stake—the presence of the biological and the biographical that body art had always taken into account. Today, tendencies in biogenetic research are reflected provocatively in a-life (artificial life) and artificial systems: technologies of life and the living creatively employed by artists and technicians who investigate complex behaviors through the modeling, computer simulation, and engineering of biological life.

This techno-scientific research on artificial life, sometimes called art or exhibited in arts contexts, attracted attention around the turn of the century. It probably has gone on for a much longer period of time, before we learned to speak of "transgenic art," as one of the more controversial practitioners, Eduardo Kac, called it. Transgenic art based on code, information, and genetic algorithms is more closely related to the strands of technological art influenced by cybernetics and artificial intelligence, and thus largely indebted to the computer and the growing impact of computer science since the 1960s. There are other strands of a newer avant-garde of practitioners and bio-artists who experiment directly on their bodies, even on the inside of their bodies, and conjoin their phenomenological bodies with tissue cultures or semi-living strange objects nursed in bio-reactors, the new studio spaces of the twenty-first century.[5]

Strange dances I have seen and will report, and postchoreographic processes may show up in biotechnological procedures. For example, *Image-controlled sound nanospheres*, an installation by DS-X.org in cooperation with the Max-Planck Institute of Molecular Cell Biology and Genetics, created for the Digital Cultures festival, reflects visual and acoustic programming performed on/with the emergent behavior of mitotic spindles. It comes no longer as a surprise that some choreographers prefer to cite Maturana and Varela rather than Balanchine or Martha Graham. The influential neurobiologists invented the term *autopoiesis* as a definition of life, arguing that living systems are autopoietic systems as they produce and reproduce their own constitutive elements including the boundaries that separate them from the environment. Now, as I suggested above, we need historians who can create a critical context for the analysis of hybrid systems of organization. My case studies can perhaps make a modest contribution to the critique of the aesthetics of digital composition. The digital, I claim, has altered artistic practices and aesthetic experiences. The current emphasis on *artistic research*, at the same time, reflects a more fundamental alignment with scientific processes and knowledge formation. *Product of Circumstances* (1999), a controversial highlight of the European conceptual dance of the 90s, addresses this alignment critically: French choreographer Xavier Le Roy performs a scientific lecture in which he reflects on his doctoral research in cellular biology while training to become a dancer. Re-enacting his training, he comments on the paradoxes of the science and art worlds, relating how he grew into the two systems, failing at fulfilling their expectations of accommodation and conforming more and more unwillingly to their rules. The outcome is biography as theory. An auto-biologist performs his research in two disciplines, his body displayed as raw material of social and cultural organization under specific conditions of production (regulation).

The fallout from these conceptual performance dilemmas will be apparent in this book. Briefly mapping its contents, I begin with two larger sections addressing conceptual moves involved in performing with technologies. The individual chapters of "Moving through Technologies" provide historical references to dance as well as to the machines of motion (camera, projector), to engineering and design, to theatre and music. They evoke baroque notions of the *Wunderkammer* (wonder cabinet) of the fantastic and the phantasmatic, as human performers, automata, and robots are at times superseded by avatars in artificial digital environments. Again, they touch on software culture, on soft skin and the erotics of performance so often neglected in studies of technology. There is always a subliminal fascination with the tactile dimension of the digital, with its *animate* side in localized feedback. Microcontrollers are intimate hardwares, while *animation* is a theme ranging across a wide spectrum of digital art works. Animation drives the molecular gaze and the microscopic imagination with which artists today observe and cut up their data. Cutting, in filmic terms, is a primary compositional method; cutting up tissue to reach for cells to be observed and made visible is a biological method, and both procedures transform the object under the lens.

In "The Interactive Paradigm" I observe how touching has gained a new sensorial significance, less perhaps for stage performance and more for bodily expressions and rhythms linked to a wide variety of kinaesthetic digital experience on many levels of social and cultural interaction. The notion of interaction, therefore, moves to the center of this book, which traces various modes of organization in interactive systems, wearable spaces and participatory configurations. In the third section on "Environments" I address the relation of the digital to architecture, built and projected environment, installation, fashion, games, and telepresence. The fourth section debates the advances of artificial intelligence and computation while revisiting the crucial aspects of collaborative research in contemporary production. The final section makes forays into science and performance from a perspective that is skeptical of neuroaesthetics and transgenic bio-art but acknowledges the growing significance of molecular biology for any advanced critical understanding of cultural reproduction and cellular performance.

When I write about dance, I keep a close eye on other theatrical and performance practices, and on the new forms of exhibition and distribution. Each of the chapters and the dialogues with practitioners can stand on their own and are interlaced with all the others, as my arguments here do not propose to formulate a full-fledged theory of performance and interactivity but rather address, repeatedly and from different starting points, the many challenging ways in which *interfacial performance* works and how the traditional paradigm of theatre is transformed. These transformations are ongoing, and how lively and diversified the debates are can be attested by the proliferation of digital communication, maillists, Websites, and blogs, which seem to have replaced stage presence with online presence. The contemporary stakes have shifted considerably, and the pathways to the future, along with the fashioning of wearable futures, do not necessarily point toward the theatre and the traditional concert stage (Zygmunt Bauman thinks of the latter as *zombie institutions*). They may very well point to the screen, the Internet, and the many runways and niches in the diversified markets of musical cultures, sports, game cultures, and lifestyles. The pathways to the future, it is commonly assumed, run across a globalized world, and even though artists rarely participate directly in the activism of non-governmental organizations or in policy decision-making, they engage in ongoing cultural and transcultural collaborations, dialogue, and the exchange of knowledge. Thus they contribute to a deeper understanding of the political dynamics of collaboration and the role media technologies play in the making of social networks.

Contemporary practitioners, developers, scientists, and theorists from the disciplines that contribute to digital performance work on many platforms and in many contexts. The main characteristic of the digital is its potential to appear in variable and multi-platform outputs. It is a ubiqui-tous border-crosser. One of the more persistent questions here addresses the shift in artmaking toward interactive systems, utilities, and environments, and thus to the programming, as well as the programmability, of virtual constellations that move us to action. Performance, and dance in particular, in this sense is a virtual event, very happily ephemeral and not exhausted at all, constituted within a matrix of possibilities, an aesthetic but primar-ily synaesthetic process unfolding in a corporeal-cognitive space. The tech-niques of interaction have begun to imply a shift from form to experience, and they are examined here because I believe them to be paradigmatic of a new understanding of embodied digital performance. The post-millennial art viewer encounters dramatically synaesthetic and kineaesthetic scenarios. If art and performance will be technological, then synaesthetic processes and corporeality need to be analyzed through new behaviors that reinte-grate body-mind consciousness and sensory functions through electrical, electronic, and digital means.

Performance Processing: The Digital Laboratory

In the mid-90s, I began to direct workshops on performance technolo-gies, incorporating new compositional ideas and instruments such as cam-eras, video-projectors, sensors, or computer software. By the turn of the century, many interests in related fields (film, digital arts, science and tech-nology, design, engineering, medicine, telecommunications) furthered an understanding of complementary thinking processes that drive new inter-disciplinary research and conceptual models influenced by the computer's information processing capabilities and the Internet's global reach. Working in the expanded tradition of site-specific, conceptual, and performance art, I embraced the sense that performance is process, that it is collaborative, and it never meant relying on one specific technique or vocabulary. At the same time, the conjunctions of performance and technology, like the folding of digital code and biology, required working with a whole spectrum of new toolsets, and new tools and interfaces result in new techniques of use.[6]

Performance organically extended its reach: stage composition and choreog-raphy became design which included spatial and virtual environments, sculp-tures, moveable light, video projection, cameras and motion detection systems, sensors, and live-processed electronic music. Performance designers, just like film editors, Net artists and DJs, had to sample and mix their tracks, shuffle online and offline experience, compose with data space, lags, asynchronized and dispersed time, signal processing. It stands to reason that nothing would be the same again, as many performers gradually left the proscenium stage and found older production processes inadequate. New performance, involving technologies and interactive design from the conceptual starting point, needed a different environment for its evolution. This book addresses some aspects I consider crucial for an understanding of digital performance, and thus also the roles of the "laboratory," digital strategies, site-specificity, networked performance, software-as-culture, processing, and real-time composition, and especially the physical aspects of interaction with sensory technologies. The term "laboratory" is not just understood as an experimental space of innovation, but also as a conceptual space.[7]

The significance of technology-centered workshops for the trajectories of digital performance practices cannot be overestimated. In the course of the following chapters I will come back to such workshops and the specific laboratory conditions for experimentation they set up. Sometimes outside of the traditional dance, theatre, music, and art schools, but sometimes also within academic institutions supporting "avant-garde" experimentation, these conditions have been vital for the growth of digital research. International workshops and residencies, which bring practitioners from various fields together for intense periods of experimentation and tool sharing, are vital for the development of new digital performance techniques. The role of collaboration—in *its* impact on how artists incorporate technologies— needs to be studied carefully in order to outline a topology of the complicated foldings between the corporeal and the digital that constitute the new performance aesthetic. The "language" of new media, as Lev Manovich called the aesthetic apparatus emphasizing the particular characteristics of the digital image and its relationship to earlier cinematic or photographic languages, is a language of forms that needs to be applied and tested in an evolving process. But this unfolding, for example in digital microsound art, implies re-processing of already processed data (sound signal)—a continuous remixing and redistribution of mutating tracks.

How the processes of working with software technologies can change artistic output, how the digital affects artists working in different cultural locations and infrastructures, or how the continuing work with the digital can re-orient a software artist such as Thecla Schiphorst toward the kind of physical-sensory production she is interested in today—these are some of the questions that drove me to organize an international laboratory on "Digital Cultures"(November 28–December 4, 2005) in the UK. "Digital Cultures" linked workshops, demonstrations, and research experiments with public exhibitions, directing attention to new work from Indian, Japanese, Latin American, North American, Afro-Caribbean, Eastern and Western European artists. The meeting was staged as a catalyst for cross-cultural research into different approaches to, and perceptions of, digital performance cultures. A language of new media has been learned, but it is not a common or neutral language. Rather, embodying knowledge and learning how new categories and concepts are derived from the computerization of culture suggest processes that make us more fully aware of differentials, and of recombinable sources in the (traditions of) cultural expressions.[8]

I believe the following chapters are instilled by the same spirit of collaboration. Digital composition and the programming of interactive environments signal a fundamental break with earlier conventions of compositional practice for the stage. Examining many of the newly emerging dimensions of mediated and interactive performance, the initial chapters elaborate the break and its consequences for our aesthetic understanding of the performing arts within new virtual and networked environments. They place their analyses into the transdisciplinary context of current debates over the materiality of the digital and the distributed aesthetics of interactivity. After a careful exploration of interactivity, the subsequent sections of the book trace new applications of digital practices in diverse art forms and cultural productions that intersect with the scientific study of motion, bodily expression, gesture, sensing and sense perception, cognition, memory, and feedback.

This study can be regarded as an introduction to a new field, written from the experience of deep practical engagement with evolving dance and performance technologies, as well as from a sustained thinking process about collaborative experiments with artists or researchers arriving at this work from different cultural contexts and methodological backgrounds. In earlier writings I looked for political activism driving such work, I am now more modestly advocating a collaborative cultural model that harbors an organizational method with political ramifications, but it is primarily research- and production-oriented. And it survives because of the energies and the passions of the people who pursue creative work. The book makes reference to numerous digital works, which suggest avenues for performance research in the twenty-first century. These works were created through transcultural collaboration and networked practice on the one hand, and from specific cultural locations on the other. The temptation to assume the homogenizing universality of technical codes (hardware/software, programming languages) and media-driven "globalized culture" is resisted here, and attention is given to different environments of production and local cultural differentiation, even though I cannot include all of the conversations recorded over the past ten years.[9]

The last two chapters evoke scientific models yet also try to see performance as a model, placing it in a social and cultural context of *human sensory activities*. This allows stepping outside some of the rather unproductive debates over what may constitute performance or live art. As technology research and development in both academic and industry settings move forward toward a future filled with multisensory interfaces and feedback devices, my analysis of the applicability of these new technologies provides a context in which the philosophical, social, and cultural implications of the digital can be debated as well. This new focus also opens up a broader discussion of *design* and of the *user* both in the contexts of interactive real-time processing (pervasive computing) and the fashion/textile design practices. Performing the "wearables" will be a journey of transformation from the analog performer to the digital performer.

Technology has decisively challenged bodily boundaries and spatial realities, profoundly affecting the relations between humans and machines. In the cognitive neurosciences, increasingly sophisticated neuroimaging techniques such as functional magnetic resonance imaging or positron emission tomography allow for distinct localizations of brain activity, while neuropsychology and clinical studies provide insight into the neural bases of motor recognition, motion coherence, self location, and embodiment. The convergence between performance and technology reflects back on the nature of movement and behavior, and particularly on the nature of "body" and our understanding of its objecthood or identity; its organization and augmentation; its physical-sensory relationship to space and the world; its immediate, phenomenological embodiedness but also the inseparability of its embodiment from the technical. Stimulation and (mirror) simulation are now scientific and artistic concepts. Whether we are in a rehearsal studio, on the stage, or in our daily habitats, we are still in place(s) among other moving bodies when we move around and interact. Navigation, a term derived from sea travel, is now widely used for journeys in virtual space and non-localizable domains. If most humans never had trouble localizing themselves within their own bodily borders, as Olaf Blanke (Lausanne Laboratory of Cognitive Neuroscience) has suggested, this sense of self location is a fundamental aspect of self consciousness and specific mental imaging. But what if the brain mechanisms required for multisensory integration of bodily regions are subject to continuing pressure or re-adaptation? What if extreme mobility, now understood in its technical and communicational sense, has affected our entire experience model?

That model now is largely technologically framed, and performance, in the broadest sense, obtains constantly evolving inputs (data) for various kinds of behavior, which enact what we can call bodily connectivity. In telepresence, I localize myself outside of my bodily boundaries. Like astronauts in microgravity, the telepresent performer lacks a stable sense of gravity. Artistic practices that respond to technical interaction in our lives have absorbed technology as a creative tool, affording performers and designers the opportunity to explore distributed environments, virtual places, and hyperconductivity. An entirely new poetics emerges when performers "navigate" interactive environments, dive into data-based information, play with digital cameras and wearable sensors; when the body becomes an instrument of a dynamic environment in which realities are generated and processed.

It can be argued that all performance traditions and their contemporary practices deploy models or maps of movement protocols and movement behaviors. What is new in contemporary art is the deliberate exploitation and critical examination of the correlation between movement, gesture, action, expressive behavior, etc., and their computational analysis—the computing models which observe the human and reorganize the data in the digital environment which, in turn, is sensed and experienced in continuous, successive dialogue (feedback loop and generative extenuation). The convergence of interface design and action observation (as it is called in the cognitive science approach) extends earlier structural explorations of the body's kinaesthetic repertoire. Interactive art also challenges the separation of work and audience, and this is no small matter for anyone accustomed to the traditions of theatre, concert music, film, and museum exhibitions. Bluntly put, in interactive art there is no audience but, strictly speaking, only users and interface participants. But the joys and drawbacks of participation will have to be carefully examined, and in the second half of the book I look at a few examples of "performed interactivity" and the new social rituals of user-participation, complemented by dialogues with artists who comment on the aesthetics and politics of digital production. Clearly there is a scientific dimension to this debate, but in artistic communities this dimension is not always addressed in sufficient depth to enhance a critical creative dialogue. As I suggested earlier, we live in the age of the laboratory. Artists work in art labs and have residencies in science labs, scientists increasingly join artists in collaborative "Research and Development" projects, and universities desperately try to merge disciplines or create transdisciplinary research centers and digital learning environments. Some artists have worked for quite some time on discovering alternate "architectures" of the body or proposing new modes of engagement with the physical, the cellular, and the microbiological. Scientific theory and the current interest in neurobiology and biotechnology have inspired notions of emergence now used widely in digital performance, yet it is not easy to point to provocative artistic projects involving biofeedback and EEG technologies that yielded insight into how the distribution of neurochemical systems in the brain are possibly affected by particular actions or movement expressions. Such insights, however, would not be gained on a stage or in a gallery, but only in a laboratory under conditions of a controlled experiment.

Emergence

There is no claim made here for the need to make art into scientific research or to ask for its problem-solving capabilities. But this book does claim the appearance of a wide range of interdisciplinary digital practices, which draw on the collaborative contributions of scientists and hard- and software engineers. From an artistic standpoint, digital performance and real-time interactivity need to develop a new body of critical cultural and aesthetic reflection—opening up its compositional languages and characteristics, its informational aesthetics, to a wide international audience interested in ideas and sensory experiences that move them. Participation in new art forms is not assumed but will be learned and adopted as their codes become more conventional. From a scientific standpoint, if human agency in reception and participation with complex systems produces emergent behavior, how can such behavior of interacting participants be analyzed or measured in regard to patterns and coherences in the productivity of the content for the aesthetic experience? Quality of experience deriving from constantly variable data and dynamically generated constellations would not be easily "controllable," however, and emergent aesthetics seem to provide particular experiences of patterns and symbolic or narrative resolutions that are nor predefined since they are, of necessity, transient. New description techniques for such transience and individually and collectively changeable content-generation are needed.

Can digital performance become a new social dance or a new intellectual or political theatre for the Scientific Age, as Bertolt Brecht once requested? Is performing with multimedia objects and databases an emerging aesthetic practice connecting process-orientation with radical and surprising potentialities which hyper-sensitize the audience, making their co-authorship and cooperation tangible? Sensitization to the digital environment and a focus on processual interaction are a major concern in all the artworks discussed below. With the rise of telepresence and distributed interaction, we can also speak of social and aesthetic experiences of being connected, if connectivity is the condition from which new mediums (interactivity, humans, media, tools, and artefacts all understood here as "mediums") are generated in the shared process of manipulating information. In such conditions, space and local context tend to become dematerialized, and I will argue that "site-specificity" gains other meanings when our actions and movements are captured, commuted, transfered and rematerialized elsewhere. To program interfaces between performers and the computer implies the creation of an unstable, open system where control parameters can be continually negotiated if collaborative interaction is the desired aesthetic effect.

Audiences are of course familiar with improvisational techniques. In complex open systems, composition or choreography will more closely resemble the improvisational "live mix" we experience in techno culture when DJs create a situation, a combinatory sound continuum, and use filter devices to modify the parameters in response to energy that is transferred between dancers and musical stream. The intensities of the event develop a kind of autopoiesis of overlapping self-organizations, as the dancing crowd and the DJ's audio machines feed off each other. In performances with interface designs based on wireless feedback information in real-time, the temporal dynamics and behavioral processes become an emergent system that is highly charged, from a human point of view, as symbiotic improvisation with the environment is open-ended and precarious.

How, then, do we introduce emergence as a critical concept into the performing arts? "In the posthuman view," N. Katherine Hayles suggests, "conscious agency has never been 'in control.' In fact the very illusion of control bespeaks a fundamental ignorance about the nature of the emergent processes through which consciousness, the organism, and the environment are constituted. Mastery through the exercise of autonomous will is merely the story consciousness tells itself to explain results that actually come about through chaotic dynamics and emergent structures." It follows, she argues, that "emergence replaces teleology; reflexivity replaces objectivism; distributed cognition replaces autonomous will; embodiment replaces a body seen as a support system for the mind; and a dynamic partnership between humans and intelligent machines replaces the liberal humanist subject's manifest destiny to dominate and control nature." Extending Bateson, Gibson, Hofstadter and other scientific studies of consciousness, Hayles sees "distributed cognition" of the human subject in correlation to the distributed cognitive system as a whole, in which thinking is done by "both human and nonhuman actors."[10]

Some of the terms used here will be familiar to anyone who has followed scientific debates in informatics and the cognitive fields. The implications of emergent social behaviors, communication skills, and aesthetic play derived from collaborative interaction are critical for a description of dynamic properties in performance systems that combine human actors and machine actors, embodied enaction and machinic processes. It is also hardly avoidable, in a study of such performance systems, to address the technical accomplishments of real-time media, computer processing, mapping, and artificial intelligence, and thus to correlate coding—and the role of software—as a form of "writing" the mediation between the mathematics and physics in computer code and embodied enaction. It is this mediation, artistically speaking, which guides the parameters of composition and what the operating environment will be. If Cage or Cunningham, half a century ago, spoke of chance operations, today choreographers and performance designers use a vocabulary that is highly fluent with mathematical and algorithmic operations. In fact, William Forsythe's well-known CD-ROM *Improvisation Technologies* (1999) offers an entire methodological meta-system of analytical approaches to choreographic principles fully cognizant of the performer's adaptation to the temporal possibilities of movement foldings and unfoldings, the mind's plasticity.

Contingencies in an ensemble's enactment of principles thus appear very relevant with respect to the phenomena I have mentioned, namely *emergent behavior* and *distributed cognition* within collectives that are connected through discrete events and unpredictable transformations of the malleable medium. The medium—performance, sound, image, space, real-time—is multiplicative. The multiplication of operative parameters in contemporary computational performance requires new critical approaches to such an understanding of "system design," and the question of *control* becomes an aesthetic one, without losing its scientific and political implications. It is also apparent, then, that the notion of *design* must be subjected to careful scrutiny, as it has gained a crucial role in artistic practices today but resonates with paradox. If emergent phenomena are unforeseen and beyond logical prediction, then an emergent aesthetic cannot be engineered. At the same time, whether we think of Robert Wilson's theatre, Laurie Anderson's or Cynthia Hopkins' multimedia music performances or Artificial Life art such as Tania Fraga's, Eduardo Kac's or Christa Sommerer's and Laurent Mignonneau's installations, the construction of complex systems always seems to work with constraints that allow the opening of passages to a dynamic, unpredictable world of which the micro-levels themselves are a part. Brazilian artist Tania Fraga works with precise numerical data, functions, relations, and logical operations in the construction of her computerized simulations of virtual and interactive 3-D objects (seen in depth with stereoscopic devices). But as the viewer moves into the 3-D world of perceptive phenomena, illusory phenomena are apprehended which transgress the laws of physics and provide unexpected sensorial experiences. When I first encountered her artificial world and performed in it, I was stunned with pleasure, slowly realizing that the phenomena I experienced did not correspond to my normal experience of mechanical and gravitational laws in the physical world.

Intangible illusions occur in the mind, and this is how we are drawn to the arts and to performance. Dance, closely associated with visual forms and rhythms, is fundamentally a multimedia system, just like theatre performance. Since the beginning of photography and motion studies, performances were staged exclusively for the camera. Eadweard Muybridge's serial photographs of the human figure in motion, originally intended as a scientific study, were first published in 1887, and they became a famous source book for artists, animators, and filmmakers. In the motion capture studio of the Computer Engineering building where I work, Muybridge's *The Human Figure in Motion* is on the shelf with 3-D Studio Max, Motion-Builder, and Maya manuals. After motion studies, filmmakers and chore-ographers discovered that dance on film is a composite medium in its own right; that choreography is editing of frames. Making dances for the camera became not only a cinematographic alternative to live dance, but motivated choreographers to re-conceive the aesthetics of dance for the theatre. The impact is evident in the cinematic quality of many contemporary works. The Japanese companies Dumb Type and OM2 literally use no less than six simultaneous screen projections in their performances of *Memorandum* and *The Convulsions of Mr K.* Frédéric Flamand's *La Cité Radieuse* turns all available moveable stage architectures into screen spaces, billboards and video rooms. Digital video effected a transition in two directions, opening up a new screen space for movement images (e.g., music television), and bringing new ideas of nonlinear editing to the practice of composition and interactive design in the theatre.

These openings, transitions, and augmentations of performance into plen-tiful systems form the core of this book which, in the first section, traces a brief historical journey of multimedia performance to arrive at an overview of some of the most widely used artistic applications of *interfaces* at the turn of the century before elaborating different types of interactive performance environments and architectures of the real and the virtual. This allows me to look at performances that are increasingly difficult to categorize but of-fer challenging perspectives on processes of embodied cognition in motion, related directly to contemporary realities of wireless technologies that have entered everyday cultural realms. At the same time, various materials (hard-ware, software) and multimedia architectures are examined with regard to performer practice, perception systems, and themes that emerge through the referent of real-time in human-machinic interaction—a deferred object of deep concern, as much as technogenesis is a symbol of our essential re-lationship to time, life, and death, which runs through many artworks and heightens our understanding of what Maria Beatriz de Medeiros, following philosophical tradition, has termed *aisthesis*.[11]

This sensing-perceiving relationship to the world, apparently threatened and yet enhanced by the constant advances in scientific research and techno-logical engineering in the age of biocybernetic reproduction, recurs in many guises of performance, wildly shifting in extremes from Stelarc's enaction of prosthetic selfhood treating the "hospitable" body as an extended, evolutionary operational system to a younger generation of women performers like Kira O'Reilly who cut into their body tissues, exploring microbiological procedures and trans-species metamorphoses (taking living cells out of the body); from Thecla Schiphorst's designing "experience models" and electrical engineering processes to create sensual gestural protocols for interaction used in sensored garments to Olu Taiwo's explorations of dynamic temporal space in the curvatures of West African rhythm linked with spiritual philosophies of collective interactivity. Taiwo stresses the importance of the "return beat" for his performance of transcultural identity, memory, and psychophysical perceptions (his interface with the orichas and ancestral spirits). Similarly, Indian choreographer Jayachandran Palazhy, who in his recent stage performance *Purusharta* collaborated with Japanese real-time sound and graphic programmers, confidently returns the most advanced computational interfaces to the basic training ground of his craft: the Indian physical traditions and body techniques, now conjoined with different physicalities, movement approaches, and conceptual tools from a globalizing world in which are embedded "our continuities of civilizational knowledge."[12]

With its emphasis, less on individual dancers, choreographers, directors, or composers, but rather on environments and the various design templates, which are, in most cases, created through collaborative teamwork and with audience interaction in mind, this book envisions an aesthetics of production which differs from stage productions of the past and from academic training practices (in the present). Based on years of sustained research undertaken during the time I was invited to create the first dance and technology graduate program in a university in the United States, and based on the experience of the Environments Laboratory I conducted during these years, in networked cooperation with partners in Latin America, Europe, Canada, Japan, and Australia (ADaPT: Association for Dance and Performance Telematics), my thinking is weary of disciplinary structures which obstruct new research and learning developments for students growing up in a globalized media culture. Meanwhile, the development of the Environments Laboratory and, subsequently, the Interaktionslabor (founded in Germany in 2003) and the DAP-Lab (founded in the UK in 2004), has nurtured new pedagogical models for digital performance.

Emphasizing the notion of *environment*, I ultimately want to point to an ecological theory of digital and communication techniques, which move us toward processes of exchange among interacting participants. The underlying search of the book, therefore, is not for the new vocabulary of media technologies, but for particular qualities of (intersubjective) interaction experience enabled by network and communication media we adapt to movement in the world, the kind of vision, feeling and form which dance, in particular, can invoke beyond other nonverbal (and verbal) art forms.

NOTES

[1] Cornelius Borck, *Hirnströme: Eine Kulturgeschichte der Elektroenzephalographie*, Göttingen: Wallstein Verlag, 2005, 13. See also, Bruno Latour, *Nous n'avons jamais été modernes*, Paris: La Découverte, 1991. For a provocative epistemological metatheory, see Stefan Rieger, *Kybernetische Anthropologie*, Frankfurt: Suhrkamp, 2003.

[2] <http://www.aec.at/en/festival2005/first_statement.asp>. See also Gerfried Stocker and Christine Schöpf, eds., *Ars Electronica 2005—Hybrid. Living in Paradox*, Ostfildern-Ruit: Hatje Cantz, 2005, 10.

[3] Giorgio Agamben, *The Open: Man and Animal*, trans. Kevin Attel. Stanford: Stanford University Press, 2004.

[4] Suzanne Lee, *Fashioning the Future: Tomorrow's Wardrobe*, London: Thames & Hudson, 2005, 16–17.

[5] For an analysis of a-life, see Mitchell Whitelaw, *Metacreation: Art and Artificial Life*, Cambridge: MIT Press, 2004. Another theoretical study of "technological embodiment" foregrounds what the editors call "material poiesis of informatics," and the implicit reference to the new biology of Humberto Maturana and Francisco Varela is hardly coincidental. See Robert Mitchell/Philip Turtle, eds., *Data Made Flesh: Embodying Information*, New York: Routledge, 2004. Among the choreographers who discuss their work in terms of autopoiesis, emergence and complexity theory, see Marlon Barrios Solano, "Designing Unstable Landscapes: Improvisational Dance within Cognitive Systems," in *Tanz im Kopf/Dance and Cognition*, edited by Johannes Birringer and Josephine Fenger. Münster: LIT Verlag, 2005, 279–91. Eduardo Kac's references to biology date back to "Transgenic Art," *Leonardo Electronic Almanac,* 6, 11 (December 1998), republished in: Gerfried Stocker and Christine Schöpf, eds., *Ars Electronica '99—Life Science*, Vienna, New York: Springer, 1999, 289–296. See also SymbioticA, the Art and Science Collaborative Research Laboratory in Perth: <http://www.symbiotica.uwa.edu.au>.

[6] My comments here are quite pragmatic, and informed by working in the theatre and in laboratories. In rehearsal workshops with media, new tools are tested all the time, and programming (as well as writing customized software for real-time interactive performance) is now second nature in digital art forms continuously mediating and remediating the live and the recorded. If I rarely glance at a more pessimist strand of criticism, such as André Lepecki's *Exhausting Dance* (Routledge, 2006), or pass over the academically exhausted debates about "liveness" and "presence" in performance, it is mainly because I don't share their melancholic obsession with

loss, ephemerality, or the "ontology of disappearance." Disappearances and deletable files are a common structural element of creativity in contemporary art making. Rauschenberg's *Erased de Kooning* is a good example for a practical attitude.

[7] Cf. Michel Gaillot, *Multiple Meaning: Techno. An Artistic and Political Laboratory of the Present*, trans. Warren Niesluchowski, Paris: Éditions Dis Voir, 1999, and Paul D. Miller a.k.a. DJ Spooky, *Rhythm Science,* Cambridge: MIT Press, 2004.

[8] A comprehensive archive of "Digital Cultures" is available at: <http://www.digitalcultures.org>.

For descriptions of my earlier workshop, "Lively Bodies Lively Machines," see *Media and Performance: along the border*, Baltimore: John Hopkins University Press, 1998, 105–44, a chapter that includes a detailed critical reflection on the seminal "Connecting Bodies" lab in Amsterdam.

[9] See, for example, "Reflexiones sobre Performance, Cultura y Tecnología," HyperMedia Studio, UCLA, Los Angeles, in 2002, <http://www.aliennationcompany.com/projects/repercute.htm>.

[10] N. Katherine Hayles, *How We Became Posthuman*, Chicago: University of Chicago Press, 1999, 288. My thoughts on emergence in the context of digital performance are indebted to Sher Doruff with whom I have collaborated in workshops and installations on several occasions. See her "Collaborative Culture," in *Making Art of Databases*, edited by Joke Brouwer, Arjen Mulder, Susan Charlton. Rotterdam: V2_ Publishing/NAI Publishers, 2003, 70-99.

[11] Maria Beatriz de Medeiros, *Aisthesis*: *estética, educação e comunidades*, Chapecó: Argos, 2005.

[12] This phrase was used by Palazhy in a movement workshop taught at the Digital Cultures Lab. Palazhy is the Artistic Director of the Attakkalari Centre for Movement Arts in Bangalore. He recently implemented the first diploma program in Movement Arts and Mixed Media in India, a program seeking to traverse beyond outer forms of diverse physical traditions to the very sources of movement principles embedded in physical traditions, focusing on their complementarity while also drawing upon the conceptual tools of digital technology. He also directed the interactive DVD production for *Nagarika*, an "Integrated Information System on Indian Physical Expressions through Technology," which compiles and categorizes movement sequences of the classical dance form Bharatanatyam and the Keralan martial art Kalarippayattu. *Nagarika* is the first such initative of creating a digital resource in India in the field of the performing arts.

MOVING
THROUGH
TECHNOLOGIES

▼▲ TRACKBACK 1:
PERFORMANCE & MOVING IMAGES

The growth of digital art and collaborative computer-assisted performance works in the 1990s, as well as the institutional and pedagogical responses to this development, triggered debates about emerging definitions of "virtual" or "digital" performance. In regard to the larger cultural impact of the Internet and the World Wide Web (the Netscape Corporation introduced the first commercial Web browser in 1994 and thus made the network available as a global channel for distributing content), "new media" art became an umbrella term for a wide variety of works incorporating media technologies. But new media artists generally adopt older media and artistic practices, and the category of the "new" is always problematic and changing. The aesthetic use of computing, software, and distributed networks in performance, therefore, needs to be looked at not from a generalized perspective of emerging media technologies but through the performers' techniques of controlling media parameters in a shared environment.

While some mainstream art institutions, museum curators and festivals began to include digital art and use the term "digital dance" in the 1990s, and while specific media art centers were created to exhibit art involving digital processes or interactivity, no such terminology was used for the wider field of the performing arts. This is a remarkable historical paradox, since concepts of performance had been consistently affected by avant-garde experiments in the visual arts and, later, in video and installation art. Video artists who today gain recognition through their installations (e.g., Pierre Huyghe) or crossover work in the theatre (Chris Kondek, Walid Raad) will remember their ancestors of the first generation of experimentalists, which included Carolee Schneemann, Nam June Paik, Les Levine, Bruce Nauman or Eleanor Antin, amongst many others who then inspired the second generation of cross-over artists such as Laurie Anderson whose work became widely recognized in the 80s. The body of work of South African artist William Kentridge is another significant example of crossovers between drawing, film, animation, and theatre. It presents a unique form of animated storytelling concerned with narrative content rather than abstract motion or the kind of reflexive "mapping" or sculpting of space depicted in Bruce Nauman's early video performances (e.g., *Dance or Exercise on the Perimeter of a Square [Square Dance]*, 1967–68). Kentridge's transformations of drawings into animated films (e.g., *Felix in Exile*, 1994; *History of the Main Complaint*, 1996) strike me as dark expressionist landscapes, CT scans of a history of violent repression and memory, guilt and forgetting. He has also used his "drawings for projection" in collaborations with Johannesburg's Handspring Puppet Company. As with Kondek's video productions for the theatre (he has worked with René Pollesch, Stefan Pucher, Meg Stuart, and Jossi Wieler after leaving his job as a lighting designer for the Wooster Group), Kentridge's contribution to the history of digital theatre and performance awaits proper acknowledgment. Eleanor Antin's diaroma-like multimedia installations, such as *The Angel of Mercy* (recreated for documenta 12), compose a hyperreal form of collage that troubles both the historians of visual art and those of theatre. As a consequence, for more than thirty years the video performances of artists like Antin have occupied an uncharted territory even though her particular use of expanded cinema, much as Kentridge's "drawings for projection," constitute a model of postdramatic theatre or installation with clear resonances in today's digital art. In *The Angel of Mercy* (1977), Antin's multiple "re-enactments" of Nurse Nightingale through video, photographs, painted cardboard, and fictional memoirs create a flamboyant feminist pantomime on a historical character and *Vorbild* (role model). It is illuminating to see the older work at documenta 12, side by side with Amar Kanwar's multi-channel digital video installation *The Lightning Testimonies* (2007), which reflects upon scenes of conflict in the Indian subcontinent through depictions of sexual violence and female survivors' testimonials that seem drawn from a huge, endless database of samples. The old role model for this installation, so to speak, is the traumatic monologue or the witness report (common to documentary film and drama), but this layered digital collage, performed as a loop with projected images on eight screens, operates within the new contextual model of the database. Its reference is not history, truth, or fiction, but the digital archive itself, with its combinatory operationality of storing, linking, reprocessing, and transforming data.

The notion of a "virtual theatre," applied to hyptertextual Websites, CD-ROMs, and virtual reality environments, did not gain much ground as it tended to disregard physical space and the techniques of the performer.[1] In the world of computer music, on the other hand, there were few problems in defining a field that had grown and expanded over several decades, from its origins in electro-acoustic and electronic music, to encompass all practices of generating or composing music with the aid of computers. The field of computer music is also well represented by many active organizations and institutions (e.g., International Computer Music Association) dedicated to electronic music research, and it has developed much of our vocabulary for the theory and application of technologies in the areas of music, sound and instrument design, sound synthesis, digital signal processing, and psycho-acoustics.

In order to introduce a term such as "digital performance," which has not yet been established, I begin by exploring the manifestations and multiple forms of digital dance as I have experienced them in the wider arena of tech-nologically mediated art. It is presupposed here that digital media and com-putation provide the technological and cultural context for those emerging performances and exhibitions under consideration. I propose that the more sustained lineage of dance on screen and live dance including projections of screen images offers a solid backdrop for understanding the compatibility between live performance and the moving image, between the polyrhythmic components of movement and the digital behavior of images and sound.

The strong interest among dance-makers in digital media hardly came as a surprise, since dance on film (cine-dance) and videodance had attracted considerable attention since the 1970s and 1980s, especially as choreog-raphers, companies, researchers, and teachers began to use video as a vital means of documenting/promoting work or analyzing existing choreogra-phies. Unlike theatre schools where actor training and text-based dramatur-gies are in the foreground, dance training often involves the study of taped choreographies as a learning tool and visual support for the memorization of movement phrases and particular choreographic patterns (for example in recreations).

Professional and low-end portable video equipment using standardized formats (VHS, SVHS, 3/4 inch tapes) had become affordable and more widely available in the 1970s. Analogue editing studios in media arts cen-ters and schools provided opportunities for post-production, which could eventually be created in any situation where a camera and a video recorder were available. The more readily affordable video camcorders replaced the 16mm and Super 8 cameras that had been used in the earlier years; those formats generally remained attractive only to film students. Some of the live dance performances of the Judson Church era included film projections on 16mm, and archival footage from this era has survived and can occasionally be rediscovered at museum retrospectives, for example of Robert Rauschenberg's collaborative work with Trisha Brown, Merce Cunningham, Deborah Hay, John Cage, David Tudor, Robert Whitman, and other artists, including the memorable event Rauschenberg and engineer Billy Klüver staged in 1966 at the 69th Regiment Armory in New York *(9 Evenings: Theatre and Engineering)*. It is haunting, today, to go to such retrospectives and hear the clicking sound of the old film projectors that may soon become extinct. On one occasion I rediscovered Trisha Brown's 1966 dance piece *Homemade,* a short piece she performed with a film projector mounted on her back. In the choreographer's notes, published in the catalogue for the traveling exhibition *Trisha Brown: Dance and Art in Dialogue, 1961–2001,* first shown at Addison Gallery of American Art (Andover, Massachussetts), *Homemade* is described as a solo of "microscopic movement" taken from everyday activities, incorporating a film of itself by Robert Whitman. During Brown's solo, the film of the dance was projected onto the wall, floor, ceiling, and audience in synchronization with the "live" dance. I never saw this work in reality, only on film and on photographs, but the image of Brown with the projector tied to her body is captivating. It is even more intriguing that Brown, in a recent conversation, remembers these early works of the 1960s as "equipment pieces." Moving with a projector tied to her back, much like *Watermotor* or the incredible *Man Walking Down the Side of a Building,* were simply, in her mind, pieces created with technical equipment.

Along with the history of postmodern dance associated with Judson Dance Theatre and Grand Union, and the participatory Happenings instigated by Allan Kaprow, one trajectory of early intermedia, audiovisual, and interactive experimentations clearly points to Brown's *Homemade* and John Cage's equally homemade *Variations V* (1965), created with Merce Cunningham's dancers who moved to activate random sound-scores through two custom-built systems designed by Tudor and Klüver (photocells and radio antennae) which triggered short-wave radios and tapes with prerecorded sounds. If one followed such a trajectory, one would observe how Cunningham engaged various media technologies as they became available throughout the many decades of his long career, how he used live interaction with mixed media early on, then started to experiment with film and video, then turned to the computer and the LifeForms software to visualize new movement possibilities, and eventually joined Shelley Eshkar and Paul Kaiser in the landmark experimentations with animation derived from motion capture *(Hand-drawn Spaces, BIPED, Loops, Fluid Canvas).* Cunningham, in this sense, is an artist whose work literally moved through the compositional technical equipments that became available.

Carolee Schneemann's *Snows* (1967) can be counted amongst the early interactive pieces although this pioneering artist's performances had a considerably stronger erotic and political charge than any of Brown's, Cage's, or Cunningham's works. A film of her legendary orgiastic *Meat Joy* performance (1964) is on permanent exhibition at the Tate Modern, carefully hidden in an alcove from unprotected viewing by young or prudent visitors. Schneemann's anti-Vietnam War performance *Snows* was performed at the Martinique Theater in New York City, involving a collaboration with Bell Telephone Laboratory engineers that enabled the development of an electronic switching system for the performance, by means of which audience reactions could trigger electrical relays to activate 16-mm projectors edging the stage, tape decks with collaged sound, revolving lights, and, in turn, the cues for six performers. Central to *Snows* was Schneemann's film *Viet-Flakes,* composed from a collection of Vietnam atrocity images she had painstakingly clipped from newspapers and foreign magazines over a five-year period. *Snows* is an early technological performance, as Schneemann taped close-up lenses and magnifying glasses to an 8-mm camera lens to make it physically "travel" within the photographs, producing a rough form of animation.

Trisha Brown's *Set and Reset* (1983) used large film projections of pre-recorded material onto suspended Rauschenberg sculptures. She then created her own "Variations" in a choreography for *Astral Convertible* (1989) which places the dancers on stage with eight movable light towers (designed by Rauschenberg and Klüver) equipped with car batteries, headlights, stereo systems and sensors responding to the movement. In *Groove and Countermove* (2000), the third part of *El Trilogy,* she had her dancers move in front of large graphic drawings (ink on vellum) by Terry Winters which look like musical notations blotted out with a tangle of bold swirling lines. Her recent stage work, *how long does the subject linger on the edge of the volume ...* (2005), interfaces with animated graphics from real-time motion capture driven by an artist-designed artificial-intelligence software (Marc Downie,

Shelley Eshkar, Paul Kaiser), which responds instantly to the dancers' movements. The software draws its own dance diagrams live during the performance, and the graphic drawings are projected on a transparent screen in front of the stage. Marc Downie refers to these digital graphics as software agents or creatures, based on his methodological perspective of biologically inspired, agent-based artificial intelligence.[2]

How long does the subject linger on the edge of the volume ... was workshopped and developed at Arizona State University's Arts, Media, and Engineering Lab, and the same project also included a new work by Bill T. Jones, titled *22*. Downie, Eshkar, Kaiser, along with Thanassis Rikakis (the Lab's director) and a team of artistic and engineering partners, used advanced real-time motion capture systems built by the Motion Analysis Corporation, tweaking their kinematic data capture for particular perceptual techniques applied to complex dance choreography. In the case of *22*, this technique was applied to a narrative solo improvisation that combines spoken language with a fluid meshwork of interwoven poses through which the dancer moves. Jones's first encounter with motion capture dates back to 1999 when he collaborated with Kaiser, Eshkar, and Michael Girard on the virtual dance installation *Ghostcatching*, a beautiful and challenging composition which troubled the notion of choreography insofar as a set of Jones's original movement sequences and movement characters was first captured, and the data then modeled into various hand-drawn virtual characters by the graphic/digital designer (Eshkar). Subsequently, in a lengthy post-production process, the data files were re-composed by a digital artist (Kaiser) and a software designer (Girard), using 3D Studio Max's Character Studio, to generate the final 3-D dance animation. Rather than attempting to do this in real-time, which was not possible with the motion capture system available at that time, the accomplishment of *Ghostcatching* was the creation of a digital aesthetic, a movement-animation in which the performance is rendered as a computer graphics representation.

I mention Trisha Brown, Merce Cunningham, Bill T. Jones, and their collaborations because they have been some of the most visible, influential, and renowned dance artists in the history of such intermedia experimentations, and their status as established choreographers helped initially to nurture the fledgling genre of videodance. I remember that when I entered my first tape to a contest, Cunningham had already worked for years with filmmakers Charles Atlas and Elliot Caplan; by the time his *Beach Birds for Camera* (directed by Caplan) won the 1993 IMZ Dance Screen award for the transformation of an existing dance into an original cinematographic work, his film was selected from more than 170 entries from 96 countries.

Festivals presenting videodance had begun to appear, and some, like the Dance Screen organized each year in different countries by the Vienna-based IMZ (Internationales Musikzentrum), have had a vital role in the dissemination of camera-based danceworks and the nurturing of the DV camera-based and digitally edited video genre that is sometimes referred to as digital dancing. Dance Screen, founded in 1994, became the preeminent competitive international festival and showcase for dance films and videos and later initiated "Dance Screen on Tour" (in 1999) to present selected programs to a wider audience around the world. Although perhaps not part of every national film or video festival, videodance increasingly entered the programming of such festivals or the public screenings of museums and independent art film centers. Moreover, dance in the screen media also received broader visibility through broadcast television, for example BBC's *Dance for the Camera*, and the support of commissions from independent TV channels in the UK, France, Germany, Canada, and the U.S., among others. In Eastern Europe, choreographer Vera Maletic already worked in film and television while directing the Studio for Contemporary Dance in Zagreb during the 1960s. She became a pioneer in the burgeoning field of dance and technology when during her many years of teaching at Ohio State University she initiated a course in videodance and, during the 1990s, began to focus on the creation of CD-ROMs and multimedia database projects documenting contemporary dance artists. In addition, some scholars and software programmers had published tools (LabanWriter, LifeForms) that attracted attention in the field of dance notation and preservation as well as among choreographers (e.g., Merce Cunningham, Pablo Ventura, Yacov Sharir, Ivani Santana) who wanted to utilize the computer for the invention and visualization of new movement possibilities.

Sherril Dodds, in *Dance on Screen,* wrote one of the first critical studies of the rich diversity of screen dance genres, pointing out that "videodance" in her view describes choreography designed specifically for the camera. Owing much to televisual and filmic techniques, and to the popular dance imagery in music video and Hollywood musicals, videodance is said to constitute a hybrid site where televisual and even promotional advertising styles act upon the dancing body but choreographers of videodance also draw on postmodern stage dance strategies, which disrupt televisual code and technological function. The latter, Dodds argues in her reference to the "discourses of technology," prompts a redundancy of the material body even as it is considered to enhance the capacities of the dancing body.[3]

The publication of Judy Mitoma's *Envisioning Dance on Film and Video* in 2002, collecting fifty essays accompanied by a DVD featuring excerpts of forty films and videos, presented an important moment for the field of performance media studies.[4] It offered the first comprehensive and illustrated reference guide to the history of dance on camera, providing an invaluable pedagogical tool for teaching the history of the collaboration between dance makers and filmmakers. Although there is no doubt that today virtually everyone working in dance uses video to record rehearsals, document performances, promote new works, or submit samples for funding requests, and although dance historians and theorists like to include dance films in their teaching, there is a surprising dearth of scholarly publications and critical reflection on dance's relationship to motion pictures. The rise of videodance festivals in the 80s and 90s indicated that the alliance of choreographer and filmmaker had generated a new genre, and with the widespread accessibility today of digital cameras and computers, along with the global resources of the Internet and its digitized databases, it is unimaginable that dance education in universities, academies, and studios would miss the opportunity to integrate dance and video more thoroughly. Theatre education has much to learn from this and can now turn to the published resources, which enable a systematic study of the aesthetic, technological, and theoretical issues in the historical relations of dance and media over the past hundred years, and specifically in the development of cine-dance or videodance as an independent crossover artform. A similar study of "videotheatre" is needed.

Intermediality and performance, the relations of live art and electronic mediation, the difference between stage and screen, the role of computer-assisted interactive design with cameras now used as motion tracking rather than recording devices—these are only a few of the challenges faced by the emerging generation of artists who draw inspiration from a diverse range of media practices. The media histories of dance, and the histories of collaboration between choreographers, performers, film/videomakers, directors, cinematographers, editors, producers, and curators, constitute a wide terrain that awaits excavation.[5] And looking at such parameters, and the relatively firm historical tracks of dance in the twentieth century, how much more complicated is the media history of performance art and its often highly subversive and conceptual strategies? Performance (live action art) not only deflected from object-based arts practices but often defied classification altogether, in spite of its filial relationships to theatre, dance, and the visual arts. Carolee Schneemann's early happenings helped to transform the very definition of art, especially with regard to discourse on the body, sexuality, and technology. Typically, she always worked in several media at once (video, film, painting, photography, performance art, installation).

Yet traces have remained, and most often these traces of the history of performance art constitute fleeting, iconic moments, caught in grainy photographs, by hand-held video or on beautifully directed film. They survive along with other relics (props) and the gossip or reports derived from witnesses of the event. In the stunning exhibition *Art, Lies and Videotape: Exposing Performance* (Tate Liverpool, 2003), curator Adrian George aimed at the photographic and filmic "record" of live art to examine how actions have been mediated, recorded, constructed, or fabricated, and how *performance images* are not not only crucial for the historicization of performance but also require careful examination of the imaging and framing (documentation) which might have been deliberately staged by the artists to create a desired effect of the event-object. In contemporary digital performance, such iconic framing would tend to be even more contradictory or even impossible, since real-time intervention in the digital is its very field of action. Real-time performance is a new medium for artistic creation, and thus also implies a different understanding of what constitutes an event, even if such a temporal object could be framed and stored (in photography, video, film). The photograph, in that respect, would not be of the event.

We need histories from many places and contexts to explore these ambiguities in the relationship of performance to its image manipulations, including for example the performer's deliberate play with camera feedback and delayed playback, as Dan Graham already explored in his 1974 *Present Continuous Pasts*.

A photograph of Graham's video installation in *Art, Lies and Videotape* shows him performing with his delayed double but also including the audience as participants: their unconscious responses and movements become part of the composition of the temporal object and the ongoing sequences of video reflections. Such early video performance works yield fascinating examples of artistic experimentation with feedback loops (Nancy Holt created a similarly impressive piece with vocal delays in her 1974 *Boomerang* performance, recorded on video by Richard Serra). They can provide further insights into today's improvisational techniques of real-time processing of media parameters. Early performance on video, arguably, also provides a rich comparative context for today's digital capturing and metadating, i.e., the computer processes which can recombine the performer's image with any other images from stored data. In the club and DJ/VJ communities, "live coding" has emerged as a practice of improvised musical and visual performance where metadating and writing code happens in front of an audience. Envisioning performance with dynamic databases, however, involves interactive media ecologies which exceed the older apparatuses of cinema, video, and photography.

Envisioning Dance on Film and Video essentially focuses on the United States (and thus the U.S.-based traditions of ballet and modern dance), with Hollywood movies, public and commercial television programs, and film festivals such as DFA's *Dance on Camera* dominating the selection of examples and case studies. Deirdre Towers, the veteran director of Dance Films Association, draws the titles of her annotated filmography mostly from entries of her recent festivals and her own *Dance on Camera: A Guide for Dance Films and Videos*. It is a good selection but among its 190 titles are only a handful of Australian, Asian, Latin American, Eastern European, and Scandinavian dance videos. No reference is made, for example, to the burgeoning videodance scenes in Brazil and Slovenia; the one Indian entry, *Circles-Cycles Kathak Dance* (1988), was produced by Robert Gottlieb in the U.S.

The emphasis on American film, film musicals, and broadcast television (with scarcely a reference to MTV and the use of video in contemporary techno and club cultures except in Larry Billman's essay on "Music Video as Short Form Dance Film") is understandable, once we look at the origins of the book. For Judy Mitoma (UCLA Center for Intercultural Performance) and her dedicated team of co-editors, the primary spring-board for the creation of this compendium was an effort by American media and dance professionals, especially producers and directors, to assess the history of mainstream dance on film and video and to gather the evidence of production, technical and creative, that could continue to foster the training of artists in the filming of dance. Mitoma combined funding resources (from The Pew Charitable Trusts and NIPAD, particularly) to generate the UCLA National Dance/Media Project in 1996 and to initiate a series of Fellowship

Programs with the help of a "Leadership Group" to which she invited distinguished practitioners, many of whom had been instrumental in creating dance for public television programs in the 1970s and thereafter (e.g., *Dance in America*, *A Time to Dance*, *Arts USA*). Jac Venza, executive producer of *Great Performances*, writes about this experience in "Setting the Record." He contributes a listing of all the dance programs that were aired during the past decades. Alyce Dissette adds the dance program list of *Alive from Off Center*, a more experimental video series that was funded by an NEA initiative between 1988 and 1996 and included performance artists like Laurie Anderson and Meredith Monk. Other very helpful surveys include Virginia Brooks's historical timeline ("A Century of Dance and Media"), Madeleine Nichols's chapter on copyright issues, and Leslie Hanssen Kopp's "Resource and Preservation Guide."

As these surveys and testimonies indicate, along with the involvement of NIPAD (National Initiative to Preserve America's Dance), the book's primary objective is an emphasis on creating a historical record of the significance of dance on film and the continuing need for preservation, on the one hand, and on motivating new generations of dancemakers to consider "best practices" for the recording of dance and the production of specialized choreographies for the camera on the other. Mitoma's contributors and workshop directors have valuable insights to share; many also write from a self-conscious position that assumes that their work had pioneering character for the dance community at large and for building a much wider audience base. Dennis Diamond recounts how he started the archival project for Dance Theater Workshop in 1975, and how he created *Dance/Video/News* a few years ago to "increase television exposure for dance companies" and help them to create "video clips that have been specially edited to make the movement sexy for television. Here we are not archivists, nor are we reverential to the choreography. We are serving the dance company by getting them exposure on television and the Internet."

A concern to legitimate dance as a significant cultural art form able to draw larger audiences runs through many of the essays, even as most of them won't go quite as far as Mitchell Rose in arguing that American audiences like a good story and have a hard time keeping up their intellectual interest in abstract modern dance. Choreographers can take valuable lessons from screenwriters, he suggests, and this attention to narrative form, content, and structure, so crucial to cinema, might have yielded a fascinating debate among the writers in this book, especially as narrative has been a neglected or even despised feature of postmodern dance in the U.S. since the days of the Judson Dance Theatre. But the editor too often relies on anecdotal testimony and personal reportage styles of the contributors to achieve a more dialogical tenor. Differences in interpretation occur rarely when choreographers' views are paired with those of their editors, as in the case of Matthew Diamond's and Pam Wise's views on the award-winning *Dancemaker*, and Victoria Marks's and Margaret Williams's discussions of *Mothers and Daughters* and *Outside In*. Williams offers a hands-on account of her camera direction and allows several pages of her storyboards to be printed. These illustrations, along with many production and rehearsal stills (those for Philippe Decouflé's videodance *Le P'tit Bal* and Peter Anderson's and Rosemary Lee's *Boy*, shown in Bob Lockyer's essay on his work as a BBC producer, are particularly helpful), have a contagious effect on our imagination.

I would argue for the desirability of publishing more storyboards and technical scripts in general, as these can supply fascinating evidence of the processes of re-organization: the "choreographic" here enters into its other medium (film, computer) and it is not merely a crossover, or an adaptation of stage to screen, of theatrical language to film language. Rather, if video-dance—or computer-generated dance, for that matter—constitutes its own site, as Douglas Rosenberg has argued convincingly, then the organizational and operational principles of the site and the digital medium have to be scrutinized on their own terms.[6] Yet *Envisioning Dance on Film and Video* fulfils its prime objective well. It establishes a record of the moving image production in and for the dance field, drawing historical lines from Broadway to Hollywood, from Thomas Edison filming Ruth Dennis's skirt dance to the Kinetoscope, animation, motion pictures, and the musical, from D.W. Griffith, Walt Disney, Busby Berkeley, Fred Astaire, Gene Kelly to Doris Humphrey, Ted Shawn, Maya Deren and Hilary Harris, from Bob Fosse, Martha Graham, George Balanchine, Merce Cunningham, and the specifically vital relationships the latter established with videomakers Charles Atlas and Elliot Caplan, to the younger generation of choreographers who took the cameras in their own hands or partnered with directors and editors drawn to the kinaesthetics of videodance.

Three of seven major sections of the book move the reader through the historical setting ("Setting the Record," "Looking Back") and particularly challenging aspects of adapting performance from the stage to the screen, analyzing ethnographic records of dancing, recreating dance from filmic records and archiving danceworks on video ("Recasting the Dance"). The sections "Seeding the Field" and "Taking Directions" address the path-breaking collaborations between television producers, directors and choreographers to advance the televisual form of dance and create a new national venue for its consumption. "Seeding the Field" offers a wider international perspective on different initiatives to promote dance on camera in Great Britain, the U.S., Canada, Japan, Argentina, and India, including the creation of major television documentaries, such as Rhoda Grauer's eight-hour *Dancing* (1993) for Channel Thirteen/WNET. Grauer describes the complicated seven-year long odyssey for the making of *Dancing*, a documentary that was shot on location in five continents by a number of different filmmaking teams. The theme of this documentary—dance in world cultures—raises many vexing questions about critical and aesthetic distinctions in the filming of context-specific dance traditions, bound to ethnographic fieldwork and issues of translation and visual representation. One would like to learn more about the research, which informs the production concept and ideology of such films, and about the important role of ethnography for performance and media studies in general.

Argentine dancer Silvina Szperling contributes an interesting biographical account of her first exposures to audio-visual media and the videodance workshop for choreographers she attended in 1993, which inspired her to pursue this "integration of two languages" further at other workshops organized by the American Dance Festival where she met some of the artists also represented in this book (Eiko and Koma, Bill T. Jones, Elliot Caplan). Returning to Argentina in 1995, Szperling focused her energies on building her own company (SZ Danza) as well as founding and directing the Festival Internacional de Video-danza de Buenos Aires. I will comment on the importance of such workshop experience further below. There are many inspirational success stories of this kind in Mitoma's volume, including David Gere's somber account of starting the "Estates Project of Artists with AIDS," using video documentation of dance as a key site for the performance of memorialization, for grieving, for activism, and for social change. Lynn Dally reports joyously on several important documentary films (by George T. Nierenberg) on tap dance and the lives of African American tap legends, while Madeleine Nichols underlines the enormous significance of the Dance Division of the New York Public Library, the largest and most comprehensive repository for dance documents in the world. She is not the only one in the volume to point out that videotapes have a limited lifespan and are not a proper "preservation medium," and that more and better moving image documents must be created to preserve this cultural tradition. The creation of digital archives has become a matter of increased concern over the past years, and many debates amongst curators in museums and practitioners online testify to this.[7]

The editors see the publication of this volume as a foundational manifesto, a wake up call, emphasizing the need for better documentation and production values and, undoubtedly, for the embrace of digital technologies at a moment in history when digital archives are being created everywhere and the dissemination of dance research will require Internet and digital media resources. Many practical insights are provided by film directors like Virginia Brooks, Evann E. Siebens, and Merill Brockway regarding the various types of dance film (simple recordings of choreography, documentary films of performance, translations, adaptations, choreocinema, ethnographic film, videodance) and especially the creative interactions between film technique and dance (camera space versus stage space, focus, exposure, framing, angles, lighting, horizon line, etc.). Brockway, in "Accompanying Choreography: A Director's Journey," sketches a tight account of his "system" how to approach televising dance with multiple cameras, and Girish Bhargava adds an illuminating short essay on the use of time code, the rhythm of shots and the placement of an edit.

The most thought-provoking and poetic essays are actually written by choreographers (Eiko Otake, Meredith Monk, Bill T. Jones) in the section "Screen Testing," which also includes Roslyn Sulcas's penetrating analysis of William Forsythe's filmic choreography and digital artist Paul Kaiser's shrewd observations on "virtual dance," choreography, and computer science. Kaiser describes his experiments with motion capture technology (e.g., *Ghostcatching*, with Bill T. Jones). Finally, there is the deliriously poetic diary by ethnographic filmmaker Robert Gardner, field notes from his journey in Africa to film the *gerewol* contest of the Borroro, which concludes the last section ("Frames and Interpretations"). Since the book emphasizes the unavoidable, complex collaborative nature of making dance on film or of using film in live performance to create a "dream-like multidimensionality," as Monk suggests in an eloquent essay about her theatre-dance-music pieces (she also created a feature-length film, *Book of Days*), it is deeply encouraging to recognize how much the integration of artistic disciplines has evolved in these composite art forms, and how perceptively choreographers adopt the language of filmmaking into their aesthetics and politics (cf. Bill T. Jones's work process on *Still/Here*).

Rather than "screen testing," I would call this a deep assimilation of visual, compositional intelligence, as in the case of Eiko and Koma's investigations of "media dance" and the poetic flow of images for their installation *Breath* (1999), one of the significant new works at the end of the last century which explored the scenographic organization of a long-durational performative installation. Eiko, in "A Dancer behind the Lens," is one of the few writers in *Envisioning Dance* who viscerally taps into the visionary, sensual, and poetic qualities of film projection as a sculptural, plastic art that can create a whole environment. Along with Monk, Jones, Sulcas, Kaiser, and Gardner, Eiko's voice will resonate profoundly with those who strive to think and experience performance through the moving camera.

The companion DVD interacts well with the book: the video excerpts are identified, numbered, and highlighted with a box in each essay, and the DVD features a corresponding table of contents that allows quick navigation. The excerpts are short and vary in length between, generally, two to six minutes. Even though they are too short to provide a deeper engagement, the DVD is invaluable as an introduction to screen dance and as an archive: the forty excerpts are diverse and evocative enough, and they span almost a century of the evolution of film choreography. Highlights among them are Maya Deren's *A Study in Choreography for Camera* (1945), often considered the first experimental filmdance; the exceptionally instructive *Nine Variations on a Dance Theme* (1966) by Hilary Harris; Bonnie Oda Homsey's stunning 1996 reconstruction of Mary Wigman's *Hexentanz*; the cinematographically beautiful *Lodela* (1966), directed by Philippe Baylaucq; the glimpses we get from the narrative dramaturgy in the work of DV8 and choreographer Lloyd Newson (*Enter Achilles*, directed by Clara Van Gool, 1996); the daring work of Victoria Marks with the mixed-ability company CandoCo. in *Outside In* (1994); or the real-time live cinematography in the idiosyncratic *Kammer/Kammer* (2000) by Forsythe's Frankfurt Ballet. Apart from the documentary films that typically use a narrator or voice-over, the main difference in the types of films we see concern the relationship of (stage) choreography and screen medium: there are those videos (recorded with a still tripod and frontal angles) that let us concentrate on the dance choreography and a "staged" view, as in Rosenberg's filming of Homsey's *Hexentanz*. Then there are the creative dance films that use real locations and the specificity of the kinetic video medium—the dancing with the camera—as in David Hinton's extremely visceral, dynamic *Touched* (1994, choreography by Wendy Houston), generating a close-up kinaesthetic experience with zooms and quick cuts which are impossible to create on a stage.

It is this impossibility, one could argue, that inspired choreographers and directors to engage the computational challenge presented by digital technologies. This implied shifting attention from the use of prerecorded video on stage or screen to the live, real-time production of mathematically-based digital images. The *performance of imaging*, in other words, includes a complete re-evaluation of the filmic medium for the scenographic and actorly understanding of theatre, introducing camera vision and camera-input, real-time composition, processing, and projection architectures into emerging systems of digital performance.[8] The arrival of coding, digital medium, and mobile (or multiple) cameras and sensors in the performance space changes the stage and the screen spaces, as we are no longer tied to the traditional role of motion pictures and the machines of motion created in the 19th century to produce the illusion of motion. The digital is not cinematographic; it produces a machinic vision, an algorithmic writing of data. Its new attributes include programmability, interactivity, and virtuality.

NOTES

¹ As I completed this manuscript, Steve Dixon's *Digital Performance: A History of New Media in Theater, Dance, Performance Art and Installation,* Cambridge, MA: MIT Press, 2007, appeared in print, promising to be the most comprehensive study to date of the use of new technologies in the performance arts. Gabriela Giannachi, *Virtual Theatres: an Introduction,* London: Routledge, 2004, is a theoretical account of hypertextuality and the theatricality of interactive technologies but hardly engages with performance practices. Christiane Paul's *Digital Art,* London: Thames and Hudson, 2003, offers an illustrated guide of artists and artworks since the 1980s, distinguishing between work that uses digital technology as a tool to produce traditional forms and work that uses it as a medium to create new types of art (Net art, software art, digital installation, virtual reality). Paul was appointed Curator of Digital Art at the Whitney Museum in 2000, and in the same year the Whitney Biennial for the first time included several works of Net art. In 2001, the Whitney exhibited "Bitstreams," and the San Francisco MoMA presented "010101: Art in Technological Times," two exhibitions that paved the way for the inclusion of digital art in the museum. In 1997, the ZKM Center for Art and Media, a major museum and research center for digital art, had opened in Karlsruhe, Germany, and the InterCommunication Center in Tokyo, Japan. Other art institutions, such as the ICA London, the Centre Pompidou and CICV Pierre Schaeffer in France, and the New Museum of Contemporary Art in New York also began to show digital art, but major performing arts venues, including The Brooklyn Academy of Music, did not follow suit. Most of the digital performance innovations created in the U.S. were shown in smaller venues (The Kitchen, PS122, La MaMa Experimental Theatre or the Performing Garage in New York, the black box stages at the Wexner Center, Walker Art Center, MCA Chicago, etc.) or in universities. The DPA (Digital Performance Archive) was created by Barry Smith and Steve Dixon to document and preserve developments in the use of computer technologies in performance. During its activity (1990 to 2000), it compiled considerable documentation about live theatre using digital projections, performances on the computer-screen via Webcasts and interactive virtual environments (<http://art.ntu.ac.uk/dru/>). In 2000, Franklin Furnace received funding to make its archives accessible online. The Daniel Langlois Foundation in Montréal also houses extensive archives of contemporary media artists. An overview of media art movements and their gradual institutionalization can be found in Mark Tribe and Reena Jana, *New Media Art,* Cologne: Taschen, 2007.

[2] Cf. in Section IV below, "Thinking Images: A Conversation with Paul Kaiser and Marc Downie" and Marc Downie, *Choreographing the Extended Agent*, Doctoral Thesis, MIT Media Lab, 2005.

[3] Sherril Dodds, *Dance on Screen: Genres and Media from Hollywood to Experimental Art*, Basingstoke: Palgrave Macmillan, 2001. Her study focuses on videodance of the 1990s, contextualizing the full emergence of the genre by looking back at the televising of stage-based dance and the commissioning context in Britain in the 1980s and 1990s, when production companies such as Dancelines or individual choreographers were invited by BBC's *Dancehouse* and *Dance for the Camera* or Channel 4's *Dance on 4*. Claudia Rosiny, in *Videotanz: Panorama einer intermedialen Kunstform*, Zurich: Chronos Verlag, 1999, writes about European videodance and its emergence as an "intermedial artform." Her case studies are mostly drawn from the entries at the Dance Screen Festivals 1990-1994, but she traces videodance back to experimental film in the first half of the twentieth century and especially to the influential work of Maya Deren. Rosiny has been a curator of dance and videodance for many years at the Berner Tanztage in Switzerland. Her role in this arena of dance and media equals that of many other women curators/producers, such as Heide-Marie Härtel in Germany (Tanzfilminstitut Bremen), Portland Green in Britain (CAPTURE), Nuria Font in Spain (Mostra de VideoDansa), Deirdre Towers in the U.S. (Dance Films Association), Silvina Szperling in Argentina (Festival Internacional de Video-danza de Buenos Aires), or Zhen Xin in China (Hart Centre of Arts, Beijing).

[4] Judy Mitoma, ed., with Elizabeth Zimmer (text editor) and Dale Ann Stieber (DVD editor), *Envisioning Dance on Film and Video*, New York and London: Routledge, 2002. My initial review appeared in *Dance Research Journal* 35,2/36,1 (2004): 176–81, and I summarize my views here as they contribute to a historical contextualization of digital performance.

[5] In this context, Siegfried Zielinski, *Deep Time of the Media: Toward an Archaeology of Hearing and Seeing by Technical Means*, trans. Gloria Custance, Cambridge, MA: MIT Press, 2006, offers a particularly provocative approach to an "archaeology" of media history understood as a dynamic process shaped by the accidental and the imaginative. Zielinski proposes that the history of "connection machines" doesn't proceed predictably from primitive tools to complex machinery, and he therefore tends to excavate lesser known events and turning points of media history—fractures in the predictable—that help us recognize the new in the old.

[6] "Video space as a site for choreography is a malleable space for the exploration of dance as subject, object and metaphor, a meeting place for ideas about time,

space and movement. The practice of articulating this site is one in which, through experimentation with camera angles, shot composition, location and post-production techniques, the very nature of choreography and the action of dance may be questioned, deconstructed and re-presented as an entirely new and viable construct. The result of this activity is what has come to be known as videodance, the practice of creating choreography for the camera." Cf. Doug Rosenberg, "Video Space: A Site for Choreography," *Leonardo Online*, 1999. Available at <http://www.dvpg. net/essays.html>. The relationship of video space as a site to theatre space as a site (in intermedial/mixed media performance) continues to be an even less theorized terrain in contemporary interdisciplinary studies of performance, which is particularly astonishing in light of the current vogue of deconstructionist readings of dance (Lepecki, Siegmund, Husemann, Kruschkova, Ploebst) and theatre (Borelli and Savarese, Fischer-Lichte, Lehmann, Schmidt, Svich), and the cultural and media-critical readings of the performative (Auslander, Bolter, Harries, Lovejoy, McKenzie, Wood). A tentative foray into theatrical intermediality, collecting essays from an academic focus group whose members share the same methodological and terminological principles, is offered by Freda Chapple and Chiel Kattenbelt, eds., *Intermediality in Theatre and Performance*, Amsterdam: Rodopi, 2006.

[7] See the "Forum on Digital Dance" and e-Symposium on "Dancing in the Digital Age" organized online by CultureThreads (<http://www.culturethreads.net/>) in 2005 to draw attention to issues of digital preservation and dissemination at the Dance Division of the New York Public Library for the Performing Arts, New York City. In the same year, London's Tate Modern hosted "Curating, Immateriality, Systems: A Conference on Curating Digital Media," a think tank examining curatorial practice that takes into account the transformative nature of digital objects and systems, as well as production processes that are dynamic, collaborative, and distributed. The discussions raised many important questions about how curators can respond to new forms of self-organizing and self-replicating systems, databases, programming, Net art, software art, and generative media, and in general to systems of immaterial cultural production. It also was emphasized that the idea of the "system" is especially important in this context in that it not only refers to the physical site of curatorial production, the computer and the network, but also to the technical and conceptual properties of what constitutes the curatorial object and the "operating system" of art: <http://www.tate.org.uk/onlineevents/archive/CuratingImmaterialitySystems/>.

[8] For helpful discussions of live theatre and video, see Thomas Oberender, "Mehr Jetzt auf der Bühne," *TheaterHeute*, 4, 2004, 20–26, and Diedrich Diederichsen,

"Der Idiot mit der Videokamera," *TheaterHeute*, 4, 2004, 27–3. My translations are at: <http://people.brunel.ac.uk/dap/daplit.html>. Both essays primarily address analog functions of representational video, not coding and interactive digital imaging or sound generation. The lack of film and live theatre studies, especially for the early history of scenic design incorporating film into theatre, is acutely observed in David Z. Saltz's introduction to a special issue on intermedia performance in *Theatre Journal* 58, 4 (2006).

▼▲ MACHINES & BODIES

In the following, I will address the shift to technical interfaces made available by programmable performance. There are a few recently published books that draw attention to processual environments, and to hybrid forms of media in performances that are not primarily screen-based. Two of them originated from international workshops specifically dedicated to digital technologies. The first, *Maschinen, Medien, Performances: Theater an der Schnittstelle zu digitalen Medien* (Machines, Media, Performances: Theatre as Interface to Digital Worlds), edited by Martina Leeker, collects essays and conversations between participants at the 1999 European Summer Academy in Hellerau, Dresden, the site of the famous early modernist Festspielhaus that has now been repaired and renovated after decades of neglect.[1]

One could regard the large book (774 pages) primarily as a documentation of the three workshop ateliers on "Theatre and New Media," which delved into various interface systems (motion tracking, camera and sensor based interactive systems, biofeedback) and examined different positions concerning "theatre with media" versus "theatre as a medium." The workshop results were presented in performances and installations at a concluding symposium summarized in the book and complemented by a wide range of essays by invited authors (including Carl Hegemann, Friedrich Kittler, Derrick de Kerckhove, Stelarc, Sybille Krämer, Gabriele Brandstetter, Joachim Fiebach, and Christopher Balme). These essays create the necessary contextual dimension for critical reflection on different discourses linked to the emerging field of digital performance and installation based on the use of interactive interfaces, especially as the latter presupposes a rethinking of the traditional architecture of the theatre, which separates the performance from the viewer. Here the viewer is often addressed as a "user"—an active participant rather than a passive receiver—and the notion of the "user" in contemporary interactive art is a critical term to which I shall return later ("Installations and the Participant-User").

Irina Kaldrack edited the CD-ROM "Interfaces - Interaction - Performance. About the use of digital technology in theatre" which accompanies the book.

Some of the video clips and texts by the participating artists are central to the workshop investigations. I choose two examples, the first one from Stelarc's spoken comments on an experiment with a participant based on his performance *Movatar*. One sees him applying electrodes of a muscle stimulation system to the female performer, and then hears his voice asking: "Imagine if an intelligent avatar could perform in the real world using a physical body, hmm [laughs], an avatar that possesses and performs with the physical body as a prosthesis for the avatar."

This idea represents one of the basic principles in Stelarc's work throughout the 1980s and 1990s, in which he uses electrical and digital/networked stimulation systems to allow for the external and remote manipulation of the objectivized body. The *Movatar* principle, he explains, functions as an inverse motion capture system. Motion capture allows a physical body to animate a 3-D computer-generated virtual body to perform in computer space or virtual reality/cyberspace. This is commonly done by placing reflective markers on the body that are tracked by cameras, their motions analyzed by a computer and mapped onto the virtual actor. It can also be done using electromagnetic sensors (like Polhemus or Flock-of-Birds), which indicate the position/orientation of limbs and head.

In the *Movatar* experiment, however, the emphasis is not on the performer moving and generating data, but on the issue of "involuntary" movement, a concept that must appear strange and uncanny to any trained performer. When I tried on the muscle stimulation system in 2001, and Stelarc sent the electrical charges to my arms, the pure sensation I felt was not just being out of control. I am not sure that one senses something not consciously perceived beforehand. I was not reacting to something nor could I prevent anything that was happening. The muscles of the body contracted and moved. The electrical energy made the arms do strange gestures I had not seen before.

The application of electrodes and wires, often seen in photographs of laboratory performances, sometimes evokes either a medical context or the various biofeedback experiments that have been made in performance interface design as well as in research collaborations between performers and neuroscientists. It also evokes the more spectacular engineering, AI, and robotic feats Stelarc himself has performed over the past years. Unlike robotics artists who build kinetic machines and sculptures, Stelarc effectively uses his own body as an instrument in transductive technical ensembles.

For example, *Ping Body* and *Parasite* tested electrophysical and telematic transductions and the engineering of external, extended, and virtual nervous systems for the body using ping data extracted from the Internet. *Exoskeleton* is a pneumatically powered six-legged walking machine actuated by arm gestures. *Extended Arm* is a manipulator with eleven degrees of freedom that extends his arm to primate proportions. *Motion Prosthesis* is an intelligent, compliant servo-mechanism that enables the performance of precise, repetitive, and accelerated prompting or programming of the arms in real-time. *Prosthetic Head* first started to be performed in 2003 and presents a virtually embodied conversational agent that speaks to the person who interrogates it. Finally, a current project envisions a *Walking Head*—an autonomous, interactive walking robot whose mechanical motions actuate and modulate the facial behavior of the computer generated human head (<www.stelarc.va.com.au>).

This fantastical "choreography" of avatar behavior, which I had noted some years ago and described as a paradoxical form of new dance, in fact highlights the historical shifts I want to exemplify with these examples and introductory distinctions between videodance (choreography for the camera) and interaction systems.[2] On a basic level, the main shift involved here is the substitution of the camera as a recording instrument and indirect interface with direct interfaces: sensing systems worn on the body which generate data in real time or produce data that can be digitally processed and transcoded. There are other shifts, involving the use of data, and an understanding of the principles of the human-computer interface and the operations of the digital medium, to which I will turn throughout the following pages. Inevitably, once I address these wider parameters of how interface design, communication infrastructure, software technology, and living bodies come together, the field of performance technology opens up in many directions that may lie outside the narrow purview of dance and performance studies. For example, Stelarc's strategic exploration of the not-conscious agent, of telematic scaling and the engineering of external, extended, and virtual nervous systems for the body undermines the humanist and rationalist conceptions of body and subjectivity, of mind, instrumental reason, and consciousness in ways that have been provocatively theorized in the recent debates on the posthuman.[3] Such theorizations have rarely been welcomed and embraced in the dance academies whose ideology is generally aligned with the classical disciplines of ballet and the privileging of prescribed aesthetic movement ideals.

Surprisingly, in the context of the shift from the machine aesthetic celebrated by the early avant-garde to the "posthuman" aesthetic in the second half of the twentieth century, the "resistant materialities of embodiment" emphasized in Katherine Hayles's influential book on virtual bodies and how "we" became posthuman could have incited choreographers and dancers to recollect their own experiences of the promise of technology.[4] Whom does Hayles have in mind when she asks how information lost its body? Which information, whose body? The promise of technological progress, arguably, was perhaps always conceived as a threat to the dance, to the primacy of the concrete bodies and physical movement, as well as to the beauty of dance's ephemerality, its constant disappearances and re-appearances. Was the power of new media as image-making technology perceived as a threat? Did dancers really ever think that digital apparitions or robots would replace them? Had they read Heinrich von Kleist's early-nineteenth-century text on the superiority of the puppet over the human dancer ("Über das Marionettertheater") and feared the superhuman phantoms of more recent science fiction? Did they not enjoy *Crouching Tiger, Hidden Dragon*, and the ways in which Ang Lee and choreographer Yuen Woo-Ping let the actors dance through the air?

In a text written for the Net Art exhibitions at Tate Modern, Josephine Barry comments on posthuman disembodiment and the apparent utopia of flying inside the Matrix:

> It seems that the crux of this problem lies in the technology itself and the highly esoteric consequences of medium-specific investigations. Indeed, just as the self-referentiality of modernist painting and sculpture met with its deconstruction and rejection in the 1960s and early 70s with social, political and contextual concerns of Fluxus, Performance and Conceptual art, so too is Net Art's supposed "techno-formalist" variant undergoing heavy critique. In some ways, this critique is connected to a wider rejection of posthumanism and its insistence on the indistinction between humans and machines, animals and humans and, perhaps most crucially, the physical and the non-physical. Spearheaded by Donna Haraway and her pioneering mid 80s text "The Cyborg Manifesto," posthumanists claimed that, contrary to customary Leftist critiques, identity within techno-scientific societies is not

becoming more rigidly dualistic but rather undergoing a general disintegration of its unitary forms due to developments such as biotechnological engineering, computer science, quantum physics and chaos theory. Within the crucible of a techno-scientifically driven identity meltdown, the opportunity had supposedly arisen for the wholesale reinvention of identity—both threatening and liberatory by turns. This would be a world without gender, race, "oedipal narratives," even embodiment. Net artists in the early 90s often combined an avant-garde rejection of the author's individuality and originality with the possibilities provided by computer mediated communication (CMC) to generate anonymous, parodic, shared, multiple and inauthentic identities. In other words, the possibility of being "whoever you want to be" in cyberspace combined with the ongoing deconstructions of authentic identity endemic to postmodern culture. Likewise, the viewer's boundaries were radically reconceived in early Net Art, now understood as prosthetically extended via personal computers and networks.[5]

The political critique of new media art, the defense of virtual reality and the non-representational nature of social reality, the techno-euphoria and the conspiracy theories, the paranoia about global dangers, and the screens that separate us from the Real—there are numerous phantasmatic scenarios implied by any performance that threatens someone's notion of the body, identity, being, the real, etc. "We" are not too sure about the virtualization of reality, and Slavoj Žižek, in his brilliant essay on *The Matrix*, suggests that it is "crucial to maintain open the radical ambiguity of how cyberspace will affect our lives: this does not depend on technology as such but on the mode of its social inscription. Immersion into cyberspace can intensify our bodily experience (new sensuality, new body with more organs, new sexes …), but it also opens up the possibility for the one who manipulates the machinery which runs the cyberspace literally to steal our own (virtual) body, depriving us of the control over it, so that one no longer relates to one's body as to 'one's own.' What one encounters here is the constitutive ambiguity of the notion of mediatization."[6] As Žižek's comment suggests, the theft of the body may present a very likely trauma to contemporary dance, and some conceptual choreographers seem to echo Morpheus' ontological confusion:

"Welcome to the desert of the real." The ontological confusion about virtual embodiment is productive, I believe, since it has introduced a range of new issues into the discussion of agency, control, manipulation, and appearance. The new theories on mediatization have crossed many disciplinary boundaries, and it is not surprising that Leeker's book acknowledges multiple perspectives and argues for a more comprehensive dialogue between the arts, the sciences, and *Medienwissenschaft* (media science).

For the history of performance, the body suspension and augmentation performances Stelarc created over the past decades are quite critical, as they manifest in a very blatant and beautiful manner some of the most problematic aspects in our experience of evolution, matter, intelligence, body, and technics, and thus in the understanding of the contemporary experience of the mobility of digital information. In particular, they manifest how the body can be probed to be "operated" upon, opened up, or extended into machinic operations, programmed and readied for involuntary motion, and many different kinds of extendable (prosthetic) expressions. There is fascination as well as abhorrence in regard to prosthetics: both the optimistic and the pessimistic critical receptions of technology need to continuously ask themselves how they understand technical mediation, and why they consider the human-technical engagement problematic. Adrian Mackenzie, in his response to Paul Virilio's critical stance toward the "displacement of 'natural capacities for movement' by sedentary teleoperative inertia," approaches Stelarc's endo-colonization in an unusually thoughtful manner by drawing attention to the "transindividual" aspect of *Ping Body* or *Movatar*, namely to a collective experience of teletechnological and biotechnological processes which includes the transduction of many divergent realities or modes of "eventuation." He suggests that a focus on temporality and technical mediation that does not fall back on pregiven ideas of subjectivity, knowledge, nature, or body can move "the focus away from the split between devices and bodies toward a less visible but vital middle ground of material practices." The idea of transduction suggests to him that "a diversity of actors, interests, institutions and practices are articulated together through specific technologies."[7]

If we look at the tools and the technical mediations in Stelarc's performance, it is therefore important, first of all, to recognize the technical ensemble (the apparatus of electrodes, cables, modem, computer and network interfaces, video screens, computer-generated sound) in relation to an indeterminate and unfolding context in which the living body is "animated," so to speak. The interfaces animate Stelarc, and Stelarc's movements and gestures are also screen-projected and become visible as if they were performed (filmed on camera). In such an ensemble, there are always multiple trajectories, and anyone who has performed with video monitors, audio monitors, and simultaneous video projections knows that such multiple dimensions can be disorienting especially since real-time transmission involves latency even though the transduction is supposed to be instantaneous. Interface performance, I suggest, always involves delays and imagined delays, however small and non-perceivable they may be. If in this case the electro-stimulation comes from outside the body, from the transducer and the network, the animated body of Stelarc also continuously re-integrates the movement: the bodymind and sensorimotor system respond and process the "information" since they are living systems. There is a very thin line, therefore, between what can be perceived as involuntary and as self-stimulated and anticipated movement, and Stelarc's playing with choreography as animation thus raises many intriguing questions about the artistic and social potential and political implications of technical mediations where the body itself can be seen as an originary technology *and* as prosthesis. Moreover, Stelarc's attitude toward automata and robotic devices is thoroughly Japanese (he lived in Japan for some years), reminiscent of the *Karakuri* tradition. His enjoyment of mechatronics is as uninhibited as Hiroshi Ishii's passion for tangible interfaces or Ryoji Ikeda's intense, minimalist compositions of ultra-frequency sound in hallucinatory white-out spaces.

In *Maschinen, Medien, Performances*, Stelarc concludes his workshop by asking us to consider how a "virtual body or an avatar can access a physical body, actuating its performance in the real world." His design for the technical ensemble envisions the avatar to be

> imbued with an artificial intelligence, becoming increasingly autonomous and unpredictable; then it would become more an Artificial Life entity performing with a human body in physical space. With an appropriate visual software interface and muscle stimulation system this would be possible. The avatar would become a Movatar. Its repertoire of behaviors could be modulated continuously by Ping signals and might evolve using genetic algorithms. With appropriate feedback loops from

the real world it would be able to respond and perform in more complex and compelling ways. The Movatar would be able not only to act, but also to express its emotions by appropriating the facial muscles of its physical body. As a VRML entity it could be logged into from anywhere—to allow a body to be accessed and acted upon. Or, from its perspective, the Movatar could perform anywhere in the real world, at any time, with as many physical bodies in diverse and spatially separated locations.[8]

One of the German writers in the book comments on this utopic vision by suggesting that such a performance resembles a *Marionettenspiel*, a game with a "living marionette" where the user can touch and animate telematically a spatially remote body. Stelarc, she suggests, fundamentally undermines the conception that one's own body is moved or actuated by a consciousness located in it (a self, a will, a mind, or spirit), that there exists an inner core that is surrounded by an outer skin. An external, alien "consciousness" impacts the body from outside. This alien consciousness is interfaced with the body and makes it move. Rather than interpreting Stelarc's conception of the body becoming the local host for different agents, which are spatially separated but nevertheless connected with each other, Kerstin Evert tends to see the telecommunicational dancer as "mehr-ortig" (many-placed), unbounded by the individual kinesphere and extended into a globally networked virtual space which exceeds the sensory organs.

Her notion of the fractal or dispersed body of course resonates with many critical readings of cyberspace and the posthuman, but if one looks at the workshop commentaries by the performers, one notices a different emphasis on the affective sensations of such a transindividual feedback loop. The reading of these commentaries is sometimes compelling, but also occasionally unnerving, as the language of explanation tends to rely mostly on metaphors of vitalism and sensory experience. Here is Horst Prehn describing his sensations as a user of the biofeedback installation *Camera Reflexiva*:

> As motion and emotion, movement and being-moved, affect each other, they give birth to unexpected and originary vital play, to creative activity, dance, scenic and theatrical stories. I am involved with body and soul in the creation of these stories. I begin to realize how I experience more subtle sensations, and how my corporeal feelings and cognitive states, and their affective experiences,

are pulled in an ever more intensive and comprehensive manner inside the flow of the event. My phantom body, mirrored and re-fracted several times, becomes an immediate figuration of muscu-lar tensions, nerve signals and brain waves, of breath and blood circulation, and of the entire emotional excitation of the partner coupled to me. In this way, the phantom figures, the diverse mir-rored fragmentations and materializations of my mediated alter ego, now become truly corporeal, animated by the activities and forces hidden in an other body. In a reflexive manner, my body and the phantom bodies generated by it now speak to each other. Their language is silent, corporeal, and we understand each oth-er in a sensual and embodied way. Indeed my medial skins begin to appear more real to me than I had ever believed possible. A hypersensual and corporeal concreteness fills me. These medial skins adapt to each form and shape, stretching over objects and performer with different aggregate states of themselves, each of them marked, colored and structured in a very specific way.[9]

Prehn here alludes to synaesthetic perceptions of the "liquid" self in per-formance with its multiple projections or *Phantomkörper* (phantom bodies), which is the term he uses for avatar. He also speaks of the feedback loop as a "perception-action cycle": the sensorial experience of the interactor evokes perception which is/becomes projection. Prehn, in contradistinction to thea-tre director Jo Fabian who participated in the same workshop on "Interact-ing versus Watching: The viewer in neuro-digital feedback loops and in the theatre," argues for an intensification of immersive self-experience inside an interface arrangement. In such an arrangement, when the performer is in-teracting with the mediated environment of acoustic, visual, light and color projections constituted in continuous feedback loops with signals generated through electro-physiological monitoring of vital data (brain functions, heart beat, breath, pulse, or sensorimotor data interfaced with computer algorithms which analyze, process, and react to the incoming data in constant modula-tions), Prehn strives to concentrate not on semiotic processes of sense-making but on the immediate physical and emotional experience of the *endo-move-ment*, so to speak, the movements inside the body. For Prehn such experiences are transcendental, ecstatic. They even resemble the hypnagogic trance states one might experience in a "ritualistic or liturgical" context.

Through the interface with the computer, these internal processes of the nervous system and the organism can be measured or read, i.e., the computer program analyses the electrical and physiological data and translates them into sonic and visual projections. The output of course is calculated by the software within the specific parameters of the program, but as with such interactive sonic and video or light projections generally, the performer is experiencing a direct visual, auditory, and tactile connection to the movement performed in real-time conjunction with the "phantoms"—those sounds, colors, lights, and images that appear on the surfaces hit by the digital projectors. In the Hellerau workshop, Prehn used the projector to project colors of light onto the performer's body (on his own body in the scene he writes down) while an additional camera (explaining the title of the experiment: *Camera Reflexiva*) instantly captured the changing colorizations on the skin and re-projected them onto the video screens. Prehn thus seems tempted to speak of *mediale Häute* (media skins), a stunning term in fact which seems quite appropriate in regard to the tendency, amongst performers using video projection, to emphasize the surfaces or membranes of the body and to include shadow silhouettes in the projections.

For a wide-angle view of performance history, it is tempting to think back a hundred years to Loïe Fuller's pioneering early-twentieth-century theatrical performances combining projections of multi-colored lights onto her flowing silk costumes. She was not only the first dancer to use Edison's new incandescent lights but also designed her own garments and experimented with different materials, lighting effects, and chemical mixes for gels and slides. Fascinating convergences could be found between dancer Loïe Fuller, avant-garde designer Adophe Appia, Surrealist painter/stage designer Pavel Tchelitchew, and the Bauhaus designers and visual artists (Schlemmer, Kandinsky, Moholy-Nagy) in the early decades of the century. Appia's spectacular lighting and spatial designs for Jacques-Dalcroze's eurhythmic performance production of *Orfeo* at the Hellerau Festspielhaus (1912) anticipates kinetic and op art which made moving light a medium for "visions of motion" and virtual volumes, as Moholy-Nagy had suggested with his moving light sculptures. Jacques-Dalcroze called the union of music and movement, of internal experience and external expression, *plastique animée*—a remarkable term that one might see echoed in Merleau-Ponty's phenomenology of the visible and invisible. I also see a correspondence to the exploration of color and wearable "skins" in Hélio Oiticica's neoconcrete works of the 1960s.

Oiticica's wearable *Parangolés* were based on an aesthetic vision, which again presupposes spiritual values for radical experimentation with matter and the dynamics of the imagination. In *Body of Color*, a recent exhibition at the Houston Museum of Fine Arts, Oiticica's *Parangolés* were featured at the conclusion of a large array of paintings, spatial reliefs, manipulable objects, three-dimensional architectural sculptures, and envionments, sketches, and maquettes. The artist's conceptual and technical explorations of time and spatial structures were delineated to emphasize how he developed a dynamic understanding of color in embodied action and participatory situations. The colored garments were at the furthest remove from two-dimensional flat canvases: they had to be experienced and worn as "habitable" paintings by the public, moving to the rhythm of samba and dynamically activating the "color-in-motion" in sensorial bodily contact with the fabrics. The *Parangolés* were interactive prototypes, textile-surfaces for supra-sensorial experiences meant to allow the participant a carnivalesque liberation from conditioned behavior. Similar to Prehn's emphasis on direct tactile sensation, Oiticica's *Parangolés* were devised to transcend the visual, to energize a flow and an expansion of individual consciousness into a kind of primeval return to the mythic. The mythic dimension, however, was understood by Oiticica as an originary moment of creative invention, of creativity as such, embedded in the discovery of rhythm, movement, bodylines, and sensuality, and thus an immediate perceptual, participatory knowledge.

What is strikingly different, in comparison to most interactive camera tracking software using a monitoring or surveillance camera for the data input, is the interface design in Prehn's work with biofeedback, which allows the monitoring of data inside (*endo*) the organism. These are physiological data that cannot be seen from the outside. Therefore the role of the spectator here is changed as well. The viewer is invited to imagine the inner physiological or neurological processes of the performance. But Prehn argues for the abolition of viewers: he wants the viewer to be the interactor inside the work. The externalization (the visual and sonic projections) is a technical and aesthetic mediation, which complicates the matter. It intensifies the synaesthetic processes at work without necessarily allowing a scientific or logical explanation or a semantic reading of the performance. At stake, in this instance, is primarily the performer's own immediate experience of multiple, simultaneous, fluid "phantoms" of self or of the body's signs in motion: the immediate sensations of mediations.

Stage director Jo Fabian, on the other hand, insists that immediate interaction with biofeedback, inviting the user-participant to affect perception without having a critical parameter of criteria for understanding the perceivability of the interface functions, is pointless. Fabian upholds a more Brechtian view of epic theatre in which the performance points up the system with which it generates its reality or its sensory processes of perception. He does not seem to trust sensory experience without critical distance, and instead proposes to work with performance systems on stage that can illustrate the perceivability of functional mechanisms of interaction and thus make them understandable and critically interpretable for the audience. In fact Fabian, who had worked at the Bauhaus in Dessau in 1989 before founding his independent production company ("Department") in Berlin and beginning to design theatre, dance, and film works in his own idiosyncratic visual language, is a critical fellow-traveler of Robert Wilson's theatre of images. His well-known *whiskey & flags* and *Alzheimer light* performances betray his visual sensibilities and his often sinister reinvention of the kind of total, synthetic theatre that the early Bauhaus artists had envisioned.

Fabian devised the "alphasystem" for his dancers, an alphabet-derived code of movement choreography which allows the performer to translate texts into precise movements and to recombine the particular gestures in infinite possible variations that can be "read" by the audience in terms of the rule system, the logistics, which they obey. To a certain extent, Fabian can be said to have invented an algorithmic or numeric movement repertoire for the dancers, which he now wants to connect with media (light, projections). Conceptually, he proposes, such is the process of interaction as he understands it: the *Verkopplung* (interfacing) of the alphasystem with another system, which can then be perceived cognitively by the audience. The audience will create meanings out of this collision, and the crucial issue is that a new meaningful experience—in a theatre based on conventions and codes that are predictable—can only be evoked through differentiations, delays, disruptions in the decoding. These disruptions occur in-between the systems.

With this dispute between Fabian and Prehn, and many pages in the book which extend the workshop investigations into very intricate conversations about intermediality in the theatre, *Maschinen, Medien, Performances* widens the scope of the historical parameters stretching from dance to installation art, from Stelarc's transductive body to the neuro-physiological research on sensory perception. Significantly, these disputes clarify to me how unspecific the term "interactive performance" is. It is crucial to ask where the interactive system is used, on stage, off stage, by the trained performer who is improvising or following a precise cue structure or choreography, by an untrained audience member, i.e., a general user or an expert user. The questions extend to: who is interacting with whom? With what? Performers with other performers using the interface or performers with the interface or performers with performers within an interface which organizes its total output via the actions of the performers? If the notion of choreography is replaced by "user experience," is it because a performative interaction environment has been specifically designed for the user? Who is the user and how does she know what to use?

Let me describe an installation which was awarded the Golden Nica award in the category "interactive art" at the 2004 ars electronica, and which has been widely exhibited at venues such as the Brooklyn Academy of Music (2001), Seattle's On the Bords (2002), the Whitney Museum (2003), the List Visual Arts Center (2004), and the San Jose Museum of Art (2006). Ben Rubin and Mark Hansen's *Listening Post* is an immersive multimedia environment which draws the audience into a kind of networked auditorium, a virtual proscenium space constituted of Internet conversations culled from thousands of chat rooms, bulletin boards and other public forums. How does the audience know how to use this work? The interaction experience, contrary to the claims made by ars electronica, does not seem to require a direct physcial activity on part of the viewer or listener. Rather, *Listening Post* invites a gentle listening on behalf of its audience and an imaginative act of unprecedented scale. You are transported into the global world of the Internet, the expansive distances of an immaterial cosmos. But you are also made to witness the performance of a system of data mining that translates innumerable wordly data into sound, capturing and recombining traces of human interaction (communication) and making them present in a physical arrangement which is breathtaking.

The installation is composed of a curving aluminum lattice hung with 231 miniature computer screens. This screen curtain comes alive as the operating system extracts text fragments in real-time from the Internet. Several computers analyze data from innumerable online conversations and chat rooms, and the software selects a range of postings beginning with "I am," "I like," or "I love." Gradually, the communiqués begin to appear on the LCD displays, illuminating the space with pulses of soft blue light. The selected texts vary in length and complexity; the simpler and shorter ones coming first, with the beep of a telephone answering machine preceding the appearance of each message. Irregular visual and audible rhythms ebb and flow, creating a stream of human chatting here translated into a technological concert of words and sounds. The language of these anonymous conversations is not only displayed, the words are also read or sung by a voice synthesizer. The sound-generating systems behave like wind chimes, but the wind that blows here is human dialogue drifting across the digital ether. The particles that move are not air molecules but words, messages, questions, answers, pauses, silences building up to cacophonies. The computer software understands the words as collectible data rather than dramatic dialogue. The software, in this sense, is anti-theatrical; it does not know the power of illusion nor does it concern itself with human subjectivity, narrative, drama. And yet, this installation has a theatrical effect and evokes theatrical conventions in the very manner in which this network performance exceeds all limits of theatre.

Listening Post, Rubin has suggested, wants to harness the human energy that is carried by all of these words, channeling that energy through the technological mechanisms of the piece. The conceptual base was provided by Mark Hansen, a statistician at Lucent Technologies' Bell Labs whose research focusses on search engines, data analysis, and the use of information systems. Hansen and sound designer Ben Rubin worked together for two years to develop the shared vision for their score of data sonification—real-time information speaking itself. The result is a unique aesthetic symbiosis of sculptural sound design and data collection and modeling. The installation, in my view, has a particularly strong musical dimension and structure, as it involves the audience primarily through listening and the almost ritual communal tendency, deeply embedded in many cultures, of tuning the body and mind's attention to the voices in the congregation.

Ironically, the work here reveals a far-reaching social and political dimension, as its relentless data mining techniques probe our acquiescence to the huge distributed consciousness of a globally interconnected world of conversations, a world congregation yearning with the desire to communicate, to have opinions, to anticipate responses. I may not know what a globally interconnected world sounds like, but when I go to visit an old cathedral or an ancient colosseum, I listen to the sound of echoes. Vast spaces with immense potential also haunt the imagination, since the architectures that create echoes are often connected to the sacred and the sublime. Massive volumes overwhelm us like the huge waves of the ocean. *Listening Post* evokes such an ocean, even if its waves of words pile up like towers of Babel, joined and spliced with truncated sentences of profane chatter about sex and everyday life, age and gender, religion and commerce. Acquiescence to such monitoring of distant echoes here means intuiting our curious involvement as listeners to private and public exchanges. I overhear what was not meant for me. If the mundane world of the network is an open source, the operating systems making these chat data available can be said to function like the chorus in the classical amphitheatres. The role of the chorus was to speak for the general population, to articulate public opinion. *Listening Post* paradoxically draws on its search engines and filter devices to capture the raw articulations of the chatters who may never know they were part of this congregation for one brief moment. To escape the ethical dilemma, must I not assume that all these postings were public after all, that their opinions were posted to be heard by the world?

Cycling through a series of six movements, each of them has a different arrangement of visual, aural, and musical elements. Although each movement's data processing logic is not overtly obvious, one can intuit a complex harmony and a structure. In musical terms, there is what one might call a symmetry of perception, and listening to the cycles I make connections and notice the aural properties. I sense patterns and rhythms. But discerning a *composition,* shaping and processing the sheer magnitude and immediacy of virtual communication, here implies both the mathematics of coding and an aesthetic arrangement. Rubin and Hansen wrote the algorithms and defined the parameters, the computer performs the concert. As one listener wrote, "the poetry of *Listening Post* derives from the fact that the communication of the chatters lives outside of the chat room, but only for a moment, and it is not archived …. The *Listening Post* has no memory, it is a monument only to the present. Its effect is hypnotic, and viewers who sat in front of the piece for a time were watching a performance for which the stage direction was provided by a filtering algorithm, and the characters were the thousands of chatters who were supplying pieces of content."[10] *Listening Post,* Michelle Kasprzak concludes, gave her the view of the future of electronic art that she had hoped for, one in which artists orchestrate systems, find beauty in the analysis of information flows, and become choreographers of data.

This idea of "choreographing data" in such telecommunicational mediation is not without its problems, as the analogue sense of working with real moving bodies and physically present subjects is of course completely changed to a decontextualized environment. The languages we use, verbal or non-verbal, are always context-dependent, and therefore our metaphoric and symbolic meaning making, our sensorial perceptions, are necessarily impaired by telecommunications. Telecommunicational perception therefore raises many phenomenological concerns for performing artists who compose with distancing techniques and digital processes, and some of these have been astutely addressed by a workshop series entitled "Dance and New Media" held at the Choreographisches Zentrum NRW (in Essen, Germany) in 2001 under the artistic direction of Söke Dinkla. The bi-lingual book, *Dance and Technology/Tanz und Technologie: Moving toward Media Productions—Auf dem Weg zu medialen Inszenierungen*, documents the phenomenological and cognitive approaches, and it will be helpful to look at them briefly because of the different areas of experimentation selected, and what they tell us about the organizers' views on the history of such experimentation.[11]

The first part of the book is of particular historical interest, as theatre, media, and art scholars explore the "genealogy" of the relationship between dance and digital technologies. After Dinkla's general introduction ("Toward a Rhetoric and Didactics of Digital Dance"), Kerstin Evert offers a short overview of some key moments in the history of "Dance and Technology at the Turn of the Last and Present Centuries," singling out Cage/Cunningham's *Variations V* as a significant early, mid-century forerunner of today's practice of interactive performance, even though she critically comments on the unequal relationship between dance and the sound design, noting that Cunningham's dancers were largely taking on a "musician or instrument function" in setting off or triggering the short-wave radios and tapes. This is an interesting observation, to which I will return later when discussing gesture control in music and dance-technology performances based primarily on the use of gestural interfaces ("instruments") for sonic production and processing, thus focusing the interface very tangibly and visibly as a mapping between performative input (gestural) and inferable output (aural). *Variations V* was primarily a music concert devised by Cage and his sound collaborators. It is quite correct to say, however, that the dancers' movements extended the movement functions and acted upon the photocells to generate sound, which was then further modulated and processed by the musicians to generate a continuous feedback loop and an interdependence of movement and sound oscillation.

Cage's interest must have rested on the particular nature of the "chance" event of human motion setting off the sound of radio waves and thus interacting with wave-lengths and whatever it was (ranging from silence to noise) that could be heard from these remote radio stations as well as the by-products of the situation as a whole. As David Toop suggests in *Haunted Weather*, Cage's compositional leaning toward "silence" and process as co-existence of everything that might happen and be heard reflects an approach to interaction that was not primarily technological but linked to Cage's natural philosophy, his desire for communication with everything, including the atmosphere.[12] The electrical engineers, in turn, experimented with the sensor-design and the many layers of accidental music, sound, noise, and distortions—the liveness of the ether and the liveness of the circuitry. Most typically for this era of early electronic music, the sound artists and engineers enjoyed tinkering and finding creative possibilities through the circuitry. Toop quotes one of the pioneering tinkerers (a member of the improvisation group Musica Elettronica Viva): "we found ourselves busily soldering cables, contact mikes, and talking about 'circuitry' as if it were a new religion. By amplifying the sounds of glass, wood, metal, water, air, and fire, we were convinced that we had tapped into the sources of the natural musics of 'everything.' We were in fact making spontaneous music which could be said to be coming from 'nowhere' and made out of 'nothing'—all somewhat of a wonder and a collective epiphany."[13]

In *Variations V*, Cage's collaboration with Tudor, Klüver, and other sound artists (including Nam June Paik) of course also involved the new technological tools to reach for the epiphanies, and they, as many other musicians did at the time, extended the notion of the "musical instrument" through various methods (contact microphones, guitar pedals, processing devices such as delays, distortion, filters, and ring modulators, special effects units, and MIDI lines running to synthesizers, samplers, sound generators, or computer programs). By the 1990s, the notion of the musical instrument had expanded to include the dancer in an interactive interface using gesture or movement to trigger sounds or control the sound sequencing. Given the musical context, it is also interesting to think of the Cage-Cunningham collaboration in relation to the contemporaneous electro-acoustic/electronic music and rock music culture. Cunningham and his dancers were dancing a reverb/feedback concert in 1965. It was completely radical in aesthetic dance terms at the time, while it invites comparisons with guitarists like

Jimi Hendrix or keyboard players like Keith Emerson (who started experimenting with the Moog Synthesizer a few years later), as well as with the
early television signal manipulations by Nam June Paik and the violin/video
concerts by Steina Vasulka in which she would manipulate the video signal
using the movement of her violin bow as gestural interface. This notion of
gesture acting as an extend musical instrument is still used by a number of
practitioners today, especially by groups which combine live musicians and
dancers and by composers and instrument designers who combine their
knowledge of musical performance, electro-acoustics design, and software
programming.[14]

While Evert's essay focuses on particular artistic works and the discourses (cybernetics, phenomenology, Marshall McLuhan's and Derrick de
Kerckhove's media theories, etc.) informing our understanding of electronic
networks and interface design, Scott deLahunta's essay "Periodic Convergences: Dance and Computers" delves more deeply into the significance
which developments in computational ideas and computer science have had
for the performing arts in order to trace the points at which computation
and choreography could meet. At these meeting points, particular computing aids (either generative or supportive) for choreographic composition
emerged. His lucid essay is an important source for information on early
developments in cybernetics, computer art, and choreography of the 1960s,
and given his own practical involvement in many significant workshops
and laboratories across the world over the past fifteen years, he has many
insights to offer both on the successful convergences between dance and
computer technologies, and also on the formal discrepancies which exist
between "the properties of the digital and the essential components of dance
practice involving human motion, corporeality and physical presence." He
knows all the tools that have been used or tried out, and thus his essay
gives us very valuable background information on interactive systems, such
as David Rokeby's "Very Nervous System" (VNS), which was introduced
by the Canadian sound artist already in the 1980s but still played a role in
the workshops at Hellerau discussed above. DeLahunta ends his overview
with a short outlook on more recent experiments in dance and technology,
involving telematics and motion capture, followed by two essays on interactive space design and interactive performance written by practitioners (Robb
Lovell and Nik Haffner), and two further essays on the history of technics
which are delightfully refreshing, as they go back to the early twentieth

century to explore the impact of electricity on early modern dance (Martina Leeker with Wolfgang Hagen), and the significance of Laban's Kinetography and movement notation, first developed in the 1930s, in the context of the history of science and media history (Hans-Christian von Herrmann).

The main portion of *Dance and Technology/Tanz und Technologie* is dedicated to critical documentations of the three workshops directed by Gretchen Schiller and Robb Lovell ("Interactivity as a Choreographic Phenomenon"), Paul Sermon ("Dance on Telematic Stages"), and Wayne McGregor ("Choregraphy—Telematics—Animation"). In an interview with Gretchen Schiller which opens the first workshop documentation, Martina Leeker asks Schiller how she moved from being a dancer to working with videodance and eventually with interactive technologies. Schiller's story is one that is familiar to many of us. At least for the generations of artists mentioned so far, who grew up training in a performance or visual art discipline (dance, music, theatre, stage design, sculpture, etc.), the process of expanding their art practice by the gradual inclusion of new media technologies was logical, even if it may have depended on specific contexts of opportunity, artistic interest, or encounters with others who inspired such expansions. Schiller simply states that she met a dance ethnologist and filmmaker while studying at UCLA who aroused her curiosity in using the camera to "produce movements that dancers' bodies could not perform." She then decided to study video art (in the architecture department at MIT) and to explore different kinaesthetic possibilities that eventually shifted her interest to architectural and responsive environments in which interactive design could create a linking between the behavior of protagonists in the space and the behavior of video.

I believe that such a trajectory in personal artistic development is indeed symptomatic of many artists, regardless of whether they are performing artists, composers, media artists, writers, or visual artists—the incorporation of time-based media and computation into performance was as organic and natural as the incorporation of actors into feature film, or of social and anthropological subjects into cinema verité, or of glass, metal, fish, and bats into sound production.

Paul Sermon's workshop on telepresence and "telematic stages" bases its approach on the history of telecommunications art, connecting remote locations with each other via video conferencing technology and placing the viewer as participant in the artwork. Sermon's reference point is the early work of cybernetic artists like Roy Ascott or Eduardo Kac, who pioneered computer-mediated communications networking. Initially it involved telephone, cable, and satellite links between geographically dispersed individuals and sites, and with the rise of the Internet such communications could involve online performance and the distributed interactions of imaging, sound, and text systems (and in grid computing the massive combination of data-processing systems or data storage banks interlaced with each other). Sermon's own well-known work, such as *Telematic Dreaming* (1992), was directed at a more personal, tangible experience of a participant communicating with someone in a remote location, and his strategy utilized video conferencing, and the mixing of video images, to create a commonly shared space for participants at separate locations. In the workshop Sermon proposed the creation of such a "third space" as the method for interface design focusing on different kinds of movements, gestures, and actions which pairs of participants could explore to acquaint themselves with the experience of their "telepresent bodies," i.e., the images of their bodies in the other site. Sermon's interest lies in the shift of the senses and a different feeling of *touch*. For him the third space becomes a stage where participants can direct a gesture, for example, to touch another body, but this implies using the hand as a "medium for positioning my sense of touch," touching "with my eyes." The workshop results indicate, however, that his own experience with installations could not be easily transferred to choreographic practice with dancers. He notes that the participants had difficulties putting aside their "knowledge as dancers," freeing themselves from the notion that they had to be concerned above all with their own immediate space, their own kinesphere. Rather than self-reference, he suggests, telematic performance presupposes coming to terms "with a virtual space that surrounds their bodies but is at the same time remote."

The issue of how to overcome this sense of remoteness—to imagine oneself in remoteness or feel projectedness—is a general problem to which I shall return throughout some of the later chapters. Leeker and Dinkla's workshop structure seems to have anticipated the differences between installation and choreography, as the third lab was given to British choreographer Wayne McGregor whose instructions explicitly address the notion of an "extended body" but start from a generation of movement material (inspired by computer animation software) and examinations of body concepts taking into account the "hybrid body" made up of combinations of the organic, the animalistic, the animatronic, the neurotic, the avatar body, etc. Only then does he begin to delve into exploring how these "fluid body" motions—movement material deliberately constructed after participants worked with animation software such as LifeForms and Poser—can be adapted to a remote location performances and webcasts.

McGregor was primarily interested in showing different approaches to working with computer programs and telematic performances. "For me," he states, "it was more important to put across strategies for working with technology than a fixed aesthetic. Teaching various methods of working is the only way to open up countless other possibilities. The interface of computer or rather digital technology seems to provide some kind of impartiality, which frees up decisions and takes away many of the inhibitions about creating dance. There is objectivity to their responses in improvisation, which removes the valued judgements that commonly restrict wholehearted participation. But above all, new media interventions provide a strong motivation to actualise the virtual choreographic ideas."

If one looks at the "virtual choreographic ideas" used in the workshop, one discovers again a historical link to John Cage's and Merce Cunningham's chance operations and also to a long-standing tradition of improvisation which values emergence and responsive fluidity in movement rather than set choreographic phrases. McGregor, similar to Schiller and Sermon, refers back to Laban's notion of the kinesphere when he speaks of the kinetic architecture of the body. It is not far-fetched to claim that the mathematics and geometry of the computer animation software Cunningham and McGregor came to use are also based on the idea of the icosahedron with which Laban developed a system of dancer-centred directions as a means of recording dance. Laban might have used the rectangular coordinate system, which can define any point in space with reference to an origin and coordinates from three mutually perpendicular axes, but he opted for polyhedral structures and the more dynamic, intuitive icosahedron system based on twenty-six directions around the dancer, and then formulated his choreutics scales to develop his spatial and movement effort analysis. It is also worth remembering that generations of choreographers and scholars have studied Laban and written dissertations on Choreutics and Kinetography, embracing the spatial analysis even as they dismissed Laban's cosmological theories as irrelevant for the practice.[15] There are re-entry points for Laban's cosmology, however; Leeker even suggests as much when she asks Schiller why she uses the yoga-based training method of Gyrokinesis as a meditative or physical-spiritual preparation for her work on interactive and responsive "kinesfields" (Schiller's Laban-derived term for the relationship between inner bodyspace and the outer bodyspace of the installation design).

Schiller responds by emphasizing the body's relationship to space in order to produce empathy in the image environment. For this reason, the workshop group practiced Gyrokinesis to train the individual to "connect and cultivate physical and imaginary spaces. This yoga, gymnastics, swimming, and classical ballet-influenced technique developed by Julio Horvath stimulates one's awareness of movement efforts. This training includes massage, repetitive undulating and spiralling movements with sitting, standing and floor exercises. Gyrokinesis conditions the physical and imaginary contact between the inner body and the environment." With regard to somatic practices and improvisation, several Caribbean and Brazilian choreographers have told me that "empathy" is an important concept in non-Western dance where the experience of rhythm and harmony can be said to involve *spiritual technologies*, i.e., mediations which connect the soul of the dancer to the wider kinesfield including the spirit world and the ancestors. The sacred dimensions of dance, and the intricate interconnections between the spiritual and the material, of course are rarely addressed or admitted in the rationalist climate of Euro-American dance or in the discourse on technology. But if it is common to assume that in African or Indian dance traditions spirituality is an ineffable subject and source of the dancer's action, and if Steve Paxton, among many other contact improvisation artists, can speak of "interior techniques" and a necessary "vision of the eastern martial arts philosophy underlying the techniques," it might be a rewarding challenge to re-consider the implications of empathy and spirit-improvisation.[16]

Schiller, Sermon, and McGregor reveal different understandings of empathy and imaginary contact improvisation, but it is noteworthy that both Schiller and Sermon speak of intimate physical relationships to virtual realities. Working with installations, they focus on the "user experience," and Schiller emphasizes the unpredictable emotional experience in the body, even as she proposes that the workshop participants can train themselves to be open to a higher physical imagination toward the "spirit" of the ephemeral environment. Although it seems contradictory that she distinguishes between the untrained visitor (the *lokaharmi*) and the highly skilled dance-*natyadharmi*, her approach to designing moving worlds in interactive environments clearly favors a non-hierarchical model where the stage is replaced by the installation as a common space. McGregor, on the other hand, enjoys the instability in the apparatus. For him, "virtual choreographic ideas" for telematically mediated dance imply a radical contingency: the technical conditions of the telematic setup lead to "something uncontrolled emerging, something that couldn't be predicted or planned for." To a certain extent, this is precisely the scenario of *Variations V*, except that McGregor uses network technology rather than sensors and short-wave radios. McGregor works with the *natyadharmi,* but his choreographic approach embraces the digital in its most transitory sense. The telematic stage harbors a state of "permanent uncertainty" as a "result of the technical conditions," and therefore different choreographies will emerge each time. A new concept of multi-dimensionality will be generated, he suggests, as a consequence of the coupling of dancers and virtual space.

As I have repeatedly alluded to videodance and dance documentation, it might be relevant to mention the problems one can envision in digital preservation methods and approaches that try to deal with the kind of permanent uncertainty and emergence in choreographic and performative practice explained by McGregor. Mike Phillips, who is working with Ric Allsopp and Scott deLahunta on the coordination of several documentation research projects based on the choreographic practices of William Forsythe, Siobhan Davies, Emio Greco, and McGregor, proposes that new interactive software tools (such as Liquid Reader) can organize diverse descriptive methods for databases of digital artifacts that emerge directly from the creative process. At the 2006 Digital Resources in the Humanities and Arts Conference at Dartington College of Arts (UK), Phillips summarized his approach to such creative dance preservation:

> This active and recursive process fits nicely to the concept of choreographic resources discussed here. For there is a co-dependency built into the type of resource creation proposed by these four projects; these choreographic resources are dependent on the choreographer-dancer not only to engage in their generation but also to reabsorb them back into the practice. As these choreographers 'step back' to reflect on their body of work and how to make dance more intelligible, they remain attuned to the needs of their own creative practice. And they are not concerned that

unlocking some of the mysteries of this practice will diminish the experience for the viewer. Quite the contrary, they seek no less than to challenge themselves and their audiences to take dance making to new places and to reveal 'the next level of imaginary trace.' Whether using technology to transfer the dynamic action of drawing into pliable data; inventing impermanent names for individual capacities and unique movements; generating creative agents informed by the thinking in movement; or asking experts from different fields to describe the information contained in choreographic work, the projects outlined here emphasize dance as a particular form of knowledge. Not as a rarefied, unknowable ephemera, but a complex and meaningful resource for understanding human perception, complex systems of interaction, and moving ideas. All of these projects make use of various forms of documentation to produce something meaningful. But the research is not taking place in the gap between dancing and its documentation, nor does it draw attention to dance's disappearance. As such, it is a form of scholarship balanced precariously at the edge of the creative practice itself.[17]

Moving beyond other digital documentation projects initiated, for example, through NIPAD or Ohio State University's dance software development (LabanWriter, LabanReader), Liquid Reader deploys new technological capabilities for more comprehensive and generative methods of re-articulation in a range of media. Basically it can be described as a digital and conceptual interface for the documentation, analysis and dissemination of live and body-based performance practices. The Liquid Reader project is a collaborative arts and technology initiative involving numerous partner teams of practitioners from different disciplinary knowledge bases. It takes as its starting point the capabilities of digital technology to integrate audio-visual, textual and graphical content, and the potential to apply these capabilities to forms of unstable or live body-based media (such as dance, theatre, and performance art) whose publication has, until now, been limited primarily to text and page-based documentation and dissemination. The project is developing a set of software and conceptual tools that enable the exploration and analysis of the process, construction, and dissemination of performance. Such research development also tells us how important it is to define more clearly the various dimensions of contemporary creative compositional practice: how have technologies altered the way we make dance and how do changing descriptions of practice affect the way performance is perceived?

In this respect, a book of considerable interest for a historical perspective on the changing notion of "design" in theatre and performance was published in the Netherlands in 2004, edited by a scene designer and a professor of computer graphic design.[18] Colin Beardon and Gavin Carver's *New Visions in Performance: The Impact of Digital Technologies* brings together a range of vivid analyses of creative work which spans traditional theatre, dance, textile design, film, and computer games. The eleven essays are written by practitioners directly involved in the conceptual and methodological development of mediated performance and interactive systems. Some of them are co-authored, as we generally expect to see it in laboratory research publications in the sciences. We are less accustomed to see research methodologies or creative experiments theoretically reflected by artists and research teams, and here the book makes an important contribution. In their concluding essay, the editors provide an eloquent synopsis of the diverse poetics and conceptual frameworks employed by the practitioners, identifying various common themes and concerns that the authors share in their use of digital systems and real-time processing. This introduction to certain core issues—virtuality, the mediated body, liveness, manipulated time-space, interactivity, and audience involvement—is put at the end of the book, ostensibly to avoid postulating a unifying theory of new technology in performance or to lump the diversity of emerging digital art and media practices together. Their careful parsing of overlapping concerns between theatre, dance, media artists, designers, and programmers is very valuable, and along with the more scholarly essays by Steve Dixon, Jackie Smart, and Christie Carson at last begins to provide a sense of historical context for these current creative research and production processes.

Digital media, even as the hardware and software potentials of computer-assisted design, real-time processing, and Internet-based communications increase constantly, are not a new phenomenon for performance, after all, as Mark Coniglio rightly points out in "The importance of being interactive," since we tend to read them through our analogue habits and prior understanding of photographic, filmic, and electroacoustic techniques such a projection, amplification, and distortion. The manipulation of time and space in imaging media has been studied and analyzed (in art and film theory), and important early philosophies of time, movement and perception, such as Bergson's notion of spatializing mechanisms and becoming (duration), now enjoy a revival of interest.[19] The transformational technological innovations of the nineteenth and twentieth centuries are common knowledge in our cultures today. "New visions" in performance are also indebted to older forms of media production, whether we think of the use of film projection and lighting in the theatre or of the many avant-garde experiments in film, electronic music, and early video and installation art. Coniglio, referring back to improvisations between jazz musicians and the essential fluidity of live performance where virtuoso artists can "invent" responses and skillfully manipulate the musical phrasing right there in front of our eyes and ears, admits that digital data, once stored in the computer, appear "antithetical to the fluid and ever changing nature of live performance" unless the programming of an interactive improvisatory environment allows the dancer (Coniglio works with the New York City based company Troika Ranch) the same virtuosic command over her instrument. He then confirms his dedication to "unrepeatable" live interactive performance, cautioning us to be weary of claims that the "use of sensory technologies and digital media offers some kind of radical shift in the nature of live performance itself."

Interestingly, Coniglio is the only contributor in the book who addresses the issue of virtuosic performance head-on, even though Dixon's "The Digital Double," with its references to several widely-known and distinguished artists (Cunningham, Stelarc, Nam June Paik, Chico McMurtrie, Yacov Sharir, igloo, Company in Space, Marcel-Lí.Anthúnez Roca), and Smart's detailed, evocative reading of the "technology of the real" in Wayne McGregor's *Nemesis* (Random Dance Co.) come close to remembering that the power of performance, to a large extent, relies on the skill and ingenuity of the performer, and not only on those of the system. Jools Gilson-Ellis and Richard Povall, in a tantalizing dialogue about their collaborative partnership ("Halving angles: technology's poem"), also remember that theatre and dance have literary and poetic ancestors. Gilson-Ellis impressively plays with language and metaphor and draws on her deep-seated interest in poetry and mystery. "My writings always had a bent for the magical, but the experience of working with technologies in this way makes me a different kind of writer.... I demand a poetic alchemy from the digital."

Povall, who programs the sonic landscapes of music and words, the "quality" of the sound which Gilson-Ellis activates and "moves" through her physical performance (tracked by cameras), argues that they build "poetic systems"—systems that can capture "the essence of the performing body, turning that information into sonic and visual gesture. In these systems, the centre of attention is not the objective body-state. The focus instead is the subjective body—the phenomenal dancer." Povall and Gilson-Ellis emphasize that their aesthetics of movement has become the aesthetics of an emergent poetic narrative, which in current work such as *Spinstren* is the result of many years of experimentation. Generating poetry in real time, playing with "voice ghosts," Gilson-Ellis argues, allows the dancer to navigate between the present tense of voicing and moving, and the past tense of writing and recorded voice, resisting the difference between past and present. This confusion of temporal realities becomes an "an unsettling enchantment."

Several artists express a similar interest in ghostly doubles and virtual enchantments, without necessarily commenting on the spiritual or sacred roots of theatre and dance or alluding to cultural traditions outside of their focus on Western sciences and avant-gardes. Dixon, opening his essay with a reference to Artaud before examining the "theatre and its digital double," finds various manifestations of "virtual magic" in the sense in which digital and telematic technologies create "other realms" through the (1) double as reflection or video copy; (2) double as alter-ego or cyborg; (3) double as spiritual emanation and phantom; and (4) double as manipulable mannequin. Avatars based on motion-capture animation, bodies without organs (a by now familiar reference to Deleuze/Guattari filtered through Stelarc's much quoted joke about the "obsolete body"), particle bodies, replicants, cadavers, mechanical dolls, and robotic manipulations make their appearance in Dixon's impressively wide-ranging analysis of figuration in contemporary performance. Freud's notion of the uncanny comes back to haunt audiences who, Dixon speculates, actually love this digital world since the double serves as a "conceptual template" for our late commodity culture's obsession with synthetic replacements, narcissism, and death. Dixon's point is hard-hitting; when he writes that "to see one's self is to demolish oneself in an autopsy of perception," he approaches the unreal through a lens that differs markedly from Gilson-Ellis's story-telling based on folk mythology, Toni Dove's endorsement of ghosts as virtual counterparts (enacted by the user) entering and inhabiting the fanatsy space in her interactive installations

(*Artificial Changelings, Spectropia*), Jorgen Callesen, Marika Kajo, and Katrine Nilsen's "Performance Animation Toolbox" which uses slapstick ghost stories in their public installation *Spirits on Stage*, or Michael Nitsche and Maureen Thomas's redeployment of computer games for real time interaction with avatar models purloined from old movies.

The design teams reflect most clearly the overwhelming tenor of this book, which is concerned less with content, meaning, and the challenges faced by performers who need to create meaningful expression within responsive environments, but with the design of interactive systems as such. Having said this, I want to emphasize that such a book on interface design for performance and participatory digital art is long overdue. *New Visions in Performance* offers a tremendous resource for opening a complex debate among performers, directors, choreographers, composers, and programmers, regarding not only the research and methodologies for interaction design, but also the potentially new aesthetic forms and compositional repertoires, performance techniques, and cultural sensibilities which may or may not reside in what the commercial industry, somewhat despairingly, calls "content development." The closest link to the market, in this book, is struck by Carson's essay "Turning conventional theatre inside out: democratizing the audience relationship," in which she argues for the educational values of the Internet and digital information systems, enabling institutional theatres (her examples are The Royal Shakespeare Company, the National Theatre, the Globe Theatre, and CalArts Center for New Theater) and cultural producers the kind of interactive portals that encourage the wider population of audiences to have a role in the process of creative production. Carson applauds the Globe Theatre's Globelink Website (with its unusual "Adopt an actor" scheme), which along with live workshops, lectures, tours and performances builds practice-led resources for the study of Shakespearean drama based on a democratic ethos of "audience-driven interactive experience."

Carson represents an educational theatre position, but content (drama), professional craft (acting, stage design), and audience interest in the theatrical process are hardly negligible for a debate on "new visions" if indeed Coniglio's claim about the "importance of being interactive" is earnest and, above all, reflects adequately the new models in interdisciplinary digital performance, which the editors summarize as being overwhelmingly predicated on "virtuality" and on the body being digitized, its movements and enunciations captured and coded for algorithmic processing. Carver and Beardon here draw a crucial distinction:

> In its early stages, any new technology will be understood primarily as technique. That is to say, the developer will communicate the intended use of particular gadgets to artists who then incorporates [sic] these into their traditional practice, or maybe exploits [sic] them in some new experimental pieces of work. As the techniques become more numerous and artistic experience grows, so a more sophisticated relationship between technology and art form develops. This is the stage we now appear to be at and, hence, it is no longer appropriate to analyse the chapters in this book in terms of the digital technologies that they employ (motion capture, Internet, complex algorithms, etc.). Rather, we need to move to a more conceptual level so that we can talk about the technology in terms of models of use.

If we follow the logic of this argument, we can assume that the emphasis in digital performance, particularly interactive or networked installations, has shifted to the design of programmable and manipulable environments. Kjell Yngve Petersen ("The emergence of hyperreality in performance") focuses on the "use of cameras, computers and video-projectors in the stage setting" to examine the visual aspects of performance "being infused by telematic and real-time technology." This infusion allows designers to develop polyfocal viewpoints and scenic montages with multiple perspectives, displacements of time, duration, and place. Stage reality, consequently, comments and redefines its own notion of reality and becomes a hyper-reality. Petersen includes illustrations of such augmented space-time, and bases his theorizations on notions of meta-fiction derived from "dynamic semiotics."

Similarly, Smart's essay on "Wayne McGregor's *Nemesis* and the ecology of perception" interrogates notions of "the human real" and "presence" as constructed concepts, arguing persuasively that the choreographer disrupts conventional hierarchies of theatrical signifying systems, for example dislodging movement from its "privileged position" within dance and giving more weight to sound, lighting design, and the virtual spaces created by video and 3-DVR projections. McGregor, she argues, does not oppose the dancing body to the electronic images and virtual spaces, but strives for an "ecology" of fluid and unstable relations. Smart's analysis of the dramaturgical structure of *Nemesis* is a brilliant and sustained reading of a stage work. She is also the only contributor who comments, with some sense of critical objectivity, on the movement language and the dancing within McGregor's choreography, especially in her concluding remarks on the performers' struggle to deal with the technological costumes (prostheses) they have to wear at the end: "The effect of the prosthetic limbs, then, works in conjunction with the video projections of the 'real' dancers ... to create a series of perceptual dichotomies between ability and disability, the human and the non-human, live presence and technological mediation, reality and fiction."

Although she doesn't follow through her references to the posthuman, which in light of her and Dixon's remarks on the post-biological obsessions in contemporary performance might have suggested a critical engagement with Hayles's influential *How We Became Posthuman*, I enjoyed reading her essay against Jane Harris's, who in her dialogue with Bernard Walsh ("Sorcerer's apprentice: reactive digital forms of body and cloth in performance") stands out as a design artist working entirely with 3-D computer graphics animation. Her digital images of moving garments, which clearly reference choreographed bodies and how such bodies move inside dresses and affect the motion of cloth, have eliminated the live body completely. Paradoxically, the invisibility of real dancers in her animation, derived from motion capture and a lengthy CG process which builds the visual kinetics of the animated garments, evokes absent body-ness: "cloth behaviour" implies bodies and other reactive objects. Harris also emphasizes her conceptual exploration of such disappearance and re-appearance, and her emerging interest in testing real-time use of animated movement data in the context of live performances.

After such emphasis on responsive environments in the design process for interfaces, the models that presuppose audience participation are much less convincing, since here the book lacks any theoretical and empirical engagement with user behavior, effectivity, emotional affect, and social or aesthetic consequence. Although interactivity is postulated as one of the distinct features of digital performance using real-time or telematic processing and feedback loops, the role of the (unrehearsed) participants, the aesthetic function of such unrehearsed behavior, and the criteria for shared authorship or a successful interface remain unexamined. Toni Dove ("Haunting the movie: embodied/sensory cinema") wants to dismantle narrative cinematic language to arrive at new methods of story construction. She builds an active viewer into her system, which responds to "natural body movements" allowing the "transient" (Dove's term for the user) to shape the onscreen action, alter and inhabit dialogues, navigate and "play the movie instrument." Again, as we have seen above, the artist here uses the musical instrument metaphor for the enactment of a gestural or kinetic interface (arms and feet, the latter moving on floor pressure pads). While Dove's explanation of her concepts is captivating, the "theatrical action by the performer" is rather unclear. When I witnessed user behavior at her installation of *Artificial Changelings* in the late 1990s, I did not see any of the subtleties and enchantment ("the trance-like state" of being immersed, lost in space and time) she claims. I saw users trying to control the movie character with clumsy gestures that sought to mirror the gestures of the movie character.

The problem, of course, is that any unsuspecting user needs to learn the rules of the interface, the algorithmic instructions. And he or she does this by staring at the screen to see how a gesture or stepping on floor pads controls the projection (or the sound that is triggered). We see this rather poignantly in Callesen, Kajo and Nilsen's illustrations and explications of their video tracking system. All the prototypes of their interaction design are based on simplistic and mundane improvisatory games ("Heaven and Hell," "SheMonster," etc.), and even if their "impersonated stage" becomes a storyteller, I fail to see what interested them in the story or the human behavior. Nitsche and Thomas ("Play it again, Sam: film performance, virtual environments and game engines") ask their students to create virtual location designs (using videogame 3-D engines) and camera positions for a scene from *Casablanca,* which is then dramatically enacted live via a LAN multi-player game engine. Although fascinating as an experiment in theatrical adaptation of a 3-D game world, fusing computer games, cinema, and acting, the authors' definition of "dramatic narrative" in performance (of Bergman and Bogart avatars) in the so-called "expressive space" of real-time 3-D virtual environments leaves much to be desired, especially after we find out that, hilariously, the game software inserts weird automated behavior that cannot be controlled by the players.

Finally, Burke and Stein's "Theatre of context: digital's absurd role in dramatic literature" makes the most improbable claim, namely that interactive "hypertext design" for theatre (using demographic data and audience responses collected into a data base via Website and interactive stations in

theatre "galleries" before the show and during intermission) can be effectively incorporated into dramatic literature and the performance architecture.
Their prototype is called "Iliad Project," and although they propose that
effective participation requires the audience community to become aware
of their presence within the play through factual information about their
identities, I cannot fathom, from the examples they give (e.g., statistical evidence of home addresses, customized to the attending audience; snapshots
of facial reactions during the show) how their dramatic text is composed,
what the dramaturgy is, and what the actors will do with the database. As
they refer to "our *Iliad*," I am not even sure whether they mean Homer's
epic, some adaptation they plan to write, or some improvisatory reality TV
punning on Bush's War against Terrorism. Their notion of the "absurd"
(linking "our *Iliad*" to Jarry, Ionesco, and Beckett) remains rather abstract,
much like their proposal that "rules and algorithms built into new dramatic
literature can define the gathering" of input and output data.

Carver and Beardon give us a rich collection of models. Many of the
analyses of virtuality, the digitized body, and interaction design in performance are provocative; there is a wealth of information on crossover
research and programming possibilities, even if the emphasis is on design
ideas (and to some extent, on functionality), and not on performance aesthetics and the experience of the dancer, actor, or musician in such responsive environments. In other words, performers will have a hard time finding
inspiration here, unless they can imagine what Gilson-Ellis' metaphor of
(almost) falling from the trapeze and catching the (song under the) breath
means. Computer scientists and engineers, but also composers and video
artists, will wonder why their discourses have been largely neglected, even
as digital sound and projective media (in installations, clubs) play a very
significant role in contemporary art and popular culture (there is not a single
mention of the role of VJing/DJing and sampling, nor of the various creative
software and open source experimentations in art made of databases). But I
am less concerned with what is missing; obviously there are more books to
be written on this subject. What is noticeable is that no one except the team
of Callesen problematizes the fact that much of the work under discussion
is practice-based research within universities and art labs, and that the design teams ought to distinguish "between prototypes used in research and
prototypes used in production and between different types of audiences for
the prototypes." Callesen's team realized the weakness of their initial virtual

design methodology: "the problem with artistic practice-based research in academic environments is that the research team often lack the practical knowledge, experience and artistic skills to be able to define the research questions and carry out meaningful experiments." They addressed the issue by inviting performers and directors into their workshop. Ultimately, their methodological formulations are sound, even if the actual work strikes me as weak and puts the cart in front of the horse, as so often can be observed at industrial design exhibitions like SIGGRAPH. There is a strange irony in this, since some of the best writing on digital performance today comes from the performers and directors themselves. The strongest models are provided by artist communities outside of the academy that network to build collaborative production processes and place their work under public scrutiny at festivals and exhibitions.

NOTES

¹ Martina Leeker, ed., *Maschinen, Medien, Performances: Theater an der Schnitt-stelle zu digitalen Medien*, Berlin: Alexander Verlag, 2001, with CD-ROM by Irina Kaldrack and Martina Leeker. For a description of the significance of Hellerau for a history of modern dance, see Johannes Birringer, *Media and Performance: Along the Border*, Baltimore: Johns Hopkins University Press, 1998, 27–50.

² Ibid., 59–77. Söke Dinkla, in her essay "Auf dem Weg zu einer performativen Interaktion" (126–40), reminds us that "avatar" is a word derived from Hindu religious mythology and signifies the incarnation of a god (especially the god Vishnu) in various human and animal shapes. In contemporary Internet chat and game culture, avatar usually denotes the 3-D figure or 3-D animation which "embodies" the user. Such avatars can have all kinds of graphical human, animal, or fantasy shapes, and represent an artificial, visual substitute of a real person in the virtual world.

³ See, for example, N. Katherine Hayles, *How We Became Posthuman: Virtual Bodies in Cybernetics, Literature and Informatics*, Chicago: University of Chicago Press, 1999; Ray Kurzweil, *The Age of Spiritual Machines: When Computers exceed Human Intelligence*, London: Orion Business Books, 1999; Ollivier Dyens, *Metal and Flesh: The Evolution of Man: Technology Takes Over*, Cambridge, MA.: MIT Press, 2001; Gregory Stock, *Redesigning Humans: Our Inevitable Genetic Future*, New York: Houghton Mifflin, 2002; Adrian Mackenzie, *Transductions: Bodies and Machines at Speed*, London: Continuum, 2002; Slavoj Žižek, *Organs Without Bodies*, London: Routledge, 2004; Alphonso Lingis, *Body Transformations: Evolutions and Atavisms in Culture*, London: Routledge, 2005; and Marquard Smith and Joanne Morra, *The Prosthetic Impulse: From a Posthuman Present to a Biocultural Future*, Cambridge: MIT Press, 2005. On Stelarc's philosophy of performance, see the provocative interpretations in Brian Massumi, *Parables for the Virtual: Move-ment, Affect, Sensation*, Durham: Duke University Press, 2002, 89–132. See also, Marina Grzinic, ed., *Stelarc. Political Prosthesis and Knowledge of the Body*, Ljubljana: Maska, 2002, and Marquard Smith, ed., *Stelarc: The Monograph*, Cam-bridge: MIT Press, 2005.

⁴ Cf. Hayles, 245. I am not sure that Hayles is critically aware of her use of the plural "we" but her location (within the globalizing tendencies of late capitalism and the technologies which drive it) presumably is the West, and thus her cybernetic van-guard is connected to the economic accumulation which Peter Sloterdijk has identi-fied as the driver, along with the modern kinetics of "mobilization" as the vehicle. See *Eurotaoimsus: Zur Kritik der politischen Kinetik*, Frankfurt: Suhrkamp, 1989,

64. Sloterdijk's critique of the accelerated kinetics of modernity includes a critique of the "self-dramatization" and "self-stimulation" of bodies, and the philosopher's cynical view on auto-mobility is perhaps complemented quite nicely by Stelarc's ironic pronouncement of the "obsolete body," which has often been interpreted to mean that it is past evolution.

5 Josephine Barry, "Human, all too Posthuman? Net Art and its Critics," 2002: <http://www.tate.org.uk/netart/humanposthuman.htm>.

6 Slavoj Žižek, "The Matrix, or, The Two Sides of Perversion," lecture held at "Inside the Matrix" Symposium at the ZKM, Karlsruhe, 1999: <http://on1.zkm. de/netcondition/navigation/symposia/>.

7 Mackenzie, *Transductions*, 118.

8 Leeker, 714–5, my translation.

9 CD-ROM, my translation.

10 Michelle Kasprzak, "Back to the Future: Ars Electronic at 25," Mute 29 (2005): 135.

11 Söke Dinkla and Martina Leeker, eds., *Dance and Technology/Tanz und Technologie: Moving toward Media Productions—Auf dem Weg zu medialen Inszenierungen*, Berlin: Alexander Verlag, 2002.

12 David Toop, *Haunted Weather: Music, Silence and Memory*, London: Serpent's Tail, 2004, 46–47. In his first chapter on "body processes," Toop recounts the story of John Cage's experience in a totally soundproof anechoic chamber: "Drawn to silence, [Cage] expected to discover exactly that. Instead, he heard two persistent noises. The engineer in charge of the anechoic chamber at Harvard University explained: the high sound was the work of Cage's nervous system, the low sound was blood pulsing through his circulation. In other words, he was hearing his own lifeforce" (p.7). In light of my earlier comments on Prehn's biofeedback experience inside the *Camera Reflexiva* installation, it seems that we need a history of twentieth-century biophysical and biotechnological performance experiments that links the work of sound artists and psycho-acoustics researchers back to Meyerhold's biomechanics, Jaques-Dalcroze's eurhythmics and Laban's kinetography, amongst other systems of movement research, and find patterns of connection that point to the contemporary collaborations between sonic artists, media artists, dancers, and neuroscientists who use specific bodily interfaces in their work or focus on the inner body. One of the most well-known immersive installations of the 1990s, for example, which extrapolated physiological data for the interface experience was *Osmose* (1995) by Canadian artist Char Davies and her team (Softimage): The "immersant" in this fully-immersive and interactive virtual environment, which uses stereoscopic 3-D

computer graphics, a head-mounted display (HMD), real-time motion capture, and live stereoscopic video projection, controls his/her movement with breath and balance. Davies has described her work as a biological process involving passage from one side of a membrane to another, "osmosis" being a metaphor for the transcendence of difference through mutual absorption, dissolution of boundaries between inner and outer, and the inter-mingling of self and world. Her view of such work, although rather more metaphysically or even mystically minded than Toop's writing, bears many interesting parallels to Toop's accounts of Ryoji Ikeda's sound installations or to environments by Francisco López, Douglas Quin, David Dunn, Michael Prime, Hilegard Westercamp, and others who collect underwater, ultrasonic, and electromagnetic sounds of various species (fish, aquatic insects, bats, and plants). For an interesting critique of Cage's notion of chance and the atmospheric, see Rocco Di Pietro, *Dialogues with Boulez*, London: The Scarecrow Press, 2001, 27–34.

[13] Toop quoting from Alvin Curran's *Writings Through John Cage's Music, Poetry and Art*, in *Haunted Weather*, 232.

[14] An example is the Boston-based group Interface, comprising composer/bass player/programmer Curtis Bahn, violinist/programmer Dan Trueman, and dancer/ flute player Tomie Hahn. Bahn and Trueman have designed their custom-built spherical speakers, and they also perform their instruments with bows carrying specially designed accelerometers. For an extensive bibliography on "Interactive Systems and Instrument Design in Music," see <http://www.music.mcgill.ca/musictech/ISIDM/>.

[15] See Valerie Preston-Dunlop, *An Investigation into the Spontaneous Ocurrence of Fragments of Choreutic Forms in Choreographed Dance Works*, M.A. Diss., Goldsmiths College, University of London, 1978. There is a growing bibliography on studies linking mathematics and dance, and it does not surprise that research in virtual reality environments emphasizes the importance of how the human body relates to the concepts of *motion* and *space*, making reference to Laban's icosahedron. Cf. Josef Wideström and Pia Muchin, "The Pelvis as Physical Center in Virtual Environments": <http://www.polhemus.com/CaseStudies/Physical_Centre.pdf>.

[16] See Steve Paxton, "Drafting Interior Techniques," in *Taken by Surprise: A Dance Improvisation Reader*, edited by Ann Cooper Albright and David Gere, Middletown: Wesleyan University Press, 2003, 174–83 [first published in 1993 and dedicated to John Cage]. See also Thomas F. DeFrantz, "The Black Beat Made Visible," in *Of the Presence of the Body*, edited by André Lepecki, Middletown: Wesleyan University Press, 2004, 64–81, who speaks eloquently on the complex rhythmicity of black music and dance, and how the interlocking rhythms, for example the call and response structure in African diaspora dance, not only have helped connect

people of African spirituality with cosmic forces that enable healing and sustenance, but also provide an interactive model for communicative desire and a communal aesthetic.

For a brilliant philosophical analysis of African-derived dance and technology, see Olugbenga Olusola Elijah Taiwo, "Interfacing with my Interface," PhD thesis, University of Winchester, 2006. See also Taiwo's "The 'return beat': 'curved perceptions' in music and dance," in *The Virtual Embodied: Practices, Theories and the New Technologies*, edited by John Wood, London: Routledge, 1998, 157–67.

[17] "Constructing Memories: Creation of the Choreographic Resource (Liquid Reader)," presented at DRHA 2006, Dartington College of Arts, quoted with permission. A full version appeared on the companion DVD of *Performance Research* 11,4 (2006) dedicated to this important conference.

[18] Gavin Carver and Colin Beardon, eds., *New Visions in Performance: The Impact of Digital Technologies*, Lisse: Svets & Zeitlinger, 2004. For another book taking investigating the design of "virtual embodiment" in a variety of creative art practices including live performance, dance, sound, biotechnology, and film making, see Susan Broadhurst and Josephine Machon, eds., *Performance and Technology: Practices of Virtual Embodiment and Interactivity*, Basingstoke: Palgrave Macmillan, 2006.

[19] See Brian Massumi, *Parables for the Virtual*, and Mark B.N. Hansen, *New Philosophy for New Media*, Cambridge, MA: MIT Press, 2004. See also Hansen's earlier essay "Cinema beyond Cybernetics, or How to Frame the Digital Image," *Configurations*, 10 (2002): 51–90. Henri Bergson's main ideas regarding the new imaging technologies are found in *Matter and Memory* [1896], trans. Nancy Margaret Paul and W. Scott Palmer, London: George Allen & Unwin Ltd., 1988.

▼▲ TRACKBACK 2:
ALGORITHMS, DANCE, & TECHNOLOGY

I will now sketch a history of such a growing international network of art-ists involved in cutting edge productions of digital performance, based on my working experience since the early 1990s and the evidence of software-driven developments in the sciences and the arts which helped to generate an environment for exhibition and installation of the new computational culture. What I want to foreground here is a brief synopsis of the interre-lationships between performance design, computation (computer science), and programming languages, which are observer-dependent or imply the integration of the audience.

Performance and technology have always had affiliations if we consider the history of stage technology in the classical and baroque eras on the one hand (including the theatre's traditional relationship to painting, sculpture, and architecture as well as its more recent proximity to film and the modern entertainment industry that Walter Benjamin already analyzed in his famous essay on "The Work of Art in the Age of Technical Reproducibility" in the 1930s), and the history of modern science and mathematics enabling the rise of the computer and of human factors research in engineering and design in the second half of the twentieth century on the other. If stage technology was mechanical, it also could be said to have an algorithmic base, as Peter Weibel and others have suggested after examining the history of procedural instructions (an algorithm is a set of instructions to act made up by a finite set of rules). Alberti, Dürer, and da Vinci were tool makers just as Lovelace and Babbage; computer literature and digital art are indebted to Leibniz (*de arte combinatoria*) and other Baroque machine visionaries like Athanasius Kirch-er. The history of a converging computational sensibility driving interactive art-making and combining performance composition with computers, artifi-cial intelligence, electronic music, and digital imaging has a much shorter life span. It can still be considered emerging and thus allows us to look at models of experimentation and collaboration which point into various directions (in the absence of firmly established canonical works) where digital performance and digital art intersect with engineering, robotics, gaming, a-life, biotechnology, nanotechnology, neuroscience, and other sectors.

Within the historical trajectories of experimental art forms, generally associated with the notion of the avant-garde, one could excavate a tendency toward invention and a science of mixture—or we might call it an alchemy of mixed media. Many examples of the use of mechanical or technological devices might be found, without that one could claim a predictable procession from simple tools to more complex machinery. While multimedia performances as we generally understand them today gradually began to inhabit stages and concert halls during the 1970s and 1980s, the imaginary "total theatre" had already existed in the minds of Richard Wagner, Edward Gordon Craig, Adolphe Appia, Erwin Piscator, Filipp Tommasi Marinetti, Josef Svoboda, and others. Performance and live art, in both Western and non-Western contexts, also owe their inventiveness to various popular cultural traditions which inform the hybrid construction of many body and media based works as well as the participatory architectures we see, for example, in Lygia Clark's and Hélio Oiticica's performative propositions, especially in the latter's experiments with ephemeral materials incorporating the viewer into the art event as a dynamic component. In the 1960s and 1970s, Oiticica constructed not only his remarkable wearable and inhabitable paintings (*Parangolés*) but also the *Penetráveis*—environmental pieces consisting of labyrinths in which the audience was invited to walk and experience sensations through bodily contact with diverse materials such as ropes, hanging fabrics, plants, sand, gravel, wood, and everyday life objects. Addressing the Brazilian artists' aesthetics of "cultural contamination," Simone Osthoff poignantly argues that

> The rapid development of the Internet since 1994 and the increasing number of artists working with digital communications technology has brought new attention to the role of interactivity in electronic media and in emerging digital culture. Interactivity in art, however, is not simply the result of the presence and accessibility of personal computers; rather, it must be regarded as part of contemporary art's natural development toward immateriality, a phenomenon that is evidenced, for example, in the works of Brazilian artists Lygia Clark and Hélio Oiticica [and the] visual and conceptual parallels between Clark's and Oiticica's

sensorial creations from the 1960s and 1970s—masks, goggles, hoods, suits, gloves, capes and immersive environments—and early virtual-reality experiments from the 1960s and 1970s, such as Ivan Sutherland's head-mounted display and the Sayre Glove. Although not technologically based, Clark's and Oiticica's works are also related conceptually to those of artists pushing interactivity in art into new territories. Both in Brazil and elsewhere, Clark's and Oiticica's participatory creations continue to yield new meanings.[1]

Symptomatically, Oiticica focused on sensorial explorations involving social, cultural, architectural, and environmental spaces through performance. The *Parangolés* could be called "wearable spaces," and they thus attain a media function and aesthetic which are remarkably close to the digital aesthetic we recognize in today's intelligent wearables which communicate with the environment and respond to the emotional behavior of the wearer. The emphasis here is not on the conception of a "total" or "synthetic theatre" but on the syncretic. As Osthoff points out, weaving a web of relationships around the body's internal and external spaces, artists like Clark and Oiticica relayed a modern European geometric abstract tradition to Brazilian vernacular culture, and such syncretic process fused two very different traditions—a Western aesthetics privileging vision and metaphysical knowledge, and Afro-Indigenous oral traditions in which knowledge and history are encoded in the body and ritual practices are profoundly concrete. The syncretic method, in my mind, also implies a computational method of transduction, which reprograms cultural questions: participatory performance, the carnivalized museum, and the samba become the site of confluences of data which previously appeared disparate and are now interconnected. Ephemeral materials and seemingly everyday objects such as clothes become sensorial images as well as manipulable color-textures exposed to light and movement. Like music and celluloid (film), they project an energetic encounter between the body and psyche of the wearer-viewer by means of direct kinetic, visual, aural, and tactile stimuli. A form of quasi-cinema, the *Parangolès* are moved to the rhythm of samba, and thus function to activate and enact the fleeting illusion of "color-in-motion."

What I am trying to evoke here is a language of digital, sensorial performance, and such a language may only evolve in conceptual or imagined relationship to processes of mediation that already have a history of representing and manipulating reality (ritual, spiritism, trompe l'oeil, optical illusionism, photography, cinema) or are based on scientific experiments which entered (or were sometimes forgotten) into the sedimented layers of civilizational knowledge and engineering endeavor over the centuries.[2] The perplexing mechanical, optical, magnetic, hydraulic, and pneumatic devices constructed by Athanasius Kircher in the seventeenth century have been archived as exotic feats of Baroque magic rather than examples of early experimental science. The "deus ex machina" is an ancient theatrical trope which stands for the machinic imagination as a promise to solve a dilemma or human crisis of communication, and in this sense technology can also be understood as imaginary. Interestingly, contemporary "media archaeologists" like Siegfried Zielinski and Erkki Huhtamo have suggested a paleontological view of media development, namely that there is no beginning, no final layer of bedrock, beyond which media archaeological excavations cannot dig deeper. In every sedimentary layer of media history, further traces of antecedent deposits can be discovered. This approach also suggests the refusal of any determinate course of future development of media in our cultures and serves to counter current tendencies at standardization and universalization of media technology and media culture proposing instead a wide range of diverse media machines from which individual genealogies can be traced.

For instance, we rarely think about the theremin these days. The instrument is at most a curiosity, long forgotten, but after the young Russian scientist Leon Theremin invented it in 1927, it captured the imagination of the RCA (Radio Corporation of America), an early giant among innovative sound recording and broadcasting manufacturers, as well as of Hollywood filmmakers and several virtuoso soloists who introduced its violin-like sound—created through hand movements causing changes in the electromagnetic field around two antennae—to audiences. After an absurdly adventurous life, during which Theremin invented a number of electronic devices, an early television, and an electronic security system for prisons, having been abducted by the KGB, forced to work for Soviet intelligence during the Cold War, and condemned to labor camp in Siberia, we see him featured in a 1994 documentary by Steven M. Martin as he is reunited with his soloist-protegée, Clara Rockmore, who had been his friend and dancing partner in the 1930s. I found *Theremin: An Electronic Odyssee* to be a spell-binding film, as I watched the historical footage of Rockmore's delicate, riveting performance technique and suddenly recognized how much today's gesture-controlled interfaces in sensor performances imply an intuitive and virtuosic, technically refined knowledge of sound waves, pitch, volume, dynamics, tonality, and the behavior of signals of the electromagnetic field. Rockmore's performances also inspired Robert Moog to build his own theremins before he went on to invent his pioneering synthesizer in 1954. As with Daguerre and Niépce's invention of photography, Edison's experiments with telegraphic, phonographic, and electric devices, and the early filmmakers' continuous re-elaborations of chronometers, chronophotographs, cinematographs, and kinetoscopes linked to physiological and psychophysiological research (Marey, Muybridge, Demeny, Méliès), such inventions or processes which are electrical, mechanical, or chemical in nature clearly have a scientific dimension, quite apart from their profound historical and cultural impact. This makes them fascinating for artists or conceptual experimenters not working necessarily on the phenomena of form, of measurement, or of intelligible relations, but on problems of transformational recasting, a method indebted to mathematics and its procedure of restating previously solved problems.

Such recastings have interesting consequences, as scientific methods are recurringly being adopted to artistic research or rediscovered as a dimension of artistic creation, even if philosophers of science disagree amongst themselves whether mathematics is experimentally falsifiable and thus belongs to the natural sciences (as Karl Popper defined them) or whether its experimental conjectures belong to the realm of aesthetics. The computational significance of mathematics for the hard sciences and engineering is undisputed, and a basis in mathematics and physics, as we shall see, is unavoidable for much of the work now done with software and inscription technologies for visual interfaces, words, images, video, and sound. Many digital designers today speak of "proof of concept" when developing a new interface to be tested in performance or in application, only to discover new problems that will require new algorithms to be written, new design formulations to be tried. Again, this should not strike us as something new or surprising, since scientific method had shaped discoveries in art and architecture in many instances, for example in the ways in which painters have experimented with the phenomena of light and color, and the architects of the Bauhaus sought to implement a systematic program of architecture clearly emphasizing the scientific method of functionalism. Galileo, incidentally, had drawn the moon and light refracted on its rotations based on his mathematical conjectures even before he was able to observe the planet through his specially designed telescope. Zielinski's interest in technological "devices for hearing and seeing," applied to a very long cultural history of *techné* (the ancient Greeks did not separate between science and aesthetics), therefore unearths numerous examples of what we would now call world modeling—artifacts that reveal how their makers *drew*, and sought to combine heterogeneous elements, manipulate natural phenomena, and transform the real.

Before the notions of mixed reality or hybrid art became fashionable at the beginning of the twenty-first century, I had become aware of the emerging "dance technology" field at two workshop-conferences, "The Connected Body?" (1994) and "Connecting Bodies" (1996), both organized by Scott deLahunta at Amsterdam's School for New Dance Development. They caught my attention insofar as this unorthodox school seemed poised to short-circuit the energies that postmodern dance, tanztheater, and contact improvisation (as well as the work of dancer-singers like Meredith Monk) had brought to the postdramatic theatre with new devices for hearing and seeing. The first workshop had a strong body-centered dimension and introduced me to somatic practices and body-mind centering, thus opening windows into less familiar movement techniques and discourses on anatomy, health, integrative medicine, or holistic psychology. The second workshop assembled an international forum of pioneers, including the software developers of LifeForms (Thecla Schiphorst), Alias Animator (Peter Mulder), and BigEye (STEIM), discussing the connections between the discourses and practices of body movement and technology. They focused specifically on the impact of algorithmic technologies on dance making/choreography, and I remember vividly that Thecla Schiphorst at that point in the mid-90s not only explained earlier work with LifeForms, a graphical, three-dimensional system for the creation of dance on the human figure which enables the user to create and edit movement, but also presented *Bodymaps*, her interactive installation activated by the viewer's touch. A parallel workshop on BigEye (developed at STEIM, the Foundation of Electro-Instrumental Music) was conducted by Eileen Standley, Lot Siebe, and Sher Doruff, introducing us to the software and its application: a video camera follows the performer and converts movements to MIDI messages which can control the lights and/or sound on the stage.

This, literally, was my first workshop with an interactive interface, and although BigEye is now an old-timer in terms of the accelerated software development over the past decade, it remains an entry point for me, and a late one for that matter, since Schiphorst, Tom Calvert, and their design team had already initiated LifeForms during the late 1980s, and interactive software, such as David Rokeby's Very Nervous System (VNS), had been used at least since 1986. Around the same time, in the early 1990s, efforts were underway at Ohio State University's Department of Dance, which also housed the Dance Notation Bureau Extension, to develop the LabanWriter software for notation/reconstruction of dance scores. The initial impetus for the creation of a dance and technology maillist originated in the context of these activities, putting OSU firmly on the list of early academic patrons of dance and new media education. Initially, this professional training was mostly conducted as course work in the areas of preservation/documentation, recreation, and videodance, the latter implying directed choreographic projects for the camera which included training in video techniques and editing. It was not until 1999 that OSU decided to implement a graduate degree program in dance and technology, thus focusing more decisively on research in the growing spectrum of digital imagery, animation, interactive and networked performance, and the intersections of dance and computer science. Around the same time, Art and Technology courses began to be taught in art schools, and robotics joined the established areas of painting and sculpture. Theatre training remained decidedly old-fashioned and actor-centered, and thus removed from the scientific advances and articulations of software culture.

The 1990s was a crucial decade for the development of the latter, and before we look at some ancestors of the dance and technology movement, let me sketch a few other important efforts undertaken during this decade. I rely on personal experience of the artistic and research practices of the digital era, and partly on written exchanges amongst the pioneers and activists of the performance technology community. It is my impression that there are several overlapping trajectories for the intersecting communities of dance, performance art, music, visual arts, architecture and design in their engagement of new technologies and computer engineering. While the interest in cybernetics and interactive communications systems dates back much further (to Norbert Wiener and the Advanced Research Projects Agency/ARPA, Xerox PARC, or related research initiatives at MIT and the University of Illinois), and while there is the important strand of electro-acoustic instrument and computer music research (developed at Bell Laboratories, IRCAM, Oberlin College, University of Michigan, the Columbia-Princeton Electronic Music Center, the Heinrich Strobel studio in Freiburg, and other music schools or composers' studios around the world), the explicit merger of dance and digital technologies found a visible public platform in a series of "Dance and Technology" conferences hosted by different institutions in North America, first at the University of Wisconsin (Madison, 1992), then at Simon Fraser University (British Columbia, 1993), York University (Toronto, 1995), followed by a fourth "International Dance and Technology" (IDAT) Conference hosted by Arizona State University (Tempe, 1999). Since 2000, the most important platform has taken place at the Monaco Dance Forum, which took the lead in organizing biannual events featuring new digital performances and installations, along with artists workshops on new technologies. In 2006, curator Philippe Baudelot announced that the Dance Forum would from now on no longer present specific technologies as tools at the service of artists in order not to question the artists' subject matter with respect to tools. Technology had become second nature, and Baudelot now wanted to emphasize the artistic dimensions of new choreography. The time had come for the festival to no longer distinguish any works that one could qualify as digital from the others.

In the early 90s, the notion of the "digital" in performance had just been discovered. The "Shadow Project" (Jackson Hole, Wyoming) was organized by Thecla Schiporst and John Crawford in 1991, followed by similar workshops at San Francisco University from 1992 to 1995. Doug Rosenberg began to teach screendance and networked performance workshops at numerous American Dance Festivals and founded ADF's Dancing for the Camera Festival. In his address to the 2006 ADF Screendance conference in Durham he pointed out that ADF's involvement with experiments in dance and media in fact dates back to 1973 and the Dance for Television Workshop produced by Charles and Stephanie Reinhart. Since the 1990s, the ADF workshops have had a growing number of participants who subsequently helped to spread the media practices to other parts of the world. In Europe, Terry Braun and Illuminations Interactive produced the "Digital Dancing" workshops in London annually from 1994 through 1998, followed in 1999 by the "Shifts" symposium organized by Barriedale Operahouse. Also in the UK, performer and filmmaker Liz Aggiss had collaborated with Billy Cowie for a number of years on films and screendance installations (*Anarchic Variations, Men in the Wall, Doppelgänger*). Influential for many emerging artists at the time, Aggiss and Cowie became known for their highly visual, interdisciplinary brand of dance performance that incorporated elements of theatre, film, opera, poetry and vaudevillian humor. Similarly, Bob Lockeyer's role at the BBC was enormously influential as he was responsible for the dance programs. Working with Arts Council of England, he created "Dance for the Camera," a series of short dance works made especially for the camera. To date over fifty videos have been made and broadcast in the UK and around the world. Lockeyer also taught many workshops in the UK, South Africa, Canada, Australia, and New Zealand.

One could trace such spiraling histories in different parts of the world, however particular and unique each local situation might turn out to be. For example, a newly organized festival, Videobrasil, was formed in São Paulo in 1983 and sought to connect the emerging local video art practices to other audio-visual sectors and developments in the electronic image field, supporting crossovers between performance, installation, and screen-based works. Increasingly, Videobrasil developed programming that featured the emerging independent media arts in Latin America, and eventually defined its role within an international context, renaming itself International Electronic Arts festival in 1993. Ten years later, Leonel Brum, founder of the Dança Brasil and Dança Criança festivals, initiated Dança em foco: Festival International de video & danca in Rio de Janeiro. Since 2004, this festival is associated with Festival Internacional de Videodanza del Uruguay and Festival Internacional de Video-Danza de Buenos Aires, jointly representing the Circuito Videodança Mercosul.

My own dance and technology workshops, "Lively Bodies Lively Machines" (LBLM) took off from "Connecting Bodies" and were held at Chichester's Split Screen Digital Arts Festival in 1996, then again at Chichester in 1998, before moving to other countries and locations around the world including Helsinki, Copenhagen, Dresden, Beijing, Sydney, Thessaloniki, and Istanbul. In Turkey a young generation of dance and performance artists founded the TECHNE Platform in 2006, then expanded the platform into their a-m-b-e_r07 Festival for artists working in the field of art and technology. On the European mainland, the Amsterdam workshop "Connecting Bodies," mentioned above, was followed by "Future Moves" at Theatre Lantaren-Venster in Rotterdam (1996). "Future Moves" subsequently has taken place in a collaboration with V2 Media Lab during the Digital Electronic Arts Festival events in 1998 and 2000. In order to provide some insight into the language used at the turn of the century, I quote from the description:

> The theme of FM3 is "Time Tracking—timing and synchronization between different disciplines" which is directly related to "Machine Times," the theme of DEAF_00. The workshop FM3-TT mainly focuses on using the qualities unique to computers (or more in general technology) which can give birth to new ideas, and new ways of working. Which offers opportunities for making pieces that are clearly beyond the capability of non-computerized methods. Looking beyond the technology one could discover another issue, which is strongly connected to the usage of technology but is rooted more deeply in the segmentation of the art world: collaborative usage of technology requires a common timing. When planning to introduce new ways of working and interdisciplinary collaboration, using the same technology, the need of a commonly understood vocabulary and knowledge about the working methods of the other disciplines is required. Since all processes are taking place in time, the timing in interactive performances and the sense of time, the feeling of "the beat" using technology seems to be the key aspect to be researched. Timing includes a whole series of elements possibly used together in a multimedia performance, just to list some examples: timing in human interaction, timing in human-machine interaction, timing in related media elements, timing in rhythm, cadence and musical feel.[3]

It is significant to realize, in other words, that the constant growth and expansion of digital practices across the vast spectrum of new media art not only affected temporal artforms such as dance, encouraging choreographers to experiment with software algorithms, sensors, and tracking devices, but moved "performance" (as a time-based medium) from the periphery to a more central place in contemporary arts courses and art exhibitions. Electronic arts festivals such as DEAF, ars electronica, ISEA, SIGGRAPH, Boston Cyberarts, CYNETart or the European Media Arts Festival in Osnabrück began to exhibit digital works that were co-authored, and progressive art schools encouraged students to experiment with time-based mediums, thus nurturing an exposure to new performance technologies which was not always provided to students in traditional dance and theatre schools. Another significant reflection of "Future Moves" or Ghislaine Boddington's shinkansen/Future Physical and Butterfly Effect Network can be found in the steady growth of interdisciplinary arts centers at universities dedicated to foster the convergence of the arts and the science and technology fields.

For example, Australian-born digital artist Simon Biggs recalls that such convergences happened in Australia already in the 70s and 80s when choreographers and directors started to incorporate computers into work that is barely remembered today since it was obscure and experimental, rarely resolved artistically.[4] Strangely, in this age of databases, we still rely on oral history when it comes to remembering some of these earlier experiments. Biggs, who emerged as an artist during this time, states that he first employed a vision recognition systems and the human body in 1984 (albeit not for performance, in the sense that the body was that of the audience/viewer), adding that "this was rough work and more proof of concept as the technology involved was so exotic and 'big' (it involved three computers, one of which was a room-sized mainframe, to crunch the numbers)," and it was not until the end of the 80s and start of the 90s that he was able to routinely implement these techniques in installations.

Biggs's work is not generally known as performance; but in his many installations he has on occasion worked with dancers and choreographers. The conceptual distinctions between performance (presented on stage) and installations or Net-based work will be addressed throughout the following chapters. Although the boundaries between these genres are porous in regard to an articulation of an algorithmic method and an aesthetic logic, the inclusion of the audience in the experience of interactive performance systems is crucial for an understanding of the distinctions between performing arts and visual arts contexts for such work. Early computational experiments, however, may never have reached a stage or an audience, since many of the earlier "proof of concept" trials most likely happened in laboratories, as it was the case with orginal tests in which A. Michael Noll, John Lansdowns, Jeanne Beaman, and Paul Le Vasseur used computers as part of dance-making processes back in the mid-60s.

Not surprisingly, the history of dance and technology is thus intertwined with the history of computer technologies and the influence of computational ideas on choreography—and on the arts in general—during the various stages at which new software was written or new computational ideas put out and then made accessible to others. For example, to return to the old-timer, BigEye, I would not have designed the workshop on Lively Bodies Lively Machines in the same manner if this camera-tracking software had not been available for application in the rehearsals. In 1996 and 1998, I invited several practitioners (including Tessa Elliott, Jools Gilson-Ellis, Amanda Steggell, Per Platou, Kirk Woolford, Sarah Rubidge, Dominique Rivoal, Joumana Mourad, Daniel Aschwanden, Scott deLahunta) to take part in the workshops in order to share their expertise with camera-tracking software algorithms. Some of them had already worked with BigEye and other custom-built software for a number of years. Many workshops throughout the 1990s were conceived in this manner bringing pioneering artists, computer musicians, and programmers together with younger visual and performance artists for a period of time that allowed setting up laboratory conditions for intensive work with coding and technological tools on an advanced level. These workshops had a spiraling effect, similar to the spread of video production knowledge gained a decade earlier in community access television. They also had an affect on art schools, music and dance schools, since some of the experienced practitioners held teaching positions or were getting invited to residencies at universities and cultural centers. One of the important democratic or grassroots elements in these workshops was the emerging notion of "shareware" and open systems which in many instances allowed not only an exchange of know-how and artistic ideas but a sharing of the software tools.[5]

Biggs suggests that at a time before the inexpensive BigEye software became accessible, there were other softwares around, not all of them available since very much tied up with the developers' own objectives (David Rokeby's VNS for example) while others had been designed to be open, available, and cheap to use (e.g., Mandala). These systems were mostly developed by lone artist-developers. BigEye was different in that it was developed by an institute (STEIM), a small operation in Amsterdam yet very focused and thus able to undertake larger R and D projects than any individual artist could contemplate. STEIM worked in collaboration with "client" artists whose main contribution was the specification of capabilities although some also contributed actual code or z-specifications, something between code and a description of what the code will do.

What surprises us is that fifteen years later things have not really moved on much. There is a new real-time camera-tracking interface, Max/MSP/

Jitter, which is a significant piece of academically (IRCAM) and industrially developed software with a large developer community, but it is not dedicated to interactive systems and performance. There is Isadora, which is dedicated in this way and has impressed many of us because it is such a beautifully intuitive system, but it is another example of individual artistic labor (created by Mark Coniglio) rather than a fully blown industrial strength authoring environment. Biggs told me that he had long wished for a study to be undertaken that would mount an in depth analysis, both technical and artistic, of all such tools and systems that have been developed over the past forty or fifty years. The outcome of such a study could be published, the objective being to facilitate the sharing of knowledge with the longer term desired outcome being the establishment of a research community in the field who are able to support all participants through the open and transparent sharing of data, knowledge and technologies. This would mean that rather than re-inventing the wheel every time somebody seeks to develop a new system (and many are used in "live coding" performances, e.g., SuperCollider, Betablocker, Al Jazar), the knowledge would be readily available, in a navigable and useable form, to ensure that the next generation of systems are an effective iteration of those that have gone before and offer really new possibilities and capabilities.

On the other hand, we must also note that a growing number of digital artists interested in performance now draw on their coding knowledge, live coding/hacking and re-tooling experiments to develop custom-built software and hardware for new work. Others collaborate with computer scientists, AI, and motion graphics designers to devise transformative possibilities for capturing movement which change static images into navigable virtual spaces or allow the digital dance object to be affected by mathematical manipulations based in algorithms developed for specific artistic outcomes. The promise of these software developments requires that we look more closely at how aesthetics of coding and performance composition meet.

NOTES

[1] Simone Osthoff, "Lygia Clark and Hélio Oiticica: A Legacy of Interactivity and Participation for a Telematic Future," Leonardo 30, 4 (1997): <http://www.leonardo.info/isast/spec.projects/osthoff/osthoff.html>.

[2] Lev Manovich, in *The Language of New Media*, Cambridge, MA: MIT Press, 2001, argues that the digital image evolved from cinema and photography. While pointing to formal and material differences between digital media and cinema, the book's prologue takes Dziga Vertov's 1929 masterpiece *Man with a Movie Camera* as foreshadowing much of what became important in the language of digital media, especially the technique of spatial montage. For studies of the hidden layers of media development, see Zielinski, 2006, and Erkki Huhtamo, "Focus on Media Art Histories," *New Media Technologies*, 12, 3 (2006): 357–360.

[3] <http://framework.v2.nl/archive/archive/leaf/other/default.xslt/nodenr-67855>.

[4] Quoted from email correspondence on the dance-tech list, January 19, 2006. Some of the other references are indebted to the extended maillist discussion on this subject that I initiated in early January 2006. Scott deLahunta needs to be credited not only for his influential activities as an organizer of workshop-conferences and research projects, but also for his consistent efforts in community building, facilitating an archive, as well as helping to sustain a dance-tech maillist. A brief historical overview of important workshops can be found in his essay "Periodic Convergences: Dance and Computers," in *Tanz und Technologie/Dance and Technology*, 66–87. This is one of the very few essays in print that sketch a history of the interrelations between dance and computer science. The archive of the dance-tech list moderated by Scott Sutherland is at <http://dancetechnology.com/dancetechnology/archive/>. Archiving began in late 1996 after a tentative beginning in 1994 when David Ralley, a software programmer in the OSU Dance Department, announced the LabanWriter and MultiMediaDance prototypes. DeLahunta and Mark Coniglio initiated discussions about dance and technology on the list and set up the Dance Tech Zone <http://www.art.net/~dtz>. A.William Smith acted as an unofficial early bibliographer of dance technology research (<http://art.net/~dtz/ohiostate.html>) and edited the IDAT conference proceedings (<http://www.surrey.ac.uk/NRCD/pub-proc.html>). Unlike such umbrella organizations as NDA, CORD, ICMA or Performance Studies International, IDAT had no formally constituted central committee; each event was organized by the volunteer host on its own terms. The largest international workshop-festival since the demise of IDAT, outside of the Monaco Dance Forum, was the Digital Cultures Lab at Nottingham in late 2005 (<http://www.digitalcultures.

org>). For a collection of writings from Digital Cultures, see the special issue of *International Journal of Performing Arts and Digital Media*, 2,2 (2006).

[5] A workshop I organized with deLahunta at OSU's Dance Department in 2002 was explicitly dedicated to an examination of the shared use of "tools" and digital techniques experienced in the framework of such a collaborative process. See our report: <http://www.dance.osu.edu/~jbirringer/Dance_and_Technology/ttreport.html>.

The reinvention of the wheel is a subject that may not trouble the theatre (theatrical production is always reproduction), but once we think of performance in conjunction with research and scientific discovery, the issue of systems design and the continuous development of the operational system or ecology of performance becomes more pertinent. "From Wagner to Virtual Reality"—the charming subtitle of Randall Packer and Ken Jordan's book *Multimedia*—of course suggests a larger arc of the historical trajectories of modern performance technologies reaching back to the 1840s and Richard Wagner's integrative vision of the *Gesamtkunstwerk* in his "Outlines of the Artwork of the Future." This vision is seen as a precursor to many of the avant-garde manifestos of the early-twentieth century, especially those of the Italian Futurists, the Russian Constructivists, and the Bauhaus artists in Germany.[1] But *Multimedia* barely glances at performance or the experiments, for example, at Black Mountain College in the burgeoning era of collaboration between musicians, painters, dancers, and filmmakers (what is now often referred to as the Cage-Cunningham-Rauschenberg model) which predated the exhilarating experiments of the Judson Dance Theatre, the gradual rise of what was to be called postmodern dance, and the astonishing engineering events staged by Rauschenberg and Klüver (E.A.T.: Experiments in Art and Technology) in the late 1960s.

Similarly, the book does not really develop its initial references to Wagner and opera, thus missing out on significant stage developments in what Bonnie Marranca dubbed the "theatre of images" of the 1970s, including Robert Wilson's collaboration with Philip Glass, Richard Foreman's, and Lee Breuer's stagings, Meredith Monk's music-theatre-dance works, or Robert Ashley's electronic operas. Laurie Anderson's multimedia concerts and The Wooster Group's and John Jesurun's experiments with nonlinear multimedia theatre collages would also need to be mentioned in this context. Instead, *Multimedia* tends to have a focus less on performance, and more on digital multimedia understood through computational and human/machine interface design developments in the course of the last century. But Billy

Klüver makes a brief appearance advocating the synthesis of technology and art, and I now revisit *9 Evenings: Theatre and Engineering*, considering the event as a series of workshop performances or test rehearsals, before addressing the wider implications of this model of science-art collaboration for the contents of this book.

After the rise of abstract expressionism and action painting, the emergence of happenings, and the workshops and performances of the Judson Dance Theatre, New York City had established itself in the 1960s as a new center of artistic activity drawing attention, in particular, to the vibrant experimentations between artists from different disciplines. Some of the new ideas flowing into performance originated from collaborations between visual artists, musicians, dancers, filmmakers, sculptors, writers, and engineers. Although the notion of hybrid or multimedia performance was not common at the time, it is interesting to remember that the inclination to perform, as we see it so prominently in the work of Robert Rauschenberg, was considered (and sometimes criticized) as a tendency "toward theatre" which opened up the plastic arts toward temporal action, projected image, random collage, and the use of ready-mades, scenography, and electronic engineering. Already in the 1950s Rauschenberg had participated in the concerted actions at Black Mountain College, then created his combines—three-dimensional works that incorporated objects, machines, and other devices—and later worked as stage designer for Merce Cunningham's dance company (touring with John Cage and David Tudor), before setting out on his own collaborative performance projects to be shown, for example, at the 1965 New York Theatre Rally or at the 1966 "Now Festival" in Washington. The inspiration for a festival on specific "technological arts" experiments, as we would call them today, arrived in 1965–66, when Rauschenberg's friendship and collaboration with Billy Klüver, a senior physicist and communications engineer at Bell Telephone Laboratories, led to planning a series of projects by artists and engineers from New York City to be presented at an "art and technology" event in Stockholm. When the Stockholm hosts could not longer fathom the process-oriented plans for artist-engineer collaborations submitted by Klüver and Rauschenberg, the New Yorkers went ahead on their own and started fundraising and location scouting. They secured the 69th Regiment Armory on Lexington Avenue and Twenty-Fifth Street (the place where the famous 1913 Armory Show had been held) and some corporate support, and Klüver and Rauschenberg went ahead to solicit the teams for *9 Evenings: Theatre and Engineering*, the now legendary event of ten experimental performances presented in October 1966.[2]

Among the artists, Rauschenberg had invited Steve Paxton, Deborah and Alex Hay, John Cage, Lucinda Childs, Robert Whitman, Yvonne Rainer, David Tudor, and Öyvind Fahlström. Klüver invited numerous engineers from the Bell Labs; around thirty eventually worked on the projects and became intensely involved in the various artist-scientist collaborations to be devised for the huge, cavernous Armory building. I don't think my curiosity in this event would have been aroused quite in the same manner, had not Vera Maletic, in early 2000, presented me with the original program of *9 Evenings* after noticing that I was printing a software patch of an interactive design on an invitation for a performance in an industrial engineering building. The program for *9 Evenings* featured striking diagrams (now preserved in the E.A.T. archives at the Daniel Langlois Foundation in Montréal) of the engineering operations and circuits for the projects. Herb Schneider was responsible for drawing up the diagrams to help visualize the arrangements and the coordination of the elements of action, film, video, sculptural objects, sound, and electromagnetic waves. Klüver in particular had put an enormous amount of work, along with several other engineers (Herb Schneider, L.J. Robinson, Per Biorn), into the prototyping of a new theatre electronic environmental modulator system (TEEM) to be presented at the event. Ultimately, many of the electronics components in the projects, as we gather from the sometimes scathing critical responses and eyewitness reports to the evenings, did not quite work, broke down, or malfunctioned the first time round, but as all the projects were scheduled to be shown twice, the performances improved as the festival moved along. Large audiences showed up each night, and we can conclude that the legendary status of this festival resides perhaps less in measurable artistic and scientific accomplishments than in the underlying vision and concept for the collaborative process, which according to Rauschenberg's idea had been focused on one-to-one peer relations, with artists and engineers sharing responsibility equally for the result.

John Cage's *Variations VII* was designed as a collage of live sounds to be piped in from numerous outside locations (via telephone lines) and sources (TV, radio, microphones), to be mixed live by Cage and Tudor who were seen sitting behind a huge assemblage of sound equipment and cables. It did not work all that well and left Cage exasperated by the lack of the engineers' improvisational performance virtuosity. On the other hand, some of the engineers complained that the delightful art projects, in their mind, had at least one thing in common, namely that from an engineer's point of view they were ridiculous. In the context of the Judson experiments, which most of the participating artists elaborated on, one can understand why this might have been so. At the same time, reading the description of some of the performances, one is amazed at the scope of the imagination displayed in these projects. Fahlström's *Kisses Sweeter Than Wine* presented a complex and often surreal environment of actions created by performers who manipulated objects amidst several simultaneous slide and film projections. Rauschenberg's *Open Score* was the most unusual work. The performance began with Frank Stella playing a tennis match with Mimi Kanarek; their rackets were wired to amplify the sounds of each hit, while at each sound occurrence one of the lights in the Armory would be switched off. In other words, Rauschenberg and Klüver had designed an interactive tennis match in which gesture controlled both sound and light. After the game had proceeded for a while, the hall was eventually in full darkness, and a special infrared closed-circuit TV projection system was turned on to throw images onto large suspended screens, while a cast of nearly 500 extras had come on in the dark to perform invisibly. Algorithmically speaking, they performed instructions for tasks, and the audience could sense their presence but not perceive anything except the ghostly images of the performer crowd on the screens. *Open Score* ended when the performers had vanished in the dark, and a single spot light picked out Rauschenberg, carrying something in a burlap sack. As it turned out, inside was dancer Simone Forti, singing in a clear voice the tune of an old Italian folk song, while Rauschenberg carefully pulled her about the empty space: a riveting ending to the strangest tennis match ever played.

What is memorable about *9 Evenings* is the collaborative methodology devised for the projects, enjoining artists and engineers in the design of performances that involved various prototypical interactive and intermedial strategies. These strategies would become central to composition in the subsequent eras of computer-assisted and digital performance, but here they also translated into thematic preoccupation with control behavior, human-machine combinations, wireless communication, and unpredictability which gave the works a particular look quite outside of the mainstream of theatre or art in general. For example, there was a noticeable emphasis on "networking" functions of objects or artists' gestures that "controlled" media output (such as lights or sounds, and to a lesser extent images) and thus acted as interfaces in a feedback system. Rauschenberg's use of an infrared TV projection system also alludes to the operations of surveillance capture systems. As we have seen in many recent digital arts exhibitions, this touches upon the more problematic sides of techno-culture. Those range from invasive military or policing technologies to everyday surveillance in buildings and public squares to the seemingly innocuous game-enjoying behavior of the (invisible?) mass audience doing their thing underneath a Big Brother regime, which in recent years has been steadily trivialized into so-called reality TV, the Internet self-showcasing of MySpace or YouTube as well as the ubiquitous blogging syndrome. People are watching themselves.

Simone Forti's folk song hummed from inside a sack, as she is pulled around like a kidnapped victim in some gangster movie, intones a macabre allegory of images that would become part of the collective consciousness of Western culture and its obsession with crime scene re-enactments. Robert Whitman's *3 Holes of Water*, featuring several cars wrapped in plastic and fitted with film projectors throwing a montage of live and prerecorded TV images on a huge screen, created a similar allegory of the drive-in movie theatre culture, critically portraying the kind of mass mobilized fascination with the apparatus of imaging and the fantasies this apparatus supplies (similar to the earlier fantasies connected to speed, the automobile, and 1920s machine culture). We don't know what induced Rauschenberg to solicit a cast of nearly 500 extras to perform a series of simple tasks ("Touch someone who is not touching you"; "Women brush hair"; "Take off a coat and put it back on"), but it is tempting to think of this mass choreography in terms of Kracauer's "mass ornament" and the implied mechanization of such a vast chorus of human beings. Rauschenberg's design of automated gestures for mass performance thus inevitably reflects on the role of the audience in the society of the spectacle: the chorus is made to mirror the invisible function of the mass audience inside the apparatus of circulating images (the culture industry).

Most significantly, *9 Evenings* publicly performed a model idea which had not existed prior to this event, but would later be redeployed by arts and science laboratories (and such programs as XeroxParc PAIR) and festivals such as ars electronica or SIGGRAPH, namely the creation of a framework for interaction between the creative arts and techno-science. Rauschenberg,

Klüver, Whitman, and the engineer Fred Waldhauer had set up E.A.T. in 1966 as a non-profit foundation dedicated to establishing "an international network of experimental services and activities designed to catalyze the physical, economic and social conditions necessary for cooperation between artists, engineers and scientists." The research role of the contemporary artist was understood by E.A.T. as providing "a unique source of experimentation and exploration for developing human environments of the future."[3] Around the same time, other Bell Labs scientists also promoted collaborative research in computer graphics and vision, music and acoustics, and a few years later composer Pierre Boulez founded the IRCAM (Institut de Recherche et Coordination en Acoustique et Musique) in Paris, based on a similar conception of research and invention as the central activity of contemporary musical creation. Not surprisingly, Boulez invoked the model of the Bauhaus as interdisciplinary inspiration for what he considered the inevitable collaboration of musicians and scientists. By the time Rauschenberg and Klüver founded E.A.T., the influence of Bauhaus teaching had of course extended to the United States since several of its master teachers (Gropius, Moholy-Nagy, Albers) had emigrated before World War II, and Albers was Rauschenberg's teacher at Black Mountain College.

The idea that a creative confluence of art and science was inevitable, however, did not establish itself in the imagination of the art world until the 1960s with its cultural upheavals and radical democratic movements. Tinguely's ironic, famous self-destroying machine in the garden of MoMA ushered in the 1960s, but E.A.T.'s grand visionary proposals for the 1970 Expo in Osaka, Japan, involving seventy-five artists and engineers in the design of a multimedia project for PepsiCo's mirror dome, reflect the utopian dimensions of a performance scenography which clearly points to the digital age and its emphasis on audience participation. PepsiCo withdrew its support to the plans just prior to the opening, having become scared of the experimental programming envisioned by Klüver, but from the diagrams we gather that the Osaka project was even more ambitious than 9 *Evenings*, suggesting a complex system of feedback between aesthetic and technical choices, and a deliberate effort at humanizing the technological architecture.

Klüver proposed to create a laboratory environment, encouraging "live programming" to open up opportunities for experimentation, rather than resorting to fixed or "dead programming" as he called it, so typical of most exposition pavilions. The Pavilion's interior dome was to immerse visitors in three-dimensional real images generated by mirror reflections, as well as spatialized electronic music, and thus to invite the spectators to individually and collectively participate in the experience rather than view the work as a fixed narrative of pre-programmed events. This outline, with its emphasis on the sensorial and experiential—reminding us of Oiticica's exhibitions of *Tropicália* (Rio de Janereiro) and *Eden* (London) at the same historical juncture (1967–69)—and thus on the prototypical involvement of the spectator-as-actor in a behavioral setting, is a remarkable document of a scientist's aesthetic credo. Klüver unmistakingly pronounces the interactive paradigm when he suggests that the Pavilion would give visitors the liberty of shaping their own reality from the materials, processes, and structures set in motion by its creators. He also places his vision in the context of a tradition of architectural utopianism that reaches back to Tatlin, and to Buckminster Fuller's designs for geodesic domes (e.g., the Biosphere of Environment Canada, Montréal) or Le Corbusier's collaboration with Iannis Xenakis on the multimedia architecture for Varèse's *Poème électronique*, installed in the Philips Pavilion at the 1958 World Fair in Brussels.

In accounting for such historical convergences of arts and science, and the more recent developments in software design, I tried to evoke a sense of the continuum of technology and art practices characteristic of the modern/postmodern era. A comprehensive examination of the notion of the "epistemological laboratory" would take us more deeply into the continuities of scientific research, artistic techniques, philosophical speculation, and poetic texts commenting upon each other, especially as scientific writers (e.g., Bruno Latour, Hans-Jörg Rheinberger) now offer intricate reviews of lab objects like vacuum pumps and gene synthesizers. These continuities are more enduring, I suggest, than the commonplace assumptions of the "two cultures" (science/art), which were diagnosed as having separated into different languages, after the fallout of Newton's mechanistic model of the universe and Newtonian scientific method, exacerbated by the nineteenth-century Industrial Revolution and the post-Enlightenment paradigm of rationalist and objectivist thinking. Even if the latter was regarded as alien to the romantic and expressionist paradigm of artistic subjectivity, it is of course pointless to deny that science matters to everything, not excepting emotions and concepts, ethics and creative imaginaries. The extraordinary upheavals precipitated by the evolution of science and technology have rendered culture—the arts and humanities—more precarious and muted. The crisis of humanism has been a feature of all critical theory of the past decades. The scientific imagination, on the other hand, knows this and hardly denies cultural reflection and symbolic mediation. Latour emphasizes the "mediation" of the laboratory, refering to Boyle's experiments as having introduced "actors," by which he means inert bodies, physics equipment. Scientists retain their claims to the objectivity of their results regarding the physical world, but they recognize that a major contribution to their success is owed to the extraordinary model-ability of the physical world itself, as opposed to the strength of the scientific process per se. The cultural modeling of the world still is an invitation to confront our (post)humanity and our choices of how we want to live in the world.

NOTES

[1] Randall Packer and Ken Jordan, eds., *Multimedia: From Wagner to Virtual Reality*, New York: W.W. Norton & Company, 2001. The reference to the "theatre of images" is indebted to Bonnie Marranca's seminal book, *The Theatre of Images*, New York: Drama Book Specialists, 1977. For a more recent theorization of experimental theatre since the 1960s, which has been most influential in Europe, see Hans-Thies Lehmann, *Postdramatisches Theater*, Frankfurt am Main: Verlag der Autoren, 1999.

[2] Cf. Sally Banes, *Democracy's Body: Judson Dance Theater 1962–1964*, Ann Arbor, Michigan: UMI Research Press, 1983. I am especially indebted to Calvin Tomkins: *Off the Wall: a Portrait of Robert Rauschenberg*, New York: Picador, 2005, 214–27. For an excellent archaeology of significant twentieth-century models for interdisciplinary art and technology research laboratories, see Michael Century, "Pathways to Innovation in Digital Culture": <http://www.nextcentury.ca/PI/PImain.html>. See also, Deborah Garwood, "The Future of an Idea: *9 evenings*—Forty Years Later," *PAJ: A Journal of Performance and Art* 85 (2007): 36–48.

[3] Quoted by Century, "Pathways to Innovation in Digital Culture," 7.

▼▲ Deafman Glance & Molecular Gaze

Performance, as we noted in the events of *9 Evenings: Theatre and Engineering*, has a particular range of possibilities for the invention of a dialectical exchange between human action and technology, which spotlights the gain and the cost of "technics." Bernard Stiegler uses "technics" (*la technique*) as a general term for technical systems suggesting that every civilization constitutes itself around a technical system, defined as a stabilizing element within the technical evolution based on previous achievements.[1] The projection of new forms, orientations and mappings—for example in Cage's aleatoric processes or Rauschenberg's science-art collaborations—offers challenges to what might otherwise be foreseeable in a stabilized economy of representation, for example the naturalism of theatre, or in an empirical world in which one had assumed to know what it means to be, or have a body, or perceive a body.

The question of how technics act upon the body in an unforeseen manner is a recurring theme in this book, and I will address specific instances in which perceptions and proprioceptions are confronted in digital performance. The results of science, and what Suzanne Anker and Dorothy Nelkin have called the "molecular gaze," offer serious provocations to conceptions of the body, mind, and life's reproducibility, from the prospects of genetic engineering (trans-speciation, cloning) and nanotechnology's neuro- and bio-medical applications to the more amorphous dilemmas generated by our society's faith in industrial engineering. Towers and bridges collapse, dams break. Yet despite the Romantic legacy of irrationalism and anti-scientific bias in Western culture, or the various religiously motivated rejections of factual truth, there are few superstitions today regarding problems that can be solved if they are susceptible to technological intervention and control.

Pierre Boulez has suggested that John Cage's indeterminism presented an enormous challenge, at first, since the musical event became entirely unforeseeable. Furthermore, electronic instruments could be considered transgressive, as they exceed the limits of what one can do with traditional instruments, unleashing new possibilities for performance and the spatialization of sound.

On the other hand, Boulez disagrees with a complete reliance on chance, faulting Cage for his abandonment of the tools of composition, the logic of grammar and the logic of organization. Humpty Dumpty had a great fall, all the king's horses and all the king's men couldn't put Humpty Dumpty back together again. The Cagean silence had dislocated Boulez's logic, as much as Duchamp's ready-made had dislocated the traditional art object, or Brecht's epic theatre had sought to dislocate the theatrical illusions of reality through new methods of interruption, later reformulated by leftist filmmakers such as Jean-Luc Godard or the Dogma movement (cf. Lars von Trier's *Dogville*). Brecht's epic method was based on an episodal narrative structure interrupted by titles, films, songs, etc.; an active separating out of the other elements of the drama from the narrative; and a detached style of acting (in "quotation marks"). He was quite explicitly advocating a science of the theatre:

> But what has knowledge got to do with art? We know that knowledge can be amusing, but not everything that is amusing belongs in the theatre.... I have often been told when pointing out the invaluable services that modern knowledge and science, if properly applied, can perform for art and especially for the theatre, that art and knowledge are two estimable but wholly distinct fields of human activity. This is a fearful truism, of course, and it is as well to agree quickly that, like most truisms, it is perfectly true. Art and science work in quite different ways: agreed. But bad as it may sound, I have to admit that I cannot get along as an artist without the use of one or two sciences.[2]

Brecht thought that the theatre of the scientific age was in a position to make dialectics into a source of enjoyment, and he proposed that the present-day world could only be described to present-day people if it were described as capable of transformation. Such transformational politics present the core of a dramaturgy conceived as a method of educational experimentation. Brecht's *Lehrstücke*, more crucially than his epic theatre plays though rarely performed today, crystallize his major pedagogy through which his model for a theatre of the future proposes to enact a practice that transforms the structure of relations of the apparatus. If one examined the pedagogy, one would find the seeds for a political interactivity. It features an "open" text, with a rigorous structure designed to facilitate insertions or deletions according to the exigencies of the particular project. Moreover, the performance of the learning plays is designed to abolish the actor/audience separation, thus shifting the focus to the process, which one could call a process of indetermination (as Brecht rejected the determinism of tragedy). The actors' learning process can convert the contradiction in bourgeois society, and its theatrical apparatus specifically, between the producers (the actors) and the means of production. The relation is contradictory insofar as the ownership of the apparatus alienates the labor of the former according to Marxist theory. In order to annul this distinction, the purpose of these performances is for the actors to acquire attitudes (*gestus*) and particular, critical relations to reality. Mimesis, in Brecht's theatre pedagody, is no longer mirroring but an acting out of a measuring: it always involves a critical attitude on our part, we are all active actors required to take responsibility for making corrections, re-determining the course of action after observation (rather than abandoning ourselves to the magic realm of mere fantasy).

In order to produce a revolutionary theatre, Brecht argued for a separation of the elements. In his *Mahagonny* notes, he distinguishes his separation of words, music, and scene from the Wagnerian *Gesamtkunstwerk*, which fused the elements into one seductive and overarching whole in which drama, music, and scene work together to engulf the spectator in the aesthetic totality. Conversely, in his separation of the elements, each aesthetic component retains its autonomy and thus can comment on the others, often in contradiction, to provoke critical insight. The measures to be taken, Brecht believed, are rehearsals for the production of revolution, learning the dialectics of historical change by educating ourselves, carrying through certain behaviors. Half a century later, in Heiner Müller's *Hamletmachine*, the idea of self-education is reduced to radically condensed matter, a few shrunken heads, an Actor Playing Hamlet who thinks he is a data bank of past failures and false moves, and now refuses to act. The machine: a few pages of surreal imagery, hypertextual samples, re-mixes, with strongly entropy-dependent material properties.

While the promise of revolution (always) remains to be fulfilled, not surprisingly, however, the notion of indeterminacy (based on Heisenberg's uncertainty principle) proved to be as fertile to the artistic and philosophical imagination as the second law of thermodynamics. Entropy—the tendency of organized systems to disintegrate over time—came to be of central interest in Robert Smithson's earthworks, mirror displacements, and "non-sites," but especially in his comments on the "monuments" of synthetic mathematics in contemporary art obsessed with the fourth dimension. Mathematician Brian Rotman, reflecting on the equally unnerving fascination with metaphors of the "virtual," added his own entropic vision:

> traditional mathematics' syntax-driven discourse of symbols, notation systems and formulas organized into linear, alphabetic chains of logic (pictureless first-order languages, axiomatization), is confronted by a discourse that is performative and driven by digital—screen-visualizable—images for which proof and logical validation are secondary. This is not to say that the classical, infinitary agent will disappear, but rather its ideality, its ghost ontology, cannot but be revealed and ineluctably altered when confronted by the materializing, de-infinitizing action of digital computation.[3]

For Rotman, the contemporary virtual, within the current technological matrix of the digital, is to be seen as re-structuring the domination of text-based culture and its systems of symbolic reference, a process likely to affect most of those entities which are the product of written mediation—either transforming them or introducing phenomena foreign or antagonistic to them. Our cognitive abilities and subjectivities are not only collective, Rotman suggests, but dispersed across heterogeneous arenas, smeared across multiple sites as, ever more connected, we navigate through an expanding universe of virtuality and encounter innumerable digitized traces, anticipations, proxies, avatars, representations, and doubles of ourselves. We'll never walk alone, we are all Humpty Dumpty.

The debate about the two cultures, therefore, may have also spent its energy. The continuities between science and art appear more basic, for example, in regard to a fundamental aspect of "theatre engineering," if we took this term to mean the progressive forging of vision, i.e., the continuous invention and reinvention of techniques for producing representations (images, words, gestures, movement, sound, space, time, etc.). When we think of theatre or the visual arts, and the various visionary changes that have been effected by practitioners over the past two centuries, technological developments were in many cases paralleled in visual or presentational techniques, and thus the production of new ways of viewing or experiencing. Jonathan Crary, in *Suspensions of Perception*, illuminates very meticulously how a new kind of spectating evolved with new visual technologies across the nineteenth century, tracing various changes in observation techniques and the emergence of subjective models of vision as well as of machinic objectivity of vision (suggested, for example, in Muybridge's chronophotography). Felicia McCarren, in her study of mechanization, automation, and the early-twentieth-century machine aesthetics, points out that Crary emphasizes the overlapping of innovations in visual modernism and the empirical study of cognition. In other words, the physiology of vision and hearing and machinic perception arrangements develop hand in hand; the research (Helmholtz's *Physiological Optics* or Marey's locomotion studies) is reflected in philosophical writings (e.g., Bergson, Kracauer, Benjamin). The early filmmakers elaborate the motion picture technology, while dancers and actors get used to the camera and what Benjamin described as "optical tests." And gradually scientific and artistic images create a new spectator who learns a new form of attention. Performance, McCarren infers, interacts with the elaboration of the motion picture camera, and thus the very possibility of looking at camera reality had become "inseparable from the effects of dynamic, kinetic, and rhythmic modalities of experience and form."[4]

If modern dance, in this respect, concerns itself with such modalities of mechanics and mobility and the newly technologized focus on movement, and if modern lighting technology, in the hands of a visionary designer such as Adolphe Appia, transforms theatrical representation by creating three-dimensional, geometric structures that could be altered in appearance by varying the color, intensity, and direction of lighting to enhance the actor's movements, it might be worthwhile to dwell for a moment on the synthesis achieved between mathematical/physical principles and architectural composition of space-time in the theatre. Appia's innovations, especially in his work for the experimental institute at Hellerau, which he helped to conceive together with Émile Jacques-Dalcroze, have often been described as fundamental for the development of modern theatre, as he provided the theoretical and practical basis for exploring the creative synthesis of the arts of music, theatrical performance, dance, stage design, and lighting. Dismissing the flat, painted backdrops of nineteenth-century illusionism, he argued for a *rhythmicization* of space through music and moveable light (light which spreads and diffuses). His concepts of lighting, in particular, were so advanced at the time that one can understand his emphasis on relationality (lighting related fundamentally to every movement an actor makes) much better through the lens of more recent visual compositions—in the *mise-en-scène* of Robert Wilson—which have made an indelible mark on our memory.

Wilson's break-through occurred in 1971, when he staged his seven-hour *Deafman Glance* in Europe and entranced his audiences, including surrealist writer Louis Aragon whose review, published as an open letter to André Breton, drew attention to the director's compositional synthesis of "gesture and silence, of movement and the extraordinary." Aragon's astonishment can still be felt when we read his attempt to describe a performance ("I have seen nothing more beautiful in this world") which seemed to resist interpretation: "because it is at once both wakeful life and life with its eyes closed, the confusion that arises between the everyday world and the world of every night, reality mixed with dream, the totally inexplicable in the gaze of the deaf."[5] The architectural and painterly vocabularies of Wilson's *tableaux vivants*, his specific treatment of the visual and the aural scores through heightened attention to the choreography of lighting, rhythm, and duration, with a slowed-down, dilated and abstracted choreography of the body in movement, began to generate a substantial and unique series of works (performances, operas, and installations) and collaborations with composers, singers, and writers over a period now of more than four decades. His theatrical aesthetic came to prominence during almost exactly the same time span when Pina Bausch's Wuppertaler Tanztheater turned the traditional ballet and dance world in Europe upside down.

Bausch's impact on the choreographic imagination of entire generations of dancers has been considerable, and tanztheater gradually became a lingua franca, whereas Wilson's performance architectures seem to have had the opposite effect. Although widely commissioned for his own work and for directing adaptations and opera productions at all the major theatres and opera houses around the world, Wilson's signature style has remained quite singular and autonomous. He is a kind of Jackson Pollock of the theatre. Although this must be perplexing for the new historians of postdramatic theatre, Wilson's first landart installation (*Poles*, 1967), his early "mute operas" with the adolescent protégés Raymond Andrews and Christopher Knowles, the collaborations with composer Philip Glass (*Einstein on the Beach*, 1976), with playwright Heiner Müller (especially in *the CIVIL warS*, the magnum opus developed over several years in preparation for the 1984 Los Angeles Olympic Arts Festival), and with Gavin Bryars (*Medea*) and Tom Waits (*Black Rider, Alice*) in the 1990s mark particular phases of a highly consistent and also highly intransigent aesthetic formalism which, including the more recent *Monsters of Grace: A Digital Opera in Three Dimensions* (after 1999), has been articulated in performance but could be placed just as convincingly within the avant-garde contexts of the visual arts (in the absence of a tradition we might call theatre science).

In the following, I construct a brief hypothesis on Wilson's technology of visual persuasion, based on my diagram of a set of his architectural compositions and structural principles ranging from *Deafman Glance* to *Les Fables de La Fontaine.* I will enumerate these principles to create a template of Wilson's formal techniques, which might help to construct a small data base or arithmetic of such a rhetorical and iconographic apparatus.

1. Wilson is an action painter who does not pour out his gestures onto the canvas. His early compositions—*Poles, The King of Spain, The Life and Times of Sigmund Freud, Deafman Glance, I was sitting on my patio*—are like black and white Barnett Newmans, cool and austere color fields, light fields with darkness, structured silence. Surface without depth.

2. First approach to performance is drawing. The stage is a flat plane, framed. Wilson's stage is always the proscenium. The Italian-style proscenium supplies an immense space for minute, intimate movements. The literary model of theatre, and illusion, is dismissed.

3. The first principle is space (mental space). Drawing is the diagram, the language for painting which is also a mathematical language. Painting the space for performance is to compose it, to organize the plane with basic elements. Lines, geometric forms, light, and color.

4. Acts and scenes are numbered. Actors are numbered. The movement of the actor is envisioned as an algorithm. Precise counts, for each line (gesture), each motion (step), each position (figure) in the landscape.

5. The drawing is chiaroscuro. Light and dark, strong contrast and clear architecture. Pictorial space can become cinematic space of black and white film (film noir). In later works (after *Einstein on the Beach*), the palette changes and theatrical lighting is used for color. Wilson's virtuosity as a lighting artist creates an increasing rhetoric of luminescence. Color sensations are explored in slow motion, from dark blue to paler blue to white. ("I can do anything with those three lights").

6. From drawing to lighting. Wilson adds and subtracts. Giving light to generate the scene, creating passages, squares, windows, corridors, lines, geometric shapes. Geometric contours are outlined, objects are illuminated

as if from within, the actor is in silhouette. Light is an actor. Objects become actors, chairs are sculptures designed to draw attention to their surreal form and their "role" as a character.

7. Actors can receive their separate light that identifies them. Their hand or their face is spotlighted. Body-lines become gestures, the hand or the arm is immobilized, and light traces the imperceptible movement of stillness and displacement. If the actor moves, the space seems to move with him or her and stillness is experienced or dreamt as moving immobility.

8. The length of Wilson's performances (many hours) guarantees that immobility is also movement, slow duration, slow space. Time is time-line. Geometries (the vertical) introduce the fourth dimension, and choreography of lines, light and movement are felt as durations, with rhythms based on a clear structure of stillness, movement, repetition, variation, and contrast.

9. The sound of Wilson's performance can be recorded language, spoken language, distributed/amplified sound (of language and music and sound effects), live or recorded music, light. The light in the later productions (of the 1980s and 1990s) is attuned to the musical libretto of the operas and gives it emotional weight. Light becomes Wagnerian, more chromatic and transcendental (*Parsifal*), yet sometimes it defies gravity. In order to choreograph and express the (musical) content within the context of his abstract formal stage paintings, Wilson adopts the Wagnerian rhetoric, slows the tempo, and to maintain the continuity of sound he makes tonal compensation. Wilson's color of the sound becomes symmetrical and repetitive, he adds trance-like weight to the sound.

> PARSIFAL: I scarcely tread, yet seem already to have come far.
>
> GURNEMANZ: You see, my son, time here becomes space.
>
> *(Gradually, while GURNEMANZ and PARSIFAL appear to walk, the scene has changed more perceptibly: the woods have disappeared, and in the rocky walls a gateway has opened, which closes behind them. The way leading upwards through walls of rock, the scene has entirely changed. GURNEMANZ and PARSIFAL now enter the mighty hall of the castle of the Grail.)*
>
> —*Parsifal*, Act I

Wagner's libretto describes the effect of music. In Wilson's staging of *Parsifal* (1991), a horizontal bar of light slowly ascends. At the end of Act I, when Gurnemanz sings these lines, a frozen iceberg has appeared.

10. Wilson's grail: the spatialization of time. "The time is a vertical line and the space is horizontal. This time-space cross is the architecture of everything, and it is the tension between these lines that interests me."[6]

11. The stage score has two main elements—the visual and the auditory—and is composed of the visual elements, the way they are painted and their stage presence, along with the textual elements (if there are any), and lastly the music. In Wilson's diagram for an opera (*Einstein on the Beach*), the mapping is written in the following code:

> I, II, III, IV; A, B, C, D; 1, 2, 3, 4, 5.... Well, that is how I make an opera. First I decide to make a work called *Einstein on the Beach*. I start with the title. Then I decide to make four acts with three themes and all the possible combinations of these three themes: A and B, C and A, B and C, and finally the three themes together. Then I introduce the interludes, which I call Knee Plays (kind of articulations). Then I define the duration, I decide that this part is going to last 22 minutes, that one 21. All together I have four hours and forty minutes. By this time I know the form, the structure and the duration. Then I decide what I want to put in A. This is the next phase. Einstein talked about trains, so I show a train that comes on stage.... Einstein said that when you fly over a train, all you would see is a line. Then, when the train has crossed a quarter of the stage, it is interrupted by a vertical line of light. Then the train continues its route. The line of light disappears. The train gets to the middle of the stage and is interrupted once again by a vertical line of light. Then the train starts up again and gets three quarters of the way across the stage, where there is another vertical line of light.[7]

12. The breadth of the horizontal is interrupted by the vertical line that gives depth and also implies, opens up and expands time-movement. The breadth allows for the breathing of the space and the gaze. Scales, disproportions (the huge Abraham Lincoln tree in *the CIVIL wars*, the tall Cycladic statue in *Alcestis*, the enormous chairs in *The Black Rider*), oblique angles (the tilted doors in *The Golden Windows*, the crooked expressionist

houses in *The Black Rider*), layering of different planes, shadows, the repetitions and shifts in perspective (the rotating stage configuration in *Hamletmachine*), and 3-D illusions (the floating shoe and bicycling boy on the penny-farthing in *Monsters of Grace*): continuous movement from simplicity to complexity.

13. The deafman glance is always the apparent, deceivingly simplistic figure of silence, inarticulate tone poems of mundane language (*A Letter for Queen Victoria*, the *Einstein* chorus and knee plays), the childlike fairy tales (the knee plays in *the CIVIL warS*), the miming of an abstract formal choreography (the actor counts until fifty, turns left, and slowly walks ten steps to stage right). The *musique concrète* of the early libretti creates extended loops of vowels and consonants, molecular word reverberations and oscillations, making voice audible and physical, creating voice-lines and delays, oscillographs without semantic meaning. An earlier version of *Listening Post*.

14. The ephemeral oscillographs are like a dance, the stage a recording machine of visual and aural time lines.

15. Counting is the Wilsonian algorithm for the automaton actor. No intention, no psychology, no emotion. Movement itself is movement of the deafman, animated lines, crossing the stage laterally, as if listening to inner count. 1, 2, 3, 4, 5, 6, 7, 8, 9. The surface of the senses is in the gaze focused on the drawings. The listening of the deaf follows the drawn line, movement in stillness and stillness in movement.

16. The code is restricted by its lack of indexicality. What is seen is, perhaps, nothing. But as in dreams, the movement appears internal, imagined, fantasized, open to speculation and thought-experiments. How do thought-experiments become persuasive?

17. In Wilson's choreography, the model actors are deaf, listening to their inner scores. They furnish the gaze with a scenario enacted by the viewer's proxy. The automaton-actor in Wilson's *tableaux vivants* are agents of what we would experience through our glancing at the silhouettes in the architecture. The glance is self-persuasion.

18. The arithmetic of Wilson's choreography is performed according to an order of operations: addition (+), subtraction (-), multiplication (x or ·), division (÷ or /), acceleration, deceleration, abbreviation, zero. Wilson's performance logic is perfectly reductive and infinitely expansive at the same time. Each gesture could be described as a potentially alienating mudra, an

abstract stylization that crosses Western painting and modern dance with Indian dance, noh theatre, and Japanese aesthetics. Wilson does not know the Brechtian gestus.

19. As the mudras mean nothing, the movement (based on arithmetic counting) exists, lives, breathes in the abstract geometries of these visual worlds, and in the long duration, they may change from the physical reality to the supernatural. In *Monsters of Grace,* an abstract opera with no actors on stage but live music by Philip Glass and 3-D computer animation, Wilson finally reaches the full digital stage of such performance.

20. *Einstein on the Beach* models its opera-structure on an additive process (four acts: A+B, A+C, B+C, ABC, and five knee plays) and on structures repeated in cyclical succession. The sound material is reduced to the most minimal terms (numbers and syllables), the repetition of very brief rhythmic and melodic modules, and a rhythmicization based on the sequence of small units. The visual process, such as the appearance of the train in Act I, Act II, and Act IV, follows the same formal abstraction culled from arithmetic and geometry. The Einstein figure plays the violin; the gestures of the musicians a continuous drawing of lines.

21. The deafness of the body in Wilson's performance is the condition for resonance, for listening to such vision, to the virtual and the supernatural. A chair very very slowly descends from the ceiling, a tortoise crosses the stage in 35 minutes, other movements happen in a polyrhythm of graphic writings and drawings, in midst of vocal litanies, repetitions, and echoes, a dog barks in the distance, King Lear abdicates and a small boy approaches on a bicycle, as if from a very large distance, closer and closer, until you can almost touch the digital image. The supernatural envelops the realm of parables: in *Les Fables de La Fontaine* (created with La Comédie Française in 2004 and first shown in the U.S. at Lincoln Center in 2007), the stage is populated with lions, foxes, and various birds.

22. Molecular language, intoned or distributed (via surround loudspeakers, as in sound designer Hans Peter Kuhn's digital sampler work for *Death, Destruction and Detroit* and *Alcestis*), ebbs and flows in the architecture of modulated light. Texts in Wilson's auditory book are sampled, mixed and remixed, become sound points or echo-traces in the space. Film projections appear as geological layers or sediments of the landscape. Visual libretto (stage), sound libretto (music, language samples), film libretto: all elements can be combined, modulated, held in tension, separated. Different screens.

A fundamental formalism is used to set in motion a whole range of operations we now call digital.

The Digital

The balance and tension of the different "screens" in the *mise-en-scène* of live performance and the digital is of primary interest for our investigations of the common ground between performance practice and (computer) science. The numerical, graphical, and computational sensibility observed in Wilson's aesthetics—to be found also in Merce Cunningham, Trisha Brown, Lucinda Childs, William Forsythe, and other choreographers—beckons toward an examination of technologically mediated art which directs its "molecular gaze" at the mechanisms and the embeddedness of codes in the new organisms created from exchanges between abstracted and transformed data, between hidden algorithms and the theatrical, human, and perceived. The algorithmic base does not necessarily remain hidden, of course, as human-computer interfaces (HCI) will precisely materialize in performance and in the enactment of the balance and tension of the screens or scores, the recombination of the elements Brecht had tried to separate. The ways in which computer programming makes available particular enactments, or invites particular chronometries, improvisations, and possible interactions that might develop, are fundamentally cultural and creative concerns. Here computer science and programming join with the model actor or dancer, suggesting functionalist models or models of emergence. The latter pertains to the less controllable realities, constraints, spasms, and contextualized expressions of the human body.

If the functional architecture of performance implies a modeling, what then is the ground for a modeling that points beyond Wilson's highly designed illusionist apparatus with its pristinely regulated, mechanized order? For the contemporary human-computer interface, it is the digital medium, its materiality and organization. This interface has no use for Wilson's automaton actor whose "freedom"—generally postulated in the literature on Wilson—consists of internalized repetition of precise information inscribed in the geometries of the scene. Rather, if the interface itself implies an operating system and operations programmable by the software, it also implies an agent curious in *becoming molecular*, exploring qualities of real-time communication with dynamic virtual environments. From the actor's point of view, such becoming suggests a coming together in the creation of the new space, participating in the digital medium of probabilities (probabilities of application), which may determine the "work" that is processed in that situation, that "real" time. The applications will provide certain appearances of the images, sounds or, generally speaking, the digital objects. The digital objects follow the logic of the programming, and they can assume various forms and vocabularies with which the new media objects are organized.

As principles of categorization, Lev Manovich has identified five primary ways in which the new digital media set the stage for computerization: 1) numerical representation, 2) modularity, 3) automation, 4) variability, and 5) transcoding.[8] Since all new media are expressed through "numerical representation" (i.e., digitization), and can be described formally (mathematically), any digital object is subject to algorithmic manipulation, lending itself to individual customization and contingent articulation in the performed interaction. Errors and unpredictable effects are part of this post-formalist contingency. Through "modularity," media objects (e.g., words, graphics, videos, sounds, behaviors) can be combined (authored) without losing their individual characteristics, therefore allowing for all of the objects to be perpetually recombined or substituted in various configurations and presented through diverse interfaces. A perpetual re-authoring. "Automation" can be seen in constellations that are dynamically generated by user-defined behaviors and preprogrammed interactions; in software agents and search engines (as we saw in *Listening Post*). Because of their numerical nature, new media and their modular structures possess "variability" that is derived from human or machine manipulation, or both. Variability also includes using information about and from the user to generate content and media composition, branching interactivity (through tree structures), hypermedia and hypertext, periodic updating and refreshing, and scalability (i.e., granularity) represented in the amount of detail presented in the media. Different versions of the same data can be generated and distributed.

Finally, "transcoding" describes the blending of computer languages (e.g., how computers model the world in bits, bytes, variables, data structures, algorithms), interface metaphors, media languages (e.g., visual composition, video editing, generative aesthetics), and other cultural discourses. Transcoding implies remodeling, for example exchanging lens-captured computer data with scientific simulations of real-life conditions (e.g., microscopic images or high-resolution 3-D medical images) or switching between game engines and different programming languages. It also implies filtering computer and research discourses into relations of interconnected technical, aesthetic, perceptive-linguistic, and social dynamics.

The re-modeling tells us digital performance lives in the world of modeling and coding techniques, and in the following chapters a closer look at the science-derived approaches to complex dynamic and nonlinear systems is necessary, especially at the ways in which the behavior or performance development of such systems is modeled as the interaction of a collection of elements. Whereas in Wilson's algorithmic theatre the actors and objects are plotted, choreographed architectures set in motion for the silent gaze of spectators, in digital performance each interactional behavior draws permutational responses, recirculating feedbacks between inputs and outputs, player and player, thus intimating a very different social relational dynamics or knotting together of organisms, living systems.

NOTES

¹ Cf. Bernard Stiegler [1994], *Technics and Time, 1. The Fault of Epimethus*, trans. Richard Beardsworth and George Collins, Stanford: Stanford University Press, 1998. For Boulez's comments on John Cage, see Rocco Di Pietro, *Dialogues with Boulez*, 27–34. For an excellent overview of the intersections between art and science in the developing arena of genetic research and engineering, see Suzanne Anker and Dorothy Nelkin, *The Molecular Gaze: Art in the Genetic Age*, Cold Spring, NY: Cold Spring Harbor Laboratory Press, 2004.

² *Brecht on Theatre*, edited and translated by John Willett, New York: Methuen, 1978, 131.

³ Brian Rotman, "Ghost Effects," Lecture at Stanford Humanities Institute, 2004, quoted with permission.

⁴ Felicia McCarren, *Dancing Machines: Choreographies of the Age of Mechanical Reproduction*, Stanford: Stanford University Press, 2003, 60. She draws on Jonathan Crary's *Suspensions of Perception: Attention, Spectacle and Modern Culture*, Cambridge: MIT Press, 1999.

⁵ Louis Aragon, "Lettre Ouverte à André Breton: sur *Le Regard du Sourd*. L'art, la science et la liberté," *Les Lettres Francais,* no. 1388 (1971), quoted in Miguel Morey and Carmen Pardo, *Robert Wilson*, Barcelona: Ediciones Poligrafa, 2002, 23. I am indebted to the illustrations in Morey and Pardo's book, an extraordinary resource for anyone interested in the computational logic of Wilson's *mise-en-scène*.

⁶ Quoted in Miguel Morey and Carmen Pardo, *Robert Wilson*, 71–72.

⁷ Ibid., 72.

⁸ Cf. Manovich, *The Language of New Media*, 27–48.

THE
INTERACTIVE
PARADIGM

▼▲ River Beds & Gardens:
The Tactile Interface Environment

In the late summer of 2000 I attended *Natur/Spur—Projects in Ecology and Art*, an open-air performance and exhibition festival in Dreieich, a town southeast of Frankfurt, Germany. The second event of its kind curated by cultural anthropologist Ute Ritschel, *Natur/Spur* took place along a one-mile stretch of the small river that runs through the town and past the homes of its residents. Twenty-one artists participated in a month-long series of installations and site-specific performances exploring the natural environment and eco-system of the river. Some of the works drew attention to its local history and the fact that it was first "modernized" in the 1970s, when engineers rectified its meandering course and forced its water flow into a concrete bed, and then "re-naturalized" it in the 1990s after frequent flooding and the grave disruption of the river's biosphere led to protests by ecologists and the Green Party. The little river now runs again in all its organic splendor and wilderness, lined by trees, plants, and flowers, feeding its insects and birds and various species-visitors.

The artists were careful not to "intervene," as site-specific actions are often construed, but approach the organic life systems of the river with aesthetic, holistic/meditative, or scientifically-inflected ideas and performance gestures that linked the chosen materials or actuations organically, as *traces* or *nutrients*, to the existing temporal and environmental flow-totality of energy transfers and biochemical cycles. Freia Leonhardt, a butoh-trained dancer, created a mermaid-like character and, walking slowly through the river for half a mile while the audience followed along the shorelines, interacted with water, bed, and shore as if she were navigating between different habitats and niches. Others built sculptural works with found materials (wood, branches, bones, glass, footprints, etc.) that created real and metaphorical continuities with the river, joined or bridged it or alluded to the mixed traces of nature and culture in a small urban environment. Referring to the river's inexorable fluidity, others dealt with the concepts of time, erosion, pollution, refuse, regeneration, and alchemical process. A very subtle, beautiful, and intimate performance (*Secret Messages*) was created by Marilyn Arsem who waited on a bench on the shore for individual visitors to sit down with her and exchange a secret while watching the flow of the river and the leaves of the rich vegetation. The images the Boston-based artist had created were very nearly invisible—she had stencilled some of the leaves to leave holes in the shape of letters that would form words and sentences— and it took time for my eyes to actually recognize these holes as shapes of an alphabet. While I tried to decipher the world of leaves, Arsem had quietly gone down to the river and disappeared behind a tree. When I looked into the stream, I noticed more letters made out of frozen ice floating by. I am afraid I do not remember what they said: my body and mind were too riveted to think straight. After a while I became aware of the scent of the jasmine.

Later that day I visited one exhibition not located at the river but in the local cultural center, where Helga Griffiths had installed a complex environment of audio-visual sculptures (*Olfactorium*). She had painstakingly collected numerous scents and aromas from the river ecosphere and built a garden-like chemistry laboratory in which the viewer could encounter liquids and distilled scents of various flowers and herbs while also observing an actual machinic distillation process. An acoustic installation of many tiny loudspeakers softly transmitted conversations with psychologists, biologists, wine critics, chemists, and researchers from the perfume industry who spoke about the distinctions between natural, nature-identical, and synthetic scents. *Olfactorium* was captivating in many ways, appealing to our sense of recognition and, above all, to our olfactory sensorium, which is probably the most suppressed mode of sociality, sense-making, and artistic expression in the contemporary arena of media technologies.

From Site-specificity to Digital Interspatiality

Symptomatic of media arts and performance at the turn of the century, *Olfactorium* provocatively conjoins the "natural" and the "synthetic," placing the viewer into an active, participatory role. As a mode of embodiment, the participation in the exhibition is not primarily visual. Rather, as in dance, the participant needs to get down on the floor. Here fragile glass bowls filled with distilled aromas were placed in a spiraling, net-like configuration: I had to immerse myself, smell, close the eyes, breathe in the scent, follow my nose, dip a finger into liquids, taste them, remember, associate—let the body enact the experience, move through it. *Olfactorium* gestured toward what Roy Ascott has hypothesized as "moist architecture"—a scenario where actual and virtual realities intersect with "vegetal reality" or plant technology, allowing access to a vast spiritual database, an expansive, syncretic psychic memory.[1]

The "moist" scenario reflects an ecological view that this chapter brings to bear on digital performances and installations. What is at stake in the era of digital media is not the body's obsolescence or disappearance, nor the dream of total immersion in a kind of unhinged cyberspace, but a new biocentric or ecological conception of the body that I want to explore here with examples from interactive performance. Historically, digital performance and interactive installation now appear to be the logical transformation of an earlier body-centred approach to performance that expounded the "real" body in its most vulnerable, immediate existence, narcissistic obsession with self, and ritualistic subjugation to various external pressures or internal traumata. A significant shift has thus occurred from live *transactions* between bodies in installations of the 60s and 70s to virtual *transmissions* between bodies in contemporary digital art. The 60s and 70s were the time when live art and tanztheater tested the limits of the body's self-assurance and self-laceration. Already by the late 70s, the impact of conceptual and video art (and, subsequently, computer-based media) shifted the focus from the flesh body to the constructed body. The constructed or mediated body appeared in its various articulations as sound echo (cf. *Boomerang*) or screen double, and this doubling has often been described in psychoanalytic terms as phantasmatic projection, as an uncanny experience of split subjectivity. On a formal level, the use of such projections and doublings became a widespread scenographic technique used both in video installations as well as in live performances with video. The performance of the body became the performance of its mediations and videated projections, stuck in the loop form that now dominates most digital video installations. Bill Viola's work invites the same deafman glance as Wilson's spectacles. In the theatre, the inclusion of film and video in live performance was extended in the 90s, as the advances of computer technology allowed hybrid dramaturgies—using motion capture animation, 3-DVR (Virtual Reality) design and interactive media—on the stage. Increasingly, theatre- and dance-makers interested in interactivity built installation and projection environments instead of using the proscenium. As live art grows more hybrid, the remediations of bodies in the terrain of digital information grow more complex, for the body is no longer its own site of performance.

Today, interactivity is the conceptual model for site-specificity, for spatial and media practices that articulate the *transactions* between event, site, and visitor. Discussing the work of Brith Gof, Nick Kaye referred to their site-specific work of the 80s as an articulation process during which the "host" (site, architecture) was confronted and dispersed by the "ghosts" of performance narratives and techniques which operated on many layers of "restless relationships" with host site and audience.[2] Prefiguring the paradox of telepresence performances with distributed action, where images and sounds are created not simply to be transmitted by artists from one location to another, but to spark a multidirectional feedback loop with participants in remote locations, site-specific performance itself can be said to have become transitory. Transactions have become transmissions. Miwon Kwon points out that in art practices over the past years the "operative definition of the site has been transformed from a physical location—grounded, fixed, actual—to a discursive vector—ungrounded, fluid, virtual."[3]

"Local" performances in the theatre and dance world are often connected to a particular place of production since directors and choreographers are bound by contract to specific houses where they work unless they are commissioned to create a new piece for a host site (e.g., festival). Experimental groups generally have their own (often temporary) homes, and companies such as The Wooster Group are known to stage their works in these home venues before going on tour. With the steady increase in theatre, dance, and music festivals as well as art biennials across the world, touring has become a global phenomenon. Similarly, stage directors like Robert Wilson, Peter Brook, or Peter Sellars have been mostly on tour in recent years. Like conductors and musicians, they cross paths with video artists and filmmakers who work in many different locations. In the era of digital and televisual culture, the notion of a local production is losing its relevance, unless the local is more narrowly defined with regard to community theatres and community arts organizations whose explicit focus is a local or ethnic neighborhood, or a river ecosphere. Even without consideration to such community-based production, it is misleading to claim that performance will disappear in virtual spaces. The visceral properties of theatre and dance do not disappear, nor is context irrelevant. Rather, the physical dimension of performance and the physical/virtual spaces it inhabits through the human-computer interfaces are reconfigured. The formal aesthetic properties of computational performance may also be reconfigured to the point where traditional categories of theatre and of temporal/spatially bound live performers are no longer useful. Mediatized performance, in other words, does imply natural dislocations and relocations.

There is a critical discourse on dislocations in the technocultural environment, and to some extent it is indebted to the critique of an exponential capitalist spectacle once pronounced by the Situationist International (cf. Guy Debord's *Society of the Spectacle*) and now recaptured by contemporary locative media projects that mix performance strategies with tactical media tools in urban settings. The notion of tactical media performance refers to the kind of guerrilla theatre activities deployed, for example, by Slovene artist Igor Stromajer whose *Ballettikka Internettikka* (since 2001) forms an ongoing patchwork of infiltrations and clandestine transmissions from within rooms (kitchens, toilets, cellars, offices) of famous theatre buildings in Moscow, Milan, Belgrade, Berlin, etc., which he occupies "illegally" to broadcast small performances to the Internet. The tactical weapons are disguise and clownishness; the equipment includes laptops, mini cameras, toy robots, and mobile digital devices (GSM, WAP, GPS) to log on to a server that streams the microperformances to a growing online audience eager to watch the subversive actor (and his sound manipulator/composer partner Brane Zorman) break and enter. Stromajer is a former theatre artist who turned to tactical media in order to explore such distributed networked activities in a truly Dadaist fashion, mimicking high-cultural operatic genres through low-tech parasitic maneuvers. His "ballet" performance in the dilapidated cellar of the Bolshoi Theatre was broadcast to the Net as a series of self-refreshing still images of strange jumps and pirouettes with a newspaper. In earlier work he sang ASCII and html code or treated such code as "libretto" for what he calls "html choreography" (<www.intima.org>).

There is of course much deliberate irony in the hacktivist conflation of virtuosic ballet vocabulary and rudimentary computer code for information exchange. ASCII (American Standard Code for Information Interchange) is vintage code, already available in the 1960s and then popularized in one of the classic Net art pieces of the 1990s, Vuk Cosic's *ASCII History of Moving Images*, which converts scenes from film noir and science-fiction TV series into short animations. Moving ASCII characters do not quite look like anything we had seen before. More importantly, the example of Stromajer's break-ins and transmissions might be considered the first known theatre practice not based on live performance and stage presence, while Cosic's digital re-animation of older films also clearly indicates a new meta-media practice. Transmission, and the use of communicational protocols, drastically redefines the concept of live performance: Stromajer's Bolshoi Internet ballet can still be accessed on the Internet, and has in fact been seen by tens of thousands of viewers. Paradoxically, it continues to remain a mobile and dislocated event.

The discourse of these *détournements*, which according to the Situationists are diversionary appropriations of urban elements with a playful aesthetic and subversive agenda, is also indebted to the anti-aesthetic and anti-modernist critique of artists like Robert Smithson whose earthworks and writings on the site/non-site dialectic stimulated debates on site-specificity and the mobilization of environment. Such mobilization is now commonly understood in a political sense. A growing number of independent organizations, media centers, and schools, in many European countries but also in Southeast Asia and South America, has helped to generate a new media-network culture which is unprecedented in so far as electronic arts festivals give many younger artists the opportunity to show new work and participate in the critical-theoretical discourse on the social design of technology. Such design involves networking or so-called techno-political tools, advocated by the activists of "Net criticism," tactical media, hacktivism, and open source groups (such as Adilkno, Foundation for the Advancement of Illegal Knowledge) mostly operating across the Internet. Open Net culture is projected as a digital commons, a third space between the state and the market where people communicate freely (email, maillists, chatrooms) and where they can organize. The Nettime discourse is not utopian but pragmatic, initially devised to counter a U.S. technoculture poised to lead the rest of the world. Incorporating older media and artistic languages, network media function both as virtual communications (globally) and are used locally by social groups and movements, and this is how I see the dialectic of site and non-site to be of continuing relevance.

These critical ideas have had an impact on projects like the Sonic Acts Festival on Digital Art, Music, and Education in Amsterdam, shifting attention from the widespread display of interactive art in museums to critical investigations of programming and the role of technology in the life sciences, the political realm, and in art education.[4] Nettime activism and new media education thus complement each other, and the V2 Institute for Unstable Media in Rotterdam has made a specific effort to draw attention to the important role of "media memory"—the collecting and archiving of memory as data that can be stored and retrieved. The question is how this continuously growing database of collected memory will be used, and how specific practices create different cultural forms of reprocessing the past. The CYNETart Festival in Dresden introduced new categories for entries in 2004 which changed the focus from computer-based graphic and 3-D works to "real-time processing," "audio-visual processing," "Net projects," and "real-time spaces"—an effort to reposition the formats of (digital) perception into actual performance spaces.

Project-based programming, for example by shinkansen, the ICA or the "Digital Summer" in the UK, the C3 Center for Culture and Communication in Budapest, Karenina in Italy, MECAD in Barcelona, Digital Media Lab in Ljubljana, or the exhibitions curated by the V2 Institute, DEAF (Rotterdam), Transmediale (Berlin), and Cyberarts Festival (Boston), often emphasize the politics of media performance over its aesthetics, thus contributing to a conception of art as discursive "platform" which was also foregrounded during the 1997 and 2002 documentas in Kassel. Shinkansen's "Future Physical" series presented one of these platforms in London in 2002 ("Virtual Incarnations"); the discussion revolved around collaboration and inter-authorship, with choreographer Shobana Jeyasingh announcing that in her new work she wants to perform in telepresence linking London and Bangalore, in an effort to focus on the social impact of digital connections in the survival of family networks living a diasporic existence. Shinkansen organizer Ghislaine Boddington underlined the need to explore the essential political importance of local and distant connectivity through Internet communications.

With roots in artists' collaborations and activist projects, such platforms imply the formation of alternative networked economies and counter-publics. It is only in this sense of a radicalized participatory democracy that the notion of interactive art for users and citizens (as in Amsterdam's Digital City project) gains a strategic value not yet frozen in museum displays of high tech art or commercially abused through merchandising. Mainstream museums now incorporate new media art, as I already pointed out, but the speed of technical development in the culture at large is such that even specialized art centers—ars electronica in Linz and the Center for Art and Media (ZKM) in Karlsruhe—cannot continually update their critical indexing and anchoring of an expanding trans-mediality. Among practitioners, some of the collaborative groups (Knowbotic Research, Makrolab, Agentur Bilwet, Raqs Media Collective, Blast Theory) explicitly publicize their "research" as a form of counter-media, "questioning the ideologies propagated by the information surrounding us," as the British ensemble Blast Theory prefaced their interactive performance *Can You See Me Now?* during the Dutch Electronic Arts Festival 2003.

After receiving much attention for their mixed-reality installation *Desert Rain* (2000), which involved visitors in a hyperreal narrative labyrinth, Blast Theory's *Can You See Me Now?* offered a different paradigm of engagement for the "user." For five days during DEAF03, online players were invited to play a chase against members of Blast Theory. These players were dropped at random locations into a "virtual Rotterdam." Using their arrow keys, they could then move around the city and also communicate with other players. On the real streets of Rotterdam several "runners" from Blast Theory—equipped with handheld computers and satellite receivers—tracked down the online players. If a runner reached within 5 meters of an online player's location that player was "seen" and eliminated from the game. *Can You See Me Now?* is a game that happens simultaneously on the streets and online, inviting the player to investigate the near ubiquity of handheld electronic devices in the general population, the presence of satellite and GPS systems, and the consequences of the blurring of previously discrete zones of private and public space. In such public space our intimate conversations are inadvertently witnessed; our movements can be tracked and located. Again, this is the techno-aesthetic paradigm of *Listening Post*. But by sharing the same real/virtual space, the players online and runners on the street enter into a relationship both playful and adversarial, there is a competitive edge. Moreover, participants are expected to identify with a digital image, an avatar, of themselves, thus recognizing themselves as data in a navigational hide and seek where their "identity" and location become digital prey. Thinking through the implications of such dislocations of the audience, one can note the distance that has been travelled over the past twenty years since the publication of Herbert Blau's *The Audience* and *The Eye of Prey*. Blau's question, "Who's There?", derived from Shakespearean drama, is perhaps still valid as long as theatres and games gather players and audiences. The critical difference between theatre and computer games, of course, is that the latter need no audience. They must be played. As with all interactive art in the widest sense, the computer game is an action-based medium.

Also at DEAF, George Legrady's *Pockets Full of Memories* presented both an online and a local, on-site installation that explored the theme of collective memory and gave insight into self-arranging data structures. The performative framework of the installation was derived from gaming, involving the player in an algorithmic process, which, like all games engines, functions via specific codified rules of operation. Visitors of the installation were invited to contribute to an archive by having a personal object scanned. Gradually, a two-dimensional map of digitized objects formed, projected onto a large screen. The objects that on an individual level worked as means of identification became detached from the persons as they were categorized according to the logic of the database. Like a building or wonder cabinet under construction, the image archive grew over time, yet the objects lost all personal associations as they became part of the larger patchwork of an immaterial database. The significance of such interactive installations does not only lie in the design of the content and the ways in which they explore scanning, surveillance, and the social and technical processes of archiving/retrieving data. The performative dimension of such installations is not always intuitive or transparent but relies on the contributor's willingness to act and a discursive frame, a kind of narrativization of the interactive interface. The emergent digital art is no longer representational but based on encoding and decoding operations, navigations, and communicative actions.

Having said this, my introduction to this chapter offered an additional perspective on sensorial action and perception, which is often neglected in the study of technological operations. The idea of the local retains a very concrete sensorial meaning, related to (analog) affective and embodied experience. But my claim is that virtualization, and the various operations that become possible in digital performance, does not compromise human subjectivity and the aesthetic or political framing of reality. On the contrary, aesthetic perception and interpretation, if considered crucial for our understanding of the role of art, are relocated through the interactivity of digital aesthetics. The technologies of virtual realities create new materialities and new appearances, and in a theatrical sense such virtualization is not a demon that spells the end of art or the end of the human, or the conversion of every truth or every thing into data, but a program that will test the future of illusion through its inseparable interactional relation to the body of experience.

There is another way, then, of looking at transmissions of site. If a riverbed cannot be transplanted somewhere else, the modeling and simulation of its biological life is possible in "a-life" (artificial life). The paradox of site-specific performances that mobilize site(s) in real-time processing of virtual and translocal space, for example by transmitting physiological data from participants directly to image/sound generators elsewhere, allows us to rethink the history of ephemeral genres such as dance in their relationship to media and, especially, to database and telecommunications technologies. The transmission of data from human bodies, as we shall see below, enables the performers to interface more directly—to experience a stronger symbiosis—with the digital machine or artificial life. Simply put, in most of the artistic works discussed in this book, the machines are not entirely autonomous. They are different from yet dependent on humans. Investigating the question of a work's re-placement from an ecological or environmental point of view, digital performance offers striking concepts of movement or live action converging with virtual environments, as well as of the preservation and sustainability of its elusive nature.

Interactivity

I use the term "interactivity" with regard to two phenomena. First, I think of "interaction" as a spatio-temporal and architectural concept for performance that maintains a social dimension even if intersubjectivity or socialization (implying morality and ethics) is reframed under digital technocultural conditions. Secondly I look at "interactivity" in the more narrow sense of collaborative performance with a control system in which the performer-movement, gesture and action are tracked by cameras/sensors and thus used as input to activate or control other component properties from media such a video, audio, MIDI, text, graphics, scanned images, etc. In the latter case we speak of an *interactive system* that allows performers or audience members (users) to generate, synthesize, and process digital objects within a shared real-time environment experienced through sensory engagement.

Before examining the behavior of such systems, I suggest that the term "interaction" is useful philosophically, both in an anthropological and psychological sense and regarding spatial practices that anticipate technological mediation of environments, for example in modernist industrial design (Bauhaus, Mo-holy-Nagy) and the machine aesthetic influenced by cubism, photography, and the complex combinations becoming possible in film editing (advanced by Vertov, Eisenstein). Historically, "interactivity" proper didn't evolve as an aesthetic category until the computer age. However, in the pre-digital era one finds avant-garde experiments with performance as live concatenation of different, sometimes conflicting media (Dadaist, Futurist, Constructivist performance) or as an instrument for provoking the audience, asking them to do things. Modernist theatre artists like Meyerhold, Appia, Schlemmer, Beckett, Kantor, Grotowski, and Judith Malina/Julian Beck (founders of the Living Theatre) also developed provocative aesthetic ideas for a theatre beyond theatre, for new models of spatial relationships. These were recognized by art critics in the 60s, and Michael Fried's infamous attack on the "theatricality" of minimalism (in his 1967 essay "Art and Objecthood") manifests anxiety over the temporality of performance, its evasion of objecthood and inclusion of the presence of the viewer. Art historians, consequently, derive their understanding of interactivity predominantly from the 1960s (Happening, Fluxus, process art, Situationism, kinetic art, concept art, "art and technology," cybernetic art, closed-circuit video installations). The progressive "dematerialization of the art object" implied a more active, physical participation of audiences in the event. Since the 1970s, interactivity in art generally refers to multimedia installations and environments that involve electronic or computer-assisted interfaces. Nicholas Negroponte already suggested in 1970 that such interfaces are characterized not only by the points of contact and interaction between a machine and the physical or information environment, but by the artistic strategies used to engage audiences in a dialogue.[5]

Compared to installations, interactive performance in the strict sense of computer-assisted design cannot claim such a long and heterogeneous history. Dance-makers in particular have largely remained committed to (re)presentational stagings of multimedia works—complete and highly structured works for the consumption and aesthetic contemplation of the audience. Theatre companies known for their experimentation with new media (The Wooster Group, Builders Association, George Coates Performance Works, Complicite, and director/writers such as John Jesurun, Robert Lepage, Mark Reaney or Jo Fabian), also use traditional stage spaces augmented with video monitors and projections of live or pre-recorded images. Interactive performance installations engaging viewer-participants are rare events that require careful analysis as there aren't any established aesthetic criteria for the evaluation of successful "audience direction" of performance process. Emphatic "audience" enjoyment of social dancing in the vibrant club cultures is as rarely discussed as interactional rivalries performed in rap, clowning, and krumping contests (cf. David LaChapelle's documentary *Rize*) since such participatory enjoyment in hip hop culture tends to belong to a realm of sociability beyond the digital interactivity of media art and computer games.

The problem for performance is the overwhelming emphasis, in professional acting, dance, and music training, on specific techniques, vocabularies, and compositional structures that have limited usefulness for an exploration of participatory processes, computation, and the integration of recipient behaviors and feedbacks. Moreover, professional practice as it is commonly understood in Western training has been largely focused on the performer's physical virtuosity, voice, psychological characterization, and bodily intelligence, shaping and disciplining the body for the execution of choreography and stage presence, and not for interaction with unstable, mediated environments. Highly coded theatre forms of Eastern traditions could offer a rich source of comparative analysis for the correlations of computational algorithms and digital aesthetics, if "coding" were also understood as the development of particular interfacial techniques (cf. Min Tanaka's Body Weather technique).

Addressing "interaction" as a spatial and architectural concept for performance, therefore, means shifting the emphasis away from the creation of scenography and of steps, phrases, combinations, physical gestures or points on the body that initiate movement (away from the dancer's internal bodily awareness, widely encouraged in today's practices of yoga, somatics, experiential anatomy, body-mind centering, and release techniques) unto the performer's environment, to a not-given space but a shifting relational architecture that influences her and that she (re)shapes. Shifting attention to touch, weight and energy transfers in partnering, as it is practiced in contact improvisation, is a good preparation for working with physically motivated sensor interfaces and wearables. Similarly, actors working with live cameras and microphones also need to re-orient their focus toward video or sound editing techniques and the vocabulary of such framing or amplification technologies. This re-orientation further

implies an initial awareness of how lighting sculpts space, and how lighting color, angle, temperature, and intensity are constituents of the dynamic
and intermediating plasticity of space that creates opportunities for movement with camera tracking. Moving bodies and changing light, along with
the crucial experience of the resonating body within a reverberating sonic
environment, are part of the collective consciousness in which performers
are enveloped and in which they are co-creative participants. This notion
of a resonating environment, in my own practice, is indebted to the plastic
sculptural process that we explored—a *plastique animée* of fluid space design integrating "nervous" media presences.[6]

I see the plastic sculptural process as a contemporary modification of
Laban's Space Harmony, of the Bauhaus principles of synaesthetic abstract
constructivism, and of Joseph Beuys's and Hélio Oiticica's enactments of
"social sculptures." In philosophical terms, a non-Western and non-Euclid-
ian approach to spatial science and geometry would complement the notion
of plasticity as it is used in neurobiology.

> There is a need for a philosophical framework that enables us to
> engage harmoniously with the contextual living space in which
> we are immersed and from which we are as inseparable as a
> whirlpool is from a water flow. Reversing the man-induced ebb
> of essential harmonies may come through a philosophy of 'inclu-
> sionality' wherein, as in the wisdom of indigenous traditions, all
> things are understood to be dynamic contextual inclusions that
> both include and are included; i.e., wherein 'self' is to 'other'as
> whirlpool is to riverflow.[7]

In other words, an ecosophical, relational concept of performance is participatory, and it does not exclude virtual architectures, as Rafael Lozano-
Hemmer has shown in his writings and artistic projects, for example his
highly charged public interface event *Vectorial Elevation* (1999–2000), a
transformation of Mexico City's Zócalo Square with enormous light sculptures created by participants on the Internet using a virtual reality program.[8]
On the contrary, performance and the changing notions of "site-specificity"
in interactive installations need to be discussed with regard to the virtualism of VR environments and such models of immersion that integrate
physical and synthetic 3-D simulated environments, in order to perceive the
connections between designs based on representational space and designs

generated from algorithms. Current developments in computer science, artificial life research and 3-D design programming (VRML) point to hitherto unimagined combinations and hybrid living environments for multisensorial performance which could have a considerable impact on collaborations between choreographers, directors, composers, and designers interested in complex, dynamic "improvisation technologies," to use the term that William Forsythe applied to his rehearsal operations.

I want to give an example of such research to clarify my point. At the 2001 "Subtle Technologies" Conference in Toronto, Maja Kuzmanovic and David Tonnesen showed a computer simulation of the "T-Garden" project they were developing with the FOAM initiative at Starlab (Brussels). Tonnesen emphasized the interdisciplinary nature of the "T-Garden" collaboration and explained its conception:

> It is a responsive/hybrid play-space where visitors can 'converse' with sound, dance with images and socially shape media, constructing musical and visual worlds 'on the fly.' The performance aims to dissolve the traditional lines between performer and spectator by creating a computational and media architecture which allows the visitors-players to shape their overall environment through their own movements, as well as their social encounters with each other. At the same time, T-Garden constitutes part of a larger research project investigating five fundamental questions:
>
> 1. How do we develop sustainable, international collaboration networks between cultural institutions, operators and policy makers?
>
> 2. How do we allow the project to evolve in the most open and interactive manner (e.g., looking at authorship and copyright issues).
>
> 3. How do people individually and collectively make sense of responsive, hybrid environments, articulating their knowledge in a non-verbal language?
>
> 4. Can play (in the broadest sense of the word) become an essential mode for cross-cultural experience?
>
> 5. How can new forms of expression be sustained by a fusion of media matter, motion and gesture.[9]

These questions point to the heart of current experimentations with inter-activity, which for theatre- and dance-makers until very recently was largely a dialogue with composers and programmers who designed MIDI-activated sonic environments for non-linear choreography. "T-Garden" suggests an expanded architecture allowing the performers or "gardeners" to experi-ence physical and tactile relationships to a virtual reality they can actu-ally modify and shape, moving through the projective, computer-generated world. Since this world needs to be projected via surround-sound speak-ers and LCD projectors, it means that the performer moves through light waves, fields of color and pulsations, floating virtual objects, etc. Her body potentially experiences ruptures of the kinaesthetic from the visual senses as all physical body-surfaces gain a multidimensional tactile extensionality. We also note that it is the audience who become the performers and "gar-deners" in this interactive installation. Its logic of interactivity in play aims at dissolving spectacle and the featured stage performer altogether, and it explicitly induces tangible, manual, motorsensory, kinaesthetic actuations and synaesthetic integrations.[10]

Such movement through generative environments posits a shift in per-ception that many theatre practitioners, used to working in delineated real space—with a forward orientation on the proscenium and toward a pas-sively spectating audience—have been reluctant to engage. The engagement requires new vocabularies informed by interactive design and VRML (Vir-tual Reality Modeling Language) and involves such notions as parameters, mapping, navigation, tracking systems, Musical Instrument Digital Inter-face (MIDI), genetic algorithms, modules, and patches based on specific programming languages such a C++, Max/MSP, Pure Data, or Isadora. It also requires at least a basic understanding of the underlying computational processes that generally remain invisible. And it prompts us to reflect on contemporary science-derived concepts of "emergent" or autogenerative systems as they are now being used by diverse artists working with interac-tive installations, a-life architectures, 3-D shared spaces, and telepresence.

NOTES

¹ Roy Ascott, "The Moist Scenario," Keynote address at *Cross Fair 2000: The Intelligent Stage* (November 9–12, 2000), a symposium held at the Choreographic Centre North-Rhine Westphalia [CZNW] in Essen, Germany, quoted with permission of the author. In popular new age culture, aromatherapy is probably part of a wide range of alternative, osteopathic medicines, and it was interesting to hear Ascott propose new links between "dry" digital media and the "moist vegetal reality technologies" he encountered during his research on shamanic practices under the influence of the *ayahuasca* vine in the Brazilian Matto Grosso. For Ascott, the transformative animism of the shamans in the Amazonian rain forests evokes a healing power, an environment in which the user enters into entirely new kinds of space to participate with other entities, a scene of action which is quite out of this world and deep into one's interior space. Such environments of psychic restructuring differ from the use of yoga, Body Mind Centering and other body work practices, and are rarely addressed in Western performance, aside from the ecstasies of techno and rave culture.

² Nick Kaye, *Site-Specific Art: Performance, Place and Documentation*, London: Routledge, 2000, 52–7.

³ Miwon Kwon, "One Place after Another: Notes on Site-Specificity," *October* 80 (1997): 95. For the complex issues of transitoriness in regard to changing notions of the art object, performance and transcultural transmissions, see Henry M. Sayre, *The Object of Performance*, Chicago: University of Chicago Press, 1989; Nestor Garcia Canclini, *Hybrid Cultures: Strategies for Entering and Leaving Modernity*. trans. Christopher L. Chiappari and Silvia L. López, Minneapolis: University of Minnesota Press, 1995; and Johannes Birringer, *Performance on the Edge: Transformations of Culture*, London: Continuum, 2000. For an evocative study of the tropes of "natural history" in theatre, see Bonnie Marranca, *Ecologies of Theater*, Baltimore: Johns Hopkins University Press, 1996.

⁴ Cf. Frans Evers, Lucas van der Velden, Jan Peter van der Wenden, eds., *The Art of Programming*, Amsterdam: Sonic Arts, 2002; Gert Lovink, *Dark Fibre: Tracking Critical Internet Culture*, Cambridge; MIT Press, 2002. On the subject of "media memory," see Joke Brouwer, Arjen Mulder, Susan Charlton, eds., *Information is Alive: Art and Theory on Archiving and Retrieving Data*, Rotterdam: V2_/NAI Publishers, 2003. For an expanded context of these developments, see Johannes Birringer, "A New Europe," *PAJ: A Journal of Performance and Art* 75 (2003): 26–41.

⁵ Cf. Nicholas Negroponte, *The Architecture Machine: Toward a More Human Environment*, Cambridge: MIT Press, 1970, 101. For a good critical overview of the evolution of interactive art, see Söke Dinkla, *Pioniere Interaktiver Kunst*, Karlsruhe: ZKM/Cantz Verlag, 1997.

⁶ "Nervous environment" is derived from the term sound artist David Rokeby uses for his interactive software "Very Nervous System" (VNS), first created in 1982. VNS uses video cameras, image processors, computers, synthesizers and a sound system to create a space in which the movements of one's body create sound and/or music. In his writing Rokeby has pointed out that VNS is not a "control system" but an interactive system, by which he means that neither partner in the system (installation and moving person) is in control. "Interactive" and "reactive" are not the same thing, according to Rokeby. "The changing states of the installation are a result of the collaboration of these two elements. The work only exists in this state of mutual influence. This relationship is broken when the interactor attempts to take control, and the results are unsatisfying." Quoted from "Lecture for 'Info Art,' Kwangju Biennale," 1996: <http://www.interlog.com/~drokeby/install.html>.

⁷ Ted Lumley, "Inclusionality: an immersive philosophy of environmental relationships," paper presented at the "Subtle Technologies" Conference, Toronto, May 20, 2001. Quoted with permission.

⁸ For an extensive critical documenation of his interactive art project, see Rafael Lozano-Hemmer, ed., *Alzado Vectorial/Vectorial Elevation: Relational Architecture No.4*, Mexico City: Conaculta, 2000.

⁹ Maja Kuzmanovic and David Tonnesen, "T-Garden," Presentation at "Subtle Technologies" Conference, May 2001, Toronto, Canada. Quoted with permission. For more information on the project, visit <http://www.subtletechnologies.com/2001/index.html>.

¹⁰ The "T-Garden" project, which included interactive performance director Chris Salter, derives some of its conceptual terminology from theatre, understood as spatial practice and social drama (Victor Turner), cultural anthropology, virtual architecture and current research in hybrid spaces and the world of 3-D game design. It is not an example of interactive digital art designed for the general "user" in clear-cut distinction to interactive dance or music performed by trained professionals. The sliding between performer and recipient needs to be carefully theorized, especially as an increasing number of artists and programmers collaborate on the design of interactive installations for audience-play. In the summer of 2002, together with 30 other artists, I participated in such a design project ("Real-Time and Presence:

Composition of Virtual Environments") at the Trans-Medien Akademie in Helle-rau, and with the exception of French musicians Bertrand Merlier and Jean-Marc Duchenne, all other teams created environments for audience interaction (<http://www.t-m-a.de>). The theoretical debate on interactivity is still in its infancy. Cf. Annette Hünnekens, *Der bewegte Betrachter: Theorien der Interaktiven Medienkunst*, Köln: Wienand, 1997; Emanuele Quinz, ed., *Interfaces*, special issue of *Anomalie digital_arts* 3 (2004); Antonio Camurri and Gualtiero Volpe, eds., *Gesture-Based Communication in Human-Computer Interaction*, Berlin: Springer, 2004; Florence Corin, ed., *Interagir avec les Technologies Numériques*, special issue of *Nouvelles de Danse* 52 (2004). The focus on the user of intelligent interactive systems and game art environments is most explicit in Scott deLahunta, ed., *Swan Quake: the user manual*, Plymouth: Liquid Press/i-DAT, 2007.

▼▲ Interactive Systems

The outside-inside relationship of *Natur/Spur* and *Olfactorium* provides an interesting link with the conceptual intersections between the physical and the digital, which characterize several types of environments. I propose the following distinctions:

1. *interactive environments* (based on sensors or motion tracking and real-time processing, and a dynamically evolving dialectic between artificial ecosystem and human agents);

2. *derived environments* (motion-capture based re-animations of bodily movement, or liquid architectures which can also be networked and reintroduced into live telepresence or telerobotic communications between remote sites);

3. *immersive environments* (Virtual Reality based, e.g., the "Cave" or panoramic installations that integrate the user, via stereoscopic devices, into the polysensual illusion of moving through space);

4. *networked environments* (telepresence, telerobotics, and on-line collaborative multi-user platforms allowing users to experience dispersed bodies or actions and to interact with traces of other remote bodies, avatars, and prostheses).

5. *mixed reality environments* (interplay of live and prerecorded audio/video, mixing and combining the parameters of the previously mentioned environment types for performers or users).

What are these intersections, and what do I mean by "ecology" or "environment" of performance? An ecological understanding of our life world and cultural systems recognizes movement practices as organisms. Dance has always been a live expressive organism, based on a fundamental physical-sensory relationship to space and the world, to perception/cognition, and to subjectivity, if we retain an anthropocentric perspective. From a biocentric perspective, "movement" can be studied in many diverse species and geographies of the world, and these performance worlds inform the natural/cultural environments of human dance practice. Think of the dance of the butterfly in a tropical garden, the stuttering walk of penguins, the arabesques of flocking birds, or the majestic swarming departure of millions of bats from a mountain cave at dusk, streaming upwards into the distant horizon. Animal movement and plant behavior have inspired fascinating experiments in contemporary robotics, microelectromagnetic (MEM) technology, computer animation, transgenic and a-life systems. Computer scientist Demetri Terzopoulos, for example, has built an entire intelligent "marine ecosystem" for his artificial fish that are animated by algorithms based on quantitative data and mathematical equations derived from fish behavior. The simulated space inhabited by the artificial ecology is computationally rendered to look like a natural system.[1] Similarly, Simon Penny, Bill Vorn, Louis-Philippe Demers, Kenneth Rinaldo, and others work with interactive ecosystems inspired by scientific theories of emergence.[2]

Rinaldo's interactive installation *Autopoiesis*, first shown at the Kiasma Museum in Helsinki (2000), consists of fifteen robotic sound sculptures (made out of grapevine) that interact with the public and modify their movement behaviors over time. The behavior changes are based on feedback from infrared sensors, the presence of participants in the exhibition, and communication between each separate sculpture. Such "autopoiesis" or "self-organizing" is symptomatic of current dance experiments with interface designs based on feedback in real-time. The compositional process is a kind of symbiotic improvisation with invisible sensor "vines" or dynamic fields in space, with dynamic characteristics of living systems. The convergence of artificial life and media art unleashed provocative research into genetic algorithms, cellular automata, tissue cultures, and behavioral robotics, which also influenced, for example, Stelarc's recent performance experiments with walking machines or the *Prosthetic Head*. In Martin Arnold's installation *Deanimated,* a method of decomposition/degeneration is applied to selected micro-narratives from older movies, subjecting them to frame-by-frame manipulation and turning actors into hysterically fluttering inanimate objects. At the 2000 ars electronica, a transgenic dance work (*D.A.V.E.*) was shown by choreographer Chris Haring and media artist Klaus Obermaier, involving some truly stunning scenes of gender-morphing in which Haring's male body images dissolved, shifted form and became warped and reconfigured in a series of freakish mutations. Digital video animation, in this case, acts as a parasite or decomposer, drawing on the human host-form to fabricate fantasies of posthuman metamorphosis.

Digital dancing, decidedly not posthuman, has nothing to do with the synthetic "engineering" of steps or movement phrases, or with copying the motion of figure animation (as Merce Cunningham appeared to do when he used the LifeForms software as inspiration for his recent choreography), but everything with the overall physical behavior of the system. Movement bridges organic and inorganic forms, it evolves as a coupling with technically expanded virtual domains. Contrary to the assumption of disembodiment often associated with VR and telematics, the interactive coupling always involves sensory synthesis in an expanded biofeedback system. It is the convergence of movement with the hyperplasticity of space enabled by multimedia interactivity in real-time processing that I define as an interactive environment. The bottom-up aesthetics of interactivity is rooted in flow, in a dynamic network of microagencies that are sensing and acting upon each other—a dialectical principle that enhances the immersive sensory experience I described in *Olfactorium*. I do not think of human performers in the interfaces as separate from an intelligent environment but treat the entire interface environment as communicative process. It is not necessarily a primarily visual one, even if the discourse on digital images tends to privilege vision at the expense of convergences that involve acoustic, haptic, and peripheral senses.[3]

In postdramatic theatre, intersections with interactive systems generally focus less on movement but on critical dislocations of narrative, actor-character relationships, temporal processes, collage and doubling, and the extension of spatial and fictional (illusionistic) architecture. Even if such theatre no longer adheres to an Aristotelian or naturalist/realist template nor seeks recourse to Stanislavski's or Grotowski's philosophies of the acting process, its dramaturgical paradigm continues to bind naturalist traits of the actors' presence and diction to the *mise-en-scène* and the plot's fictional reproduction of life. If the fracturing and dislocating of "reproduction" imply non-realist and hypernaturalist techniques, or perhaps, even, not-acting techniques, then how can one understand the operational code of interactivity and technical mediation in the theatre? How does interactivity affect acting?

The Wooster Group, in particular, has established a significant reputation for their deconstructive dramaturgies, the mixing and sampling of heterogeneous texts, personal narratives, popular cultural materials, and brilliant use of film/video and audio processes within live performance. The group is also known for their re-writings and subversive re-stagings of appropriated and collaged image/text materials, from their works of the early 80s (*Route 1 & 9, L.S.D., North Atlantic*, etc.) to *Frank Dell's The Temptation of St. Antony* (1988), *The Emperor Jones* (1995), *House/Lights* (1997), and the more recent touring productions of *To You, The Birdie!* (2001), *Poor Theater* (2004), and *Hamlet* (2006). Their live performances have a particular technological style which I am tempted to call "live post-production," as they have developed a performative set of video and microphone/ audio strategies clearly characterized by video and sound editing techniques that a producer would use in a television studio. Their theatre space, the Performing Garage in SoHo (New York City), functions as a sound stage; the use of scaffolding often makes it look like an installation. And given their presence on the scene for so many years, their technical and artistic method has also had a considerable impact on younger companies such as Builders Association (director Marianne Weems had worked with the Wooster Group before), Elevator Repair Service, Cannon Company, Big Art Group, Radiohole, Les Freres Corbusier, Cathy Weis, and Richard Maxwell.

When I saw *To You, The Birdie!* at the Wexner Center in 2002 and compared it to an early version of *Route 1 & 9* witnessed at the Yale Drama School in 1981, I was struck by the extent to which the Wooster Group had perfected the integration of theatre and video techniques. But it was not exactly apparent how the actors engaged the interface environment as an open communicative process. Rather, their digital aesthetic approaches the stage as a programmable environment, with all actions and video images tightly cued and conceptually fixed. However, the "live editing" or illusion of real-time live processing is maintained, certainly in the audio production if not in the video editing, turning this performance into a cunning theatrical pun on interactivity as well as shifting the Wooster Group's experimental theatre aesthetic closer to dance. *To You, The Birdie!* is such a complex, interesting work that I want to sketch its template here, first drawing attention to the commentary given by the company in the program notes. Director Elizabeth LeCompte introduces the notion of "dancing with technology," which no longer comes as a surprise, as the group's audio-visual (re)production strategies seem to have evolved to a point where media choreography approaches the complex fluidity so characteristic, for example, of William Forsythe's dance works.

TO YOU, THE BIRDIE! allows us to further our explorations of the possibilities of "dancing with technology" in three specific ways. We work with live feeds from on-stage cameras, which force the performer to simultaneously consider both the framed, mediated space of the monitor and the actual stage space simultaneously. We are also creating sequences that rely on the performer dancing a *pas de deux* with their own prerecorded image, yielding movement that is psychologically evocative as well as physically captivating. A third approach involves the use of existing videotapes—including Marx Brothers films and dance pieces—on monitors visible only to the performers, who then translate physical actions and camera moves through their bodies onto the stage.

The performance is ostensibly an adaptation of Racine's seventeenth-century tragedy, *Phèdre*, centering on the obsessive sexual infatuation of Theseus's wife with her stepson Hippolytus (the rewritten text is by Paul Schmidt). The title of the performance, however, refers to the game of badminton, and the "players" of this elegant and athletic game open the performance with a live video-produced duet, which prepares the audience for much of the splitting and doubling of actors/video-actors devised in this staging. The set design is a mobile, grid-like landscape with gliding screen panels, hidden video cameras, and television monitors that make intimate meetings between the actors/characters easily visible. The badminton court takes up the whole width of the upstage area. It is presided over by Venus (Suzzy Roche), a goddess as referee, and a monitor high above her recapturing her facial expressions and judgements. Across from Venus's monitor, behind the audience, hangs another monitor that can only be seen by the actors. On this invisible monitor, films are played which cue the performers to imitate particular dance steps or movement expressions (in one sequence, I imagined seeing a performer "copy" Martha Graham's vocabulary from her early mythic dance dramas). Perhaps these are training films for the athletes.

In the beginning, as Theramenes (Scott Shepherd) and Hippolytus (Ari Fliakos) enter to face off in the court and set the tone for the physical choreography in this performance, they come downstage to prepare themselves. They sit down, as if in a locker room, but we don't see them whole, as their lower body halves remain hidden behind a large screen. On the screen, a pre-recorded projection of their lower halves merges with the action of their upper bodies. The men chat with each other, their eyes following the action on the invisible monitor, and as they fidget, reaching down with their live arms, their video hands simultaneously show up on the screen below as they fiddle with their exposed genitals beneath their kilts. The screen images are larger-than-life and appear slightly out of sync with the live bodies.

The group here establishes the paradigm of the typical split/mixed realities pervading the entire *Birdie* environment. Not quite as perversely uncanny as some of the bodily mutations in Matthew Barney's films, the collages and mutation shift perspective back and forth between the upper and lower bodies almost as if to comment on the classical theology or metaphysics of the higher and lower regions of Man. The source material for *Phèdre*, of course, is mythological and full of the kind of unsavory mythic permutations Barney explores through his satyr-body in the *Cremaster Cycle*. Phèdre's mother, Pasiphae, gave birth to the Minotaur after her affair with a bull, as we recall, and in the Wooster Group's *Phédre* the realm of bestiality and transgressive love has become an underlying psychosomatic trauma mediated, in numerous scenes, through the dire scatological images and medical paraphanalia surrounding the protagonist in her wheelchair. But whereas Barney's *Cremaster 5* creates a perverse lyrical atmosphere through its operatic arias sung to the floating testicles of a "Giant" submerged in the thermal bath underneath the Queen's throne, the Wooster Group's *Birdie* strikes a more mundanely gurgling and sluicing tone, with manipulated and neurasthenic bodies out of sync with their images and their sounds. The players pass the microphone to each other, and as the actors' voices are miked, so is the badminton game with its pops and whizzing sounds permeating the space. The extraordinary game choreography, with Shepherd and Fliakos whipping the "birdies" through the air and expertly playing under-the-leg shots and back-hand top-spins, looks like a real game, not a choreography, and again this confusion is mirrored by the continuous suturing and undoing of voices: Shepherd, who acts as if he is Hippolytos's best friend, speaks Kate Valk's words.

Most of the voices are amplified and they come from loudspeakers, dispersed and dislocated from the subjects who speak (similar to the Wilson template above), and at the same time reproducing and redistributing the characters of sound as we come to associate the granularities of voice (for example the sonorous but sometimes nasal voice of Willem Dafoe's Theseus) and particular rhythms of articulation with particular performers. The performers, in a Brechtian manner, use the gestus of (amplified) voice to comment on the characters who are, at the same time, reframed by the video screening technologies.

It is possible, then, to speak of the Wooster Group's application of the gestus in a technological fashion: "character" is always mediated or alienated, video and textual fragmentations are (re)combined to illuminate the sick world of the court which overexposes narcissistic masculinity—Theseus contorting himself to show off his muscular body—conflated with a voyeuristic and often pathetic eroticism. But Valk's Phèdre is stiffly corseted and needs help from her nurse Oenone (Frances McDormand), feeding her, walking her, assisting her in her obsessions with shoes, fashionable clothes, and her stepson, relieving her of her fluids, with grotesque enema sacks being attached via long, snakelike tubes to Valk's lower body. The dripping fluids ("I had Venus like a virus in my blood," Phèdre suggests) drain all eroticism from this organism. The queen's existence, surrounded by the vain tools of (dis)pleasure, is slowly filtered out. The various sources of myth, tragedy, and their technological "reproducibility" come apart at the seams. The sound of dripping water, whizzing birdies, birdsong, cars crashing, walls of glass shattering, etc., takes on a hypnotic quality: radio intimations of a stricken world we barely see but imagine through all the other senses heighened by the technological plasticity set to work in this performance. The analog audio world has a subterranean quality, which echoes Cocteau's film *Orphée*, in which the radio functions as transmitter of mysterious signals from (Eurydice's) underworld.

The Wooster Group's "dancing with technology" therefore can be taken almost literally. *To You, The Birdie!* plays havoc with sensory perceptions of the sources (of tragedy, of narrative, of desire, of the subject's identity/character). However, their sensibility cannot be compared with Robert Wilson's abstracting mechanical/algorithmic aesthetic. Rather, the use made of technological strategies in *Birdie* points to a performance style, which fragments and collides medium with medium, and also demonstrates in a particularly strong manner how technology must not be understood as disembodying. The Wooster Group's use of video and audio technologies produces a hyperphysical bodiliness, and their production style in *Birdie* quite often foregrounds this bodiliness on a microbiological or microelectric level, for example in the badminton game where players wipe off their sweat from various public and private parts of their skin, or in the scene in which Theseus admits his remorse lying down in front of a screen which amplifies, sometimes asynchronously, his face and the "movement" of facial muscles during his speech. Phèdre's muscles seeem distressed, cramped, as she dances awkwardly to the vocal ventriloquism of Theramenes's rendering of her lines of thought. These doublings and distortions create a loopiness, which reflects on technical mediation but also on biological motion itself as the basis of all perceptual experience.

The Wooster Group's "dancing with technology" thus exemplifies the mixed reality of technological performance and especially the framing operations afforded by the on-stage use of camera and microphone feeds. On one level, the company works with live cameras feeds that capture the actors' actions and transmit the input to the monitors on stage. The actors thus perform both to the camera and to the stage audience, doubling what Walter Benjamin called "optical tests" (for the film actor performing to a camera without any audience present), since in the Wooster Group's staging the actors have to remain continuously aware both of the framing created by the video camera and the larger stage frame. The live optical tests are a double framing implying a mediation between different acting techniques required for each medium. To bring the face or the hand to a close-up on the video screens means that an actor must be aware of how to place the body in relation to the camera eye, while the theatre audience can view both the real size actor's face or hand and the amplified images on the screens. The audience in fact is invited to perceive the mediation of shifting perspectives as such, observing the alternation of the framing devices. A continuous tension exists between the televisual imagery of the actor/character and the production techniques for the live mediated representation. Arguably, the Wooster Group here use a Brechtian *Verfremdungseffekt* to play with the space of seeing and the different or contradictory projections of (technological) embodiment, self-display, enhancement, entrapment, displacement, and deformation—thus also various permutations of the fleshly anatomy as they are implied by Phèdre's corseted and medically encumbered persona.

On another level, the dance with technology in *Birdie* calls for a *pas de deux* between actor and pre-recorded video image. This peculiar coupling, as LeCompte suggests, affords a psychological self/image or movement/image combining a live/technological representation, which heightens the

Beckettian spooling. Yet unlike *Krapp's Last Tape* or its psychedelic echo, frantically performed by the late Ron Vawter in *Frank Dell's The Temptation of St. Antony* (when he runs his tape in the hotel room and lip syncs to his video image and the images of other actors in a fake cable TV-show, or when he asks the video technician to rewind or fast forward the tape so that he can "rehearse" the talk show), the *pas de deux* indicates a shift to real-time simultaneity. However, the Wooster Group's technique only mimics the digital interactivity. In one scene we see Kate Valk's upper body, while her feet perform a dance shown on the monitor placed in front of her. The prerecorded feet appear slightly asynchronous with her body; they may belong to the wrong body. They are discontinuous with her real body, but these are interactive trickeries, since the perceptual illusion of course controls the scene. We still read the video feet as her feet. The images articulate the motor body and biological motion but our eyes most likely are drawn to the picture-framing device. The isolation of the feet on screen here reflects a more "classic" video art strategy of discrete framing (so often practiced in earlier video work by Bruce Nauman, Vito Acconci, Dan Graham, Gary Hill, and others, including Bill Viola in his 2003 cycle of *The Passions*). It also reveals a flatness of the closed box markedly different from outwardly expanding interactive and immersive real-time projection environments, as they are used by Frank Castorf and stage designer Bert Neumann at the Berlin Volksbühne, for example, and by directors deploying massive projectors for cinemascopic effect.

The particular framing used in the Wooster Group's technique seems owed to its tele-theatrical strategies and presentational performance style. Not unlike Richard Foreman's use of framing devices and scenographic strings, lines, and barriers (in the work of his Ontological-Hysteric Theatre), the Wooster Group delights in complex and mind-twisting edges—segmenting televisual and "real" acting in front of the eyes of the audience and constantly disquieting what in some fashionable and widely exhibited contemporary video installations (e.g., Shirin Neshat's *Rapture*, 1999) has become an engulfing experience where the viewers are very nearly entrapped, caught in the middle. In Neshat's *Rapture*, for example, the audience is literally sandwiched between two opposite, facing screens, and deep emotional engagement is provoked by dramatic filmic composition and the diegetic soundtrack. Nothing of the kind takes place in the Wooster Group's work; the video images do not embed the viewer but are used, in a quasi-Brechtian manner, to distance and alienate, to unsettle a clear identification with the split subjects. The Wooster Group's filtering and framing style is always dissociative.

Finally, on a third level, *Birdie* offers an exchange of video and actor hiding the interactive control directing the actor's movements from the audience. Perhaps it is only possible to speak of control in an ironic sense here, as the Wooster Group does not employ a computer-programmed environment or surveillance system. Their references to controlling agencies operate on a more literary and grotesque level of (badminton) games where fate is the referee calling the shots as *deus ex machina*. The metaphysics of such fate are mocked when the audience sees the actors/re-enactors perform to hidden film excerpts, translating "forbidden" knowledge or source code (Marx Brothers, Martha Graham) to the spectator. Both the Marx Brothers' antics and Graham's high seriousness would be perceived as quaint today. Those performance styles have already been filtered through the Ridiculous Theatre, and watching such a Wooster pantomime might appear bizarre to an audience unable to access the control monitors. The logic for such re-enactments is elliptical, both hidden and infered by the spectator at the same time. The interaction between actor and screen creates a compelling pattern of meta-media, based on the inference of older media, silent-era movies, expressionist dance, classical dramaturgies, forgotten tragedies. Acting is based on acting, but the Wooster actor seems displaced in video and performance simultaneously, enjoying the dangerous liaison of reduced telepresence, strange segmented bodies and part-objects, screened genitals and projected heads, perverse desires, out of focus and recycled, falling behind the perfect mediatization promised by the televisual. The deadpan Wooster style of dissociated acting conjures up a discrete aesthetic form of post-production: the meshing of body/machine is mindful of the theatre's trauma (vis-à-vis technoscientific culture) of poor reproducibility.

It offers us performance at a close distance, approximating the present and presence of sutured subjectivities, which always interact with their screenic images and older data. Certainly the work of the Wooster Group confronts the problematics of the simulacrum, as they specifically engage it also in *Poor Theater*, with its re-productions of Grotowski's and Forsythe's aesthetic techniques. Their simulation of past and present performance techniques, drawing attention to the disintegrationist operations of acting (non-mimetic, not-mirroring), thus provides a significant ideological commentary on both sides of the contemporary advance of interactivity—the representational/simulational capacities of new media and the enactive potential afforded by interfaces whose rules are not determined.

In large metropolitan theatres like the Berlin Volksbühne, where stage designers have enough funding to build enormous "film sets," the theatrical commentaries on the simulacrum can be trenchant when Castorf, in his adaptation of Dostoyevsky's *The Idiot* and *The Humiliated and Offended*, not only uses continuous splitting and roaming of view-points (via live camera feeds) to create multiple scenic presences, but also treats the intimate close-up ironically as a humiliating device, rendering the actors highly vulnerable, exposed to a particular style of low-tech, low-res video associated with "trash TV," soap operas, Big Brother, and porn movies. Christoph Schlingensief's direction of Wagner's *Parsifal* for the Bayreuth Festival used a similar approach, aggressively overpopulating the stage with flickering videos, trash, and kitsch objects which turned the sensory overload of the mediums onstage into a kind of voodoo-TV-laboratory. Some of these productions in the new decade have pushed the interactive use of hand-held cameras to a delirious edge, but there are also astonishing revelations like Chris Kondek's *Dead Cat Bounce* or Hotel Modern's *Kamp*. In Hotel Modern's staging of a miniature scale set of the Auschwitz concentration camp filled with thousands of prisoners and their executioners (represented by tiny handmade puppets), three actors move through the cardboard "film set" like giant war reporters, shooting horrific scenes of bestiality (which are created with their fingertips moving the puppets) with miniature cameras, thus generating an unimaginable collage of puppetry and live film.

In dance-theatre, such a critical and ideological edge is often missing, as the emphasis here resides more directly on the feedback control of interactive systems, and therefore on the dynamics of proprioceptive and kinaesthetic space. In *The Secret Project*, presented by half/angel (Jools Gilson-Ellis and Richard Povall) at the 1999 International Dance and Technology Festival (IDAT) in Arizona, one could sense the flow in the gestural interaction between dancer and the invisible topology of the empty studio-space. The space was not empty, even if the mapping of the active environment could not be literally seen. It could be intuited through Gilson-Ellis's left and right arm movements, the motions of her fingers, her position in space, and the dynamics and direction of her physical movement.

Using motion sensing (BigEye) and other interactive softwares, *The Secret Project* explored how choreographic improvisation and voice can generate or locate soundscapes and respond to the attenuated, resonating environment. Rather than attempting to "control" a virtual stage space, half/angel sought to extend the actual and metaphorical motion of the performer into sonic and poetic rhythms, evoking a reciprocal sensorial environment. As the physical space became sound through the body, Gilson-Ellis challenged us to experience movement as live musical composition and vocalization of the poetry she had written. In movement, she literally danced with her arms and voice as extended musical instruments pushing, plucking, and caressing the textscapes/soundscapes (programmed by Povall) triggered through her interaction with the camera-sensor. The performance was so subtle and moving that at times we could not tell whether Gilson-Ellis had found her voices or knew where to find them in the virtual landscape, or whether her agitated (amplified) breathing hinted at an unpredictable environment. Some voices perhaps were lost, hidden, occluded.

And yet, the question of control and variability in an interactive system needs to be explored more deeply. Like music before it, dance-theatre incorporates "instruments" (cameras, video-projectors, microphones, sensors, microcontrollers) and software tools, which allow it to structure and control the various components of any media event, i.e., sound, video, 3-D animation and motion graphics, biofeedback, light. The convergence of choreography and system design with the languages of programming, electronic music and film editing in interactive, real-time processing constitutes what I call the "performance system." But what role do software programs play and can they also be performers of choreography?[4]

In the first generation of interactive dance-theatre, when "mapping" (gesture to sound, gesture to video output) was explored in the interface design for performer and reactive environment, such understanding of the system was inspired by the cybernetic vision of feedback control and the modeling of the machine on the human actor. Direct interfaces (flex sensors, accelerometers, micro switches, pressure plates) required specific techniques of use which sometimes led choreographers to argue that the dancer acted as a live video editor or musical instrument. But aesthetic and conceptual concerns regarding the performer techniques within preprogrammed parameters (which were criticized as limiting in their "triggering" function) eventually led to a search for alternate interfaces. Dance-technology or music-technology collaborations involving direct, gestural interfaces have declined even though some practitioners argue that the interface should remain tangible so that mappings between performative input (gestural) and output (video/ sonic) are easily inferred.

An analysis of specific artist-instrument combinations suggest localized technique development which combines choreography and improvisation, and one can also identify a common set of software techniques (e.g., granular synthesis) and filtering parameters perceived in the digital video/sonic output. Especially with regard to digital dance/music collaborations on stage or in interactive installations (and music technology's concern with analog/digital sound production and transformation), both the gestural and the software parameterization techniques should be given equal recognition. If there were a larger spectrum of works available for analysis, one would be better able to distinguish the range of sensor data values (able to be transformed by the reactive environment) from the particular aesthetic performance technique—or *through* the style of choreography/improvisation harnessed for a particular emergent output.

Let us look at a few examples. The first type of interactive environment translates physical gestures via sensors, motion-tracking cameras, and analog/digital converters into a signal representation inside a computer program. Looking at the Max/MSP software as an example, one encounters specific design features that organize the relational architecture. Max is a graphical programming environment that allows the building of controllers for real-time synthesis and signal processing. The gestural data, received via a sensor system, is mapped to the control of a given sound synthesis parameter. The continuous MIDI data—generated by physical gestures of the dancer or musician (playing instruments with sensor devices)—affect the performance parameters of the Max/MSP patch which runs on the computer and effects the sonic and graphic output. As a programming language the Max software primarily controls the source materials (the sound and video files stored in the computer or synthesizer), sound parameters, and the dynamics of real-time synthesis. It can harbor considerable complexity since patches might be constructed in the manner of a "nested" design—enfolded entities that are in a continuously fluctuating state of unfolding to activate the modular parts. What is crucial about the interaction is the range of responsiveness of the controller with regard to the dynamic range of expression of the performer. Beyond simple cause and effect, I should think that the system only becomes challenging and valuable to the performer once she can play with it and modulate the sonic space and musical parameters around her to allow herself and the audience to perceive the real-time conversions of movement into sound.

Given the limitations of control in the programmed environment, we must ask how performers and musicians regard the physical relations between performance and controlled parameters, and how dancers can see their (self)movement as a form of topological "mapping" of the body's experience and proprioception within the interface. Tomi Hahn, a dancer and musicologist trained in Japanese traditional dance, collaborates with composer/bass player Curtis Bahn and violinist Dan Trueman on performances with movement sensors which react to her arm and hand motions and allow her to negotiate all aspects of the sonic structure of a virtual sonic geography consisting of a large array of synthetic sounds and non-linear poetry. In their performance of *Streams*, there is no pre-set structure or duration. Hahn slowly enters on a diagonal and begins, almost imperceptibly, to make music with her fingers, the most subtle textures and nuances of sound recalling bodies of water and land. It becomes quickly apparent that she has improvisational freedom to manipulate the micro and macro elements of the sonic structure. From glacial stillness to a vast imaginary landscape of flows and gurgling percolations, her dream-like minimal movements play with the haunting ephemeral quality of sound and acoustic memory.

As the musicians told me after a performance, the computer system for *Streams* is basically a digital model of the filtration characteristics of the vocal tract; all sounds are passed through this sonic model evoking the impression that the dancer "speaks" the music. The sound is realized using a spherical speaker array that creates unusual spatial effects and casts individual sound elements into particular locations forming unique, physically locatable "sound-characters" in the sonic space. Hahn herself has noted that the interactive technologies used in *Streams* altered aspects of the group's collaboration on movement and sound composition. Rather than structuring time, as in conventional dance/music collaboration, Hahn sees *Streams* as a process of "composing the body," using physical modeling synthesis algorithms in the Max/MSP/PeRColate patch (including granulation, delay, filtering, and mixing of numerous palettes of sampled sound) to analyze particular expressive gestures. As Hahn pointed out, the sensor interface in this performance allows her to tap into her personal embodied knowledge of the tradition of Japanese dance in which she was trained, yet the technological interface also lets her integrate an individual vocabulary of her contemporary body. This is brilliantly exposed in her performance of *PikaPika*, a drastically different piece based on Japanese *anime* and *manga*, in which she wears a glittering costume and arm-mounted speakers, embodying movements from Bunraku that generate thundering explosions of sound which wrap the audience in a frighteningly turbulent sonic storm. Hahn delights in this, taking full pleasure in a powerful torrent of dense technological noise that drastically turns the tables on "feminine" or cultural etiquette. For Hahn, this interactive dance thrives on intensity that allows her to question the gender mapping of her bi-racial body.[5]

Streams and *PikaPika* point to the equivalent of extended vocal techniques (practiced by singers such as Joan La Barbara or Pamela Z) in interactive performance, since until recently the use of gesture as a control component in music composition/performance for dance was largely limited to simple musical parameters: presence or absence of sound, volume control, and, more rarely, pitch control. Although much work has been done in the world of computer music by composers who write for gestural controllers, dance has remained somewhat isolated from these forays. Only through collaborative rehearsal can we expect to understand better how the dancer's physical and cognitive relationships to real-time interactive systems evolve. The technical goal is to integrate an image-based recognition system or a motion sensor interface (e.g., the MidiDancer, a wearable device Mark Coniglio built for dancers) into a unified Max, VNS, or Isadora environment. But what does "technical" integration mean to the dancers? How do they integrate diverse parameters into their movement intelligence and increasing awareness of tactile image projection spaces (as they are used in extreme close-up scenarios for telematic performance)? How is partnering done with projected image-movement?

From a choreographic point of view, the dancer within an interactive environment resembles the "player" in "T-Garden"—she will need to familiarize herself with the response behavior of the sound and video parameters, and both player and composer will strive to create an exponentially more sensitive, articulate and intuitive system. In a shared environment this could mean refinements in sensors, filters, and output processors, but also an attenuation of the performer's spatial-temporal consciousness. How does the performer-musician-system relationship evolve to sidestep perspectival space and detached vision, foregrounding different sensory modalities? Can one get rid of the screens for projection, and allow the performer to modulate and remodulate the entire space as image? How does this relationship compare to jazz-improvisational structures (aural), video game action structures (tactile-kinetic), and different cultural contextualizations of virtual environments?

For example, dance and theatre artists in Tokyo and São Paulo have explored interactive environments as conceptual systems through very different metaphorical mappings. The Japanese multimedia group Dumb Type often creates dense, quivering, and pulsing image projections, taken to the limits of maximum acceleration, and the computerized "image system" appears like an automatic machine moving outside of anyone's control. The dancers appear as mapping modules of the image machine. They are completely permeated by its effects, by the video-light and the intensely loud sound, and their physical presence is no longer autonomous but integrated into the machine. In Brazil, artists and performers such as Renato Cohen, Tania Fraga, Ivani Santana, Lali Krotoszynski, or Diana Domingues are approaching interactive environments as transitional stages of consciousness, multidimensional, and transformative poetic worlds or shamanic trance states. In her recent dance work, *Corpo Aberto*, Santana performed a one-hour solo with cameras attached to her body, continually shifting her and our awareness between her physical gestures, her movement trajectories-as-camera-eyes, and the (preprogrammed and live-circuited) projections of the contours and shadows of her body. The immediate feedback she danced with was her *doppelgänger*, but her projected figure gradually lost its human form and, near the end of the performance, mutated into otherworldly shapes and animated skeletons. She finally replaced her camera-generated double with animations created with the LifeForms software.

Such intricate physical performance techniques with mini-cameras are also used by the New York City-based MeibeWhatever company. In *Wear + Tear* (2005), the company's young artistic director, Mei-Yin Ng, danced a ferocious solo in the nude during which a mini-camera attached to her hand acted as an intimate tactile eye occasionally "touching" her skin and the cavities of her body in unexpected ways. The live images were projected in a curved fish-eye shape, flickering in the unstable rhythms of the wireless transmission from her moving body. The performance showed how much she endeavored to elaborate her investigation of wearable cameras, now focussing the fragility of the (protective) skin and the seemingly intrusive sensory device she turned on herself. *Double Vision* (2004), her earlier collaborative work with Eric Koziol (who is responsible for video design and integration), was remarkable for its performance technique. Mei-Yin Ng here worked with Peking Opera performer Ge Bai who showed great skill in manipulating the technical devices and a very accurate timing and awareness of space/distance. Perhaps due to his traditional Peking Opera training, Ge was able to freeze at the same point in space every time when the company wanted to reveal the camera's point of view (matching that POV). This skill seemed essential in achieving the perfectly precise visual image needed in the live projection setting. The matching, however, often had a profoundly humorous effect, since the company used the video images as commentary on a series of mundane domestic behaviors and physical obsessions that plagued the performing couple.

One of the most innovative companies working with the integration of performance and live interactive video is kondition pluriel (Montréal-based) whose work has been shown at numerous festivals around the world. Co-directed by choreographer Marie-Claude Poulin and software artist Martin Kusch, kondition pluriel is widely recognized for its very distinctive use of physicality and distributed video-feedback in responsive environments. Creating carefully designed performative spaces that integrate media and choreographic concepts, their presentations are not restricted to theatre spaces but have been shown in galleries, public spaces, and museums. This versatility often allows kondition pluriel's practice to be received in a visual arts context (much like contemporary sound art), drawing attention to the hybridization of performative and sculptural languages heightened by the fluid code translations, the bricolage of movement and movement-images. The sculptural emphasis is most evident in their construction of moveable screens and the architectural dynamic in which projective space is deployed.

Kondition pluriel's works, for example *schème* and *schème II* (2001–2002), *entre-deux* (2002), *myriorama* (2004), *recombinant* (2004), and *the puppet(s)* (2005–07) are sometimes called "choreographic installations" by the artists, and this contradictory notion encapsulates their emphasis on "time-specificity" (the temporal diffusion and permutation of movement through real-time camera vision and re-projection) within unstable architectural structures, namely the interactive projections scattered around the mobilized screen-spaces. At the same time, their most recent work deliberately experiments with the conjunction of the two presentational modes, installation and performance, increasingly drawing the audience physically into the unfolding event.

Poulin's dance experience, and her extended research into somatic technique and kinanthropology, during which she analyzed movement with respect to the nervous system, underlies the work's unusual physical style. In *schème*, the five performance sequences are linked together within a clear conceptual framework: the place where the performer is located, his or her physical presence, the space and time. In terms of the image and the sound, only those sources coming either from the space itself or the performer are used. In terms of movement, only those sequences demonstrating a clear relationship to space and to media-based time are selected, and the sound sequences originate from what the artists call the "room tone" of the space. The sounds of the dance are recorded and manipulated interactively via the sensor-system. The projections are created of images of the performer, the performance space and 3-D simulations of the same space. *Schème* was the first major work of the company, and for Poulin it was her first confrontation with the virtual. "I was obsessed with the idea that as a dancing body, I could only access this virtual world by projecting my mind-thoughts into it," she told me. "And while I was doing so," she added, "my physical body was getting very internal, as if the visualisation of this other architectural space was leading me to an internal visualisation or the inner architecture of my own body. It did not make sense to me to start traveling around in the 'real space,' since I was travelling with my mind in the virtual space and at the same time with my mind-body in the inner space of my body."

Schème offers a fascinating parallel to what Dutch architect Lars Spuybroek has described as the "surfaces of action" and the convergences/incorporations of surfaces in the material event—event here understood both as architectural organization (movement) and material presence (textiles, walls, spatial volume, relations between walls, floor, corners, etc.). In Spuybroek's own work, using techniques of morphing and topological mobilization in the architectural formative procedures, he has created numerous projects which deploy radically experimental methods of modeling which are both analog and digital. In shifting from one form of modeling to another, and including interactive sound (in *Son-O-House*, for example), he never loses sight of the organic synthesis of bodies and space, and of the way the tracing of bodily movement can be traced in the production of volumes.[6] If *Son-O-House* can be described by Spuybroek as a "house where sounds live" and as a structure for living and for movements which inhabit space, perhaps we can look at kondition pluriel's performance-installations in a similar light and note how the bodies are here intertwined connectively with the "virtual sites" (whether schematized or realistically textured) generated from the performance.

There is a considerable contrast to the Wooster Group's dislocation of video-actors and part-objects, since *schème* does not show prerecorded temporal objects but comes alive through embodied enaction, performance inhabiting space by making the performers' bodies become the material support for those forms of technical inscription of memory (video, digital media) that are themselves threatened with immediate obsolescence. Among contemporary media philosophers, Mark Hansen has most clearly articulated this relationship of human embodiment to real-time mediation, arguing that the body in such performances is the medium of time itself. In *schème*, there is a continuous intertwining of action and projection, and thus a continuous succession of perceptual experience as the projections are not "fixed" but shift position on the surfaces of the site. Poulin and Kusch succeed in creating a multidimensional rhythm and dialogue between the presence of the body, the sound environment, the projected virtual image, and the actual space.

Whereas *schème* is almost entirely floor-bound and explores impediments to articulate movement (the performers use crutches) which make the bodies appear inapt and suffocating, *recombinant* draws the audience close up into intimate proximity—circulating around and amongst the two performers inside the installation. This proximity can create a certain amount of tactile anxiety, on part of both the performers and the audience, but such proximity also induces the spectators to be physically active and become aware of their bodily positions, their own being-in-the-way of others. If the space becomes a convoluted body, as Poulin suggests by disorienting any clear perspective, the mingling of performers and spectators becomes an unsolvable impediment to correct positioning of perspective as such. Architecturally, the artists have set up four surfaces of mobile projections, curved and angular, opaque and transparent, with which the performers reconfigure the performance space. These manipulations reveal continuously changing schemes of architectural arrangements, which invite the spectators to move around. Kusch's interactive programming of the video heightens the sense of a shared dislocation of the bodily images that are scattered onto the screens, and I am tempted to speak of image-presences since kondition pluriel's deliberate dis-focus pushes the transformation of the real physical presences to a new level. The convolution of moving bodies and moveable space, and the fluidity between body and media in the unfolding of time, creates a cycle. The difference between causal and non-linear relationships of the living presences, images, and sounds appears insignificant vis-à-vis the continious sensory immediacy of this cycle of body and time. The issue of control therefore disappears, if *recombinant* indeed intimates a phenomenological reality in which bodies and digital media are exhaustively interpenetrated. This interpenetration can also be called a network or, to use Spuybroek's term, a machining-architecture constructing itself over time, a scenic evolution in which everyone participates. Two performers, a visual artist, a sound artist and a light designer perform and improvise live for the duration of fifty minutes with approximately one hundred spectators.

But in their latest work, *the puppet(s)*, kondition pluriel go one step further. By using the dancers' bodies as quasi-interfaces and entry points to the work, they examine notions of interactivity, intimacy, proximity, and the relationship between public and private space in ways that have rarely been attempted. Readers familiar with the history of interactive installations may recall a well-known installation by Jeffrey Shaw, *ConFIGURING the CAVE* (1996, created with Agnes Hegedüs and Bernd Lintermann), which was designed as an immersive VR environment using projections on three walls and the floor. Visitors would enter the CAVE and manipulate the image and sound environment by tilting a wooden mannequin constructed by Shaw as the direct interface device. For *the puppet(s)*, kondition pluriel built interactive sensor-costumes for the dancers and asked them to play the role of a live *übermarionette*, literally inviting the spectators to touch them and thus activate the sensor-interface. The performers, however, also were asked to stay within "character" of their choreography, so to speak, and to shift in and out of different physical states. Another complex feature of this work is the compositional arrangement: the work is a choreographic and participatory installation which not only involves the physical engagement of the spectators but also deconstructs traditional choreographic structures by organizing the movement material in a non-linear manner mixing three choreographic signatures (Marie-Claude Poulin, Dominique Porte, Benoît Lachambre).

In other words, different personal choreographic styles of expression are here made to interpolate tactile invasiveness (the spectators are made to touch and to be "invasive" on the bodies of the performers) as a sinister but also humorous commentary on the ubiquitous presence of invasive technologies in our culture. Lachambre, for example, confronts the dynamics of human communication through the absurd and the theatrical, while Porte explores the same theme through a strictly formal movement, precise and rigorous. Within the framework of *the puppet(s)*, the choreographic signatures combine to create a bank of behaviors and movements that the dancers will draw from, according to pre-established rules. The respective qualities of the choreographic approaches respond to the different needs of the narrative construction of the piece, which is relatively open, so to speak, as the behavior of the active audience cannot be predicted. The role of the observer or passive consumer of the spectacle is thus transformed into that of an active co-author of the artistic process. This is a very daring proposition, and the results are difficult to fathom or generalize, since the unique choices of the spectators will resonate differently in the environment each time this event takes place. The installation therefore must be understood as live art, creating a unique experience for each participant. More significantly, the constellation offers up a tactile interface, an intercorporeality between performers and performing audience members, which breaks the rules of etiquette. Such unprotected sensory skin cannot but create a charged tension; yet it also can generate critical reflection on the perception we have of the "bare life" (Agamben) embedded in highly mediated, invasive, and virtually punitive societies.

As such examples illustrate, dancers, composers, and designers can interpret the relational architecture of interactive systems in many different ways, depending on a work's emphasis on dance gesture-to-music synthesis, or dance gesture-to-video synthesis. Discussions of mapping have been controversial within the performance-technology community, and some artists have complained that mapping strategies should address the basic problem common to most intermedia pieces which place stage performers in the role of musicians, namely, how to create an interdisciplinary work that succeeds from all the choreographic, music-compositional, and filmic perspectives. What this implies, of course, is that the dancer becomes the "musical performer," or, in Santana's and Ng's case, plays with being the eye of the camera, which is not the same as interacting with a dynamic multisensory environment that may respond in unexpected and uncontrollable ways or that, as in the case of kondition pluriel, incorporates a proactive audience which may behave in unexpected ways. Yet the question remains whether choreographers and composers have different or conflicting goals, or whether there is an aesthetically stringent co-resonance between movement, sound, and video that can transform the entire environment kinaesthetically. I will mention two other interactive works, presented at CROSS FAIR in Germany, which connect the first and second types of environment.

Scanned, conceived and directed by Christian Ziegler, is a performance-installation that consists of video projections of a dancer's scanned movements. To create the live work, Ziegler first asks a dancer (Monica Gomis) to perform movement phrases lasting from one to fifteen seconds, which are taped by a video camera. A program he wrote for the computer allows him to let a digital video scanner unfold the movement-images over time, controlling direction and speed of the scan as well as resolution and tempo of the scanned material. In performance, the scan projections slowly emerge over a period of time, as if we were watching a painting come into life. The "choreography," according to Ziegler, can be seen by the imagination of the viewer. One could also argue that there is no choreography, but that the interface with the computer creates temporally dilated paintings of human gestures and movements, completely reorganizing the time and space of the dance frames.

Yours, a collaboration between Polish composer Jaroslav Kapuscinski and Frankfurt Ballet dancers Nik Haffner and Antony Rizzi, is performed as a dialogue between a pianist and a video projection of a dancer, accompanied by percussion sounds and a female voice (reciting from Beckett's *Texts for Nothing*). Kapuscinski enters the dark center of the room, with audiences seated on both sides of the Disklavier placed there, with a film screen suspended above the instrument. As he begins to play his composition, a dialogue evolves in real time: every strike of the piano keys manipulates the digital video image on the screen by intervening in the order and speed of the dancer's movements. Rizzi was filmed in the nude, his movements based on Haffner's choreography. The interface here is the piano: Kapuscinski "scratches" the video samples of the dance, as well as additional audio samples, via a computer that "reads" the key strokes and even senses the particular articulations in the playing. The composition is newly interpreted in each live performance, and the piano interface is also open to audience exploration, as Kapuscinski suggests after his forty-five-minute performance. He invites the audience to "play the dancer." On opening night very few people actually tried it, being aware that Kapuscinski was working from a structured score that allowed him to develop the digital dance in a deliberate, dramatic manner. Those of us who did try the piano realized that the interactivity was based on relatively simple MIDI trigger (on/off) signals that allow the pianist to play the video image track backward and forward, freeze-frame the motion or advance it, literally, frame by frame, thus controlling the image of the dancer down to the finest atom.[7] It is the same method that Arnold applied in *Deanimated*.

Conceptually, the aesthetic of interactive digital art is necessarily indebted to such "MIDI performances," exploring the potential "pastforward" connections that can be made between instruments and media, as well as directing critical attention to our unstable relationships to sound and image environments that seem to have a life of their own. As in the case of Dumb Type's image machine in *Memorandum*, the fast-forwarding and rewinding of movement images in *Yours* plays tricks with our memory and optics, and digital artist/programmer Michael Saup went so far as to argue at CROSS FAIR that technologies are not our tools or extensions but autonomous intelligent systems: we ought to be interested in what they do to our psyche.

Collaborative work such as *Ghostcatching* (Paul Kaiser/Shelley Eshkar/ Bill T. Jones), exhibited as a stand-alone virtual dance, along with *Yours* and *Scanned*, already points in this direction of a certain autonomy of the system that runs processed and derived data. *Ghostcatching* is based on optical motion-capture, a system of multiple infrared cameras, computer hardware and software that enable digital 3-D representation of moving bodies. Recording involves the placement of reflectors in strategic positions on the performer's body; cameras surrounding the performer track these sensors in time and space, feeding the information to the computer for consolidation into a single data file. Mocap data subsequently drives the movement of simulated figures on the computer, where they can be mapped onto other anatomies in an animation program. With the animation tool one can draw out and reconfigure the abstracted motions and trajectories of the dance. What we see is the ghost of the dance or, rather, animated motion pictures and drawings.[8] Captured movement phrases thus become the digital building blocks for virtual dance or interactive performances that explore possible, emerging, and always newly manipulable relationships between live and synthetic presences, forms, images, micro-frames, sounds, and their resonances in our imagination. The promise of motion tracking technology and real-time digital signal processing (also now available in motion-capturing) is the simultaneous exploration of a fluid environment in which dance can generate sound and animation, sound can affect video images, and captured images inform new movement and a new form of action painting. The re-programming of captured data with machine-learning technique allowing autonomous intelligence opens up new pathways for "thinking images" to which I shall return later.

My last example is from the international Interaktionslabor, a media lab which takes place every summer in an abandoned Coal Mine at Göttelborn (Germany). In July 2003, the gigantic Engine Room was used to receive the public for an interactive sensor-dance, which dramatized the breathing organism or correlation of dancer-landscape. Upon entering a door leading to a staircase, the audience glanced down thirty or forty feet to an empty space where one of the two winding engines of ten thousand horsepower had stood, the remaining one now facing a gaping hole, a deep resonance body, with the western wall serving as film screen. The collaboration between Lynn Lukkas/Mark Henrickson (Minneapolis), Paul Verity Smith (Bristol), Marija Stamenkovic Herranz (Barcelona), and Kelli Dipple (Melbourne) opened up some striking possibilities of the sensor-interface, pointing to "spaces" in-between the aural, the rhythmic, the visual, and the visceral.

In this interface environment, the body's actions were measured not only as sound (via microphone) but as the most subtle variations in the biomechanics: the pulse, breath, and heart rhythm in the body itself (via a Bioradio attached with electrodes). The electrically measurable signals were transmitted wirelessly as data to the computer, where they affected not only the sound processes in real time but the rhythm of the image movement of the projected film sequences stored in the computer (Macromedia Director and Max/MSP). Marija Stamenkovic performed the dance of breath, first improvising softly with extended vocal techniques as she descended the staircase in midst of the audience, then purely with heavily amplified breathing as she moved onto the flat plane of the engine room, and finally with her whole body and staccato voice as she propelled herself into an untrammeled trance-like flurry of movement. Her voice crept under our skins, the magnificent resonating sound in the huge room entering through our pores and stomachs, and as we listened we realized how her breath controlled the image movement and thus the dramaturgy of the story. If Stamenkovic stopped her breath, the film's motion froze. When she breathed, we saw her (on film) walk across the slag heap of the Mine, descending into a hollow path.

Lukkas had filmed her outside movement differently in each section, the third one using a hyperactive zoom. In conjunction with Stamenkovic's accelerated breathing, this final segment materialized as pure hyperkinetic sensation, transforming the entire space-volume into an irregular pulsating body-machine of continuously unfolding exhaustive yet libidinal intensities. A performance of this kind is hard to describe; it appeared to produce an extended three-dimensional space where pure sensation broke the continuity and stability of her own image (on film) even as she entered into a feedback loop with remembered movements she had enacted outside. Additional sound began to grow inside the building, transforming sense perceptions of spatial images even further, or allowing the audience to recognize how their own sensations framed or pulsed the virtual images. Image-movement of landscape and figure, sound clusters and pebbles, breath and body, echoed and transformed one another in recursive couplings.

If one looks at the documentary photographs of such performances, they must disappoint. Generally, one sees a dancer and a screen projection, which in this case is nearly meaningless since all the other sensations and the volume of the space itself are lost. The sensorial coupling of interactivity and real time also tends to get rid of the conception of a "work"—there is no *Titled On*. It does not survive as an object or a choreography. Its event structure implies that the digital performance is entirely contingent on the concrete situation and the interlaced process which produces itself in real-time before a public.

Immersed in Invisible Writing

I will discuss "immersive environments" by mainly addressing them as a new knowledge and training space. Creating interactive virtual reality is a heavily research-oriented endeavor and requires appropriate laboratory conditions which can rarely be re-constituted in a theatre or gallery. Apart from the CAVE environments that were created at ars electronica and various computer science labs, I am thinking of the groundbreaking Art and Virtual Environment Project conducted at the Banff Center in Canada (1992–94), which featured nine complex VR works including *Dancing with the Virtual Dervish* by Diane Gromola, Marcos Novak, and Yacov Sharir. *Osmose*, a VR environment created by Char Davies and a team of engineers from the SoftImage company, gained notoriety when it was exhibited at ISEA '95. *Osmose* was subsequently shown at several other venues and received considerable critical attention due to its successful composition of a breathing and motion interface with its immersive virtual environment. Unlike the film projection mobilized by Stamenkovic's breathing in *Titled On*, the participant in *Osmose* wears a stereoscopic head-mounted display and a vest that tracks breathing and balance. The immersant can, through breathing, float through the symbolic life-world created by the computer-generated artificial environment. In Davies's conception, virtual space is a spatiotemporal arena wherein mental models or abstract constructs of the world are given virtual embodiment (visual and aural) in three dimensions, animated through time.

Her interactive design strives to heighten proprioceptive bodily awareness. Avoiding hard-edged objects that drift in empty space (a common feature in conventional VR), her multi-layered and semi-transparent forests and pools of shimmering water evoke an almost mystic realm, for lack of a better word. This realm can be kinaesthetically explored through full body immersion, even while the digital constructs retain their immateriality. Davies's early work as painter already reflects her interest in luminosity and interlaced picture planes. In *Osmose*, and her later work *Ephémère* (1997–98), she explores the body's fluid interfaces with immersive virtual space. The computer-generated environment becomes a participatory medium for the body's convergence with itself, an inwardly directed movement, so to speak, a convergence in which the immaterial is confused with the bodily-felt, and the imaginary with the strangely real.

Virtual reality was hailed as a new medium in the early 90s, but due to the immense computational labor and arrays of equipment involved, the creation of immersive environments understandably has not yet become a common language, even as choreographer Yacov Sharir describes his own experience in very provocative terms:

> What artistic, intellectual, kinaesthetic, and emotional issues could be addressed using this Technology? ... Virtual technologies allow us to manipulate, extend, distort, and deform information as well as experience of the body. They are vehicles that enable us to extend and color work in many ways, some of which may not be possible in the physical realm and/or by traditional means. They offer a way to augment and extend possibilities creatively, experientially, spatially, visually, sonically, and cognitively.[9]

The augmented interface he recounts is a conflation of the interactive principles I described above and an immersive experience within a real-time, 3-D graphic and aural environment generated by computers. Sharir refers to it as a "distributed performance environment" which he entered and inhabited with a head-mounted display and dataglove. The three-dimensional world, created by Gromola, projected on an enormous scale the torso (skeletal spine, pelvis, ribs) and inner organs of her body built from X-ray and MRI data. Sharir notes that when moving through the virtual torso he also encountered digitized images of himself dancing, which diffused and multiplied his sense of being *inside* an other body.

Much could be said about the psychological and cognitive effects of navigating immersive environments, and literally moving into someone else's (virtual) body also strikes me as a politically and ethically charged process. While the literal involvement of the performer's or audience-interactor's body and neural system in the *image* of Gromola's medically scanned body raises many culturally sensitive issues about contemporary biotechnology, Sharir's experience of the distributed self-as-image refers us back to the motivations for such performance research in the first place. He is clearly stating a desire to provoke questions about human beings, subjectivity, perceptual systems, and how we re-envision and re-configure ourselves through technology. On the computational and formal level of making work, however, he seems largely content to explore "possibilities" for a new spatiotemporal aesthetics, asking where one can locate his performance. In the real space or the virtual world?

In the pursuit of knowledge about the body and its movement possibilities I detect a cybernetic impulse that surely drives the software development. The interactive, multisensory, and reflexive body developed in our artistic training is merged with an informational conception of the body. The "bio-apparatus," as Sharir calls it, is tracked, and the data it offers are computed and then extended outward into controlling devices that simulate and regulate the behavior of an organism, a virtual world or any simulation system through feedback. Given current advances in transcoding and biomedical imaging, you could easily envision performing inside 3-D computational fluid dynamics (CFD) simulations of your own blood-flow or aneurysm. Sharir and other choreographers are fascinated with the transmutational potential of the software to project a body immersed in fluid, non-linear and non-mimetic environments. There is intense spatial ambiguity, since the immersant retains a felt body that is, however, mapped quite differently than the seen bodies that may float through the animate virtual environment. There are many representational dilemmas when interfacing with dataworlds, but our main question here will be where to locate the dance. Scott deLahunta has pointed out that we cannot avoid to pay more attention to software development for artists by artists. "The process of computation is invisible in the simplest sense that the labor of the software programmer or engineer is largely taken up in the 'writing' of an instruction that tells the computer hardware and connected peripherals how to execute an operation."[10] This writing and rewriting is part of the creative process whereby an interactive virtual environment is made. It is revealing, in this respect, that choreographers have been working with code that was by and large written by and for musicians (BigEye, Image/ine, Max/MSP, VNS). Such code may not be ideal for physically rich and complex action.

Consequently, there has been much debate about dance making and interactive systems, especially with regard to "transparency" and the receptivity of an audience to the aspects of the work that might be invisible. What is being considered "invisible" in this context is the mapping from input to various forms of output. Mapping is not a spatial representation, it is an operation that assigns continuous MIDI data received from a tracking system to control DSP functions such as filters, low frequency oscillators, distortion algorithms, etc. The interpreted data provides information about the speed, direction, and location of moving objects in the software's video window. That information is used to provide input control data to music-generating software. This is essentially a first-generation definiton of interactive systems.

Mapping, therefore, has been the crux of the creative process as regards these systems. However, deLahunta argues, it is the manifestation of mapping that enters the field of perception of the viewer/listener, not the mapping itself. Once completed, the instructions that comprise the mapping itself are relegated to the invisibility of computation. How this invisible mapping works is of interest primarily to those who are engaged in its construction. Although deLahunta is correct in observing this gap between computation and choreography, he may underestimate the curiosity with which some dance companies have approached the relations between software writing, algorithmic composition and movement creation. Forsythe's companies, Jo Fabian, Frieder Weiss, Wayne McGregor, Pablo Ventura Dance Company,

Kinodance, Kinkaleri, Yacov Sharir, Isabelle Choinière, among many others, have developed rehearsal systems influenced by computational thinking. What remains to be seen is whether artistic work with interactive systems allows audiences access to all facets of the systems—input, mapping, and output. It is true that performances using interactive systems tend to give an audience access only to the output, while interactive installations allow access to input and output. DeLahunta proposes to "include exposure to the mapping itself during performance." This corresponds to my early experiences with motion-capture technology. In the initial stages of the capturing process performers generally cannot see the data that are recorded, nor can they experience in real-time, while they perform, how the recording data might be mapped onto a character or figure animation. This becomes possible, however, with real-time magnetic and optical capturing systems that wire the hardware/software to video projectors, which display the data processing and mapping *immediately* to the performers and to audiences.

A real-time closed circuit relationship to the mapping could afford the performer who practices with these systems a training environment for more complex interactions with them, thus combining input measurement that responds to a higher level of detail and subtlety in performer action with more complex mappings. Confronting proprioceptive and cognitive questions about the immersed body requires intensive practice with interface methods that manipulate the intermingling of self and virtual world, and a more in-depth understanding of the programming language itself. This reference to learning begs the question: where in the dance field do we discuss notions of dance training overlapping with the development of interactive systems? Where do we create learning environments in which performers and musicians could practice in depth with coding, interactive lighting, sound and video projection systems, or entirely different architectures, especially if the latter (MIDI and DMX operated) depend on fine tuned lighting and calibration of camera sensing systems, as well as on lighting design choices that are an integral part of multimedia projection spaces?

DeLahunta argues that there is a small number of practitioners whose efforts over years are accumulating richness and depth through personal determination. A company such as kondition pluriel is a good example since their artistic work is predicated on sustained periods of research. SWAP, a young company from Portugal, has followed a similar course, fusing several artistic disciplines with the science of computation and writing their own software for each new project. Introducing *Dynamic Painting* (2003), *Displacement* (2004), *Swap* (2005), and *Edge* (2006–07) to their audiences at European festivals and workshops, Rudolfo Quintas and Tiago Dionisio refer to these works as "Augmented Reality Interactive Systems," designed for "user-participants" (installation) or "interpreters" (stage shows). Inquiring about their approach to immersion or interaction, they replied that their research experimentation focuses on the body as concept and sensory place, as the problematic central element where the visual and musical contents emerge in a dynamic feedback adaptation process.

> During our process of experimentation, we develop artistic software and human-computer interfaces, researching how those increase the emotional and intuitive relation that is established between a user and the system. These interfaces are developed using studies in such areas as phenomenology, psychology, perception, semiotics, anthropometry and human motion, with the aim of absorbing and capturing the implicit messages of body gestuality and what Hashimoto calls *kansei* (emotion design). Following this, the interfaces explore computational modules of gestural expressiveness with the aim of capturing the user subjectivity and intimacy, perceived by others as expressive content. The relation between image/sound and body movements that result from interaction is caused by perceptual-motivated mappings. These mappings explore synaesthesic qualities that address infinite variation, extreme plasticity, formal imagery and deep feedback loop interaction. We transpose the limitations of physics and time with the computation as support for meta-physicality and extra-temporality, where different artistic disciplines are linked in synchronic and asynchronic processes (for example, the intensity and expressiveness of a body gesture can correspond to the color or the animation path of a visual object).[11]

What is most interesting about SWAP's installations is the departure from the undifferentiated oceanic-symbolic world encountered, for example, in Davies's *Osmose* where the immersant is induced to feel a dissolution of the demarcations between self and environment. The "interpreter" (João Costa) of SWAP's augmented reality environment learns to intuit how a musical relationship (using basic parameters such as frequency, amplitude and velocity) is translated through his gestures to the motion of abstract silhouettes or colored digital objects in the digital environment. In *Swap*, the interface radically augments the motion beyond what can be seen: a camera vision system captures the performer's silhouette in real-time and immerses the performer in a virtual space where he interacts with thousands of small particles. The particle behavior and composition is modeled in real-time by the generative nature of the system, responding to the interpreter's motion. This collaboration initiates a real-virtual dialogue embodied in the projection space or, rather, embodied in a recursive correlation between self-moving performer and augmented environment. The performer can learn to interpret how every perceptual experience (even of abstract particles or shapes) refers back toward an action of the body on itself, and thus toward the dynamics of proprioceptive space. The image projection enables the visualization of this relation that results in a motion graphics composition representing image-movements of a body—not the body representation of the interpreter but the merged "body" that is the outcome of the performer's expression and the system behavior. Quintas and Dionisio argue that this originates two different body knowledges, and that the interactive space domain becomes hybrid and probabilistic, not only implying a switching between figurative and abstract imagery, but also a reorientation from a predominantly visual sensory interface to a bodily or affective interface.

This reorientation is complicated by the fact that the motion graphics or virtual actions might be understood or sensed as disparate visual data, which do not coincide with the performer's felt experience of his body's motions. Much of SWAP's work aims at this complicated overlap or "augmented" overlap, since they know that dancing implies that the performer can imagine himself to be out of his body and "in" different shapes. The artistic challenge of the work arises precisely with their attempt at motivating the performer to experience augmentation as affecting a change of their movement and effecting an emotional expression. A considerable part of the psychological impact resides in the extra-temporal dimensions of the digital: the captured gestures continue to live on in the virtual space, as the software augments them in time and thus regenerates—continuously—the traces and memories of the performed actions. Past gestures are extended into the present and into the future. Looking at the installations from a technical point of view, one could say that the artist-designers want the interpreter to experience the software abstractions.

However, even if interactive performance is focused on aesthetic or sensory experience, rather than training of new performance techniques, the role of the user or interpreter is a problematic one. Kondition pluriel emphasize performer research in their work; SWAP often create installations for the general public, inviting untrained, non-professional participants to be users. This difference in the form of address is a critical one; it is also obvious that there is a difference between experiencing an immersive VR environment as the immersant and observing the immersant's behavior. This latter distinction can be drawn in all interactive installations that privilege a one-to-once interface. In the case of *Osmose*, the visitor makes an appointment and is given twenty minutes to wear the interface and become fully immersed in the 3-D space, while other audience members can "witness" a video projection of what the immersant might be seeing or hearing. One would think that observing someone else go through a deeply affective interface experience might be pointless, were it not for the fact that such strangely (and falsely) vicarious instances are now becoming more and more prevalent in our digital culture.

In addressing the invisibility of computation in relationship to physical performance and performer training in interactive systems, deLahunta cautions us about "the long-term outcome of creative activity that is proportionately shifting its center of labor from the physical spaces and composition to the virtual spaces" and mapping configurations (e.g., in Max/MSP). As he rightly argues, any performance artist working with interactive systems knows that the amount of work involved in "getting the technology to work" is immense and seems disproportionate to the amount of work done in the studio, rehearsing and perspiring. A shift away from the physical is by consequence in aesthetic terms a shift away from formal expression to the conceptual or, as implied above, the ad-hoc improvisational and the vicarious. DeLahunta therefore wonders whether we will see future audiences develop a taste for mapping and for complex yet transparent interactive architectures, coming better prepared and interested in watching or contemplating choreographic choices for dancing in interactive systems. Once dancers or actors begin to inhabit and play with multidimensional mapping environments, the invisibility of computation is harnessed by the physical intelligence and the consciousness of new performance techniques in augmented reality environments. If interactive systems offer new bodily experiences, performers need to become good interpreters and spend more time in them in order to create new expressions and enactments that may only be possible within such interactive worlds.

NOTES

¹ For Terzopoulos's artifical life systems, see <http://www.cs.ucla.edu/~dt/>. Ken Goldberg's *Telegarden* (1995) exhibited a telerobotically tended garden accessed through the Web, allowing visitors to join the web community of "gardeners" and remotely maneuver a robotic arm via a Web interface, planting and watering seeds and monitoring their growth. They became caretakers, so to speak, and the interactive design here involves a fascinating reflection on social or ecological responsibility. Cf. Ken Goldberg, ed., *The Robot in the Garden: Telerobotics and Telepistemology in the Age of the Internet*, Cambridge, MA: MIT Press, 2000, and <http://telegarden.aec.at>. See also Peter Lunenfeld, ed., *The Digital Dialectic: New Essays on New Media*, Cambridge, MA: MIT Press, 1999, 126–27. For provocative reflections on what is happening to concepts of the self in the presence of the robotic-informatic web of media systems, external memory devices, and digital procedures, see Brian Rotman, "Going Parallel," *SubStance* 91 (2000): 56–79. Rinaldo's "Emergent Systems" Website is at: <http://www.ylem.org/artists/krinaldo/emergent1.html>. For a comprehensive study of a-life, see Mitchell Whitelaw, *Metacreation: Art and Artificial Life*, Cambridge, MA: MIT Press, 2004.

² Cf. Steven Johnson, *Emergence*, New York: Scribner, 2001; M. Mitchell Waldrop, *Complexity*, New York: Touchstone, 1992.

³ The emphasis on digital image, and the use of cinema as a means to theorize digital visual culture, is particularly striking in Lev Manovich's *The Language of New Media*. For an attempt to recover sensory affectivity as the crucial phenomenological experience of the digital, see Massumi, *Parables for the Virtual*, 2002, and Mark B.N. Hansen, *New Philosophy for New Media*, Cambridge, MA: MIT Press, 2004. The suppressed multi-sensorial dimensions of art were highlighted in a provocative exhibition, *Sensorium: Embodied Experience, Technology, and Contemporary Art*, presented in two parts from October 2006 through April 2007 at the MIT List Visual Arts Center. Curated by Bill Arning, Jane Farver, Yuko Hasegawa, and Marjory Jacobson, the exhibit was accompanied by a book of the same title, edited by Caroline A. Jones, Cambridge, MA: MIT Press, 2006.

⁴ Software systems used in performance include: VNS (written by David Rokeby), BigEye and Image/ine (Tom Demeyer, STEIM), EyeCon (Frieder Weiss, Palindrome Inter-media Performance Group), Max/MSP/Jitter (David Zicarelli et al., Cycling74.com), Nato (Netochka Nezvanova), ChoreoGraph (Nick Rothwell, Barriedale Operahouse), EyesWeb (Antonio Camurri, InfoMus Lab, Genova), Isadora (Mark Coniglio, Troika Ranch), and Keystroke (Eric Redlinger, Sher Doruff, WAAG). PD (Pure

Data) is also now a popular alternative to Max/MSP. An overview of software development for performance is offered by Scott deLahunta: <http://huizen.dds.nl/~sdela/transdance/report/>. He organized the path-breaking workshop "Software for Dancers" at Sadler's Wells Theatre in London (October 2001), which was followed by "Performance Tools: Dance and Interactive Systems," at Ohio State University in January 2002. At "Absent Interfaces," (Tanzquartier Wien 2005), deLahunta proposed to examine other approaches to media performance which no longer rely necessarily on human-machinic relationships and the older model of the relations between body as input, computer as processor and audio/video media as output.

[5] The group Interface (Bahn, Trueman, Hahn) presented these two performances in a collaborative concert, "Moving Voices," at the end of an international workshop on dance and interactive technology at OSU, June 30, 2001. For more information on their work visit <http://www.arts.rpi.edu/~crb/interface>.

[6] See Lars Spuybroek, "Machining Architecture," in NOX: Machining Architecture, London: Thames & Hudson, 2004, 6–13. See also Mark B.N. Hansen, "Embodiment: The Machinic and the Human," in aRt&D: Artistic Research and Development, edited by Joke Brouwer, Arjen Mulder, Anne Nigten, Laura Martz, Rotterdam: V2_Publishing/NAi Publishers, 2005, 151–65, and his inspiring new book, Bodies in Code: Interfaces with Digital Media, New York: Routledge, 2006. For kondition pluriel's performance work, see: <http://www.konditionpluriel.org/>.

[7] For a more detailed discussion of the Cross Fair event, see "Thinking Images" and my essay "The Intelligent Stage," Performance Research 6, 2 (2001): 116–22.

[8] Cf. Ann Dils, "The Ghost in the Machine," PAJ: A Journal of Performance and Art 70 (2002): 94–104.

[9] Yacov Sharir, "Dancing with the Virtual Dervish: Virtual Bodies," in Immersed in Technology: Art and Virtual Environments, edited by Mary Ann Moser with Douglas MacLeod, Cambridge, MA: MIT Press, 1996, 281–85. Virtual reality works don't travel easily because of the complex hardware/software set-up. Sharir was able to perform in a new version of "Virtual Dervish" recreated by the National Museum of Contemporary Art, Athens, Greece, on October 14, 2002. Visitors experienced the work (one by one) by wearing a head mounted set and an electronic glove designed to assist them in the navigational process.

[10] This passage, and some of the subsequent observations, are indebted to conversations and an unpublished manuscript, "Invisibility/Corporeality," which Scott deLahunta presented in my Environments Lab during his residency at the Interactive Performance Series (April 2001), Ohio State University.

[11] Workshop presentation by SWAP at the Center for Contemporary and Digital Performance, Brunel University, February 28, 2007. Quoted with permission.

▼▲ Between Mapping & Artificial Intelligence

Although I have not resolved the question of performance techniques, I introduced a range of examples that reflect different emphases on composition, improvisation, and embodiment. While the term "embodiment" is now commonly used in reference to sensory interface experience, it tells us little about the techniques, which might be acquired to perform more effectively within an interactive environment. Major performance works that have been shown repeatedly on the stage tend to reflect a compositional integration of performance techniques and interactive design which may be lacking in less significant works relying on improvised input to activate the transformative potential of a particular software in an interactive environment. Designing interactive installations for audience participation tends to prioritize multisensorial or synaesthetic "experience" over performance aesthetics or particular figurations, gestures, movements, and expressive content or qualities.

When I looked at the potential and the limits of mapping, I was mindful of compositional strategies for interactive choreographies that can be repeated as performative process within the various states of the system. Yet again, it might be contradictory to speak of repeatable choreography when introducing the second generation of interactive systems where the continuity of computer processing co-evolves with the choreography and generates its own creative behavior. Whereas the first interactivity understood human-computer interaction on a stimulus-response or action-reaction model, the second interactivity emphasizes sensorial dialogue insofar as human enaction and machinic processes each have their own autonomy, being able to self-reorganize in constant dynamic relationship.

The second-generation interactivity heightens the experience of human embodiment and sensorial performance as the coupling of performer and virtual environment evolves in noncausal correlation with one another. Ideally, both performer and system respond to the other's enaction by undergoing self-permutations on the basis of distinct operational rules (a new form of "post-choreography") that are internal to them. Moving toward indirect interfaces (optical, magnetic, and ultrasonic sensors or machine vision), however, creators of such performance systems often prioritize the development of software techniques over physical techniques. In innumerable performance experiments of this kind one sees mediocre or underdeveloped dancing/acting. In such cases, perfunctory physical techniques are used to patch the interface rather than expanding the transformational capabilities of the system or developing new re-organizations of the body and its expressive metabolism. The situation tends to be worse, I think, in interactive installations inviting the unprepared public to move and become "co-authors."

In an indirect interface, the performers (or participants) are challenged to re-organize their motional, affective, perceptive, and proprioceptive behavior in the environment. The desired aesthetic aim would be to anticipate direct *dance transformations* or *acting transformations* in real-time. In other words, the more complex the technologies behind the interface become, the more attention, creativity, and originality need to be applied to transformative techniques and synaesthetic processes.

Trisha Brown's stage work, *how long does the subject linger on the edge of the volume ...*, recreated for the 2006 Monaco Dance Forum with its fully active intelligent environment, interfaces with animated graphics from real-time motion-capture driven by an artist-designed AI software which responds to the kinematic data and generates particular behaviors. Marc Downie speaks of "choreographing" these extended agent-bodies, but he carefully distinguishes such motion behavior from human, physical intelligence. The artificial intelligence software draws its own dance diagrams live during the performance, and the graphic agents are projected onto a transparent screen in front of the stage. The agents are software creatures, acting according to their artificial intelligence. They have their own autonomy. Their imagery comes about as they picture things to themselves, trying to make sense of what they see onstage in real-time as the dance unfolds. Brown's choreography is not improvised but carefully rehearsed, and thus a composite work is created in real-time, which conjoins a specific sedimented performance praxis with an equally specific intelligent creature system.

For example, *how long* opens up with a triangle creature, whose intention is to move from stage right to stage left. It performs this task by catching a ride on points in the motion-captured dancers' bodies; it guesses which ones are moving in the right direction and must discern a motion pattern. It extends a line out to a likely point, and is then pulled that way if it has guessed correctly. Sometimes it guesses wrong; then it has to let its grip on that point lapse and await another opportunity. During the course of the performance, we notice a pattern in such lapses, as in each case the line is left as a trace. Aesthetically, this could be considered a drawing process over time, which constitutes a larger image (just as a choreographic structure evolves to form larger patterns, repetitions, and variations). As a line progresses, comparable to what I mentioned earlier in regard to SWAP's extra-temporality of past, present, and future gestures, it creates a history of its attempts. This "virtual choreography," in other words, has memory.

The Monaco Dance Festival gave testimony to such surprising advances in performance technology, as we watched the physical intelligence of Trisha Brown's dancers interact with the artificial intelligence of Downie and Kaiser's "thinking images." In a post-performance discussion, Downie emphasized that the computer is an embodied agent, deeply coupled to its environment such that its actions on its environment must be very carefully calibrated, and its perceptions of its environment (dependent on its limited sensory apparatus) must be very carefully maintained. The machine is learning from dance, and it can be trained to do so. Its sensory apparatus sketches the relationships it is programmed to perceive as soon as it starts making them out. Its tentative grasp of the onstage choreography keeps its frames in constant flux, for it can continually re-adjust itself as it advances its ideas. This recogniton, in the computer science underlying this work, is generally referred to as pattern recognition, but in Downie and Kaiser's artistic collaboration for the stage production of *how long* it gains an astonishing poetic or calligraphic quality which reminded me of the extraordinary use of ink calligraphies in Shen Wei's choreography *Connect Transfer* and in Cloud Gate Dance Theatre's *Cursive* (all three parts of this masterful work were shown in Berlin in 2006), where the visualizations formed an organic whole throughout the length of the choreography. Cloud Gate uses a movement form and a kinetic expressivity, which seems intimately inspired both by calligraphy and martial arts (intermixed with ballet, modern dance movement, t'ai chi, and Peking Opera styles). The dance "writes" an emotional graphics, so to speak, which is culturally located (in the ancient Chinese traditions of calligraphy as a visual and narrative art), thus also makes a political statement, as well as abstracted in the overall stage pictures of "flowing ink" or floating forms—and thus thoroughly modernist. To describe Trisha Brown's piece in modernist or postmodernist terms is more difficult. Her vocabulary does not break new ground, it bears the typical look of her formal, organized choreography, which sometimes feels light and relaxed, with dancers stretching their arms into simple extended horizontal lines or swinging them loosely, while at other times there is a flurry of complex partnering, knotted-together bodies, and floor work followed by plain walking and strolling. As in many of her previous works, for example the aptly titled *Unstable Molecular Structures*, the movement is characterized by a fluid yet unpredictably geometric style. Interestingly, the dancers perform as if completely unaware of the interactive intelligent capture system. This caused a certain surprise amongst those in the audience who knew about the real-time motion capture engaged in the action. The virtual performers, in other words, seemed to choose to interact with the dancers, and not the other way round.

Downie's creatures (irregular triangles, squares, rectangles, and lines) focus not on individual dancers, but rather on the patterns they form together. One such pattern is the spatial composition the dancers make at any given moment on stage—the spaces between them, the similarities and differences between their shapes, the composite shapes of the duets or trios created when the dancers lean against each other in the frequent freeze-frames Brown uses. Given the history of Brown's choreographic explorations (since her early accumulation pieces), there is undoubtedy an algorithmic sensibility already inscribed in the dance, which now finds itself fully embedded in the motion-graphical environment designed by Downie, Kaiser, Eshkar, and ASU's scientific team. The creatures' bodies and their physics are purely imaginary, of course, as an audience may read all kinds of "figures" or meanings into the geometries. It is noteworthy that the software artists prefer indeterminate images, lingering between abstraction and figuration. On the other hand, I cannot avoid noticing the dulling effect created by the front scrim, which encloses the stage with its transparent fourth wall. There are times when I become very aware of the front screen projections while losing "touch" with the performers. The sensory digital interface, in other words, has the opposite effect of the touching explored in kondition pluriel's *the puppet(s)*. The dancers in *the puppet(s)* inevitably become more real to me, their actions capture me, whereas Brown's dancers nearly disappear behind a veil.

How long was shown alongside *22*, a new solo by Bill T. Jones, which, compared to Brown's abstract movement vocabulary, had a much stronger narrative content and featured the "creatures" in an artificial dialogue with the gruesome story of a childhood incident Jones was telling as he moved through twenty-two particular postures and their variations. The story, overheard as a child, is doubled by another story Jones heard on the radio (concerning a photo-journalist's experience in Rwanda). The dance is an interweaving of these tales. But even in this performance, which made me feel captivated particularly through Jones's voice, his emotional delivery, and the exhaustion audible in his breathing, the flow or articulation of the dance itself was not necessarily enhanced or counterpointed by the graphic images. This was perhaps due to their large scale and their porousness. I perceived the images almost as a separate world, and I had to slowly tune into this world and take my eyes off Jones. Then the images (e.g., a door, a man climbing a ladder, a child pushing a box) gained a mysterious power, their semi-blurred and distorted appearance (deliberately off-setting the photo-realism we find in commercial motion graphics) conveying an eery quality or dream-like sensation that grew stronger as the dance went on and thus provided layers of subconscious resonances which took Jones's *narration* to other shores.

There is a complex connection between what I just described as narrative images and the narrative figuration in Jones's storytelling performance, and this kind of relationship tends to be explored much less frequently in contemporary collaborations between choreographers and software artists. Downie and Kaiser themselves appeared more at ease in their artistic experimentation with abstract geometries, developing a complex artificial intelligence system for embedding digital sensing and projection into Brown's motional choreography. The maintenance of the motion analysis and real-time rendering system for this concert involved a huge technical effort, unlikely to be repeated too often on Brown's busy touring schedule. It could be argued also that the mathematical complexity of the analytical operations driving the intelligent agents aren't perceivable by the spectating audience, and thus the scientific basis for the performance cannot be fully appreciated. On the other hand, the difficulty of touring with the real-time system will prevent the Trisha Brown Company from using it, and thus it's likely that the graphic image projections will be merely "played back" from a DVD, as it has already happened when Brown showed *how long* in Paris, London, and New York City. Such a canned version of the piece would seem to defeat its interactive purpose.

Distributed Space, Distributed Choreography: A Global Kinesphere?

In telepresence environments, which I describe here from the point of view of performers, we become conscious of the deep structure of affective interfaces, especially as visual, oral, and haptic senses drift apart, and perception of movement (in the body, in the image) no longer coincides with what we hear or what our bodies feel. The nervous system of dance practice, basically, involves various motor and sensory modalities, tactility, memory and, especially, proprioception—the sense that tells us where the boundaries of our bodies are. Connected to inner-ear mechanisms and internal nerve endings, proprioception enables us to feel we inhabit our bodies from the inside. As we know from astronauts' experiences in zero gravity, proprioceptive coherence in gravity refers to how these boundaries are formed through physiological feedback loops and habitual usage. As communicative experience, movement interacts with organic and inorganic environments, with space and time, the natural and artificial rhythms of the body-mind and spirit's awareness of the cultural languages and climates that affect them. Dance as an expression of culture involves the organization of energy and empathy according to the affectual apparatus and internal memory systems that have been shaped by the forms of corporeality and participatory movement vocabularies of a given cultural context. Thus, dancing bodies necessarily always rub against other bodies and spatial realities as tangible categories of physical culture. They traverse boundaries and write their gestures into various landscapes of cultural meaning-making, perception, knowledge.

Interactive network technology has changed these boundaries and spatial realities. It requires that we adopt new physical and mental patterns as we learn how to negotiate cameras, sensors, and projective environments (reaching us from remote sites), moving within the dynamics of virtualized space and accelerated, unexpected, or random events that may occur, interrupting vision, restructuring consciousness. In telepresence, the role of affection in the feedback to our orientational system becomes vital, especially as it concerns movement interaction with streaming images of partners not physically present. Dancing with streams offers unprecedented expansions of affections felt in the whole body and through the body's "virtual synaesthetic perspectives."[1] As movement artists, we know how to negotiate space; we are highly aware of the different speeds of the body, we train sensorial focus, spatial awareness, and coordinative perspectives. In our expressive work we try to amplify perception or illuminate how we receive changes inside and outside the body. These changes, if we dance with *streaming image environments*, can produce the collapse of the sensorimotor logic of images, and thus an affective experience of haptic space within the body rather than outside through optical perception. Vision and proprioception disorient each other, and this sensory disarray can be enormously exhilarating.

When I first saw Company in Space (in 1999), they performed *Escape Velocity* as a duet between two dancers, two cameras, and two projection spaces through an online connection between a Web café in Tempe, Arizona, and a performance space in Melbourne, Australia. The telematic environment effectively merged the two dancers, layering the choreography and the bodies in a spellbinding, transparent symmetry across a vast spatial and temporal gap. When Hellen Sky started her dance in front of us, I saw the projected image of her sister dancing the same choreography in Melbourne. Gradually I began to imagine the dancers being at-one, the sisters now a couple floating in a third space created by the overlaid projections which included film footage of a forest, a desert. Sky's slow and intensely focused movement was tactile or, rather, conflated with the tactility of the image spaces; she seemed to sense the presence of her sister with her whole body. Her inwardly turned performance style resembled butoh dance. She rarely ever looked at the screen, but her body and the other body apprehended each other effortlessly, now submerged in the blue and green colors of the outdoor landscapes, now foregrounded in close-ups that slowly mutated and trembled in color and resolution. I could not tell whether the two living beings transformed the digital space or whether the changes in the "physicality" of the images were caused by the medium, the camera-work or the real-time synthesis, which included delays or degradations in the Internet transmission. The degradations were haunting and visceral, they made this precarious dance across vast distance seem real and organic.[2]

When I met Sky and McCormick again at the Digilounge workshop in Chelmsford, Essex, their experiments with telepresence took a more complex conceptual direction toward real-time dynamic systems in which the composite mediated space, no longer figurative and representational, is generated by the crossing of several networked morphogenetic processes. Collaborating with British artists Ruth Gibson and Bruno Martelli (whose company is called igloo), Sky and McCormick tested a telematic performance based on the idea of visual world-modeling. Movement data, captured in real time from Sky and Gibson (in exoskeletal motion-sensing suits), were transmitted and processed to create "soft bodies," that is, the data were not mapped onto animated figures but stretched, folded, and manipulated to create space-models. These images act like the congealment of the space in-between the two dancers performing in distributed locations. McCormick thinks of the composite mass of the dancers as *shared volume*. The representation of the mass, the visual shape, is made out of the connection between the dancers' motions (e.g., the motion of hands, pelvis, or upper body). As I watched the projected environment of warped space, I was perplexed by this performance, which had been utterly transformed into a kind of biomorphic architecture. The changing shapes of volume were a direct expression of the movement and distance between the dancers who were generating the motion data, but "bodies" here became spatialized energy, floating topologies in torsion.[3]

Dancing in responsive environments that use telepresence and 3-DVR interactivity means participating in virtual, distributed space: to enter *into* image-space and experience the body somewhere else requires different kinds of intuition. The term "sensing" gains a dimension beyond the physical and organic understanding of bodily anatomy, musculature, cellular consciousness, and proprioceptive spatial awareness of moving within the individual kinesphere. The convergence of interface design and networks extends Laban-derived structural explorations of the body's kinespheric repertoire for movement with regard to space, shape, effort, dynamics, rhythm, and expressive qualities. Laban suggested that we should neither "look upon a site simply as empty space divorced from movement, nor understand movement as occurring occasionally; for movement is a continuous current with placedness itself, and this is the fundamental aspect of space. Space is the hidden principle of movement, and movement is a visible aspect of space."[4] However, if movement is indeed a "continuous current," a new understanding of "interspaces" or "interplacedness" in telepresence is required. The idea of real-time flow bridging spaces across the network exceeds Laban's physics; on the side of temporality it also involves delays in the uplink/downlink teleoperation. Musicians who have engaged networked performance to play musical concert across the Internet worry about the latency. At the 2007 Sonorities Festival of Contemporary Music in Belfast, several composers (including George Lewis, Alain Renaud, Pedro Rebelo, Chris Brown,

Devolution, Australian Dance Theatre, choreography by Garry Stewart, with robotics design by Louis-Philippe Demers, 2006. Photo: Courtesy Chris Herzfeld.

Listening Post, Mark Hansen and Ben Rubin, Whitney Museum of American Art, 2002. Photo: David Allison. Courtesy Ben Rubin.

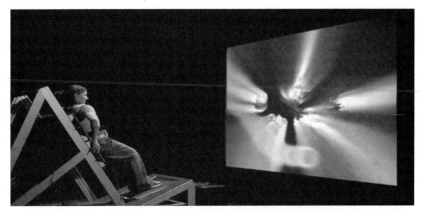

Intimate Transactions, Transmute, 2005. Photo courtesy Keith Armstrong.

Apparition, Klaus Obermaier, with Robert Tannion and Desireé Kongerød, 2004. Photo: Gabi Hauser. Courtesy the artist.

16 (R)evolutions, Troika Ranch, 2006, featuring Johanna Levy and Lucia Tong. Photo: Courtesy the artists.

TransPort, Sarah Jane Pell, Live Video Feed, 2004. Photo: Courtesy Korin Gath.

Genesis, Eduardo Kac, 1999. Transgenic work with artist-created bacteria, ultraviolet light, Internet, video (detail), edition of 2, dimensions variable. Collection Instituto Valenciano de Arte Moderno (IVAM), Valencia, Spain (1/2). Photo: Courtesy the artist.

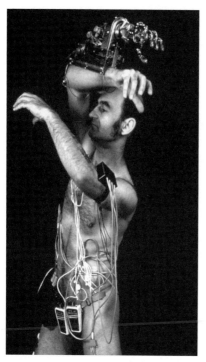

Stelarc performing *Third Hand*. Tokyo, Yokohama, Nagoya, 2003. Photo: Simon Hunter. Courtesy the artist.

Helenna Ren manipulating her partial garment in performance of *tedr*, 2005. Videostill: J. Birringer.

Here I come again/Flying Birdman, ADaPT, multi-site telepresence performance, November 25, 2002. Videostill: J. Birringer.

Ruth Gibson wearing Gypsy motion capture exoskeleton Animazoo, Workshop "Sharing the Body," Monaco
Dance Forum 2002. Photo: Courtesy Bernd Lintermann.

Alejandro Ahmed and Nina in *Pequenas frestas de
ficção sobre realidade insistente*, Cena 11, 2007.
Photo: Courtesy Cena 11/Cristiano Prim.

Robert Wilson sketching a scene of *Einstein on the Beach*. Still frame from *Visionary of Theater*, 1996. Photo: Courtesy Paul Kaiser/The Byrd Hoffman Watermill Foundation.

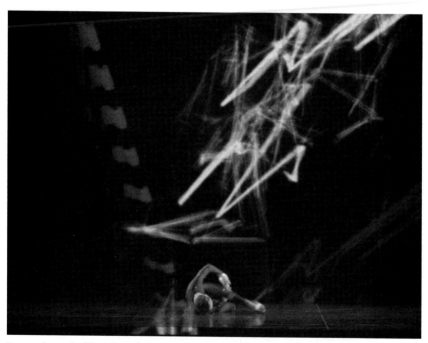

Dress rehearsal of *how long does the subject linger at the edge of the volume ...* Trisha Brown, 2005, Arizona State University. Photo: Courtesy Paul Kaiser and Marc Downie.

To You, The Birdie! (Phèdre), The Wooster Group, 2002.
Photo: Courtesy Mary Gearhart.

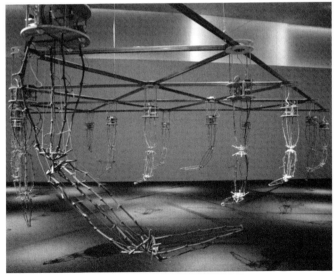

Autopoiesis: Artificial Life Installation, Kenneth Rinaldo, 2000-2005.
Photo: Yehia Eweis. Courtesy the artist.

Helenna Ren, Katsura Isobe and Olu Taiwo in front of digital dunes in *Suna no Onna* (Woman in the Dunes), Dans Sans Joux, 2008. Photo courtesy DAP-Lab /Hans Staartjes.

Predator, Fabian Marcaccio in collaboration with Greg Lynn for the Wexner Center, 2001. Photo: Courtesy the artist.

and Chris Chafe) debated current technical efforts being made to reduce the latency, but they barely addressed the particular aesthetic advantages of asychronicity, of the delays and degradatations characteristic of the network medium. Real-time networked performance challenges us to compose with the particular unstable plasticity of the medium.

Asynchronicity and deferral affect kinaesthetic perception, if the performer sees her image trying to catch up with her or transmute into dimensionless topological forms. The intervention into the ecology of movement that happens here is a dis-location, and subsequent re-distribution, of movement as captured, sampled, and processed data. Movement is not only movement. As its generated data is used in networked performances, it is not only a "continuous current with placedness itself" but continuously crosses into or between data-space, projected space (video/animation), or other virtual contexts (VR, nongeometric virtual space). Space is dematerialized, movement is captured, commuted, transferred, and reconfigured elsewhere, and we interact with force sensation or sensory information such as video, which simulates three-dimensional kinaesthetic perception of movement energy, position, direction, and velocity. What, then, is the ecology of networked environments?

If we think of the World Wide Web as a global environment, then telematic performance implies the network itself becoming the total volume of the body's potential movement. The only difference might be that we cannot feel it in our bones and muscles; our minds strain to comprehend global scale. But performers working with telepresence focus precisely on the physicality of virtualized body and environment, intuiting a new bodily processing or "mapping" of sensation and proprioception within the interface, while also confronting cultural assumptions about scale, complexity, proximity, and interactive meaning in controlled and emerging environments. As I suggested in regard to Tomie Hahn's performance of *Streams*, her motion may be precisely controlled and exact, but it is a tactile choreography, which transcends the sense of motion as she touches movement between sonic dimensions. She performs a kind of infrasensory sense, touching invisible sound waves as her transduced sensor data collaborate with the signal processing designs within the interactive environment. Sounding here is a living system, manifesting processes of continuous change, adaptation, and evolution, and the designers use a spherical speaker array that creates unusual diffusion effects, casting individual sound elements into particular locations. *Streams* evolves as a kind of hovering, which can also be considered in its critical relation to "real-time," namely as a continuous deferral that makes the audience *listen* to the micro and macro gestures in the emerging sonic universe. In the absence of a global controller, there is an unstable balance in the system.

Compared to the derived virtual world of *Ghostcatching*, in which Kaiser's redrawing of motion data is complete and non-interactive, the interface environments of *Streams* and *Escape Velocity* have much greater stratification or diversity because each level of interaction is open to improvisation, changing inputs, outputs, mixing and re-mixing. To abandon choreography and control over sonic design means to approach fluid states of communication for which older aesthetic principles of dance or music cannot account. Networked environments imply that the limits of what constitutes presence or place will never be as clear again, since all the coordinates of movement control and proprioception have changed.

There are two ways of looking at telematic performance, which I have explored in my Environments-Lab. They raise different questions about the actual and virtual contexts that are being connected. Firstly, "telematic performance" needs a telecommunications network to create links between (at least) two remote real spaces at the same time and to present the activities in those two separate spaces variously as single performance events. In this case, the structure and environment of both performance spaces will most likely resemble each other, and the linking of remote sites primarily concerns the collaboration between the producers of the performance who play with their physical-sensorial relationship to the virtualized real. The important difference between VR and telepresence lies in the fact that the latter is not pure data space but a transmitted "actual action," however manipulated and filtered through data streaming. Secondly, the performance is transmitted to make use of the Web as a third performance space, a composite virtual site potentially accessible to a global audience. The transmission not only effects the disappearance of the original, "natural" environments but also furthers the asynchronous construction of a synthetic environment where the interface between observer (user) and transmitted performance is accessible for manipulation. The "distributed dance," in other words, becomes a "social dance" that makes the user a part of the system if the user responds by altering the action, adding to the call and response, improvising with the images, rhythms, and meters of the performance. In engaging virtual space as a medium linking producer and user through actions affecting our realities, we change. We create what we see (what touches us and what we can touch). In fact, touch is undoubtedly the most fundamental sense in our performances. Telematic environments are the opposite of VR: we engage connectivity as a form of sensuous contact improvisation.

How do we prepare for this sensuous contact improvisation with the digital? I suggest we try to make the virtual organic, and engage more deliberately with the actual environment we plant for communicating a tactile digital dynamics. The rehearsals at the Environments-Lab (1999–2003) were conceived as plastic, sculptural, and engineering processes on the one hand, and as motional and image-movement processes on the other, linking constructed and transformable space to the exploration of movement narratives and their digital recomposition. The sculptural and plastic elements in the environment themselves are the textures onto which we project images, experimenting with three-dimensional video-spaces that also move, inflate, shrink.

Creating intimate interfaces based on touch and proximity, we interact with real space and tactile video projection—sensual digital spaces—in order to rehearse telematic form-giving and bodily spacing inside the streaming. Performing now is intuiting the entire spatial, plastic, sonic, lighting, and digital video projection-environment, the habitat we arrange and mold so that the spatial installation itself moves and becomes transformable. In this sense, environments are not "natural," they are artificial life worlds addressing the human body and its environmental memories. We perform with concrete elements—earth, glass, water, steam, ice, air, cloth, plants, rubber—and inflatable costumes that become prostheses. Our building: an old industrial foundry full of pipes, aluminium airshafts, and corrugated metal. Our sculptural constructions deal with suspension, flow, and transition, and we seek to fold the digital images back into the physical. Like the receding industrial culture, the new digital forms have their own detritus and residue. We "choreograph" the residue and manipulate its data, finding ourselves at the beginning of a huge conceptual undertaking. It means reorganizing ourselves, thinking through all the dimensions of such ecologies of "environment" and how they can be transported, via the network, to remote sites that also breathe and house residues.

NOTES

¹ Massumi, *Parables for the Virtual*, 97.

² Company in Space, directed by Hellen Sky and John McCormick, are recognized as one of Australia's most innovative companies using computer and network technologies to access new pathways between performer and audience. *Escape Velocity* was performed at Arizona State University, February 27, 1999, with choreography by Hellen Sky (Arizona) and Louise Taube (Australia), computer design and operation by John McCormick (Australia), original score and interactive sound design by Garth Paine (Arizona), and camera performance by Luke Pither (Arizona) and Kelli Dipple (Australia). Using teleconferencing systems to bring dancers in the two locations together in the same virtual space, the composer in addition used VNS and Max/MSP to sense the video image of the choreography and create a layer of interactive sound fed into the mix with pre-structured material. Paine also used Supercollider to generate material that was controlled by an audience member at IDAT moving a mouse around on the screen of a browser at that end. He then converted those mouse positions into MIDI and a Supercollider patch at the other end, which was also fed back into the mix. With these performance experiments it is vital to recognize the teamwork that underlies the aesthetic production.

³ *Sentient Space* was first created at Digilounge in Chelmsford (UK), February 2004. Another performance at the workshop was conducted by Carol Brown and her dancers. In their collaboration, Brown and digital architect Mette Ramsgard Thomsen devised an interactive environment (*SPAWN*) to explore how kinetic information informs the behavior of virtual architectures. The dancers created duets or trios with the projected light of the architectures computed by the software Thomsen had written. Their bodily contours were tracked by the camera and processed by the computer program; they could affect the morphological shapes of the image-light and image-color as their movement dynamics became embodied architecture. They literally enacted the virtual spatialization of their bodies.

⁴ Rudolf von Laban, *Choreutiks: Grundlagen der Harmonielehre des Tanzes*, Munich: Florian Notzel Verlag, 1966, 19 (my translation).

DIGITAL ENVIRONMENTS, WEARABLE SPACES

▼▲ Architecture & the Digital

I not only think that we will tinker with Mother Nature,
I think Mother wants us to.

—FROM THE PROLOGUE TO *GATTACA*

Performance Design

Suite Fantastique, an architectural exhibition at the Wexner Center for the Arts in Columbus, Ohio (January 27–April 15, 2000) gives occasion to this chapter, and the musical title that its curator chose for the exploration of contemporary design arts also alludes to a performative dimension in architecture and digital media which I want to subject to a few careful, and at times speculative, reflections. Promotional writing announcing the exhibit was hardly restrained, promising us "spectacle and drama," an opening night event with film screenings, DJs, music, food and all-night dancing, with the scenography of the exhibition staging a "suite" of events mixing the classical postmodern with the popular avant-garde of the "rave." The museum as performance space? An art exhibition disguised as, or rather transformed into, a live techno mix?

When I received the invitation to the show and its opening night with DJ Spooky, I concluded that performance and the new digital media had finally, and perhaps irreversibly, taken hold of the imagination of the contemporary museum. This is something I don't regret. The Wexner Center, in any case, belongs to the category of contemporary art centers that don't have permanent collections but focus their curatorial philosophy on the parallel programming of temporary exhibitions of visual art, film/video, performance, and design of the twentieth century and beyond. It houses no collectibles but installs events, so to speak. Its extraordinary ambience, created by Peter Eisenman's architecture (completed in 1989), already draws attention to perceptual experiences of a present, and presence, playfully mixed up with traces of an excavated past that has become decorative, fake—mediated, in other words.

What is astonishing about *Suite Fantastique*, however, is that its performance is not presented in the black box or the video theatre, where we regularly see independent or foreign films, emerging projects in media and Internet art, as well as experimental dance, theatre, and music, but that it has been devised by the curator of architecture and design for the main galleries. The "Suite" is an assemblage of works, both virtual and concrete, inviting the visitor to navigate the spaces and re-construct or project the events that may be implied by its narrative.

Before I question the application of the concept of "performance" to a design exhibition, let me briefly describe the facts, since the museum has not yet entirely replaced the material object with electronic reproductions and simulations, nor forfeited the practice of displaying static, inactive works as cultural treasures in glass cases. What exactly has shifted from "object" to "experience," as Hilde Hein suggests in her book on *The Museum in Transition*, needs to be determined very carefully.[1] In this case, the initial space, threshold to *Suite Fantastique*, is refered to as "Overture" by curator Jeffrey Kipnis, and it is easily the most provocative installation of the entire show, featuring a continuous screening of opening movie credits created by the Los Angeles-based motion graphics firm Imaginary Forces.

In a darkened gallery, we watch a loop of the title sequences of seven contemporary, not necessarily well-known science-fiction movies (*Gattaca*, *Sphere*, *The Island of Dr. Moreau*, etc.), projected onto a huge screen and accompanied by thundering soundtracks. An additional five-channel video remix of the same sequences, using footage not shown in the final film versions, is projected onto a series of staggered screens suspended in mid-air. Here we can clearly say that the object has been transcended; the display features time art—animate forms and image movement that are ephemeral and contingent on the "site" (movies) in which they perform their function. The function, in this case, corresponds to the logic of commercial advertising and music television: the visuals are intended to seduce, to captivate, and to transport the viewers into an emotional and narrative space.

The transition into the next gallery space could not be more startling. A narrow, triangular room gradually opens out, featuring framed ideas and drawings by Daniel Libeskind hung on the wall behind glass plates. It is a considerable shift in tone, from the hyperdesigned commercial Hollywood spectacle to the silent, meditative, and private world of the architect marking the page with condensed, indecipherable diagrams. "Chamber Works:

IV Horizontal," drawn in ink on paper, appears to be a largely abstract composition of lines that reminded me of some of Robert Wilson's black and white sketches for his visual theatre.

The entire middle section of the exhibition, titled "Perfect Acts of Architecture" (1977–1987), takes us into the conceptual world of theoretical architecture and diagram diaries by some very well-known artists, including Libeskind, Peter Eisenman, Rem Koolhaas, Thom Mayne, and Bernard Tschumi. On the walls and in glass cases, we can study Tschumi's collages and graphic experimentations, and Koolhaas's savagely ironic and fictional montage "Exodus, or The Voluntary Prisoners of Architecture." As we walk up the gradual incline of the Wexner building, we also increasingly encounter the unusual forms and design constructions of Scott Burton's sculptural furniture. The curator refers to the Burton chairs as "Scherzo," and in another small room we also see a video of Burton sitting on his "Perforated Chair" at an elongated granite table and chatting about his early conceptual performance experiments. We see a clip of an action from the early 1970s in which he had performers walk around a room to explore physical relationships, proximity-relationships, and body languages in an empty space. Interestingly, the exhibition pairs the very concrete materials of Burton's stone, aluminium, and steel fabrications with the 80s conceptual or virtual architecture, here refered to as "paper architecture." But it doesn't provide any explanatory or interpretive context for the existence or prevalence, in late postmodernism or during periods of sluggish world economy, of "virtual" architecture—or a drawing process which performs an excess of ideas without representing actual buildings or without harboring the potential or interest in physical manifestation.

Is the architectural drawing a design technology which reads as a score, "between the lines" (Libeskind), not waiting to be executed, or, like John Cage's *4:33*, is it the score for a silent musical performance, not played yet not silent either, full of chances, starting points, or possibilities for deformation, superimposition, layering, and transformation? A score for the fantasy of potential performers/interpreters? Is such a score (*4:33*) not also a model for what we now call "interactive art?" Even more interesting is the fact that the exhibition displays these hand-drawn sketches and collages from the 80s, thus returning to the pre-history of more recent digital diagrams and 3-D models of electronic architecture, namely the contemporary use that most architects now make of computer-aided design systems. We have seen them in Eisenman's and Greg Lynn's recent publications or installations: the computer allows the possibility of constructing "objects," spatialities, and visual perceptions that one could not do directly from the mind to the hand. Geometry and perspective are no longer needed to create architecture. CAD modeling can provide infinite possibilities of spatial manipulation and modulation, and designing begins to look phantasmatic.

Finally, we ascend to the last room of the "Suite" and enter a tropical room full of color and sound (DJ Spooky's remix). Our eyes have to get used to the unusual shape and texture of the raving thing or blob that seems to have grown here. Entitled "Predator," the fantastic whale-like vacuformed plastic that snakes around the room is a collaborative concoction by Argentinian painter Fabian Marcaccio and architect Greg Lynn, inspired by the setting and the digital special effects sequences of another *Predator*, Arnold Schwarzenegger's sci-fi movie. The whale-house has an opening through which one can step, glancing into the belly of this enormous object, which appears to be a kind of "transgenic species," as Eduardo Kac might call it. It is a hybrid of painting, architecture, and digital technology that has come alive as a vigorous and visceral organism.

Technologies of World-making

Architecture and design, film and television, undoubtedly play a major role in today's world of visual imaging technologies in a competitive marketplace. More crucially, information and communications technologies have begun to profoundly transform the role of design. Compared to the clear and functionalist language of design in the Bauhaus and subsequent schools of industrial design, today's design is more comprehensively related to environments, event-flows, and the modulations in the ongoing stream of form production tied to capital. Information processing is commodity production, in this sense. It is a medium of capital that now operates on a global level. This is how we learn to understand the spread of electronic communications. The ecology or environment of the Internet is a new infrastructure, and designing information for global access can perhaps be compared to the older roles of architecture in the creation of inhabitable and traversable metropolitan space. If Walter Benjamin lived today, he would not study the boulevards and passages of nineteenth-century Paris, but the interminable flows and sitings of the World Wide Web. Information architecture, therefore, could be considered a form of world-making.

Suite Fantastique approaches these current phenomena from an artistic, not an economic, viewpoint, proposing that artists, whether they are painters, architects, composers, or filmmakers, imagine or reflect upon new worlds, and that the instrument they use, whether it is a pencil or a computer, intimately shapes the world they imagine. Drawing and digital methods of composition are examined in the exhibition, and the show implies that world-making is now defined by digital processes.

One of the consequences, of course, is the role of speed, the acceleration of transmission. "Under a market system whose mode of being proceeds through expansion and increasing mobilization," writes Branden Hookway in *Pandemonium*, "the more easily disseminated forms of information will be selected and privileged over those that resist easy translation into the digital realm of compunicational abstraction."[2] Introducing the term "compunicational," Hookway is referring to Daniel Bell's suggestion that miniaturization (nanotechnology) in computational information processing has led to a new order of technologies. Communications networks have developed to the point where information processing has become indistinguishable from the act of communication itself. Mediation thus tends to become invisible, since our technological vision and sound machines have become the collective architecture, shaping, forming, and locating all information in the realm of technological reproduction and simultaneous transmission. This, it appears, is a more cumbersome way of describing what actually happens at a rave when the DJ performs the continuous live mixing of hundreds of samples of musical information, with an audience that is participating and thus interacting with the flows and rhythms of energy.

The change that I have encountered, for example in the field of dance, is that we are now describing movement and expression as "movement information" or data that can be recorded, captured, and re-transmitted via video projection or live transmission across the Net. Performance, in this sense, becomes data that can be processed and modulated, and this has implications to which I will return. For *Suite Fantastique*, the language of world-making in architecture is no longer one of geometry, proportion, perspective vision, symmetry, or organic wholeness. The link between mathematics of form and transcendent architectural values is considered obsolete, and architects already deconstructed geometric language in the

80s. Typically, younger architects such as Greg Lynn or Lars Spuybroek compose with non-architectural softwares on their computers and are more likely to be influenced by film and computer animation than by Palladio's villas or by Le Corbusier. Or by utopian modernist projects, for that matter.

Eisenman now speaks of "folded projects," and Lynn has written about his ideas for blobs and curves, dynamic and emergent systems, a moving architecture that articulates itself within the context of the life sciences, bio-engineering, informatics, chaos theory, and genetics. Lynn also deliberately refers to Leibniz's *ars combinatoria* as an epistemology founded on the dynamic nature of combinatorial changes in identity that take place with increasing degrees of complexity. This interest in complexity reflects an attitude toward contemporary realities in the global culture marked by a desire to understand, and compose with, the organizational principles of cybernetic and informational technologies. The attitude tells us that our situation is volatile, and our environments unstable and predatory. We need more intelligent machines for crisis management, surveillance, and control.

Perversely, architects today echo the analysis that has been proffered by writers such as Manuel de Landa (*War in the Age of Intelligent Machines*). Bernard Tschumi's collages, in the exhibition, make specific reference to dis-integrated metropolitan space, the "pleasure of violence" and shock, arguing that architects must manufacture "shock" in order to communicate. This was evidently written before 9/11 yet anticipates the wild commentaries Karlheinz Stockhausen made about the stunning decomposition of the World Trade Center. If violence is a key metaphor for spatial relations in Tschumi's work, for Eisenman and Lynn the challenge now lies in imagining a "fluid architecture" where shapes become data fields, thus enabling architecture to rewrite and manipulate reality as it used to be done in avant-garde performance. Experimentation in architecture, suggests Luca Galofaro in his book *Digital Eisenman*, stems from the desire to create a space that breaks through the boundaries between real and virtual, dislocating vision and dislocating the observer.

Performance Camouflage

Now I can address the question of the relationship of performance to architecture. The vocabulary used by the architects implies notions of process, manipulation, disjunction, fragmentation, and non-linearity, which are familiar to us from the recent evolution of postmodern literature, performance art, and film/video. It is also obvious that compositional method in architecture has moved from drawing to digital processing and modeling, and *Suite Fantastique* implies that the theoretical drawings of these architects already include a critique of older conventions of realism and representation. The fictional, critical, or theoretical diagrams suggest alternatives to drawing as spatial representation, and to the "notation" and "documentation" of buildings and built space. The new digital processes, like DJ Spooky's remixes, reflect the contemporary environment of information, digital files, a new digital syntax that can treat a "building" as a file in a way a DJ treats music samples as files that can be instantaneously mixed, layered, and fused. The digital process of "imagining space," in other words, can be seen as a performance. It functions as a kind of online art that can also be transmitted: a design can be sent from Japan to France and be modified and executed, in situ, or it can be recomposed and sent back as a blueprint in progress, for example.

DJ Spooky addressed this issue at the Wexner Center, in a symposium with Imaginary Forces, Lynn, and Marcaccio, suggesting that he uses "source files," just as digital artists today use source codes as shareware that gets dispersed, each one mixing and using it in her own way (e.g., Napster). DJs are the contemporary troubadours, working with a soundculture and image culture in migration and dispersion. Provocatively, Spooky argued that today's music is a digital folk culture consisting of fragments, each DJ making her own mix out of them, expanding or reinventing what Duchamp once did with the found object. After Duchamp and Rauschenberg, then, we still inhabit an era of collage/montage and combines, but now software and samples are our generative syntax, and we have other models, not the generative syntax of a Noam Chomsky but of Dr. Dre. We perform amongst "discourse networks," and techno culture/rave culture communicates online but also along the lines of word-of-mouth/oral culture dissemination. I give you my mix-tape, and you give me yours.

DJ Spooky also suggested that sound functions as "camouflage" in a biomorphic shape, only apparently enveloping us but, rather, constantly changing and adapting. He refered us to Andy Warhol's interest in mass culture and the religious connotations of the "mass," implying that techno contains a quasi-religious or spiritual dimension performed in the trance of the communal event, the mass celebration of music and dance as ecstatic transformation. If the machine culture of camouflage mimicked cubism, for example in the military application of camouflage to uniforms, canons and tanks, so do today's post-cubist digital industries use information camouflage. This idea of the digital camouflage allows me to speculate on the evolution of "performance," remembering that live art and site-specific installation over the past decades have had an strong impact on an increased understanding of open-ended concept and temporal, experiential process in art. The physical, vulnerable, erotically charged body in performance art thrives on its concrete acting out, in the here and now, with the body itself becoming the "site" of the work. Installations often create complex environments or negotiate local-historical contexts in ways that heighten our sensory awareness of the relations between physical properties, material site, and the images, sounds, memories, and experiences that are evoked when the visitor enters into the "loop cycle" of the installation. Ilya Kabakov is a master of such ceremonies. Christo attempted it in his vast Central Park installation in New York City. Olafur Eliasson succeeded brilliantly with his *Weather Project*, transforming the Tate Modern's Turbine Hall into an ocean of diffused light, an orange-golden glow that mesmerized thousands of visitors over a period of months. The visitor, by necessity, is the performer in installations that organize the manner in which the elements in the site can be interactively experienced, inferred, or processed. During the *Weather Project* installation in 2004, I observed people lingering under the atmospheric spell of light, lying on the stone floor, standing still or wandering about, sometimes as if following the internal cadences of a dance that transcended all logic. There were solitary figures, couples, and families who spent hours under this light, silently gazing up at their pale reflections or—if seen from a distance—forming distinct patterns of movement, their contours in silhouette against the yellow fog. When I walked closer onto this crowded beach, the people seemed like dervishes who had stopped their spinning and were now lost in reverie.

Perhaps unwittingly, Eliasson's work became an interactive movement installation. One hardly needed Cunningham's company performing its *Event* there in November 2004 to realize that the space, under the transformative light, had become a stage. Not a dance stage in the sense in which Loïe Fuller's *danses lumineuses* transformed space through moving light sculptures created by her costumed body. Nor a proscenium on which a Robert Wilson or Saburo Teshigawara paint their abstract landscapes and carve mysterious paths of light into darkness. But a wide-open panorama, an immersive, perhaps even transcendental world of the kind the architects of Gothic cathedrals, nineteenth-century painters of the sublime or twentieth-century light artists like James Turrell envisioned.

Historically, installation art now appears to have superseded earlier body-centered performance that expounded the "real" body. At the end of the day of conceptual art, computer-based media and imaging technologies have shifted the focus from the immediate body to the digitally dilated body. Simultaneously, one observes what is now an accepted fact in the artistic and popular cultures, namely the relentless hybridization of all theatrical, visual arts, and media practices, to the point where "performance," today, is not only a general term that applies to innumerable contexts and functional applications of media, but also a theoretical model for site-specificity, spatial practices, and media practices that articulate the transactions between the work or event, its materials, context, site, and viewers.

Ephemeral performance events or activist interventions, as they were known, no longer take place. If they take a particular place, they are most likely conceived with other channels or platforms of (media) transmission in mind. Someone is beaten up on the street so that the image shot on the cellular phone can be transmitted on YouTube. Such hooligan architects of shock experiment with fake torture and the common ironies of humiliation now prevalent also on daily television, where millions watch them with vicarious pleasure. This shift, and this horrific critical paradox of site-specific performances that mobilize the site as a process of discursive or recorded, reproducible, and transformable image-narratives, forces us to rethink the "architectural model" (design, diagram) along the lines of the movie trailer or the "previsualization," as it is called in commercial advertising. When *Suite Fantastique* exhibits movie title sequences as video clips, it performs a cunning commentary on virtual culture. At closer inspection, it turns out that these motion graphics were digitally remastered and then projected along with the original cut, rather than in the form in which they were shown in cinemas. They are virtual trailers, recombinant versions, and alongside the multiplicitous forms of television commercials and MTV clips, they hide the fact that there is no distinct object that matters or remains. Nothing of consequence. "Fallujah" is now a play, performed in London with special costume designs sporting multicolored camouflage hoods.

I assume that DJ Spooky awards a positive value to this flow when he suggests that the culture of the industrial has undergone a final transition into the digital age, and the critique of formalism has been replaced by appropriation, and appropriation by DJing as a critique of conceptualism. Architects as DJs? Spooky claims that the DJ generation grew up deeply immersed in digital media: the "ART OBJECT" has long since been dematerialized. This is the age of digital syntax, of club architecture, he suggests, and the music of the rave is like a stream of consciousness narrative, permanent flow, constant fluidity of several simultaneous beats and rhythms. At the Wexner symposium he showed a collaboration with Tschumi, mixing sound to a QuickTime movie of architectures/design fragments of an unknown building. Like the music, the digital film generated a fluid syntax of blurred grids and structures, folding and bending its insubstantial space into a pure design-in-motion.

This, I might add, is also one of the peculiar effects of contemporary experiments in dance composed interactively with computer software or derived from motion-capture technology. Computer-animated dance is another model of performance camouflage, extracting and manipulating movement data from the dancer's body and then superseding the body. The body that matters, the intelligent dancer bearing specific cultural memory and individual gestural expression, is filtered out and animated as abstracted and modified form. We began to see some very strange and fantastic dances, but it is also true that practitioners in the dance technology field strive to make these interfaces between humans and machines transparent, aiming at a model of interactivity in which the compositional process is a kind of symbiotic improvisation within a dynamic field of sensors and capturing systems. Moreover, interactive performances can engage the viewer/participant who, in turn, affects the system's evolution and emergence.

Suite Fantastique fails on that level of interactive participation: it is organized as a display exhibition, expecting no physical input from the audience, and thus falls short of investigating the audience's experience of navigational interfaces within an environment of digital architecture. Paradoxically, the museum still relies on its familiar real-world architecture of spectacular display and its odd filtering devices (visitors were not allowed to sit on Burton's furniture!). It does not actually know yet how to perform its digital art. However, *Suite* raised many interesting questions that will keep me preoccupied as I read Spuybroek's *Machining Architecture* to learn about animate or liquid buildings and continuous surfaces that are invaginating and exfoliating. Lynn suggested that "The Predator" is an installation in which painting and architecture look at each other, there are short-circuits, transfers of information, like in a multimedia performance. The work becomes a mutational machine for design and rapid prototyping, and from Marcaccio's perspective, materials and ideas are thus merged in a huge image program. Painting becomes digitally edited. The sensibility of work, it is obvious, comes from using softwares and from the graffiti-like rhythms of contemporary image scapes.

The performance dimension thus implies that artists are working in a field of constant (dis)integration, and continuous re-constellation. It is a technique, far beyond Rauschenbergian combines, that now implies a continuous admixture of analog and digital materials, fully theatrical in ways the art critics of the Pollock era could not have imagined. For those working in temporal art forms, Marcaccio's hybrid "time-paintants," as he calls them, elicit an important, lingering question regarding the everchanging digital environment of information. He is interested in duration, the space of the work over time. This raises the question of where the viewer positions herself in relation to such a space-time, the long "duration" of the ephemeral, and how these many fleeting perspectives can be integrated into the world we imagine as our digital future.

NOTES

[1] Cf. Hilde Hein, *The Museum in Transition*, Washington: Smithsonian Institution Press, 2001.

Suite Fantastique was exhibited at the Wexner Center of the Arts from January 19 through April 14, 2001 (<http://www.wexarts.org>). Other recent exhibitions featuring digital art and information design include *010101: Art in Technological Times*: <http://www.sfmoma.org>; *Bitstreams*: <http://www.whitney.org>; *Telematic Connections: The Virtual Embrace*: <http://www.sanfranciscoart.edu>.

[2] Branden Hookway, *Pandemonium: The Rise of Predatory Locales in the Post-war World*, New York: Princeton Architectural Press, 1999, 79.

▼▲ Installations ℰ the Participant-User

Although perfectly common in the world of scientific research, engineering, industrial design, and commercial product design, the idea of laboratory tests and "user testing" in the world of art appears an anomaly, unsettling our aesthetic assumptions about artworks as well as the established cultural mechanisms of their display and distribution. We generally encounter a new artwork at its first exhibition or premiere on the stage, in museums, galleries, concert halls, or cinemas. In spite of numerous boundary-crossings and reformulations of art as art-process over the course of the last hundred years, especially with the historical evolution of live art, conceptual art practices, and new media art, the notion of an original event which initiates reception (and subsequent reconstructions of the "event" and its manifestations and recordings) still governs our thinking about authors, artworks, and audiences.

But in the contemporary context of digital art, the research and development process is significantly different from earlier paradigms, and the notion of "authoring" has changed in a field that ranges over a heterogeneous collection of technological, scientific, and artistic disciplines. Its cross-disciplinary techniques for interactive design of human-machine relationships are almost always collaborative, and the outcome could be called a "model" of a premiere. The nature of the event-manifestation is altered when the focus is on programming, executable code, and public interaction with computer interfaces or distributed content. The role of observation and evaluation informing the design development moves to the foreground. A shift in the aesthetic constellation of artistic production and audience reception is presupposed in installations for human-computer interaction. They aim at an active "user" who experiences not a static completed work, but an intelligent, responsive environment. Such a system requires the participant to engage the various interfaces that control and mediate the aesthetic as well as psychological processes the work harbors. The system is designed in explicit anticipation of its user: it is always becoming and never completed.

The dissolution of the separation between "show" (spectacle) and passive audience is the direct result of the scientific and technical accomplishment of real-time performance and installation. As I pointed out in the previous chapters, these participatory installations are often conceived as performance, and they have grappled with allocating new "roles" to the former audience now called active visitor, user, immersant, participant, interactor, co-author, player, gardener, etc. Defining such installations in regard to their conceptual design, their interaction models, styles, and interface metaphors, one draws from a vocabulary closer to prototyping and marketing than to art. Such prototyping implies an informational economy, in the post-Keynesian sense, which is no longer based on a hierarchical and regulated model but on complexity and variability, on modulations of the ever increasing flow of abstract information under global capitalism. Technology development for the arts is a small niche, perhaps, but software design for "aesthetic functionality" has a potentially wide market if we think of the public interaction models of cellular phone, iPod, games, and new interactive wearables (see "Design Futures: Wearables"). The software development for such performative scenarios now has a user-centered design focus emphasizing different goals or the appropriateness of different kinds of interfaces, depending on what types of activities need to be supported, what kind of efficiency and usability or pleasurable enjoyment in the user experience is desired. Usability and evaluation (testing) are inextricably linked. In a standard professional handbook for *Interaction Design* mostly directed at technical and commercial markets (addressing students and scholars in computer science, information systems design, psychology, and cognitive science), we learn that a user-centered approach to interactive product designs involves three key characteristics:

> 1. *Early focus on users and tasks.* This means first understanding *who* the users will be by directly studying their cognitive, behavioral, anthropomorphic, and attitudinal characteristics. This requires observing users doing their normal tasks, studying the nature of those tasks, and then involving users in the design process.

> 2. *Empirical measurement.* Early in the development, the reactions and performance of intended users to printed scenarios [...] are observed and measured. Later on, users interact with

simulations and prototypes and their performance and reactions are observed, recorded, and analyzed.

3. *Iterative design.* When problems are found in user testing, they are fixed and then more tests and observations are carried out to see the effects of the fixes. This means that design and development is iterative, with cycles of 'design, test, measure and redesign' being repeated as often as necessary.[1]

Even though instrumental aspects of optimization dominate commercial product design as well as the so-called "conceptual models" (based on the idea of a person conversing with a system where the system acts as a dialogue partner), it is noteworthy that the *Interaction Design* handbook distinguishes between objective usability goals and more complex, subjective user experience goals. The latter pertain to issues of educational and aesthetic experience, fun, or pleasure. Here the lines between business, entertainment, and art become more blurred, even as computer science literature generally never addresses user experience design in interactive installations. Again, whereas cognitive science informs the design process from conceptual models to physical design, say in the case of cellular phones, understanding users who carry out tasks with mobile phones may not prove helpful for an evaluation of what constitutes successful or unsuccessful user behavior in an art installation. We also need to separate such user models from the performative dimensions of interactive art, which is staged *for* an audience and does not require the audience to become active. An interactive dance or music piece performed for a spectating audience may involve similar interface designs in its programmed environment, but its sensors or motion tracking devices are only there for the expert performers who have trained and rehearsed with them.

In the following, I discuss examples of performative installations designed explicitly for the experience of the visitor, i.e., they depend on the presence of the visitor inside the system. I begin with a brief overview of the conceptual field of interactive installation and the circumstances which motivate designers to treat the development of such work as a sequence of prototypes opened up for "testing." It will help to outline a spectrum of aesthetic, critical, and sociological theses, which respond to the particular principles of collaborative installation design. Following Roy Ascott's suggestion, one needs to consider these principles (e.g., art as processual system, the activation of feedback loops, the negotiation of behavior contingent on feedback) as a larger phenomenon in today's digital cultures. Interactive, systematic processes of cybernetic art, Ascott proposed already back in the 1960s, can be seen as interconnected components in the larger system of feedback loops that constitute culture. The integration of cybernetics and telecommunicational networks into aesthetics therefore suggests that art, science, and society are interconnected systems of feedback loops.[2]

Such an understanding of digital installations opens up narrow aesthetic notions of the artwork to larger sociological theories of interactive behavior, communicative situations, and the cultural production of meaning as the result of information exchanges. Some writers consider such artwork as belonging to a history of science and technology rather than to an exclusively aesthetic realm, having moved well beyond early computer art of the kind exhibited in *Cybernetic Serendipity* (1968) to various areas of research in neurobiology, the cognitive sciences, communication studies, and social anthropology.[3]

From the Theatre to the Transmedial Laboratory

Theorizing user testing and the social aesthetics of interacting indicates the changed conditions under which such work is created. Designing interactive installations differs from creating a piece to be performed on the stage or shown in a gallery as the audience behavior has to be taken into account. The notion of "user testing" is still unfamiliar, even though there is a time-honored tradition in the theatre to present new work to "preview" audiences (sneak previews are also known in the film industry, but the movies have already been completed and what is shown is the final cut, to test audience reactions). Yet previews are more of a warm up for the final premiere presentation, allowing director and actors some small changes or finishing touches in a production, which is practically completed after months of rehearsal (as far as dramaturgy, scenic, sound, lighting, and costume design, or acting choices and role interpretation are concerned).

However, there are forms of experimental performance art that use intermedial strategies and flexible dramaturgies that can be adapted to particular situations or even need to be adapted in order to effectively include the social and political matrix surrounding the action. They originate from the historical avant-garde, the Happenings, environmental and participatory theatre of the 60s, and the politicized activist performances that utilize various modes of intervention into public space. These practices were theorized by the Situationists or by theatre pedagogues such as Boal or Freire who believed in performance as social transformation, which, by necessity, implicates the audience. Such adaptive performances are relevant to our discussion here since they often explicitly "stage" an anti-illusionist encounter with the audience. They highlight playful or provocative demands of participation and instruction for the audience which reflect on issues of control, surveillance, privacy, or the very concept of "direction" involving processes of selection, arrangement and exclusion.[4]

Furthermore, in the history of performance theory the theatricalized real "encounter" signals the shift from aesthetic contemplation of the object to an aesthetics of experience locating the essential affect of a work in the transformation of a situation and the perceptional/emotional experience of the recipient, also pointing beyond the ancient notion of catharsis in Greek tragedy. What it implies is an interactional scenario of exchange in which the audience is no longer the passive receiver and, ultimately, no single authorship is attributable since the encounter depends on dialogical processes of interaction. The current production model of transmedial performance process is the laboratory: it links software writing (alpha and beta versions) and scientific development with performance insofar as the interactive environment to be produced follows principles of complex systems sciences aiming at emerging behaviors in the self-organization of parts and wholes and their relationships in such a system. The interactive behavior of the user is included in the construct, and the latter therefore presupposes a dynamic software configuration capable of simulating a "living system."

Interactivity, according to such a basic understanding of a complex system, implies the coupling or reorganization of particles or agents in a system. The agents exchange information which activates new information, and new patterns or aggregates evolve which display certain characteristics common to all complex systems (adaptation, mutation, replication, expansion, etc.). Christa Sommerer and Laurent Mignonneau, who are well known for their interactive computer installations which invite users to interact with a-life creatures (e.g., *A-Volve*, 1994; *Life Spacies*, 1999; *The Living Room*, 2001), have described their process of "emergent design" on numerous occasions, suggesting that even if there is no exact definition of what a complex system is, there is agreement among scientists that when a set of evolving autonomous agents interacts, the resulting global system displays emergent collective properties, evolution, and critical behavior with common characteristics. The idea of emergence has attracted artistic attention precisely because new global patterns of properties have been observed which seemed unpredictable and non-deducible from the pre-existing components.[5]

Dampf Lab

The production model examined here is the DAMPF Lab. Dance and Media Performance Fusions (DAMPF) was conceived as an interdisciplinary initiative supported by a partnership involving tanzperformance köln, the ars electronica Futurelab Linz, V2_Lab Rotterdam, and the Animax Multimedia Theater Bonn. This European partnership facilitated a series of ongoing events in 2003–2004 within the framework of two complementary strands: 1) co-productions and 2) research labs. The co-productions were aimed at the nurturing and realization of specific art works that integrate interactive computer technologies with performing arts practices. One project involved collaboration (*Rebound's Lab*) between choreographer François Raffinot, percussionist Roland Auzet, and the programmers Yan Philippe, Sven Mann, Niels Elburg, and Bernd Bleßmann. A second project was led by composer/director Klaus Obermaier collaboratimg with programmer Christopher Lindinger and the ars electronica Futurelab to investigate the effective implementation of interactive technologies in the context of a stage performance (*Apparition*). The third was led by choreographer Angelika Oei collaborating with the V2_Lab on the creation of a series of prototypes heading toward the production of a large scale interactive media installation (*Kurort*).

A research component for DAMPF was organized by Scott deLahunta, assembling a team of practitioners and scientists to help generate a range of diverse and shareable outcomes to include: drawing questions from and in turn supporting the creative work of the co-productions; the development of reusable technology solutions (found in extant or newly developed hardware and software); and the devising of unique dramaturgical and user testing approaches to the artistic process. In addition, the research labs aimed at disseminating documentation and writings that can contribute to conceptual, theoretical, and educational approaches to this area of work (<http://dampf.v2.nl>).

Three research labs took place over a period of months, the first in the context of the ars electronica Pixelspace conference 2003 in Linz. Pixelspace focused on the relation between the programmable (as different from the navigable) interface and interactive physical environments. It offered several DAMPF related research lines to be developed within this theme; e.g., connections between code and choreographic processes, complex perceptive/receptive modes, generative performing systems, etc. In the second lab, held at the Animax Multimedia Theater in Bonn, Raffinot performed on the intelligent stage of the Animax. The third lab was held at V2 in Rotterdam in early 2004. A show of resulting artistic prototypes took place in the context of the DAMPF Festival (June–July 2004) created by tanzperformance köln.

Programmable Interactivity

Besides the computer science approach to interaction design, the conceptual aspects of live art/performance and interactivity for a theory of "interacting" inhabit a wider context of practices. For a critical understanding of the contemporary nexus between participatory performance and technology, it is important to define the parameters for the aesthetic and social construction of multimedia work promoted as "interactive" or "networked" especially at a time when the academies begin to offer courses in "digital theatre" based on design concepts generally derived from gaming, 3-D animation, and VR design. Such design concepts are somewhat removed from the performing arts. But the general shift toward computational imaging and simulation, as we also see it in artificial life research, the biological sciences, archaeology, and the computer-generated models of contemporary architects (FOA, Diller + Scofidio, Frank Gehry, Peter Eisenman, Greg Lynn, NOX, etc.) is surely irreversible.

Not surprisingly, artists and programmers therefore work in laboratories in order to develop prototypes of the programmed environment that will eventually become the sensory architecture for the users. This prototyping is a form of system design, using the process from conceptual model to physical design. The interfaces in this architecture, whether they involve screens and keyboards, mouse, joystick, or magic wand, microphones, wireless sensors, or tracking cameras, need to be tested for functionality in order to allow for the development of the desired effect. Testing for functionality and for aesthetic effect may overlap by necessity. I will come to back to the question whether "aesthetic testing" is in fact possible under laboratory conditions rather than in "the field," and whether it is useful to distinguish different levels in the design process which may require specific testing methodologies in order to determine accuracy of functionality and a variable range of "user satisfaction." Speaking to industry professionals, interaction designer Renn Scott (who works for a Toronto firm specializing in mobile telecommunications devices) confirmed that different prototyping cultures are emerging in corporate organizations. Her task is that of a "user experience architect," and her observations and test analyses contribute to the constant refinements made in the product design process.

The process is thus inherently dependent on the user's real and imaginary relationship to the form and appearance of a device, in addition to functional use, which in our case creates a difficult paradox, since on the one hand interactive art must rely on hardware, software, and advances in engineering, while on the other hand any art form which does not liberate itself from its carrier, the technological parameters and their instrumental aesthetics, risks being judged in instrumental terms and falling into decay. Decay is the necessary aging and cultural devaluation of a carrier as we have seen it throughout the history of technological features which end up (at best) as sentimental objects in science museums or are simply forgotten in the course of constant upgrading. Emergent technologies of interactive design thus belong to industrial culture and its inevitable cycles of decay and redundancy. This throws a shadow on aesthetic and conceptual presumptions, if programmable interactivity indeed can also be read as a scientific communications project or database project which banks its conditions of artistic effectivity on, say, a sociological or psychological method of operation. The end-user of artworks is probably not interested in interfaces that malfunction or do not withstand the test of time. In a revealingly sarcastic report on his visit to the 1992 Melbourne Experimenta, Warren Burt points out numerous glitches, practical problems, and perceptual dilemmas in the way in which many of the programmed art environments bogged audiences (and gallery staff) down as they tried to figure out how each work "worked," how it structured the time/duration of interaction, or why a piece like Bill Seaman's *The Watch Detail* might have been very effective, "but like a computer game, you had to be willing to spend considerable time learning how it worked to get the maximum pleasure out of it. I wondered about the seeming contradiction of placing a single-user intensive interactive piece like this into a multi-user public space such as an art gallery, though. Maybe we need to develop the art world equivalent of the video-game arcade, where one can engage with a whole series of interactive electronic environments without being surrounded by the contradictions of the gallery."[6]

The elevation of the "laboratory" in current discourse on performance and new media reveals another risk. A hundred years after Duchamp, it seeks to redefine again the aesthetic criteria for, in this case, not a found object but coding, the speculative research and anticipatory design of a (data)space which may or may not also be a perceptible aesthetic product yet announces itself as art. Within the conceptual currents of a history of art that has recently embraced performance, interactive art inherently states itself as performative action, locating its aesthetic operation in the provisions for social interaction as such, for emotional and sensual communication between persons or, in the case of *Kurort*, for emotional and sensual communication between persons and "system." *Kurort* (in German) means health spa.

Interactive art and networked performance, two areas of computer-mediated production that are most relevant to this expanded concept, often overlap but are not equivalent. Translocal interaction through multi-user online performances and games, described by Sher Doruff as "collaborative culture," indicate the deployment of an aesthetic of playfulness. Pragmatically, it entails using webcams, software, game engines, and databases for creative cross-media synthesis, with the goal of developing interactive, dynamic artworks in which such databases and cooperative multimedia software carry an active role in the creation of play.[7]

Programmability and immediate playful communication (between users) are at opposite ends of the interaction design spectrum. From the point of view of the interaction designer, a precise set of usability and user experience goals initiates the prototyping to assess effectiveness. But even a well-known design principle such as constraints (determining ways of restricting the kind of user interaction that is possible at a given moment), classified by D. Norman into the categories of "physical," "logical," and "cultural" constraints, may not be effective for time-based installations designed for the art world in which reception is highly contingent on context and in which it might be better to exceed users' expectations than to fall below them.[8] It could also be ineffective for Doruff's players who might prefer inconsistency over logical consistency and a non-commonsensical attitude toward actions and the effects they trigger. If one is concerned with effectivity, it stands to reason that designers would want to offer training and hands-on demonstrations on how to use the (prerelease) system: user testing of alpha and beta versions of a new work thus becomes very time-consuming since it involves the organization, management, and control of user involvement and problem solving ("frequently asked questions").

The spectrum widens. It is often noted that computer scientists and artists don't necessarily speak the same language or understand their work on a common aesthetic and technical ground. There is also no reason to assume that artistic visions and programmability (with code and software applications) can find solutions that satisfy engineers and artists equally. However, the transcultural development of interactive genres in the current context of globalization, and the integration of interactive tools into theatre, dance, and music production, suggests that we look at the historical conditions for the current use of interactive design processes. A focus on design implicates both aesthetic-political and technical questions regarding the contingencies of the performing body in its coupling with technological systems. It allows us to formulate new criteria of interacting which offer alternatives to representational theatre and to the dominance of the image in contemporary media performance. In particular, such alternatives concern the role of kinetics, synaesthesia, and behavioral play in transmissions. Playing with artificial creatures or remote sensing in distributed, virtual spaces (multiple rooms, the Internet) implies new phenomena of proprioception and feedback in displaced actions. Such alternatives imply low constraints, low viscosity. To put it differently, if the system is designed with high constraints, it will require extra work from the player.

Interaction Beyond Spectacle

The notion of interactivity—connecting bodies to digital interfaces—gains its aesthetic sense if we read it in the context of design processes, which build an extended nervous system with high variables. In artistic contexts, a theory of interacting has peculiar consequences for interaction design, if I am looking at the "nervous system" from a dancer's point of view, for example, who wants to move in it not based on choreographic principles of constraints but on low-viscosity principles of free improvisation and kinetic exuberance. Interactivity points to a new understanding of environments of relations and a relational aesthetics based on interhuman exchange or physical interaction as well as a new technological kinaesthetics. Designing digital interfaces thus means organizing a sensory and intelligent space for communicative acts that are inherently changeable and unpredictable. The space is not "set" for a fixed task, but programmed for potential interactions in which partners behave within a network of relays and responses, and in which media generate perceptions of reality. Interaction thus involves the whole environment. Partnering maps the "world" through the continuous biofeedback it receives via direct sensory stimuli, which are also technically mediated.

In terms of compositional operation and outcome, interactive art is predicated on process. Process as interactive play or playful ritual can be associated with a wide spectrum of behaviors in social, pedagogical, therapeutic, gaming, and sports contexts as, for example, in the activities of on-line game players participating in gaming worlds where numerous people playing roles make up the plot in the process, trading and chatting, joining or building separate clans, adding to the environment or altering it, while the software of the game engine provides the parameters of play. Interactivity here means tinkering and community building. The traditional notion of composition no longer applies. Rather, programming resembles a kind of continuous post-production of recording data, as the interactive system uses input from the tools of connection to manipulate and process the output. What I described for interactive dance in the previous chapters is explored today in the gaming world, with EyeToy and PlayStation programs providing a dynamic environment for physical interaction. The emphasis has shifted entirely from the object of representation to the emergent situation or playground/playstation, and the materialization of technology, itself. Interactive real-time computing in installations relocates "process" in the physical-emotional involvement of the user. It alters all conventional distinctions between "artwork" and "observer," which is not the case in interactivity staged for an audience, as in Obermaier's *Apparition*. His aesthetic is still indebted to the notion of spectacle, even though he argues that he would like his audiences to enjoy the interactive play between dancer and system and not just the aesthetic appearance of the performance.

The proscenium is the dilemma, as long as theatre practitioners remain committed to the presentational staging of multimedia works for the consumption and aesthetic contemplation of the audience. It is an unresolved question how audiences will behave, and understand the theatricalization of a social-communicative space, once intervention into the performance is expected and becomes conventional. At this point, we can observe how interactivity is explored either on stage, or how it is explored ostensibly without a stage.

The Interactors

According to Erving Goffman and other social anthropologists who have studied social behavior, ritualized actions, and gestures, the "players" become agents in a social scenario in which behavioral action-patterns are available to be used and—on occasion—be re-interpreted and altered.[9] Specific cultural contexts influence the values and beliefs that determine the behavioral patterns. After Marshall McLuhan's media theories, such physical and psychic behavioral role-playing has been examined in relation to media and how media, as extensions of human behavior, affect our environment and our interactions. Goffman's ideas of "interaction rituals" and face-to-face behavior—especially his fascinating analysis of the extraordinary repertoire of maneuvers humans employ in social encounters to "save face"—deserve to be recuperated for a methodological examination of the kinds of behavioral patterns observed in audiences' interaction with programmed environments. One could argue that an interactive installation inevitably sets up both a social-interactive and a theatricalized context, since the visitor who enters an installation, marked as an artwork, enters an extraordinary space outside of the everyday context, and she will to some extent behave according to the rules of heightened self-consciousness that apply in aesthetic contexts. The particular venue for such work (gallery, museum, theatre, club, etc.) will undoubtedly influence the reception behavior, even if the installation seeks to suppress the aesthetic and emphasize the social or technological context. Of course there might be strategies to create the illusion that one has entered a particular space, which is not perceived aesthetically (a playground, a chill-out room, a library, a bathroom). Another important consideration in such installations is the element of time, i.e., the temporal dimension of such work and the durational aspect of the encounter. The visitor enters into the "time" of the interactive work, and many intermedia installations today use the loop and hyper slow motion as structural elements of filmic or sonic textures. Becoming immersed in different (and self-repeating) flows at the same time, encountering different kinds of simultaneous interfaces, generates an increasingly complex interactive environment filled with streams of material and immaterial data. The user needs to create an awareness of where she is and what she can do, what might be expected of her, how she will relate to the potentially infinite duration of the loop form (cf. Bill Viola's *The Passions* or Douglas Gordon's *Psycho*) or to potential changes her behavior might cause in the sequencing.

This inevitably creates complicated psychological reactions, since understanding the world, in this case, does not simply mean understanding what digital databases or sensors can or cannot do. The environment will entice the visitor to explore it in certain ways or it may alienate, frustrate, amuse, titillate, undermine, distract, or bore the visitor, along with innumerable other possible reactions we can think of. From the point of view of the interactor, there will be choices that are induced, there will be expectations that are deduced from the way the environment reacts to or sensorily and intellectually affects the visitor. The user may act automatically and intuitively, following already formed and learned behavioral patterns, or she may act like an explorer or as someone who enjoys playing with (tampering with) the interfaces, perhaps using them against their "intended" function. Other users may be inexperienced, unfamiliar with such interactive installations and unsure about the degree to which their active participation is required, too self-conscious or shy, or too embarrassed. One can only speculate to what degree such installations have a therapeutic dimension built in, since as a social space, especially if there are groups of people engaging at the same time with the interactive environment, the behaviors will inevitably become theatrical to the extent that they mirror public and private gestures, codes, expressions, conduct, emotions, skills, intentional actions, and unanticipated responses. If numerous people are inside an installation, there will inevitably be some who are more active and boisterous than others. Some will play and others will become observers, and these roles of course are interchangeable.

Lindinger, working on the design for *Apparition*, suggested the example of game design's use of different levels that seek to hook the user to become familiar with the game environment. This model may not be equally appropriate for artistic purposes, but in game design the programmer generally follows the logic of three levels: 1) the attraction level, allowing the user to become interested and slowly comfortable with the environment and the rules; 2) the engagement level, which draws the user into the game and allows quicker and more competent actions; 3) the experience level, involving increasing complexity to sustain curiosity, energy, and excitement with the player. This model is built like a pyramid. It challenges the designer to start with a very modest complexity that can be progressively enhanced to achieve higher levels.[10] The task for interactive installations, thus, could be to find the initial "attractor" or hook which makes the visitor curious and involved enough to want to progress to more complex levels of interaction. The "user experience architecture" thus intrinsically harbors a learning curve.

The Expert Performer as Interactor

Obermaier's artistic vision for *Apparition* is a departure from his previous work, which extensively integrated digital video projection into the choreography but was not interactive and relied instead on a precise dramaturgy, prerecorded film and exact cuing for the dancers. In *D.A.V.E.*, the dancer moves between back-screen projections and front projection onto her own body: the digital images and animations are mapped very precisely on top of the body, connecting the physical presence of dancer into the projection. The same approach was used for *Vivisector*, except that in this piece there was no back screen and no other light source except the video projector. The dance was visible only through the light of body-projection, working with very real bodies but streaming, so to speak, the video into the body. The performances have a very strong osmotic and anamorphic quality, and in this sense they play of course with theatrical and filmic illusionism (the two-dimensional surface oscillating with the three-dimensional bodies of the dancers). These dance works are spectacular, literally, and there are some extraordinary sequences of projections of (images of) stomachs on real stomachs, gender disturbances, virtual images on real bodies, which confuse our perception of space and time, especially as Obermaier manipulates the time code of video to accelerate the speed of images, reverse the flow, or insert quick animations and numerous jump cuts to disrupt the linearity of the image movement. Physical and image movement are in perpetual conflict. Obermaier's dancers interact with the digital video system in a highly precise manner; their choreography is fixed, it is itself a precise system, and the dancer follows the projection script without feeding back to it.[11]

Obermaier's goal for *Apparition* is to work with Lindinger on the design of a new interactive stage-work, extending further his aesthetics of the mutual penetration of body and digital media but giving the performers the freedom to improvise and play with the system in real-time. The focus is less on precise image superimpositions than on the physical possibilities of movement feeding into the "physical movement possibilities" of computing, exploring physical modeling of the computer, as well as expressive behavior and personality interrelating with expressionist graphic projections (models generated in real-time) which will be seen on a screen behind or above the dancers. Obermaier and Lindinger are also interested in using multiple projections with the EyesWeb interface, so that some rendering can happen on the screen, while other real-time images are mapped onto these images until no edges remain. Working on design problems and the first protoype, they ask themselves how much one can get out of the human body (which data), and how one can integrate these data captured from a camera which stands in the same position (frontally) as the projector. The design involves a series of parameters, and the research focuses on the correlation of data to the aesthetic vision of apparitional bodies.

During a discussion of these plans in Rotterdam, Obermaier repeatedly pointed out that he prefers to focus first on simple outlines, needed for masking, and that the pure physical motions are the basics for him, before beginning to hang the goals higher and develop interfaces for gesture recognition and more complex and subtle tracking choices (from multiple angles). Both Obermaier and Lindinger also agreed that all the key questions in the development of the work involve both levels, the technical and the content, always at the same time. Obermaier's choreographic aesthetic is visual, and when Anne Nigten (director of V2) asked him whether technology always coincides with aesthetic questions, he admitted that he finds it difficult to speak about user testing before knowing if his artistic vision can be satisfied. "Usually I work alone, in this case I depend on programmers, and as a team we need to know how far we can go. Our strategy is to define an achievable goal. In the new work, the dancers have to be in a dialogue with the responsive environment, and the audience will have to perceive the difference, namely that the dancers are not restricted and are not following a prescribed choreography."

What is often missing in design discussions is the point of view of the performer, so rarely articulated in the available literature on interactive performance created by a steadily growing number of artists, including Troika Ranch, Pablo Ventura Dance Company, Company in Space, half/ angel, Dumb Show, Wayne McGregor, Emio Greco, Sarah Rubidge, Anna Ventura, Isabelle Choinière, Christian Ziegler, Nik Haffner, Susan Kozel,

Gretchen Schiller, kondition pluriel, Lisa Naugle, Carol Brown, Ariella Vidach, Sonia Cillari, Kinodance Company, and others.[12] Dawn Stoppiello, in a recent essay written with her Troika Ranch partner Mark Coniglio, speaks eloquently about the slow learning process she underwent, adapting to wearing flexible plastic sensors attached to the joints of her body and a smaller transmitter box that allowed less restricted, more fluid movements: "On a technical level, we wanted my gestures to control the musical score, the playback of images from a laser disc, the movement of a robotic video projector, and the theatrical lighting for the piece. We realized that this was ambitious, but we wanted to see how far we could go. We wanted to find out how much media one performer could play … During the process of creating and rehearsing *In Plane*, I became acutely aware how information would flow back in the other direction. I would see the video move in response to my gestural control, and my dancing would be influenced by my playing…. Each day felt a bit like my first dance class, overwhelming because I was not yet familiar enough with the instrument to keep track of all of its parts. But perhaps the most important experience for us both came late in the creation process, when the elements had begun to coalesce." She argues that eventually she began to feel as if the video images were not an external object (to which she was linked by some interface) but seemed like "a hand or a torso or some other part of my body. The medium wasn't separate from me any longer." Stoppiello speaks of "entwinement" with the projected images; they become like phantom limbs.[13]

Addressing such entwinement as kinetic, temporal, spatio-architectural, and emotional performance experience means shifting the interpretive emphasis away from choreography and representation to the dynamics of intermediality and interconnection, to an immersive imagination or unconscious. Moving bodies become hyperextensive and hyperintensive. This notion, in my mind, is indebted to the plastic sculptural process that artists have explored—a plastic process of designing fluid space through movement that incorporates projected space. The plasticity of the mind is also an important concept now gaining attention in neurobiology. Design plasticity and soft constructivism, at the same time, are the new key words in contemporary architecture. Linking software and performance in this sense, aesthetically speaking, means positing a *transformative space*, allowing for the integration of nervous or sensitive media presences, just as Rokeby had imagined when he wrote the "Very Nervous System" software.

The relational performance architecture involving the performer becomes a laboratory for technical apprehension and new techniques, which means that a performer learns new behaviors and how to interact with virtual image-spaces that may bear no resemblance to familiar physical (self)images in the mirror. Furthermore, Bodo Lensch (director of ANIMAX Theater) pointed out that Raffinot danced on a floor that had multiple low-resonance speakers built into it, while being surrounded by a twenty-eight-channel sound system affording the spatial dislocation of sound and highly complex manipulations of acoustico-dramatic events. The sound diffusion allows playing with the effects of virtual space and its narrative and emotional implications for the dancer's psychogeography. Performers, composers, and designers interpret the relational architecture of interactive systems in many different ways, depending on a work's emphasis on nonlinearity, gesture-to-music synthesis, gesture-to-video synthesis, or depending on the dancer's dialogue with moving images and sonic geographies. The behavioral literacy in such systems cannot necessarily be expected from a non-expert "user," and thus the design of an emergent environment that can "learn" from the unsuspecting visitor presents a considerable challenge. However, Maturana and Varela's theories of cognition precisely posit all behavioral organisms of life as *processes of learning* involved in the self-generation and self-perpetuation of living systems.

User Test

Many of these questions about behavior were raised before and after each of the invited guests visited the prototype of *Kurort* installed at the V2 Institute in Rotterdam. The creative team, Angelika Oei, René Verouden, Erik Kemperman, and Stock, had shown earlier versions in Glasgow and at the Banff Center. Inviting visitors to the third prototype was motivated by the idea that continuous testing of *Kurort*'s open-scripted environment was necessary for the development of the artificial intelligence engineering, providing real-time analysis and comparison (using statistical analysis techniques) for the representation of the system's emotions, thus allowing for the refinement of the algorithms which make decisions influenced by these emotions. These decisions are then mapped onto actions by the system toward the visitor. Since the testing of iterative design is barely developed in the artistic field, the creative team looked for feedback. Can more effective methods of "testing" participants in interactive installations be derived from other areas such as the product design field? Or maybe from dramaturgical approaches adapted from the world of theatre? How can sociologists and psychologists contribute useful ideas to more effective artistic development processes?

The DAMPF Lab invited input from three scientists from the fields of psychology, sociology, and communications studies. Their input included presentations of their research activity to provide a context for the art and science interfaces. Gerd Ruebenstrunk spoke about emotional computing and gave an overview of its possibilities in the content industry. Johan de Heer addressed cross-modal interactions, attentive environments, and usability testing with some references to participatory design. Loet Leydesdorff sketched his theories of interhuman communication systems, knowledge production, observed and expected communication. In a reader prepared by deLahunta, there were some pages on "participatory design" (<http://www.cpsr.org/program/work-place/PD.html>), an essay by David Mamet on directing film and the viewer's attention to story/narrative, and articles from the Noah Wardrip-Fruin and Nick Montfort's *New Media Reader* on historically important materials like Myron Krueger's original essay (1977) on responsive environments.

In wide-ranging discussions we compared performance with interface-design and the scientific ideas sketched by Ruebenstrunk, de Heer, and Leydesdorff. We tried to delineate methodological approaches to "user testing" before we had actually seen the prototype of *Kurort* or spoken with the programmers to find out what they themselves were expecting to observe during our tests. But we lacked an initial framework of requirements and a clearly articulated set of data-gathering techniques (e.g., on-site observation, interviews, questionnaires, focus groups, procedures and rules, etc.). This led to some confusion since interpretation of the prototype was not based on a specific task analysis. After each of us had experienced the prototype (for a relatively short twenty minutes), we met again on the following day to give feedback to the design team. Most of the invited users approached the installation with an expectation that all dimensions of the prototype— technical, aesthetic-artistic, psychological, sociological—would be experienceable to some extent. The feedback session showed that most of us had responses to the technical and psychological dimension of *Kurort* but hestitated giving an aesthetic judgement other than allowing that we could imagine the work's potential as a *mise-en-scène*.

One reason for this was the emplacement of the *Kurort* prototype in the unaltered office space of the V2 building—Oei and Verouden had not chosen, at this point, or were not given the opportunity to build a specific environment. The work title suggests a health spa, which commonly provides the visitor with physical/mental relaxation and recuperation in a sensual, healing ambience. Here the architecture of the work existed only as rudimentary interface stations (monitors, screens, keyboard, mouse, microphone, desks, and a few objects such as paper, broom, chocolate). Curiously, the non-tech (or placebo) objects attracted more attention, but there was no ambience or atmosphere, and no *inszenierter Raum* in the sense in which, for example, Ilya Kabakov defines various aspects of a "doubled," "open," or "total installation," or in the sense in which other aesthetic characteristics of site-specific, kinematographic, or spatial design could be assessed.[14] The laboratory set looked detached from any physical design vision. The withholding of aesthetic responses among the users was also mingled with a certain frustration in regard to the simplicity of the present interface structure and especially the apparent lack of the system's responsiveness. It was generally noted that the system's voice (as the main "attractor") was commanding and director-like rather than inviting or seductive. Regarding the banality of the office environment, we found out that already at an earlier stage of the prototype Oei and Verouden deliberately had chosen an everyday prosaic space, using the banal as a tactic in their effort to work with social behavior as a material.

Following Anne Nigten's suggestion, we sketched a list of criteria or "keywords":

–design of environment, effects of the setting
–states of the environment
–evaluating/assessing the aspects of being directed or left free
–narrative content
–coherence, clarity
–simplicity/complexity
–aesthetic aspects
–social aspects
–duration, and involvement in the design experience
–dramatic aspects, choreographic aspects
–interaction levels, learning curve

–(three levels of testing)—attraction, engagement, experience
–modalities (sensory experiences) related to specific media
–mapping of information
–feedback of the system
–emotional aspects, believability (person, character)
–levels of control, agency in the environment
–how the ecosystem touches you
–art as communication (expression): has the artist been able
    to code something that is beyond the personal relation
    (beyond the contingent)
–anticipation (anticipatory/reactionary system)
–surprises, disturbance (can the system anticipate the state of
    observer)
–astonishment (aura and kitsch)
–metastablilization
–setting, situatedness (context)
–kinaesthetic stimuli for senses
–when (if) does emotional affect happen

Every user responded to these keywords and articulated their experience, actions, and sensations. It soon became obvious that many of us were telling stories of our qualitative impressions, emotional responses, and concerns about the missing sensual, aesthetic aspects. The software engineers Kemperman and Stock were more concerned with quantitative data. They had monitored how long someone stayed with a particular interface and what the amount of input data was. They were interested in functionality, whether the sensor did what it was supposed to do, and whether the system could observe a particular user, store this information and feed it back into the system as it evolved. Basically, the programmers observed what they had designed as a communication system: a circuit between communicator (the system they named "Lizzie"), recipient communicator and systemic observer. Oei then addressed many of her conceptual queries, elaborating her research on neural networks, cognitive and emotional response behavior within self-organizing systems. Perhaps not surprisingly, she tended to anthropomorphize the "Lizzie" system, imagining the health spa to receive a single visitor and engaging him or her in a dialogue (with Lizzie's computer-generated female voice), a process that might reveal layers of whatever it is a person needs for her or his "health" in the imagined healing space. The "personalized" system talks and makes offers, inviting feedback and response. A conceptual decision was made from the outset: the installation would only be accessible to one visitor at a time, creating intimacy but also rendering the space more restricted, private.

Oei stated that functionality is of course not where her process ends but where it begins, where all the artistic refinements are set in motion. What is needed in the collaboration with the engineers is a language that facilitates the production process and collects the three levels we distinguished, for heuristic reasons: the level of design (programming), the design of artistic experience, the psychological level or the user's social experience. Kemperman noted the discrepancy between "crisp" (computer science) and "fuzzy" logic (art) at work in the design process, whereas Oei elaborated on her metaphoric ideas about what *Kurort* can mean as a "health spa of the mind." To summarize some of the disagreements about these levels, Leydesdorff used the example of the use of objects in interactive installations. How would an apple function in such an environment? There is a distinction between the apple as design object, letting the system learn something or validate the behavior of the user in the system, versus perceiving the apple as a cultural object with many symbolic associations. This led to a longer discussion of the role of objects as interfaces, and how people might handle objects in a system on the psychological level and with aesthetic perceptions. At this stage in the user testing, Stock and Kemperman argued, the system needs more scientific information regarding the technical design of its "learning development." A fascinating debate ensued about the role of the "trace," i.e., the "footprints" or data input left by previous users which would be encountered by subsequent users of *Kurort*. For the system, the function of the trace implies observation of user behavior and translating it back into the system. One could also think of the notion of a "trail"—a sign post into participatory design allowing the user to influence the future look of components in *Kurort*.

Nuria Font and Madeline Ritter imagined that "Lizzie" could be perceived as a character whom you visit more than once. The data traces we leave serve to build "personality" into the system and, in exchange, we would be recognized upon return. "Lizzie" could become a mirror of different human personalities and emotions, along the lines of Ruebenstrunk's and de Heer's comments on emotional computing in experimental psychology, which might follow the recognition model of emotion perception/identification/interpretation (simulation of emotion/generation of emotion/expression of emotion). In such modeling of emotion parameters, there are numerous distinguishing indicators like facial expression, voice intonation, gestures/movements, posture, pupillary expression, as well as other indicators (respiration, heart rate, temperature, muscle action, blood pressure, physiological data) for which sensors could be used.

Ruebenstrunk pointed out that emotions are always person-dependent, thus "Lizzie" would have to develop pattern recognition and also learn moving-objects detection, a technique not yet fully developed in emotional computing which generally uses static sensor devices for measurement (expression glasses, touchphone, seats, voice analysis, mouse, Ekman's FACS, neck sensors, trunk sensors, arms and legs sensors). Ruebenstrunk then explained the OCC simulation model (simulating emotions in the machine) and other models based on this method of determining emotions as valenced reactions to events, agents, or objects and how these events, agents, objects can be appraised according to an individual's goals, standards, tastes/attitudes (compound emotions). If the installation system is to communicate emotions, it becomes important to note what the human observer recognizes. For example, it has often been the case in robotic installations that observers project emotions on the behavior of little machines. We tend to narrate the world to us in terms of stories and characters.

Ruebenstrunk encouraged the *Kurort* designers to give "Lizzie" a personality by providing coherence and consistency to objects and "characters" in the installation, providing them with visible cues to support visitors in their attempt to narrate an account of a character's action. He also pointed out that some simulation models (SCREAM, Prendinger and Ishizuka) take into account social context and circumstance to measure narrative intelligence. What is most important in the framework of the psychological model is the user's reaction to machine behavior, whereas Leydesdorff, in his talk on "Autopoiesis of Interhuman Communication Systems," emphasized a more systemic approach to evolving communication patterns, following Niklas Luhmann (*Die Kunst der Gesellschaft*) and posing the interesting question of how social systems can invent new media of communication or how an anticipatory system might contain a model of itself or even entertain several competing models of itself. Different kinds of health spas for the mind. Oei responded that "Lizzie" is a system which also has the character of a therapist, yet someone with a personality which forms itself after the visitor. "She" is continuously acquiring personalities according to the users' behaviors and the expectations they bring along. Some of us questioned the system's believability. An artistic environment, which one would consider an artificial space, inspires a higher degree of self-consciousness allowing us to play (lie, tamper) with the system, which is not the same as going to a doctor's office or a health parlor. Oei suggested that this is true for "Lizzie" as well, who sometimes gets annoyed and treats the user with irony, as it happened when the voice in the installation invited me to taste the fine chocolate, only to tell me moments later that the chocolate was poisoned.

Lizzie in the Sky

At the end of the feedback session, we agreed that the installation prototype, at this stage, was ambiguous and unresolved about its internal dynamics, its negotiation between need management (if I have need for food I want someone to take care of me) and aesthetic/cultural desire (I love music), between denotation and connotation. Furthermore, the users did not notice that "Lizzie" actually learnt something from the input, since the voice that addressed the visitors mostly repeated a small set of phrase loops in different sensor areas of the space, apparently not able yet to access the larger data pool of phrases Oei had written. Visitors were invited to use a drawing program (on screen): the traces of such writing should appear on one of the projection films that can be seen when sitting on a swing. The swing interface did not work properly, nor did the users recognize the purpose of a microphone that was set up in the space to record voices (the microphone volume was turned down). Almost everyone noted that the system hardware, sound mixer, etc., were left in the open, which meant that we could see some of the Max/MSP/Jitter patches on the screens, but it was not at all clear what we were meant to do with the exposed code. I also noted an over-abundance of text (written sentences lying on the table) and text projection (video) cluttering the room, while a semantic correlation between text, music, and film projection was not yet apparent.

Kemperman insisted that there is a friction between designing an experience and designing a system that can produce the experience. Oei confirmed this assessment and accepted our critical feedback: even if the functionality of the system was ready to be tested from the point of view of the program-mers, the artistic installation did not make its content cohere. *Kurort* had not completed its formal exploitation of the medium of interactive design, it had not determined, in Luhmann's terms, its "marked space"—formal decisions, which constitute art as a social medium (produced for an ob-server) and make it aesthetically perceivable. The science-based process goes through iterations, gradually implementing the engines of content into the program, but without aesthetic form superseding the operational interface, the installation may flounder. As an unmarked space, it does not allow us to be touched on any level of intensity and qualification, through corporeal rhythm, movement, affect, energy, and empathy. A systematic approach to the physiological and psychological levels of user testing needs to take into account a measure of aesthetic responses, yet at this stage of AI software engineering, participant behavior is measured quantitatively, relying on sta-tistical calculation.

Emotional computing thus tends to operate with particular observa-tional schemata, and the *Kurort* team chose four emotional axes for the system, each ranging from a positive to a negative emotion (at their respec-tive extremes): joy-distress, hope-fear, satisfaction-"fears confirmed," relief-disappointment. "Lizzie" is basing its own emotions and decisions on the psychological data sets it learns to analyze. This is obviously a tremendously challenging goal as the learning potentially crosses over into the psycho-physiological context of synaesthesia where "recognition" of emotion refers to complex sensory processing. The cognitive engineering for *Kurort* creates a synthetic machine for the translation of sense into sensibility—a machine that approximates subjective human behavioral forms which are organi-cally based on somatosensory integration and recognition, including the integration of inhibitors. Following cerebral action from the sense organs, neuroscientists have shown that the frontal lobes of the cerebral cortex are associated with motor and inhibition functions; the neocortex facilitates in-tellectual processes connected to specific cultural behaviors. In the parietal one finds the activities associated with primary somatosensory recognition, including that of body image, body boundary, touch, proprioception, and pain.[15]

For the wider neuroscientific context into which interactive performance inserts itself, Massumi's plea to look at the different logics of affect and emotion needs to be heeded. He describes, for example, how *intensity* is "embodied in purely autonomic reactions most directly manifested in the skin—at the surface of the body, at its interface with things." The tactile dimension of *Kurort*, therefore, requires a more careful study of the various kinds of connection we make to physical design and material surface, content (via language, image, sound, visual form, sculptural materiality) and its effect on the visitor's curiosity in experiencing healing sensations. Massumi searches for a way to address the *quality of experience*: "An emotion is a subjective content, the sociolinguistic fixing of the quality of an experience which is from that point onward defined as personal. Emotion is qualified intensity, the conventional, consensual point of insertion of intensity into semantically and semiotically formed progressions, into narrativizable action-reaction circuits, into function and meaning. It is intensity owned and recognized. It is crucial to theorize the difference between affect and emotion."[16] Especially for performative installations of the kind under examination here, with tactile interfaces, images, voices, and implied physical action, an aesthetic response, which registers affective sensation (and the category of "intensity" proposed by Massumi) seems inarguably important.

Although the testing of "Lizzie" hasn't provided a conclusive model of user-centered design process, the criteria we assembled generated a very useful template, affording the design team and the researchers to reflect on method, collaborative praxis, and critical frameworks needed to identify common formal and thematic concerns. Such criteria are needed to allow sustainable interpretation of participatory art as an evolving creative practice, particularly in light of the growing diversity of contemporary digital art and its intersections with videogames. The prototype testing revealed the complex nature of user observation and the challenges that come with systematic scientific approaches to an experiment. While Massumi's philosophical emphasis on bodily sensations is closer to art theories of reception, the application of neuroscientific concepts from the computing and cognitive fields opens up criteria of measurement that are very valuable for the creative work in development, if we posit that user testing can have systematic features of research in which a hypothesis is tested and all variables are recorded.

Research experimentation with interactive systems would strive to discover new knowledge, whereas the modeling of user behavior serves to predict user performance. The evaluation of user performance is needed to improve usability design. In the latter case the operational and functional side of the prototype needs to be foregrounded, and quantitative results were precisely what the *Kurort* programmers had in mind. The system designers had worked hard to complete the software "scaffolding" for Lizzie. Now they needed to see that the system worked: it knew visitors were in the space, and it started to make calculations based on a small number of parameters that it could interpret.

The qualitative issues of user involvement, on the other hand, highlight the range of theories which inform such installations as models of social interaction where the system's "purpose" may not be clearly defined or cannot be limited to aesthetic responses alone. The differences between usability and sociability can be considerable, and artists and designers will now develop concepts with which to address complex user experience goals involving emotional responses, excitement, trust, discrete levels of participation, etc. There is a clear socio-anthropological dimension, but the concepts may also revert to dramaturgical notions derived from theatre, dance, and film, especially in regard to narrative (multilinear, nonlinear, hypertextual), performance writing, choreographic notions of rhythm, dynamics, proprioception, and sensory rather than visual cues, the use of sequence and loop, etc. Extending ethnographic observation of cultural, industrial, and scientific performance, one can revisit concepts of theatricality developed in aesthetic philosophy, art criticism and performance theory in order to describe how installations theatricalize social encounter and play, and how they exploit the ambiguities of play in non-competitive contexts (cf. Xavier Le Roy's latest conceptual work, *Project*, which examines precisely the stable/unstable conditions of rule behavior in games).

That is to say, interactive users of such installations resemble players of videogames, and game structures (challenges, levels, control methods, progress/feedback, reward, etc.) provide fascinating semantic models (quest, pursuit, play, narrative space, or other spatial typologies, multiplayer experience) for a critical reflection on performance action. Instead of criticizing interactive installations shown at museums or galleries for their lack of content, narrative complexity, and psychological depth, we may have to look at how they construct a socio-cultural space for play—"interaction ritual," to use Goffman's term—as symbolization, physical and mental interaction, and interpretation; how they redefine cultural phenomena, in other words, and how they explicitly emphasize the observer's active assistance in forming the play itself. This inevitably raises further questions about presence, levels of engagement (competition, collaboration), and responsibility witnessed in such art.

Intimate Transactivity

I conclude with a closer look at an award-winning interactive installation, *Intimate Transactions*, which not only thematizes the role of collaboration amongst the interactors but also resonates with the ecological motif discussed earlier in the chapter on the digital extension of the *site-specific*. I am particularly interested in psycho-geographical aspects of site as they seem to be evacuated by extra-spatial and extrasensorial dimensions of the digital. However, there is a dialectic between site and user, and between site and non-site (displaced, dematerialized space), which has reverberated through the major works of land artists, architects, or light artists like James Turrell who make the visitor travel to the furthest regions of some desert to experience the sublime void of their compositions. This dialectic concerns affective intensities while harboring, perhaps, the kind of therapeutic effects *Kurort* places onto the private interlocution with Lizzie, or Janet Cardiff's audio walks induce in the listener to her recordings of whispered stories. It can also incorporate references to political-philosophical issues (e.g., Mel Chin's *Revival Field*) that are just as difficult to "locate" directly.[17] British sculptor John Newling claims that art is always "site-specific" because the contextual relations of place, materials, and public reaction are always uncertain and subject to negotiation. He writes

> When an art form becomes part of a place a situation is formed. The work may not necessarily be part of the assumed context of the place but the situation that is made between the placed and the place changes our contextual view of that place. Situations are bridges by which we learn and challenge the conventions of a given place. The cognition of the placed and the place, as a situation, can challenge the etiquettes of both place and art form.[18]

Newling refers to this negotiation as a "transaction" between the artwork and its site, a condition of its coming into being. In *Intimate Transactions*, the distributed interactive installation by the Australian Transmute Collective, what is at stake are precisely the etiquettes at play between the sites of this work and the people who *participate in the situation* and thus walk on the bridge. A shared world comes into being through this walk.

But are we justified in making this transition from situated practice to interactive digital art? What is meant by "shared world"? To answer these questions, I propose that the user is "placed" into the installation, and the interface offers a form of address to enter the virtual environment or play space. The user, inevitably, is "tested" in regard to the operational system that has also been placed there. In many instances, where artists explore the deformation of representational realism, the system "replaces" the visitor by decoupling the visual markers of identity or any analogical relation to the visible body. The software meets the arbitrary behaviors of visitors who will no longer recognize themselves. What they learn to recognize, as a new etiquette of interactivity, is the exhilarating or disturbing potential of digital technology to create living abstractions, monsters, hybrid creatures, and miraculous artificial worlds (or health spas with "poisoned" chocolate). Even if directly captured from the visitor's motion or bodily data (breath, voice, pulse, temperature, etc.), the system's real-time synthesis may create fantastical molecular graphics, warps, striations, particle phantasms. At the 2005 ars electronica festival (where *Intimate Transactions* gained major exposure and was awarded the Grand Prix), such becoming of hybrid biomorphologies was celebrated as a "way of life."

Secondly, interactive performance design can "host" the user's body with all its transactional capabilities— its expenditure of energies. Through pervasive dimensions (networks, wearables), bodies provide data to touch sensors. But the technical description does not tell us much. What is more interesting is the role or quality of "gestures": how the body touches and what this touch generates. This is a crucial dimension of Transmute's work. *Intimate Transactions* produces a networked performance that continuously leaves the host, flowing away to come into touch with a whole (a-life) ecology. Bodily movement affects the virtual world and the species that live in it. What emerges here is a new composite form of human-machinic performance as the streaming media is produced by the user's physical action but affects an environment of artificial life. Keith Armstrong, Lisa O'Neill, and Guy Webster conceive of this resonance as immersive: transactions between participants make us sense our role in a wider web of relations and possibilities that connect living forms.[19] This is the philosophical aspect of the work. It extends Joseph Beuys's notion of social sculpture, Nicolas Bourriaud's relational aesthetics, and Hélio Oiticica or Lygia Clark's propositions for a "resonant body" into the digital.

If we investigate the question of the user's re-placement, Transmute's installation offers striking concepts of *bodily movement* converging with a virtual environment as well as, from an ecological point of view, concepts of the preservation and sustainability of its elusive nature. Within *Intimate Transactions*, interactive performance no longer assumes *control* of digital image and sound animation but interaction is emergent, dynamic. The mutation of media forms is interdependent. Bodily energy is the ghost in the restless relationship. In "Interactive Systems," I distinguished various types of interactive environments (sensory, immersive, networked, derived, hybrid or mixed reality environments). *Intimate Transactions* is a networked transactive environment, involving telematic performances that jointly catalyze the behaviors of creatures in a virtual ecology. The "place" of the participants becomes a transactional collectivity: fluid, transitory, ungrounded.

As a user, how did I confront the uncertainty of the situation and negotiate the *experience* of the artificial world? I will now address the physical/virtual interface and bodily experience in the installation created by Armstrong and his collaborators. Paradoxically, the "local" performance in the networked installation is a very personal one, first re-turning physical and sensory attention to my own, subjective body. I enter the space alone and am "placed" on the Bodyshelf. But the task explained to me is to walk onto a bridge: to collaborate with a remote, unknown partner via the screen-world. Physical gesture will drive the emerging digital species-avatars. In its operation, *Intimate Transactions* surprises with an interface design which is unusually thoughtful, sensual, and challenging from a synaesthetic perspective, as the Bodyshelf combines various motor-sensory, tactile, and haptic dimensions. It detects shifting balances of weight and different types of back pressure when leaning on it. The ocular focus on the mediating visual world (computer imaging) is maintained, but the transitive sensory relation to the screen is rather complex, as I operate in the virtual world through the soles of my feet, shoulders, and spine. With another participant, situated in a different physical location, I will transact with the work through peripheral surfaces of the body, not the obvious limbs such as the hands. Reclining within a new form of furniture that reacts to peripheral bodily movements, we are simultaneously surrounded by immersive soundscapes and engage flowing combinations of digital imagery (ghostly, ethereal shapes and avatars) by moving the feet or rubbing the back and shoulders against the shelf. Using the physical interface, gently swaying our bodies on the "smart" surfaces, and by working both individually and collectively—observing our avatar-species float in space, connect and disconnect—we are able to create convergences of movement which in fact influence the evolving "world" created from digital imagery. This world, however, also exists without us.

How do I experience my relationship to this world? The situation that is formed is a paradoxical one. I cannot see or know the other person with whom I am connecting. I am in a dark, closed space, while a visually projected world opens up and develops behaviors. In this intimacy, I forget entirely that my condition is distributed to another site, and that another human actor elsewhere is going through my motions. I become self-absorbed, beginning to "lean" into the interface, as I had to first learn the transactive behavior (tilting my feet, the rubbing with shoulders and spine) that moved my avatar into contact with the other avatar. Thus I explore coordinating my movements in such as way that the life forms in the virtual world emerge and merge. Only at this point can I imagine changing my orientation. This is the learning curve, a process of adaptation. The initial self-absorption is the first kinaesthetic affect of the installation. The first level of engagement is one of orientation, literally of proprioception. This auto-referential sensory processing is not directed at the outer world. As I concentrate on my sensations, I am cognitively innocent (I don't know what to do, what I am looking at) and I await "instructions" which arrive and tell me the rules of engagement. The instructions of course increase my uncertainty. I start again, stop and start again (I did the wrong footstep, the unfolding world folds back). As I slowly begin to trust the relation of movement to world, I gain confidence. My slight problem is that I get confused by the avatars (who am I—the bright one or the dimmer one? I try to catch the brighter, only to realize that I may very well be the brighter one myself). This is tricky identification: I forget which one is mine and which one may belong to another player.

The sensory intimacy with the other, far away person is, of course, purely an illusion. This is not telematic dreaming or consensual hallucination but hard work. The erotics of transactivity may lie entirely in the realm of fantasy, yet there is physical feedback, and also a certain amount of cognitive thrill once the mind recognizes the plural movement in this world. My body's perceptual relationship to this environment of movement patterns is subjected to the "digital phenomenon" of the swirling, unpredictable creatures. I am not fully aware of what I do, I don't know their rhythms and cannot place myself in the virtual world, but on an unconscious level I am rewarded. Through a pouch in front of my stomach, I sense vibrations when I am able, stumblingly, to connect my avatar-creature with other creatures. It feels as if my energy—connecting as it does with the digital world and my fel-low creatures—is radiating from the center of my body. As Lisa O'Neill's Suzuki-inspired choreographic vision for the work unfolds, such energy streams, physiologically and emotionally, from the bodily center into all spatial directions.[20]

The stomach vibrations create a sense perception of "streaming" which I have rarely experienced before except in heightened moments of telematic performance, when the sonic energies of multi-channel sound, white noise, and flickering pixels pulsate through the networked studio and resonate deep inside the bowels of my body. On the sensorial level, what resounds most strongly, however, is the motor-somatic activity in *Intimate Transactions*. The interface activates my body in a way I do not normally activate my muscles. When I step down at the end, I almost can't walk any more, my muscles are cramped, sore. How much I must have focused on some parts of my body (feet, calves, thighs, shoulders, back, neck) and not oth-ers. I enjoy this, as I enjoy muscle ache after any practice, dance or sport. But I only notice it after the fact as disequilibrium in my cramped body. The cramping could also be a psychological effect. This complex installa-tion, more explicitly than any of the interactive artworks I have seen in the past, challenges my affective sensory relationship to the constantly evolving virtual world to which I become oriented. I wasn't as fluid or experienced in its navigation as I would have liked to be. I couldn't fully perceive it. Facing the animated flows of the virtual creatures, I never fully understood how my physical behavior and emotional attitude affected their world, and how it affected me. Can one be too immersed to even realize one's body as a source of action? Following Bergson's theory of perception, how can I experience the digital media environment from within? And, if I'm affected in my body through my motor-sensory action, can I process such perception without recourse to the representational content of the media? The challenge of *Intimate Transactions* lies precisely in the uncertainty I have about the digital world even though I sense my connection to it and to the other person who is (not) there.

Digital projection is image space, after all, and not a world. It thus can-not behave as the physics of 3-D space, and the convergences of our bodied perceptual rhythms with the behavior of the digital creatures are without consequence. Yet, I could say that I moved through the image-world, with the soles of my feet and my back and that I felt it in some way, but not explicitly. I also sensed it acoustically, but again not consciously. The affectivity in this work appears necessarily subconscious. This accentuation of the physical and the virtual contradicts conventional analytical ways of interpreting which, dominated by the transference of the linguistic to the non-linguistic, make the body a secondary phenomenon and sensation redundant. In this artwork, the sensual immediacy and presence of the physical/virtual bodies, their co-evolution or adaptation in a hyperplastic media environment, are made the focus of interpretation.

Intimate Transactions is an exemplary work requiring us to reinterpret the correlation between the participant's body ("placed" in action) and the digital situation. In the terms I evoked earlier, the artificial world ("non-site") of virtual ecology is not external/preconstituted but irreducibly bound up with our (collective) movements, the transactions of energies between another's and my own body. This installation is carefully programmed, designed, and aesthetically formed for the specific use of two simultaneously interacting participants. Like *Kurort*, it underwent a long iterative design process collecting user feedback and commentaries along the way (this has been documented on DVD). The sensory interactivity in this work exceeds a representational account of the image-based virtual world, and this suggests that phenomenological investigations into the sensing body need to be revived in order to value complex transactive media environments, especially interactive performances which use sensory processing involving haptic feedback and tactile perception as primary articular impressions.

NOTES

[1] J. Preece, Y.Rogers, H. Sharp, *Interaction Design: Beyond Human-Computer Interaction,* Hoboken, NJ: John Wiley & Sons, Inc., 2002, 285. In this excellent textbook (Website: <www.ID-Book.com>), the authors lay out the different approaches to human-centered interaction design, before offering five chapters with very detailed analyses of evaluation frameworks, user and expert testing, design evaluation, even including examples of applying ethnography in design. The characteristics quoted above refer to J.D. Gould's and C.H.Lewis's "Designing for Usability" [1985].

[2] Cf. Roy Ascott, *Telematic Embrace: Visionary Theories of Art, Technology, and Consciousness,* edited by E. A. Shanken, Berkeley: University of California Press, 2003, 26–27.

[3] Cf. Stephen Wilson, *Information Arts: A Survey of Art and Research at the Intersection of Art, Science and Technology,* Cambridge: MIT Press, 2002; and Oliver Grau, ed., *Media Art Histories,* Cambridge: MIT Press, 2007.

[4] German choreographer Felix Ruckert's 1999 piece *Hautnah,* for example, required each viewer to spend time one on one with a dancer in a small tent-like space. His *Secret Service* (2002) and *Love Zoo* (2004), invited visitors to play with the dancers and engage in extensive physical contact.

[5] Cf. Christa Sommerer and Laurent Mignonneau, "A-Volve: Designing Complex Systems for Interactive Art," in *aRt&D: Artistic Research and Development,* edited by Joke Brouwer, Arjen Mulder, Anne Nigten, and Laura Martz, Rotterdam: V2_Publishing/NAi Publishers, 2005, 208–23.

[6] Warren Burt, "Installation at Experimenta: Fighting the 'So What' Factor in Electronic Art," in *Electronic Arts in Australia,* edited by N. Zurbrugg. Special issue of *Continuum: The Australian Journal of Media and Culture* 8,1 (1994): 58–69.

[7] "There is no need for visual metaphors anymore," the creators of the 1994 "Handshake" online project argued, implying that net space and data-archives "become one and the same thing: there is no need for one to be translated into the other. The information reaches the recipient as a symbol of a technological space. The space itself is information; any movement is symbolic." Quoted from Gerrit Gohlke, "Restored Revolution: The net.art project 'Handshake': Antecedent to a Critique of Instrumental Aesthetics," in *Media Revolution: Ost-West Internet,* edited by Stephen Kovats, Frankfurt: Campus Verlag, 1999, 70. For Sher Doruff's workshop on collaborative culture, see *Making Art of Databases,* edited by Joke Brouwer, Arjen Mulder, and Susan Charlton, Rotterdam: V2_ Publishing/NAI Publishers, 2003, 70–99.

[8] For Norman's categories, see *Interaction Design,* 20–23.

[9] Erving Goffman, *Interaction Ritual: Essays on Face-to-Face Behavior,* New York: Pantheon, 1967.

[10] All references regarding the user testing are to my transcript of the discussions at the Rotterdam DAMPF Lab, January 17–19, 2004, held at V2 Institute for the Unstable Media. The "soft" office and laboratory space for the V2_Lab, incidentally, was designed by Lars Spuybroek's NOX architecture firm.

[11] <http://www.exile.at>.

[12] How quickly the field of interactive dance, performance, and installation art is expanding can be surmised from the more than 140 projects submitted to the Multimedia Section of the 2004 Monaco Dance Forum (<www.monacodanceforum.com>). In 2006, there were 110 submissions from 32 countries.

[13] Dawn Stoppiello, with Mark Coniglio, "Fleshmotor," in *Women, Art, and Technology,* edited by Judy Malloy, Cambridge: MIT Press, 2003, 440–50. Coniglio, a musician/software programmer known internationally for his work with Troika Ranch, wrote two interactive programs, Interactor and Isadora, which map data input to control a variety of media outputs, e.g., sonic, video, lighting, and robotic. Troika Ranch conducts regular Live Interactive workshops to give participants the opportunity to explore the use of interactive computer technology in performance (<http://www.troikatronix.com/>).

[14] Cf. Juliane Rebentisch, *Ästhetik der Installation,* Frankfurt: Suhrkamp, 2003, 162–78. Rebentisch offers a comprehensive philosophical theory of the aesthetics of installation art, gathered under the three main leitmotifs of theatricality, intermediality, and site-specificity. In her chapter on "Raumkunst und Zeitkunst" she refers to Kabakov's definitions of "total installation" which evoke the idea of immersion. Kabakov's fully designed installations, she suggests, appear like abandoned theatre stages, houses or places where people perhaps just stepped away and could return at any minute. The visitor now is "inside this abandoned scene."

[15] F. Scott Taylor, "Synaesthesia and 'The Name of Silence' in the Work of Steven Heimbecker," in *Songs of Place,* Montréal: Oboro, 2005, 55–70. Taylor is currently completing a scientific study of the effects of telecommunications multimedia on perception.

[16] Massumi, *Parables for the Virtual,* 28.

[17] In the case of Smithson's *Spiral Jetty* (1970), the dialectic between material site (the entropic site, the Jetty's submersion under the water and exposure to the elements) and non-site (its representations or pictures in the art gallery) are particularly interesting, as Smithson's notion of the "non-site" suggests a kind of abstract mapping: the

non-site "designates" the site, while the site itself is open, unconfined, and constantly being changed. Mel Chin's *Revival Field,* in which the contaminated earth of a toxic landfill in St. Paul, Minnesota, is "reclaimed" through hyper-accumulator plants, is an artistic and a scientific project highlighting the issues of habitat devastation and environmental restoration.

[18] John Newling, *John Newling's Writings 1995–2005,* vol. 1, Warwick: SWPA Limited, 2005, 55.

[19] Transmute's evolving world of creatures symbolizes inter-species behavior, and there are interesting parallels to other contemporary experimentations which link performance and cellular biology, for example in Eduardo Kac's transgenic art and in SymbioticA's work with tissue cultures: <www.symbiotica.uwa.edu.au>.

[20] Tadashi Suzuki's training method, sometimes called "grammar of the feet," helps performers to realize unconscious patterns for movement and posture, which they will then be able to alter. Interestingly, the quality of contact of the feet with the floor, in this method, determines the quality and energy of spiritual, mental, and emotional expressiveness. The presence of the group in this training method generates a physical pervasiveness that allows participants to experience a sense of fictional space. The interactive design of Transmute's installation is meant to provoke this transindividual energy, connecting the player to the virtual world.

▼▲ DESIGN FUTURES: WEARABLES

Performance Wearables / Wearable Performance

The notion of *design*, as it was understood in fashion and fine art, film, the graphic arts, and product design, has expanded in many directions and is now infused with new developments in information and communication technology, ubiquitous computing, biotechechnology, and nanotechnology. These mediating technologies have profound effects on perceptual systems and the habituated knowledges to which we are adapting today amongst highly technological living patterns. Designing our environments, and the tools through which we communicate with them and experience ourselves in the real and virtual world, therefore must be considered to have vital cultural and political stakes. The role of fashion and clothing, although marginalized in contemporary critical theory and performance studies, cannot be overlooked as it directly relates to complex social as well as theatrical concepts of "performance." The latter are also influenced today by the impact of computer and video games on our understanding of participatory player culture and the various scripts that are followed by gamers to configure settings, characters, plots, and the modifications of avatar appearance. The fantasy worlds of games are a primary example of shared design, and in some instances (*Second Life*), all the 3-D content and appearances are entirely user-created. The sharing of fantasies is an activity particularly encapsulated in fashion.

To give attention to the "fashionable" or to performing fashion does not necessarily mean talking about fashion styles or trends. Rather, in the context of highly technological living patterns under late capitalism, and thus under what Deleuze (after Foucault) has called "societies of control," performative fashion can be linked to disciplinary power in Foucault's sense of social organization, insofar as fashion coerces the body to shape and rearrange itself in accordance with ever-shifting social expectations.[1] The skills required to adapt to such internalized expectations—including the ability to diet, apply facial cosmetics, arrange clothes, and wear ornamentation—are in the service of aesthetic innovations that continually reinvent subjectivity and body-image. Foucault's often-cited notion of the self-regulating "docile body" indicates how elements of a fashionable lifestyle, which also include the urban habits of reading fashion magazines, engaging in body-sculpting practices such as dieting, gym work-outs, cosmetic surgery, etc., are techniques for transforming the body into a commodity. One could even connect this performativity to the training standards (doping) amongst competitive athletes and the publicity standards of pop stars who embody the fetishized icons our societies like to worship and emulate. These celebrities are our avatars: we pay for the entertainment in which our role models perform. The red carpets are laid out. The transformable body becomes a training site of aesthetic innovation, a projection site or *tableau vivant* for fetishistic desires, and like our other technological accessories, it is subject to periodic upgrading. Redesigning the look of the model is to give it a new lease on life, specifically by submerging its use-value into its appearance-value. The notion of iterative design, common in prototyping of interactive products as well as interactive artworks, here echoes with strange ironies as body transformations or body prosthetics are now often critiqued within the political and ethical contexts of biotechnology.[2] Redesigning life or human enhancement no longer looks as innocent as the other spring collections on the scientific catwalk. In the artistic context of wearable performance, mobile control of transformability subverts the commodity aspect. The wearable rather points to fashion in the sense of re-fashioning, not just "controlling" surface functionality in the interface, but challenging digital transformation of the materiality of the body to provoke a new language through which discrete representations of the body can be generated and re-invented. Interface design, therefore, is contingent on many specific articulating systems.

I will discuss the collaborative "Emergent Dress" project to point to such articulations and demonstrate how the performance, media, and fashion design context intersects with computer science, engineering, and new developments in human-computer interaction design.[3] The project is also fuelled by new material technology—new fibres, fabrics, and innovative processing techniques that allow the integration of sensors or smart functionality into clothing. This introduces the category of the "wearable" into the field of performance, drawing attention to the sensorial affect as interface, while it also alters the meaning of "designing wearability" for fashion, as I am here addressing cutting-edge developments in wearable computing at the beginning of the century. Since this area is still very much experimental, there are few mature commercial products with a wide user base that could be evaluated. Artistic works deploying wearables and reaching a wider audience are equally rare.[4] This chapter therefore proposes design principles and maps the ground for a speculative description of how performance transforms design strategies for wearables, and how the wearable experience affects highly mediated performances.

The type of mediated performance which stimulated the project—interactive, telematic performance—implies the experience of being present at a location remote from one's own physical location, generally involving a camera-based Internet convergence between two or more sites. Someone experiencing telepresence would therefore be able to behave, and receive stimuli, as though at the remote site. The work requires networked audio-video convergence, with the scenes at two distant sites becoming one. The architecture of such convergences in a studio or gallery involves multiple screens and sound diffusion for the live Web streams and real-time 3-D Virtual Environments. Such an ambient, immersive environment exponentially expands what we normally comprehend as our immediate sensory environment or "kinesfield."[5] The kinesfield is extensive of the tactile experience of the garment as well. I want to suggest that such tactility can interfuse multiple telepresent bodies, making fashion an intersubjective experience. At the same time, the wearer of the wearable acts to enframe digital information, giving body to digital processes and thus to her or his own intimately and affectively experienced sensation of "wearing the digital," of becoming digital(ized).

For current theories of embodied information processing, digital performance marks a significant shift toward a tactile, haptic aesthetic, away from an ocularcentrist mode of perception to embodied affectivity. Digital performance is also theorized in terms of the disjunctions it opens up in the experience of reality, time, and digital space which no longer have an analogical basis. In the following, I examine how emergent design works with this and facilitates disjunction and continuity. First, I address the notion of wearable in movement, focusing on gesture and body movement. Secondly, I describe the prototypes of emergent design within telematic environments for performance augmented by particular fabrics materials and motion analysis as well as by gesturally nuanced computational media.

Digitized Movement

Wearable computers are devices worn on the body. The convergence between the miniaturization of microchips (nanotechnology) and the growth of wireless, ubiquitous computing emphasizes mobility. Computing devices are small enough to be carried around or integrated into clothing or the human body at all times, providing continuous access to a personal wireless network (LAN) or Internet and satellite networks. Industrial mobile devices are *prêt-à-porter,* but the "Emergent Dress" can neither be industrially mass-produced nor understood as *haute couture.* Rather, it is intended to be mobile in a very personal and creative sense, practical and informal, ready-to-wear but also elusive and precious, evolving and changeable. It is meant to have a "digital" quality.

The research context which connects digital performance with new fabrics and interactive textiles therefore requires not only new fashion content for wearable lifestyles and mobile creativity, but perhaps places the emphasis of design somewhere else entirely, namely to different qualities of "performance" addressing not functionality but character, emotions, memory, fantasy, and experiential or psychological dimensions along with a heightened kinetic awareness of bodies as intimate communicators. These qualities, once considered a domain of theatre anthropology and social science research, now intrigue product designers looking at how artifacts elicit emotions. At the same time, there is a microscopic trend among performance artists to devise very intimate transactions and exclusive one-on-one encounters with their audience.[6] The collective potential of intimate transformative ecstasy experienced in wearable fabrics (*Parangolés*) enmeshing the participants, enveloping them in carnivalesque play of spatial and social relations, was advocated by Hélio Oiticica in the 60s. Lygia Clark's sensorial masks were created in Brazil around the same time; her "relational objects" were primary artistic vehicles for her sustained exploration of the client or receptor's experience of a micro-sensorial intimacy.

More recently, Lucy Orta reinvigorated these principles of intimate architectures of cloth, devising her "collective wear" into interactive shelters and modular habitations (*Nexus Architecture*) drawing in the collaboration of local participants. Extending the lineage of sound art, kinetography (Laban), and contact improvisation, recent experiments in dance and music technology point to a stronger interrelationship between gesture analysis (biophysical data) and the design of responsive architectures for emergent behaviors. If psychoacoustics research speaks of the subjective visceral nature of experiencing sound in the body, so is "Emergent Dress" directed at the intimacy of the wearable experience. It is directed at the desire and erotic sensuality attached to the clothes we wear on our skin, the frivolous, extroverted but also secretive (even anti-aesthetic) dimensions of fashioning appearance, and the physiological processes and patterns through which the proprioceptive systems attend to the body's wearing of itself.[7] This emphasis on intimacy to some extent features a design conception opposed to Hussein Chalayan's "Remote Control Dress" collection, which like his earlier Aeroplane and Kite dresses seems preoccupied with futuristic design shapes inspired by aerodynamics, architecture, furniture, and mobility (speed and the conquest of space). The "Remote Control Dress" was meant to interact with the built environment and was created with hi-tech materials, including glass fibre and resin, with glossy panel-like shapes (front and back panels were held together with metal clips) and translucent plastics. These dresses look more like armors, façade-like exoskeletons that appeared to be protective skins for the wearer who is envisioned maneuvering through hostile habitats with a smart garment able to detect changing weather conditions or security alerts. These dresses were only shown as prototypes intended to relay information from the outside to the wearer—the wireless system was to be developed by Starlab (the same company that worked on the "T-Garden" project described in "River Beds and Gardens") but was never completed.

Crucial for our concern with close-to-the-skin technology are the affective and perceptional processes working both ways in the interaction, as the wearable here is not only a garment but also the interface. While there is indeed a noticeable tendency in the West toward an "experience economy" and a cultural privileging of intensities and (emotional) participation, the question of what is meant by "experience design" needs addressing, as the increasing use of sensor technology in our environment reveals little about *how* people do make use of "feedback from an information technology" (Baurley), how they integrate the machine intelligence emotionally and cognitively, or how such intelligence influences clothing experienced from an expressive/psychological point of view (as protection, modesty, ornamentation, articulation of desire, etc.). Linking fashion to the pleasure principle, one wonders how the interface becomes charged with elements from the catalogue of eroticism and seduction, and how a particular style of wearing it can be decoded if the "image-clothing" implies an endless number of ambiguous possibilities or private secrets not determined through its semiological structure (as myth or message). Roland Barthes's analysis of the "fashion system" points to the complexities of fashion's mobility, for example if one looks at the vestimentary system ("dress") and its variant replications of attributes of the body (sexuality, desire), as well as at the circumstantial modes of behavior ("dressing") adopted by wearers.[8]

Dressing-performance in the digital context is all about articulating such mutability and exploring subtle or frightening exaggeration. Some fashion designers, like Rei Kawakubo of Comme des Garçons, have also contradicted the idea of decorative intensities and proposed unexpected, deconstructive designs which complicate the conventional premises of congruence (measurements that follow fit, like the glove to the hand), proportion, vertical axis, and the contouring of the body's outlines. For example, in 1998 Kawakubo produced a collection of disconnecting parts; the clothes were broken up, fragmented and incomplete, sides and backs missing, left and right not matching, etc. This strategy points to a diffusion and metonymic fragmentation of units that capture the sense of the digital we experience in the interface. Similarly, the recent photographic work of Zoren Gold with fashion model/designer Minori (*Object that Dreams*) is a *tour de force* of extraordinarily surreal and fetishistic images, digitally manipulated to the extent that Minori's doll-like appearance either seems textured into the surrounding environment or mysteriously alienated from it. Critical investigations of what might be called "feedback design" and its effect on "dressing" in movement are needed, and although Barthes's fashion theory tends to privilege the "written garment" over "real clothing," his inventory of elements ("Variants of Existence") provides many insights.[9] His "variants of movement" are particularly helpful in understanding how the body animates the garment (e.g., he considers movement values such as rising, upsweeping, hanging, plunging, falling, swaying, etc.).

For wearables to become meaningful in artistic and playful social settings, the affective experience in human-computer interaction needs to go beyond simple "actuators" and those expressive interactions often referred to in terms of sensorial qualities (touch, sound, taste, smell) which are outside of the visual but whose significance is not brought home. How do we make sense in a haptic relationship to a certain material (glass, soft fabrics, leather, metal)? What is sensed? And what cognitive and aesthetic processes are engaged when, for example, a garment can measure the beat of your heart or transmit your emotional disposition toward your partner? When it hangs loose or plunges forward to "act" like a magnetic or chemical attractor, playfully dominating the partner or the voyeur, toying with excess, then withdrawing, swaying and folding? When it remembers your touch, as in Joanna Berzowska's "Memory Rich Clothing" prototypes that sense and display visible markers of events such as whispering and groping?

In our group's examination of the kinaesthetic wearable we started out with a particular interest in remote communication (telematics) and the proprioceptive relations to the virtual. We refer to this sensory relationality as "exo-processing," and "ScreenDress" (Prototype 1) was tested in performance improvisations by Helenna Ren and Nam Eun Song with a particular garment material and the motion graphics, which are digitally printed/projected onto it. The graphics also represent the continuous, infinitely changeable feedback design, in line with the fluidity of the moving shape of the body. We then focused increasingly on the dancer's immediate experience of sensors on the body, and the wearer's proprioceptive relationship to sensorimotor and internal biophysical data (heart rate, pulse, breath), analyzed and transmitted in collaborative telematic "play" with interacting partners. This sensory relationality is called "endo-processing," but the performance involves both an internal and an externalized dimension, as the dancers are pushing the data into the visual screen displays and image flows. Body, flesh, skin stretch into the screens. The different outfits of "SensorDress" (Prototype 3) drive our investigations of the subjective experience of the garment when touched and "exposed" in dance. The experience of the performer is modeled for the camera but also activates an avatar for a game environment, which playfully invites participation in the game-fantasy. The *Klüver* installation of Prototype 3 (exhibited at various festivals including the Prague Design Quadrennial 2007), the completed exhibition of all prototypes in *Suna no Onna*, and the live game *See you in Walhalla* provide the context for reflections on emergent design and the audience's empathetic relationship to the emotional character of the body-garment interface.

Emergent Dress

Our ideas on intimacy evolved from Helenna Ren's telepresence performances with partners in Arizona, Italy, and Japan over the past years

(2004–2007). She tested all of the versions of the transformable body-garment and the digitally manipulated garment-body. In the development of the new prototypes, the "corset" became our first vehicle—conceptual metaphor and material object—along with other parts and fragments of pink, yellow, and black cloth that Ren put on, assembled and disassembled in performance, and thus composed into her improvised choreography of wearing, gesturing, folding, stretching, unbinding fabrics and needles, moving and re-moving gloves, shifting elements of the garments into and out of focus, while interacting with the "physical camera" (moved in close proximity by the camera operator). In these performances, created in real-time telematic contact primarily with performers Natalie King, Keira Hart, and Joe Willie Smith in Tempe, Arizona, "characters" also emerged gradually as the dancer began to shape the information composed with the *corsetbody*. We called them "Zorro," "Houdini," and "Klüver." While Ren moved with the garment, her video image was sent to Arizona's screen environment (constructed as a garden of large hanging leaves) and projected onto the remote screens as well as onto a luscious white Victorian dress suspended from the ceiling and functioning as the centerpiece of our partners' experimentation with haptic memory.

Helen Raleigh, AJ Niehaus, and Galina Mihaleva devised the conceptual strategies with which our partners in Arizona used this memory-rich garment as a "stand-alone" sensory sculpture which could be projected upon, and then stepped inside and worn, which the Arizonan dancers did during the rehearsals shedding their other clothes and embedding themselves inside an older (historical) garment concept. One might say they inserted themselves into a kind of "habitat" that enveloped them.

The telematic performances challenge the double bind of the literal and the virtual garment. We experience the suspended dress as a receptacle, a sensory surface that functions as a mnemonic landscape and an instrument responding to touch, its built-in sensors producing a sonic text (words recorded in Joe Willie Smith's voice). The "Victorian" dress flares into temporary focus, historical images, or fragmented film stills from a natural landscape appearing on it, then all discrete traces disappear again, and now as Ren's telepresent body-image remobilizes it, distance and proximity become interwoven. John Mitchell, who directed our partner team in Arizona, suggested that such a dress is viewable from *the inside out*; its porous quality "evocative of ancient shadow plays and early cinematic devices that created viewer intimacy through subtle perceptual and sensual shifts. The resulting experience is expansive, contractive, enveloping, and yet non-enclosing."

At our end of the telepresence, it became apparent that Ren's movement itself contributed to this evocation of a living dress-sculpture or vessel. Wearing pink corset and rose-colored stretches of fabric, she used her breath to work with contractive and expansive rhythms, continuously changing the shape of her body as the tight-laced corset shifted flesh and muscles, inflating the shoulders, exaggerating the wide-narrow-wide silhouette of the female form. At the same time, the compressions and deformations of fleshy tissue were distracted by the layerings of fabric Ren whirled around herself. As the camera captured her movements and stretched the fabric into the virtual space of Arizona's suspended dress, we began to see Ren animating the distant garment: her body clothed in undergarment streamed into the latter's faint blue apparition, the outer wear in the distance. Silhouette intermingling with silhouette, real and virtual bodies compounded into an illusion of a (digitally) composited whole. These rehearsals prepared the ground for the development of the ScreenDress prototype, which elaborates the real-time compositing effect of the digital media.

ScreenDress: The Two Forms of the Garment

ScreenDress is constructed from Chromatte, a technical light-reflecting cloth for chroma key production in TV and film. This material, designed to work dynamically with a LiteRing (a camera mounted device featuring LEDs) utilizes the retro-reflective properties of its fabrication for live effects/image replacement, fusing motion graphics with onscreen performance. The *technological garment* is a real garment, the physical form of the garment, existing in the real world and in its isolated state (uncoupled from the LiteRing), is gunmetal grey. Here the focus is on the material facts of fashion, the applied aspects and technical solutions to produce an artistic result. We are concerned with the cut and the fabrication, the detailing and finishes, and the overall silhouette statement, the structure of the garment and how the body engages with the piece, i.e., how it is worn/performed and choreographed into movement. Pleats, expanding and contracting layers, seams and a modular approach to garment construction are used. Garment and movement are inseparable, in that one extends the other, becomes the other.

The moving body has an impact on the form of the design and the form of the design has an impact on the moving body.

The garment, according to Barthes's analysis of the body-garment relation, is extended as a body.[10] He explains this through his study of Erté's fashion drawings and specifically the Ertéan silhouette where the woman becomes the garment, is somehow biologically fused into the woman-garment. The body can no longer be separated from its adornment and decoration. The woman and the garment become one. ScreenDress, with the anamorphic shards of motion graphics projected onto it, is extended as a body, poetically shifting its surface of moving patterns and textures. It invents and substitutes, simultaneously masks and reveals, is animated, becomes alive and organic with multiple juxtapositions of image and color. The live "camera eye" removes us from one reality into another, one where dancers, organic tissues, and animation become fused into expressive visual statement: an indissociable mixture of body, garment, and graphics, bleeding forms, one into the other. This is a dialogue between the natural and the artificial, brought together in an intimate relationship to create a new object or artifact, the *iconic garment*. The iconic garment becomes a spectacle in its own right, a mechanism for display and experience.

Interaction with Cloth and Partial Design States

Generally, the design process begins with the design sketch and the static form. From here ideas are developed two-dimensionally in preparation for 3-D realization. However, working with the "Emergent Dress," we do not start with the design sketch or static state. Instead we choose movement narratives, introducing partial garment structures and cloth to the initial frame: inviting the performer to move with the cloth, exploring and experiencing the qualities of the cloth (in front of our eyes/the camera eye), its potential and design possibilities. We observe the movement reactions initiated by the tactile stimulus of the cloth and consider how garment form and structure might begin to emerge.

In the case of the Chromatte cloth, Song was invited to discuss with designer Michèle Danjoux how she felt about the cloth; what type of movement behaviors it began to generate; structures and scale. Song found the touch of this particular cloth somewhat harsh and aggressive, it felt hostile to her movements and unforgiving. We explored slashing of the fabric to ease the sensation of restriction and tried coiling and wrapping cut lengths of the cloth to produce rudimentary sleeves and other garment features. The designer responded to the cloth's structural dimension with pleats, creased stitched folds in the fabric, which created an even more structural surface; one that could now expand and contract, open and close with each affected move. There is a fusion of designer and dancer in this process-based methodology of iterative design.

Song experimented with different movement qualities and energies to explore how the "digital sketches"—incorporating the digital graphics into her movement consciousness and proprioception—affected her ability to frame the constant flow as time-image and image-movement. A particular screen poetics evolved, and although Song's unconscious experience cannot be verbalized here, it is apparent that she investigated the ScreenDress as an interaction instrument, a kind of membrane between the real and the projective, between herself and her other. However, the relative stiffness of the chromate material and its dull appearance in real space gained mysterious textures and luminosities in the animated screen graphics. The fabric material thus created a contradictory pleasure. Or, rather, the motion graphics behaved in a paradoxically counterintuitive manner, concealing the true nature and identity of the fabric and revealing a more organic, biological, emotional response. A confusion of sensation, control shifting from fabric to dancer and back: the experience became visibly more visceral and sensually involved as the relationships shifted in motion.

In one particular improvisation, Song decided to use her voice (to spit words out and suck them in) in a complex breathing pattern to modulate the dressing performance, to emphasize the contradictory interplay between inside-out and outside-in motion. Her movement vocabulary is a mixture of ballet-inflected soft-flowing phrases and harsher martial arts punctuations, and throughout her dance with the wearable, she carefully allowed her sensory perception to guide her. Rather than looking at the screen and the transformed digital images of herself, she performed through being touched (by the motion of the stiff chromate fabric) and through kinaesthetic sensing of the pulsating digital graphics—almost as if she could viscerally feel the digital animation. The kinaesthetic sensation of this dance is primarily proprioceptive (inner), which astonishingly becomes quite visible in the screen images of her movement. Her "dressing performance" looks entirely different from Ren's much more extroverted, sardonic, and outer-directed movement, which tends to toy with the voyeur-camera and also exaggerate both the stereotypical associations one might have with erotic gestures and the more grotesque aspects of her volatile characters.

These character studies or narratives formed the basis of constructing the digital movement composition for *Suna no Onna,* the exhibition we created from our storyboard adaptation of Hiroshi Teshigahara's 1964 film. In test rehearsals involving Ren, we explored further the impact of garment form constructed with Chromatte. Ren shifted her focus from the characteristics of the fabric to the constricting corset structure she wore (tightly laced and reinforced with spiral steels), then to the fragments of cloth that began to adorn her body and the influences these began to have on her movement behaviors. She rotated her hips, displaced her weight seductively, and used her hands to further cinch in her already diminished (effects of corset) waist. The clothed body became the eroticized body. Clothes are the form in which the fashioned body is made visible. Ren's response was equally important to the designer, as it revealed the intense kinaesthetic stimulation of the garment or accessory, in this case the corset, for her. It demonstrated the "touch" of the garment, the relationship between body and garment, and how this permeated the surface beyond skin deep. Ren's movement also acknowledged some of the conditioned movement behaviors carried within our bodies and social expectations of dress. She communicated to us her own erotic fantasies, the private lived experience of wearing the corset, whilst also displaying learned movement behaviors; the way we move in a tightly laced corset, or a loosely fitting pair of combats, an identity-concealing hooded top, a fluidly cut silk dress—all those countless internalized movements and knowledges.

The process is taken one stage further with the integration of the motion graphics and the dancer's intimate engagement with her own animated self, the likely interaction of control and submission. The garment becomes capable of mediating interaction and encouraging new social relationships (between online partners). ScreenDress is ornamental and expressive, a union of design and technology. Its transforming patterns grow and contract, interstitial forms, and pulsating rhythms move across the surface, digitally emulating the biological body, the nerves and membranes, and natural flows of energy. It is a shape-shifting kinetic form, constantly morphing, moving from concave to convex; one minute the dancer is wearing herself, her own emotions, the next she is displaying a (remote) partner's imagery, becoming interwoven and intermeshed. ScreenDress is directed at the notion of watching and sensing, the intrigue of knowing more, of seeing beneath the surface. As a "relational" wearable, it enables us to engage with ourselves and to touch the other (and be touched) intimately at a distance.

SensorDress and Digital Dunes

Barthes's theory of the different structures involved in the fashion system—the real garment, the iconic structure, and the written garment—can now be extended to include the digitally animated garment and, inversely, the intelligently worn film. The shifting between forms of the garment in *Suna no Onna* (The Woman in the Dunes) is effected by digital technology and real-time transformation. The various garments prepared for the production are transposed from cloth to moving graphics and a fluid, sculptural, kinetic, and cinematic form that resembles the visual kinetics of earlier experimental film (Moholy-Nagy, Léger) but also breathes the spirit of contemporary futurisms in the world of hip hop, games, power advertising, kung-fu and sci-fi movies. We deliberately chose a classic Japanese film noir to explore such a digital real-staging of our performers' interpretations of the characters and their behavior in the dune environment. Our stage adaptation uses color and a range of textures, intermingling real objects with digitally animated environments. The data for the animated landscapes were motion-captured from our performers.

The notion of "wearing the film" was first used by Jane M. Gaines in her analysis of specific film dresses that draw attention to the elaborate design in excess of the narrative or diegetic function.[11] In our case, SensorDress is a garment constructed with intelligent fabrics allowing the motion with the garment and the body to transmit wireless signals to the computer. Rather than re-appearing as an iconic garment in the screen environment or virtual space, SensorDress allows the dancer to animate directly all the events that happen in the dunes environment projected as a responsive world now activated, ruffled and moved in real-time. The woman protagonist in *Suna no Onna* spends her entire life in the dunes, her body almost literally fused with the sand habitat. In our treatment, the garments worn by her become the interface with the digital sand. She is embedded, she wears the space in the sense of continually affecting the flow and motion of the generated live filmscape.

What does the dancer control? How is the dancer's experience controlled and affected? In the expanded kinesfield of a three, four or five-dimensional "unstablelandscape," the dancer is wearing and carrying the fabric of the film, so to speak. Her body, clothed in sensor-rich garments (using orient, flex, tilt, rotation, photocell sensors), directly mobilizes the image-movement, and thus also our eyes.[12] As the first-person eye, she controls the "camera eye" in the programmed environment of the virtual world, through her own body motion and manipulation of fabric on skin, the underfabric of the digital data. The lifestyle and perpetual habits of the female protagonist (an entrapped woman, continually shoveling shifting sands that threaten to bury her home) inform our design and performance processes for sand habitation. Katsura Isobe, who interprets the role, and the worn garments become "dissolved" into emergent states of the psychological existence of the woman, her labor, endurance, and expectations. The colors and textures relate to the space as a whole, the surrounding scenic space, and the digitally projected space.

For additional design inspiration, Michèle Danjoux studied the organic photographic images of Edward Weston and the multi-layered, multi-textured knowledge based dress systems of the Japanese Samurai Warriors and traditional kimono. The layering and tying of these systems afford design potential that offers the dancer the scope to alter the nature of the garment statements during performance. Garment surfaces were treated with a sandblasting finishing process to give the impression of time and effort and of a wearing-down in the dunes. Color palettes range from tones of sand, ochre, sienna, and rich earth colors. The garment states are not fixed, but in a fluid state of transition. For instance, a utility coat with hood becomes a sculptural, organic, and abstract form when wrapped differently around the body. Each shifting form of garment brings about a new form of interaction and movement behavior.

Both underwear and overwear are sensitive to touch, but in the interactive world of this performance, the cloth also is the camera or the "controller" of the movement-images, and thus the tilts, the swoons, the falling and rising, the drift of the 3-D world that projects itself. When Isobe turns in a 360-rotation, the filmic motion enacts the same rotation. The wearing of the shifting, moveable, moldable kimono reveals and dispels a world of images that floats, turns, collapses, and rises: motions of floating forms, sometimes congealing to a recognizable Gestalt, sometimes flowing as graphic and geometric abstractions, anamorphoses, distortions of space. Digital insects appear to crawl out of the sand and move about (motion-captured from the dancers who "become" the insect avatars). Each garment part employs a different digital-body interface allowing different techniques and gestures to be combined to explore the interface between the real and the projected. The layers of cloth become prosthetic impulses, carnal and entomological projections hovering between the phenomenal and the biocultural, grains of sand, grains of sounds, insect antennae, colors and folded cloth and bodily animations feeding back from the screen world, the digital modulations of her figure in a suspended landscape.

The dancer is the sensorimotor actor of the movement-image, but the question of control, in the sense of cause-and-effect, can never be fully answered, as the programming of the interface allows the sensor-rich dress to move the frames (forward, backward, fast forward, slow down, freeze-frame, jitter, etc.) within algorithmic parameters that also allow the computer to interpolate or generate movement/stillness and various "masks" that act as overlays or filters of the images. The audience has the impression as if they are floating into and through the landscape, perceiving the dancer's kinetic movement in fluid contact with the audiovisual landscape, but of course the actual sensors are invisible (incorporated into the garment) so that no particular triggering motion is discerned. Movement is continuous, subtle behavior as if becoming one with the film, a diver submerging in water and becoming indistinguishable from the liquid environment.

Ermira Goro, during separate rehearsals for the live computer game *See you in Walhalla*, enacts her role of a real/physical avatar in front of a 3-D projective urban environment. The avatar and the remote players (streamed into the triptych video projection architecture) are participants in the game, which consists of hundreds of scenes filmed in several European cities merged into one (the fictive Walhalla). Goro is wearing fourteen different sensors distributed all over her body-suit, from head to toe. In performance, she is re-choreographing her movement continuously, incorporating the sensorial processes on her body, which allow her an immediate, direct relationship to the virtual worlds (digital film and animation) in front of which, into which, she literally moves and navigates. As one would navigate an avatar in a game, the performer in this live production is navigating her own character into the digital world, and she is also responding to the programmed interactions she does not control, such as the appearances of the other players streamed in from the remote webcams.

Her vocabulary and the subtlety of her gestures direct her first-person perspective into the animated world manipulated through her body and garment. This requires a deep practice and immense dexterity (rehearsing with the sensorial fabric). At the same time, our production rehearsals with the SensorDress have shown that the embodied garment-character itself is partly responsible for the affective and responsive proprioceptional processing of the dancer in action, her physical and affective relationship to the garment and the image of "character" created in the wearer. The emotional relationship and expressional exchange between dancer and garment, in turn, affect the projected world and its behaviors that can be felt by the audiences. This exchange directly affects alterity, the other person or persons in the same space with the performer, and we do not distinguish here between "real" temporal space and disjunct "real-time" space. The consensual process takes place in telepresence. Other persons, creatures or digital landscapes partner the effect, respond to gesture or action, modulate perceptual experience, as in any call and response situation in a social context. The wearer is the caller, responding. The behaviors of the responsive environment are keyed to the motion in wearing.

New research into the impact of human behavior on design practices suggests that typically we do not realize how and to what extent we are participating in and therefore shaping culture. It also suggests that the products of design engage humans both through their utility and their cultural location—their situatedness. While such context-dependency and the high social variability in the connotations of dressing performance are obvious, the question of how sensorial design is experienced and interpreted has barely been answered. But our performances point to sensorial and tactile affect as primary experience of movement within the body, which inhabits intensive (internal) and also extensive space. The artistic use of fashion and game scenarios can create its intimate complexities precisely through the way in which it modifies or perverts the codes it seems to be using. At a time when we seem to move casually between real habitats and digital, virtual domains, busily reconfiguring cultural differences and boundaries, it is useful to pay attention to small details, especially when microelectronics become fused with the tissues of the human body as exotic add-ons or when iPods become cool personalized jewelry, enabling private listening expression. In the realm of clothing and sensor performance, the small, minimal cues can have large consequences. Blatant erotic messages can turn into their opposites, sand can turn into water or bury you. With the Emergent Dress project, explorations focus on extending the wearables into an understanding of constantly moving environments. Embeddedness means living in a permanent state of emergency.

NOTES

[1] Gilles Deleuze, "Society of Control," *L'autre journal* 1 (1990):<http://www. nadir.org/nadir/archiv/netzkritik/societyofcontrol.html>.

[2] Cf. Joanne Finkelstein, "Chic Theory," *Australian Humanities Review* 5 (1997): <http://www.lib.latrobe.edu.au/AHR/archive/Issue-March-1997/finkelstein.html>; Alphonso Lingis, *Body Transformations. Evolutions and Atavisms in Culture*, London: Routledge, 2005, and Marquard Smith and Joanne Morra, eds., *The Prosthetic Impulse: From a Posthuman Present to a Biocultural Future*, Cambridge, MA: MIT Press, 2005.

[3] I wish to thank my collaborator Michèle Danjoux for her invaluable contributions to this chapter and the joint productions of DAP-Lab. The prototype development of the "Emergent Dress" collection (<http://www.brunel.ac.uk/dap>) includes "ScreenDress," featuring design concept for garment by Michèle Danjoux (fashion) and Jon Hamilton (motion graphics); "CaptureDress," and five versions of the "SensorDress" conceived by Michèle Danjoux (fashion), Johannes Birringer (composition, film), Paul Verity Smith (sensordesign), with Helenna Ren, Nam Eun Song, Katsura Isobe and Olu Taiwo (dance). The "Emergent Dress"collection was featured in the installation *Suna no Onna* produced for the Laban Center, London, in December 2007. "Walhalla" is an avatar design for a live game performance with garment concept by Despina Makaruni. *See you in Walhalla*, featuring dancer Ermira Goro, was tested at Interaktionslabor in the summer of 2006 (<http://interaktionslabor. de>); the premiere was in Athens in September 2006, and the production is now touring internationally.

[4] For a provocative concurrent experiment in wearables, especially focusing on the somatic aspect of sensor technology integrated into fabrics, see Thecla Schiphorst's description of her *exhale* exhibition in "Breath, skin and clothing: Using wearable technologies as an interface into ourselves," *International Journal of Performance Arts and Digital Media* 2, 2 (2006): 171–86, and her collaborator Susan Kozel's book, *Closer: Performance, Technologies, Phenomenology*, Cambridge, MA: MIT Press, 2007. Jane Harris' work, on the other hand, explores the presence and portrayal of characters through dress and textiles in the realm of 3-D computer graphic visualization. The digital animations *(Potential Beauty)* she exhibited in the UK in 2002–2003 focused on the poetic and dreamlike movement of the dresses alone, insofar as the actual wearer of the garments is "deleted" in the final screen version. See <http://www.janeharris.org/>. For an overview of new materials technology, see Blaine Brownell, *Transmaterial: A catalog of materials that redefine our physical*

environment, New York: Princeton Architectural Press, 2006. The "Remote Control Dress" collection (spring/summer 2000) created by Hussein Chalayan is described in Bradley Quinn, *The Fashion of Architecture*, Oxford: Berg, 2003, 127–30. See also, Bradley Quinn, *Techno Fashion*, Oxford, Berg, 2002, chapter 5. For Zoren Gold and Minori's work, see *Object that dreams*, Berlin: Die Gestalten Verlag, 2006.

[5] Gretchen Schiller, "Interactivity as Choreographic Phenomenon," in *Dance and Technology/Tanz und Technologie: Moving toward Media Productions—Auf dem Weg zu medialen Inszenierungen*, 164–195. In describing the architecture of her collaborative work *trajets* (with Susan Kozel), she speaks of the particular "kinaesthetic responsivity" in highly mediated, sensitive and interactive environments (*kinesfields*) which integrate movement and digital media (see also "Machines and Bodies").

[6] Cf. "This Secret Location," an exhibition of installations at the 2006 *In between Time Festival*, Arnolfini, Bristol, or Kira O'Reilly's performance *Untitled Bomb Shelter* at the 2005 New Territories/National Live Art Review in Glasgow. Similar one-on-one encounters have been devised by Fiona Templeton (in *YOU—The City*), Willi Dorner, Felix Ruckert, John Jasperse, Leung Po Shan, among others.

[7] Sharon Baurley's "Interaction design in smart textiles clothing and applications," in *Wearable Electronics and Photonics*, edited by Xiaoming Tao, Cambridge: Woodhead Publishers, 2005, 223–43, provides a broader context by introducing some of the advances in technical textiles production but especially in pervasive computing and the shift toward wearables, mobile devices, and the embedding of computer intelligence within everyday objects and environments. The growing interest in the sensorial and emotional affect in design was widely reflected in the 2006 Design and Emotion Conference at Göteborg's Chalmers University of Technology: <http://www.de2006.chalmers.se/>.

[8] Roland Barthes's *Système de la mode* first appeared in 1967 and has been much overlooked. Within the emerging context of digital performance and wearable technologies, reviewing Barthes's semiological study seems long overdue, while it must be kept in mind that Barthes himself later revised his "brutally inelegant" structuralist approach, aware of the complexity of ambiguous undercoding through which fashion continuously modifies what it seems (not) to be saying. In the 1970s, Barthes's interest increasingly turned to the body and away from the "written" garment.

[9] Roland Barthes [1967], *The Fashion System*, trans. Matthew Ward and Richard Howard, Berkeley: University of California Press, 1990, 111–43.

[10] Whereas Hegel seems to have preferred a formless surface as "ideal" in clothing the body for the expression of the "spirit," Barthes critiques Hegel by way of the silhouette in Erté's alphabet-drawings of women, suggesting that for Hegel the

garment is responsible for the transition from the sensuous (the body) to the signi-fier, but the Ertéan silhouette performs the contrary movement, making the garment sensuous and the body into the signifier. The body, in other words, is the support for the garment.

[11] Jane M. Gaines, "On Wearing the Film," in *Fashion Cultures*, edited by Stella Bruzzi and Pamela Church Gibson, London: Routledge, 2000, 159–177.

[12] Marlon Barrios Solano uses "unstablelandscape" to describe generative hybrid performance systems (for humans and computers) for digital real-time interaction in which participants complete the feedback loop improvisationally. All the elements in the environment are inherently changeable and unpredictable within computa-tional parameters. See "Designing Unstable Landscapes," in *Tanz im Kopf/Dance and Cognition*, 2005, 279–91.

▼▲ LEVEL UP:
GAMES & THE THEATRE OF TELEPRESENCE

Level Up

Theatre culture and video game culture may not appear to form a natural symbiosis, at least not in an historical understanding of dramatic and choreographic practice. But having introduced the relationship of performance to interactive media, it is unavoidable to ponder the interactive "action design" in video or computer games. Moreover, the significance of gaming as a cultural form, its global reach in the market of a burgeoning games and entertainment industry with players worldwide numbering in the millions, is undeniable. The link between games and movies grows ever stronger, and so does the popularity of those games (and their social networks) being played together online. It is commonly known that multiple-player online games, sometimes referred to as massive multi-player online role-playing games (MMORPGs), are community-oriented and generate active player communities or clans. These have now attracted attention from researchers concerned with social interaction and group dynamics in artificial environments. In these communal environments there are tribal and machine-operational etiquettes, genres, and conventions (such as the experience points awarded for the completion of quests, defeat of opponents, mastery of the character's level, etc.), allowing comparisons to sports, business, theatre, and ritual traditions.

Moreover, subversive gamers lurk around the corners and hack into games to make their own individualistic versions (machinima); artists hack into game technologies; bartering and trading goes on in the civilized suburban neighborhoods of the *Second Life* metaverse. Lately, concerts and live performances have been rumored to take place in *Second Life*. Regarding the role of the participant in interactive art, much can be gleaned from the action-driven scenarios of gaming. Online virtual spaces such as *Second Life* have become so popular (its user base currently stands at approximately nine million accounts) that more artistic uses will undoubtedly emerge.

The connection I want to sketch here concerns telepresence performance, also referred to as telematic or networked performance. It shares the digital design and actions of configuration that underlie the creation of artificial environments and "on-line"/"off-line" game-play. In particular, it shares several online role-playing characteristics and powerleveling strategies with MMORPGs. Even though networked performances may not aspire to be computer games in the literal sense, they bear conceptual affiliations with gaming and navigation structures. Furthermore, there clearly is a growing interest among composers and digital artists in game engines and what Mick Grierson refers to as "interactive composition environments."[1] Grierson's *Noisescape* shifts the idea of playing a game to musical interaction, but as a performance environment it harbors many parallels to typical multi-user game landscapes. It places the player in an abstract virtual world complete with physical modeling, collision detection, and three-dimensional movement. But unlike many virtual worlds, there are no predetermined constraints on the environment, object properties, or interactions. Players can create, destroy, and combine elements with varying physical attributes in order to structure algorithmic music systems. The objects and the environment can respond to user behavior in real-time using adaptive algorithms.

The participation in a responsive game world can be understood as a form of navigation in a 3-D virtual environment, yet the player of course maintains a corporeal presence and "plays" throughout the game with her or his body, thus involving cognitive and sensorimotor processes active in any engagement of spaces that can be seen (traditionally in first-person POV), heard, felt, and intuited with the bodily intelligence. But instead of a wrist/hand interaction with the interface, whole-body engagement opens up more provocative design challenges for the proprioceptive, cognitive, and physical processing of temporal and spatial experience (as it is fundamental for dance) in 3-D performance interfaces. Game design or the design of online virtual environments faces the same challenges I described in earlier chapters on interactive installations and wearable sensors. It requires an effective control interface in order to navigate a particular set of parameters or codified rules of operation. In 3-D games, control interfaces are largely based on paradigms of movement in space in order to achieve an intuitive immersive experience.

In regard to gamic visuality, the subjective shot in cinema served as a model for the typical camera perspective of first-person shooter games in which precise eye vision of the player character is mimicked by computer vision (and in many instances a weapon is added to the foreground of the frame). But unlike conventional cinema, which uses montage of distinct shots (for example general POV; the look of a single character; shot/reverse shot; pans; tracks, etc.), digital game aesthetics emphasize active vision and continuous-shot technique subjective to computerized space—the fully rendered virtual-actionable space of the game world. This has in turn influenced contemporary digital cinema (e.g., *Robocop*, *The Matrix*, *Minority Report*), and it is noticeable that Neo's training scenes in *The Matrix* seem copied from the training levels that mark the beginning of many games. As the continuous-shot movement implies, the purposeful visuality of games resides in a quasi-predatory forward propulsion or search and destroy mode. It is a predatory mode with a long cinematic history of horror movies and psychological thrillers preceding it. In most cases, the predator's POV tended to alienate viewer identification, but in action-oriented games the subjective shot movement creates the opposite effect. Besides first-person shooter games, there exist numerous other game genres with fictional narratives and social worlds in which the vector graphics are used differently or depart entirely from the "realism" of *Halo* and *Quake*-like "ego-shooter" (as they are called in German) or real-time strategy games.

It is tempting, therefore, to ponder artist-made game mods as an alternative design of gameplay in which non-realist visual form, animation and invented physics introduce different kinds of performance involvement which, in strict game terms, might be considered counterintuitive. The countergaming design deliberately breaks with the "theatrical" illusion of representational modeling, invites nondiegetic acts such as illegible code, slowdowns, temporary freezes, or disorientations, and opens a window for collaborative audiovisual immersion as well as improbable kinetic ironies. In the following, I look at interactive constellations in performance applied to networked, distributed environments. These environments will be examined through the lens of interactive online computer games and the collaborative culture of multi-player experience.

In my case studies, *Saira Virous* and *Flying Birdman*, the game-like environment acts as a "theatre of operations" where various levels are engaged by players who interact with each other and the streams. The notion of "choreography," again, undergoes a conceptual reorientation as it is applied to live Webstreams with digital exchanges of images, sound, graphics, and chat. Such performance writing/composition, in accordance with the language of computing used in programming real-time interaction, will be *generative* and *emergent* rather than fixed. The physical interaction depends on input and sensory feedback, which in turn continuously modulate the emergent composition. The projects' conceptual development owes much to recent cross-currents in game design and interactive media art, but the focus on physical performance inside networked environments expands compositional ideas in the field of performance technology. However, telematic performance also offers suggestions to game designers and artists who recontextualize game culture through machinima, mods and console-based subversions.[2] The concept of generative composition I propose explores performance in virtual environments which are dynamic, non-deterministic, and variable in terms of navigable space, zones, levels, and role-playing. They therefore yield a different approach to game constraints created by rules and goals. The rules in *Saira Virous* are entirely fictive or poetic: they offer no real constraints. The rules in *Flying Birdman* playfully revisit the poetics of earthworks.

Networked Interactive Composition

Aesthetic theory has generally foregrounded the parallel evolution of "interactivity" in new media arts and sound art, while Internet-based art, networked performance, electronic writing, locative media practices, games, and virtual world design only now gain slow recognition in art theory and criticism. Choreographers, having joined forces with musicians and programmers over the last decade, were noted for their readiness to explore computational processes and virtuality, since movement capture and abstract motion were easily compatible with data manipulation within cellular models of emergence. Such models, influenced by the discourses of artificial life, cybernetics, AI, and biology, have largely replaced dramatic or realist models of representation. While these models undoubtedly offer a stronger stimulation for digital artists, it is astonishing that hardly any experimental theatre companies (including the Wooster Group and Builders Association) have attempted live, networked performances crossing different sites. The Builders Association came close to it in their 2003 production of *Alladeen*, created jointly with the London-based motiroti company, in which they thematized global connectivity and media culture by depicting a surreal world of international call centers and telemarketing where Indian operators learn how to pass as Americans. The digital scenography of *Alladeen*, however, is constructed as a closed world in which all cues are tightly prechoreographed.

Beyond the basic HCI (human-computer interaction) common to all computer systems and consoles, the design of telematic performance involves pervasive dimensions (networks, servers, communications protocols including TCP/IP). In physical performance devised for networked composition, the interactive design emphasizes techniques of audiovisual data production and manipulation, often on a microcellular level. Production is always coproduction, as incoming streams from partner sites are synthesized in realtime. On the other hand, since the creation of audiovisual streaming media primarily involves aspects of the digital aesthetics mentioned above, specific modes of camera POV, MIDI networks, voice transmission, and synchronization tend to dominate. Performance is necessarily glued into screenic projection. In telematic performances with distributed action, where images and sounds are created by multiple site participants, the screenic environment with its multidirectional feedback circuits creates a hybrid digital cinema.

This networked quasi-cinema operates on a different logic from the theatre, using a transactional, branching language rather than dialogue or linear narrative, and a turn-based "interludic" game structure, which also deviates from the realism of filmic *mise-en-scène*. Its action is a form of acting aparttogether, but synchronization is of course subject to latency and degradation—a welcome nondiegetic incursion of the anonymous network itself. In telepresence, the relationship of acting body to remote body, avatar, or various prosthetic data extensions of physically generated synergies, is not troubled by humanist and realist anxieties. On the contrary, the initial fascination with animation software (LifeForms, Poser) allowing a denaturalized re-composition of a bipedal skeleton, as with motion-capture derived animation and its immense potential for graphic abstraction, encouraged digital performers to explore playful graphics within a "posthuman" dynamic system space, rather than worry about character or expressive faculties of a mimetic body. This interest in abstraction, denaturalization, fractalization and computational calculation, witnessed in many performances that integrate "virtual bodies" in the *mise-en-scène*, contradicts the general emphasis on realism in video games where the logic of action games has favored a clear relationship between the player's viewpoint (performed by an avatar) and the "figures" in the virtual game world.[3] Physical laws are adhered to: there is a one-to-one relationship between controller action and resultant action in the game world. A leftward motion results in a leftward turn. There is an emphasis in the mainstream game industry on designing interfaces which construct a direct view of the screen scene through the player's own eyes, matching and synchronizing player actions with changes and movements on the screen, thus producing a sensation of being "in the scene," regardless of whether it is a hardcore shooter game like *Halo* or role-playing game/quest games like *Sim City* or *EverQuest*. It has often been noted that the environments of these games are rendered in highly realistic detail, with naturalistic surface texture, dramatic lighting and sound effects, and subtle use of color. As Andrew Darley and others point out, the "majority of adversaries—monsters, zombies, aliens and so forth—are rendered and animated with the same high levels of surface accuracy and increasingly this is combined with a persuasive anthropomorphism."[4]

The human tendency to anthropomorphize provides further clues to our understanding of interactivity, both generally and in regard to game performance. Before one gets carried away by the thrill of anti-realism and indirection, it may be necessary to distinguish what I want to call "hot interactivity" from shallow clicking of buttons or triggering a reaction from a programmed sequence. "Cold interactivity" is ubiquitous in our daily lives; we encounter it all the time when we operate the automated ticket dispenser in train stations or visit the cash-dispensing machine, even if such interfaces can be satisfying as well as frustrating, inviting emotional responses against our better knowledge. Interactive, networked systems always have a basic functional structure of input-output. The operating system implies gestural and visual conventions we are supposed to know. Connecting to a server from my laptop, using Bluetooth or wireless AirPort, requires merely a mouse-click. Surfing the Web, clicking through a series of screens and links or engaging a database, again indicates little more than a functional interface common to all product design. Such cold interactivity entails purposive decision-making and effectivity. The desired response is getting a result. Compared to commercial interaction design based on the conceptual paradigm of the desktop (CPU, monitor, keyboard, mouse, pad), and even the new generation of sexy iPods or colorful iPhones, the artistic rhetoric surrounding interactivity has been high-minded and often misleading. Complex interactivity draws on metaphors of social interaction adding many layers of human behavior and emotion which reflect the grey areas of play, performance, and theatricality, all those hot zones of indecision, frivolity, irony, and confusion that affect the nature of action-reaction. Acting with computer-mediated reaction raises the question of how the machine is given "character," how the human agent listens to the unspoken, the body language, the "inter" (between-the-lines) behavior, as one would say in the theatre where qualities of gestural expression matter.

Game controller design pays attention to expressive acts, on the level of motional control and activity in the pretended play world. It borrows freely from mythic or cinematic plots that deal with life and death, betrayal and recovery. Games play on fantasy, and they seemingly fetishize control/power (and, interestingly, health), as the player must internalize the protocols in the universe constructed by a particular video game, and in fact must learn how to predict the consequences of each move. Learning to control the power relationship with the hidden code/algorithm in the interactivity does not necessarily make the user a co-author nor allow the kind of active role and freedom of expression that is implied in an interactive exchange involving autonomous development. The artistic promise of interactivity implies creative composition as collaboration, while game controller design suggests the fantasy fulfilment of knowing how to win. Knowing how to operate the game system, in this sense, means that every player executes their own conquest at their own risk. Any ideological critique would have to start with this premise. As a sacred cybernetic model of control, therefore, *game* is our central cultural metaphor of the digital age. We play our heroes and role models, and we are willing to accept their continuous, ever-repeating death, their sacrifice or their punishment when they do not perform up to speed. Each game is programmed to be repeated and thus reproducible as systemic patterns with variables. In the game *America's Army* you are also offered the option of self-sacrifice ("Your body may absorb enough of the blast and fragments to allow the rest to escape damage and avenge your heroic death"). You receive rewards for liberating hostages.

Although the dexterity of a game player using a console, like the technical skill of a dancer performing with sensors, does not yet tell us much about the aesthetics or immersive experience of the performance, it reflects the qualitative input the player may have in the "doing" of visual, auditory, synaesthetic, and narrative events. Hard-core gamers who enjoy *Grand*

Theft Auto III would probably find artist-made game mods unsatisfying if the flow of doing is interrupted. The promise of non-realist/abstract countergaming and modified *Quake* engines, briefly glimpsed in the work of Jodi and Cory Arcangel, has been overestimated, as attention is shifted to visual design rather than to a different kind of game action. The British company igloo is an exception; their recent *Swan Quake* game installation invites players to journey through mysterious landscapes and find various disguised characters.[5] Humor-filled collaborative behavior here reflects uncannily on powerleveling in shooter games. Powerleveling in telematic performance has had a shaky start as defeating high level challenges has not come easily. The early networked performances I participated in were often marred by naïveté regarding the promised land of connectivity, when all that could be experienced was the equivalent of a hand-shake across space and time, the waving of hands (hello/good-bye) Laurie Anderson had parodied twenty-five years ago. The myth of the telematic embrace, thus, has to be measured against the notion of "pleasure" proposed by games analysts who argue that genuine interactivity needs to meet some conditions for successful play and an increasing attachment to a game.

Naturally, if artistic game mods seek to critique such attachment, they may encounter their audiences' incomprehension. French choreographer Xavier Le Roy, who gained recognition with stunning conceptual performances (*Self Unfinished*, 1998; *Product of Circumstances*, 1999), recently toured a work called *Project* (2005), a combinatory of ball games—soccer, handball, cornerball (?)—played according to idiosyncratic sets of rules that are imposed upon the players or have been chosen by them. The game even seemed open to spontaneous modification, but its real problem was that the audience could not play it nor identify with it.

Following the logic of game action, the main difference between networked performance and stage performance, therefore, is the absence of spectating. Multiplayer online performance only makes sense as direct live action involving the participants, whereas migrating theatre or dance performances to the Internet is a form of cheating if it requests an inoperative audience of spectators. Understandably, there is no canon or repertoire of telepresence performances, and their action design cannot be put into a box and sold. It is difficult to speak of a history of such performance as the essence of its eventhood is its complete contingency on the network and the collaboration of players connected via the network at a specific time. Each telepresence performance is a singular product of its circumstances. It might be structured after the logic of games but it cannot be replayed like a game on PlayStation. It is neither a game nor a performance. Since it needs no audience and no theatre, the redundancy of spectacular parameters calls the ontology of "performance" itself into question.

The Pleasure of Gaming and Telematic Pleasure

In terms of a general definition of what constitutes a video game, without entering a larger philosophical and sociological study of game culture and *homo ludens* (Huizinga), one might propose that "game" or "play" creates a separate frame from the real world. Rules and behaviors apply to this frame. Most computer games have a theme, i.e., a subject matter that is used in contextualizing the rules and the player procedures and mechanics they allow. The game theme provides a meaningful context for everything that takes place in the game world. Game environments provide the space for components, procedures, narratives, and actions. It is obvious that the game environment is critical, as it is specific to each individual game. In its defining features, a computer game can be described as "a rule-based formal system with a variable and quantifiable outcome, where different outcomes are assigned different values, the player exerts effort in order to influence the outcome, the player feels attached to the outcome, and the consequences of the activity are optional and negotiable."[6]

While the attraction of games may reside in their theme, characters, and aesthetics of the game environment, the immersive quality of gaming resides in the player activity. A computer game has to challenge, it must provide exciting situations to experience, stimulating puzzles to engage with, and interesting environments to explore. "Gratification," James Newman suggests, "is not simply or effortlessly meted out." The pleasure of such play, furthermore, "is derived from the refinement of performance through replay and practice. Consequently, it is essential that obstacles, irrespective of the form they take, must be 'real' in that they must require non-trivial effort to conquer them." The centrality of participation and the sense of "being there" also suggests that players demand interaction in order to effectively feel they are enacting the fantasy, moving toward gain or loss. Newman notes that "it is the primacy afforded to doing and performing that renders 'non-interactive cut-scenes' so unappealing to players," as such movie sequences prevent direct control or interactivity.[7]

The question of "doing" could be elaborated if we looked at different types of environments and spatial narratives, since the cognitive processing of the game environment and its challenges (e.g., its investigatory or exploratory dimensions), especially so in the collaborative multi-player games, will vary from case to case. Communications between players in multi-player games, using voice-over IP tools rather than the older text-based forms, build a more vivid sense of mutual awareness, attention, and enjoyment. What is particularly relevant for our contextual shift to collaborative telematic performance is the fact that the pleasure of gaming excites the body, and that current research shows how multiplayer online games also generate "affective alliances," social formations, on and offline information networks, and communal relationships for the sharing of resources.

The pleasure of telematic performance is based on very similar processes of socialization and self-organization, and along with my fellow members of ADaPT I believe that after several years of shared online performance our group has formed a digital community.[8] ADaPT's practitioners come from diverse backgrounds but share an interest in performance, dance, new media, and collaborative experimentation. Together, we have developed hybrid models of networked interaction that combine learning through the iterative pattern recognition of dense multi-layered environments (physical and virtual). Most importantly, acting in such mixed-reality environments has not just challenged our body-perceptions and proprioceptive awareness, it also requires a very specific studio architecture and knowledge of tools allowing for the interplay of performer, "physical camera" (a camera that can dance), precise lighting, sound distribution, and the computing environment which includes various interactive media controllers. Performing together-apart across different times zones in international collaborations which also involve writing and chat-windows not only raises practical questions, namely determining degrees of collaborative agency in distributed multi-user platforms, exploring perceptual learning curves and organizational strategies. It also stimulates our pleasure to experiment with playful scenarios that wouldn't have occurred to us on a theatre stage.

The Plasticity of the Telematic Game

The telematic computing environment involves both hand-held physical cameras as well as a computer-controlled movement sensing system. The global media controller organizes the sonic and graphic output for the sensing system. It is an instrument that primarily controls the source materials (sound and video files stored in the computer or synthesizer), sound parameters, and the dynamics of real-time synthesis occuring between performers and physical camera. Moreover, interactive multimedia performance generally uses interconnected systems (linking the computers through the network) to drive several patch programs for sound, video, and motion tracking simultaneously. The studio architecture needs broadband network access points so that outgoing and incoming webcasts can flow. The streams are displayed as video projections; in our studio we use multiple screens (suspended from ceiling to form a curved or angular space) for large, human-size projection. All instruments for the real-time generation of the streams are inside the space, close to the performers and operators. We use surround sound, and in a telematic performance there usually are multiple channels of streaming audio in operation.

Given such complexity in the telematic architecture, operators are challenged to play with the plasticity between performance, network, and controllable parameters, and to discover how performers see their actions as a form of topological mapping of the body's experience and proprioception within the interface. This quest, at the same time, allows speculation on the particular spatiality of the intermediated player-world we are constructing for the performer who enters "into" it. In terms of game theory, this would be the point of entry that creates the affective bond between player and game world. In telematic terms we can call it "immersive connectivity." The programming goal is to integrate an image-based recognition system (e.g., a computer running Max or Isadora) or a motion sensor interface (e.g., the MidiDancer or I-Cube sensors) into a unified interactive environment.[9] The technical integration implies that the performers understand the system underlying the theme of the game and integrate parallel parameters into their actions with the tactile image projection spaces (generated through extreme close-up shot sequences).

How do the players act with body images, avatars, and high-speed data? From a choreographic perspective, the performer within a networked environment familiarizes herself with the response behavior of the sound and video parameters, and with the immediate stream-image that the physical camera generates of her close-up. Here the performer is taking in at least two image fields, one of her own locally generated stream, the other of the incoming stream(s). There can be varying degrees of *consensus* or *dis-sensus* in the projected streams, depending on how images of self and other are mixed, layered, partitioned, or distorted. Performers and programmers strive to create an exponentially more sensitive, articulate, and intuitive system, allowing the continuous re-organization of the haptic spatial environment projected from the frame compositions of the camera. The physical camera operator is in very intimate proximity, to the extent that performer and camera act as a duo. At the same time, the performer creates data. In a networked environment this also requires of the programming a constant, iterative rendering process, refinements in sensors, filters, and output processors, while it suggests an attenuation of the performer's spatial-temporal consciousness. If she wears multiple sensors, as well as acts in a duet with the camera, she needs to do a great deal of parallel sensorimotor/cognitive processing, developing an extreme awareness of her movements and which movements control what parameters. The perceptual challenges of "inviting being seem," as Deborah Hay calls such performance practice, extend outward, as the telematic performer and the networked streams are conjoined in a feedback loop with each other, forming a conscious flow of multiple perceptual occurrences unfolding continuously.[10] Performing with synthetic or 3-D projections, she animates these virtual image spaces that are constantly emerging and also unpredictable. Her action "plays" the computerized visual movement, crossing real and virtual space.

The plasticity in the telematic architecture distinctly intertwines numerous agencies (gestures, bodies, machines, media flows, data): the player moves in real space but also enters into screen space, her corporeal action is digitized, her voice is transmitted and received (it returns as echo, with a slight delay) along with the responding stream and the fluid images generated by the partner site(s). The interactive environments allow the real-time synthesis of various media forms, but this synthesis is part of a larger synaesthesia. The technical system is only a feedback system in which information travels and transduces bodily activity into computation, which controls the instant media outputs. But this system is not an environment that affects proprioception, vision, hearing, smell, and haptic sense unless we understand the sonic and the projected images, in their behaviors, as transformative, acting upon the sensing body and intensifying unaccustomed connections, deformations, or interferences with the functioning of the body that now, and continually, must adapt to the unpredictable dissipative states.

For example, I wanted to include a level in the game in which the players perform with eyes closed, activating bodily modalities apart from sight. The process (proprioception, tactility, affectivity) through which human perception constructs "images" does not depend on the visual mode, and telepresence is not directed at an audience watching a scene, but at players enacting a fantasy. Entering virtual worlds opens up perspectival flexibility in computerized space, which is not necessarily Euclidian. Our response to the surface, the grain of sound and the skin of the images, intensifies. We "wear" the projected textures differently, we touch and sense the video images with our whole body. This "wearing the digital" challenges composition to imagine the relations between play action and projected world in different ways.

Noticing how open, complex, and evolving this networked scenario is, I became interested in the function of playful constraints as a way to invent an interactive dramaturgy based on a "game engine" rather than prolonged improvisation which proved ineffective in online collaboration. At that time (2003–04) I had joined a group of gamers in Nottingham who organized the annual ScreenPlay festival featuring independent games, mods, and interactive art. Many of our discussions at the festival focused on the relationship between games, play, ritual, fun, and learning—questions raised in equal measure by game developers, educators, psychologists, and artists using reverse engineering to subvert game consoles. I had also become aware of Blast Theory's efforts to take games into the street to test the notion of ubiquitous computing in streetplay. When I developed the dramaturgy for *Saira Virous*, jointly with our ADaPT partners in Tempe, Detroit, and Amsterdam, I used "game engine" as a metaphor for a scenario in which players enter online to engage remote partners in an exploratory journey. I wanted to make the entry a physical journey based on fictive tasks, whilst our partners in Arizona, who named their part of the game *Viroid Flophouse*, chose to work with an iconic "board game" designed to look like a grid labyrinth mapped with hieroglyphic signs. Josephine Dorado, on site in Amsterdam, joined in the programming and execution of the interactive gamescape. In the following, I describe the different dramaturgies of the game and theorize the notion of a telematic performance game.

For *Saira Virous* I sampled and remixed a few moments from the language/plot of David Cronenberg's *eXistenZ* (1999), a film which opens with a designer's live demonstration of a new virtual reality game, except that unlike the video games of our present day reality, the games in *eXistenZ* are delivered directly into the player's nervous system via the metaflesh game pod, a surreal coupling of amphibian nervous systems and technology. Things go wrong during the test, and the film's plot, similar to *The Matrix* and *The Thirteenth Floor*, develops its ever more perplexing confusions of reality-within-reality-within-simulation. Its most interesting aspect, the melding of technology and biology, had an almost viral effect on our imagination, especially as we were intrigued by very quick "cuts" (level changes) between scenes. The biomorphic contorsions, or grotesque torque, in which the players find themselves resembled the digital motion animations we had developed in our interactive rehearsals. We proceeded to invent our own dramaturgical devices and set up a level structure, which potentially can be extended much further:

1. Welcome by MC.

2. Second intro by Mystery Figure (Saira) preparing Players for training session.

3. Level One: Moving in all directions: boule game/rolling dance.

4. Game-journey begins.

5. Level Two: Obstacle: game only works when you double up.

6. Level Three: Intimacy (Blind scene, listening to Inner Voice).

7. Level Four: Final Fantasy arrives for *kosupure* (dress change), character must change identity.

8. Level Five: 'Infection' starts mutation process. Texas desert landscape. Players must cross desert or swim across the channel to reach ocean.

9. Saira must tell players whether she loves them or not, otherwise they dry up/drown and shrivel. Love and infection go hand in hand. Hand dance.

10. Level Six: Obstacle by Particle Systemics (Lycanthropic movement: hands dematerialize).

11. Level Seven: Playing with very small object (*kawaii*). Location changes to underwater.

12. More Bad Things surely happen.

The subsequent rehearsals and written exchanges between partner sites developed the levels and changed directions. Our Arizona partners introduced the idea of self-sacrifice: the gamers must express their devotion to the obstacle (virus) through the act of self-destruction. The environment is a metaphor for the gamer. The gamer must destroy or dissolve the environment within specified parameters (motion sensing triggers). The virus then can accept or reject the act of self-sacrifice based upon these parameters. In the event of acceptance, the gamer is regenerated and proceeds to the next level. In the event of rejection, the gamer goes back to the first level. *Flophouse* is a pun on the idea that in gaming environments the death of a character doesn't constitute non-existence. The character is regenerated by starting the game over again. In *Saira Virous*, players in Nottingham and Detroit used an "empty space" in which all visual and sonic elements were created on the fly using live camera work and sampling (prerecorded media) to generate the immersive context for the journey from level to level. The navigable space is constituted by the image-movements the partner sites enact through affective bodily interfaces. The Arizona and Amsterdam sites both had the same spatial configuration. The first level of the game consisted of a projection of a sculpture garden. Both gamers had to step "through" the door, thereby triggering the motion capture region associated with that area, in order to move to the second level. When the movers in one space occupied a square within the "region map" of Level 2, that area was highlighted on the game board in the remote partner's space.

Each square had a distinct and characteristic sound that accompanied the movement of the players. This sound was shared between the sites. When a hidden square was activated, a special sound indicated to the performers that they had found one of five hidden squares. Once all five hidden squares were uncovered, the board changed to one of five winning messages and the game was over for those participants. The original idea for the viral fiction was for remote sites to infect each other using digital telepresence. Initially the performance took the form of a cooperative game, where players on each side of the Atlantic either learnt a specific fictional task that allowed them to invent a role or used motion sensing to control a graphic environment in the partner space. Over time the game engine was developed, based on the action of the remote and local gamer "sharing" the same space. In *Saira Virous*, the gamer in Nottingham and the gamer in Detroit learnt to navigate surreal landscapes with unconventional movement or perceptional tasks, such as moving only with one arm, listening to a song inside the head or swimming across the channel to Japan wearing goggles. In *Flophouse*, the gamer in Arizona and the gamer in Amsterdam had to position themselves in the same virtual gaming space in order to get to the next level. The performers then worked together by means of their virtual location in the performance space to cooperatively solve the puzzle in real time. A master of ceremonies in a third remote location (Nottingham) made casual or irritating observations, gave encouragements and subtle warnings to the performers throughout the performance.

What I have described is the beginning of an ongoing multi-phase project shifting between "collaborative" and "competitive" forms but primarily exploring the physical and programming dimensions of such online multiplayer environments. The game is a useful step for us into the realm of augmented reality using multi-modal performer interaction and information streams to connect sites over distance in whole-body, movement-based teleactions. One important aspect of the work is that it is participatory: it really only makes sense to be involved in the game, rather than sitting down to watch it. In this sense, the notion of composition applies to the interaction design and the player operation, allowing not only trained performers but any player to engage the play-world. It is an embodied play world, which cannot be experienced at a console or computer but actually needs to be entered literally. "Embodied" means full physical participation in the interaction and an engaged interrelational sensibility toward co-located presences.

This is precisely how I understand telepresence—to be present in a distant image world which is being created as I become present in it. Here we also observe the particular challenge of camera work (framing, angle, motion) within the frame compositions of the virtual space. *Flophouse* had its virtual map designed, but does not exist as a "world" until the physical game gets under way and the role-playing movers and their actions are transmitted via cameras. Digital real-time dramaturgy implies that the player is integrated into a moving architecture generated with real-time data. Telepresence or tele-action also means entering into the streaming images of the remote site, thus affecting the reality or virtuality perceived at that location. It is crucial to recognize that such live action, unlike avatars in synthetic computerized environments, brings corporeality as dynamic material energy to a remote physical location.

Another critical difference, for example between telematic performance and telerobotics, is the motivated physical action that travels from one location to another. It operates on the remote action and changes its reality. Since it is not artificial, it can understand irony. This surely distinguishes the telepresence game from MMORPGs and the priority of "rewards" in commercial action games. I can play with the distanced body images or actionable objects and have ironic relationships with the processing of my action and the fictive rules it breaks, enjoy the thrill of the exchange of energies and strange fantasies with performers in the other sites, and savor the natural precariousness of temporary networks with their lags, interruptions, and collapses. These network environments, after all, behave like the weather. The materiality of its temperatures makes such live game technologies exciting: to be streaming together teaches us a great deal about living organisms and the humorous aspects of the "control" of a game. In telematic performance, we like to lose control.

The Earth Game

My second example is *Here I Come Again/Flying Birdman*, created collaboratively online in 2002 and co-produced by seven ADaPT member teams sited at Tempe, Los Angeles, Columbus, Salt Lake City, Madison, Brasilia, and São Paulo. It reflects a more theatrical configuration, as the networked performance, in this case, didn't just link seven studios but sought to display the game to audiences. Each site announced the performance locally (as well as on the Internet) and invited audiences to join the event, deliberately exploring the capability of online performance to connect "sites" and "nonsites" in the manner in which Robert Smithson had experimented with the distributed nature of his earthworks and "mirror displacements." In a sense, *Flying Birdman* was an homage to land art and an earlier era of media art (Vito Acconci's audio composition "Here I Come Again" was recomposed for the performance), associating telepresence with Smithson's art as a form of traveling across spatial and temporal boundaries. Looking back at Smithson's *Partially Buried Woodshed*, *Incidents of Mirror-Travel in the Yucatan*, and the famous *Spiral Jetty*, my dramaturgical concept for an "earth game" was based on the idea of tele-reversals, namely the relationship of diffused online and concrete urban spaces, the latter being suffused today with wireless communications and nomadic media to the point of oversaturation and entropy. In an urban world of continuous acceleration and entropy, in which nomadic interfaces require reception in constant flows of displacement, how can telepresence be conceived as an art form that situates itself in-between varied and simultaneous, but not synchronous, action-interfaces?

Flying Birdman was based on short narratives and structured spirally like a Japanese *renga*, a poem of live performance, real-time audio and sound processing, prerecorded film, still images, spoken voice, and graphic text communication exchanged by participants and audience during the live event. The performers in the various sites were asked to play with the theme of "left-overs"—debris, decomposition, and the idea of recycling. The anchoring voice of the Flying Birdman ran through the entire telematic performance, but this voice of the fictive Birdman was also under-scored with subtle audio mixes and other traveling, whispering voices that functioned like echoes. These word echoes were randomly chosen by the participating players, picked up and digitally transformed by the other collaborating multisite partners. The run-on voice of the Birdman was recited live by five sites while the other streams were created, with the Brazilian players from the Corpos Informáticos group concentrating primarily on writing. The Birdman's voice changed and transformed from one language to another (altogether there were five languages used by different native speakers).

Each site functioned both like a film set and a gallery for the local public. The Website links for the online performances were announced on the Internet so that online visitors could join. Each site was free to design their environment for the production and transmission; we agreed that each locality would have panoramic screens allowing the participants to see all streams dialogue with each other in the spiral. This cinematic arrangement also allowed on-site viewers to see the intersection of public and virtual spaces, and how the local actors constructed the dialogues with remote partners in real-time. The game dramaturgy for this telematic earthwork included an ambience act (default mode) and, once players start, a spiraling dialogue—between sites and non-sites—with at least two sites dialoguing with each other at any given time during the ten levels. Each level had a six-minute time frame. The dialogue was passed on and moved around, and the Internet visitors followed the movement of the dialogue by opening the respective URLs.

Although the Internet is a new medium, we are re-adapting existing forms and media to the interface of distributed action-synthesis. With the media responding to each other over large distances, an aesthetics of transmission must take into account the imponderable and the unexpected, as well as the interplay between player action and code. There is a reversal between performer actions and their avatar-presence in the virtual space of this "digital earth": I cannot see what others see elsewhere. The game is performed in real-time through multi-authorial operations. All partners are physically co-present but also discontinuous, not in one location, yet moving in and out of phase with each other. What we learn from systems theory and the concepts of autopoiesis and emergence addressed earlier are the creative implications of such real-time translocal composition. Networked performance profoundly affects the way we imagine our autonomous bodies in their spatiotemporal placedness in relation to the world. Thus it also impacts the understanding of aesthetic transmission and reception of such individual, collective and technically mediated connectedness.

Interauthored composition here means entering the stream. This leads to a re-scaling of existing aesthetic operations. While the professional experience of most of the ADaPT members is dance, theatre, digital art, and programming, telepresence performance also adapts live camera-editing/framing and thus a form of live filmmaking and soundmixing, accompanied by textual communication (chat) or improvised writing that functions as a commentating medium (like subtitles). There are other forms of online performance that involve interactive storytelling or hypertextual narratives as platforms for direct visitor collaboration in fiction development or in spatialized narrative wherein the interactive user takes the role of camera person and editor. There are also translocal compositional environments which construct *performative co-presence* quite differently, not using live dance or physical action but data performance, for example with software applications like Keyworx which were developed for real-time, distributed, multimodal media processing.[11]

Initially, our collaborative ADaPT work experimented with connectivities, infrastructures, and languages we could use. We had to decide on shared software and agreed-upon protocols before improvising together, following the model of free jazz or hip hop jams. *Flying Birdman* suggested a more concise dramaturgy built on cybernetic principles of the feedback loop. As "roles" were passed on from site to site, the behavior of the digital objects was unpredictable and thus affected the behavior of the system they constituted. The loop narrative was translated into streaming video and audio, and different components of the story were developed by the participating sites. In this sense the narrative became a Rashomon-like spiral, distributed among the participants. Each site would observe something different, for sure. The dramaturgy only referred to the time frames of each level and the equal distribution of roles/media, not to the evolving content. One of the challenges in such telepresence performance is the incorporation of the camera interface into the performance, with dancer and camera operator working very closely together in a restricted area that has to be well lit. Camera and microphones are the key interface between performer and network technology. They are the basis for linking the different site-environments into meaningful relationships between the visual and kinaesthetic/ kinaesonic forms and digital outputs.

Taken together, the seven sites produced a form of real-time digital compositing, since some of the partner sites also used video mixers and compositing software. In terms of the skills involved, dance and acting here become a live filmic practice, since much attention goes to the phrasing and framing of the action, the choice of camera angles, camera movement, and in-camera editing or mixing. The live sound does not have to flow directly into the webcast but can be filtered and modified through software. Another challenge is the strategic use of the small delays in Internet transmission (how small depends on the network traffic at any given time) and the degradation of image and audio transfers. Depending on the choice of thematic content, the occasional break-ups and fragmentations of the video stream become part of the (out-of-control) indeterminate aesthetic. What is indeterminate is the transmission and the evolving interplay of the autopoietic creative behaviors.

So far I have outlined the architecture of the environment, both on the formal and the technical level of mixing the streams and producing the distributed content. The involvement of the public both on-site and online, and the transcultural integration of different platforms and behaviors, proved to be more complicated. And it is difficult, of course, to make any claims for the reception of such translocal events. The local visitors witnessed the actual processing of distributive content, the expressive construction in front of their eyes, which became the webcast on the screen mixed with the rhythms of other incoming streams. It was more difficult for online audiences to feel the resonating synergies of these constructions and to follow the spiral, even though the Website provided a map for its navigation. Strong expressive moments occurred when the performer (Birdman character) was moving with or—seemingly—through the urban landscape or architectural filmspaces constructed by another site, becoming "present" to act in a virtual space. The camera work (framing, angle, motion) transports the actor into the frame compositions of the virtual image received through the network. The performer then finds herself inside the moving rhythms or, rather, polyrhythms of the received "places" in this earthwork, making choices as to how to behave, hesitatingly, urgently, attentively responding to features of the image, allowing the viewer to make particular associations.

The performer feels and "touches" the digital landscape, the sense of touch here understood as unconscious vision and orientation, stroking and inhaling the distant surfaces, contours, and edges. The interfusion of the senses, sometimes referred to as synaesthesia, is fully at play in the networked event. You listen to the streaming images, the granular sound drifting by, filled with subtle noise of the network, the light and shadow of intimate sensation, breath drawn in from the edges of acousmatic experiences. Hearing articulates the emerging spaces. You can picture the performer to be on the edge or inside a waking dream or moving through a digital land, changing direction and expression, but all the while the space is motioned by other players. There is an element of playfulness, but also of psychological and affective intensity, since the virtual spaces are unfolding unpredictably. This indetermination can be intuited, and the intensity of sensation is graspable. Abstract images, in such moments, might have considerably less affective resonance than narrative space. In *Flying Birdman* there happened to be (thirteen months after 9/11) several discrete visual references to the dumping (the displacement) of the rubble and earth from Ground Zero at the Fresh Kills landfill across the Hudson River. There were other intricate moments of such complex montage of interactive figure and ground, echoing with an ungraspable concreteness heightened by the poetic rhythms of the refrain ("here I come again"). When such figure-ground relationships become synaesthetic relations, when their proportions are measured by our sensory bodies, they become part of our physical existence and then close the gap between tangible and abstract architectures.

The contradictions in this "theatre of telepresence" are obvious. There is a televisual side to the live performance (onsite), which tends to make the composition aesthetically conservative. And there were obvious efforts made in *Flying Birdman* to prepare meaningful levels of interaction that reflect on the poetic charge of the surreal Birdman character who has been "under" the earth, emerging again but unable to tell what he/she witnessed there. A return from death, which cannot be spoken except by repeated deferral of its mythic role as a messenger. At the same time, all performers were open to improvise with the conditions that would arise under the protocols of the *Birdman* spiral, making choices of behavior when confronted with or embedded within a remote physical environment. As a networked game with multiple players distributed in different sites, unaware of the emerging composite meanings and acting through aleatory processes apart-together, the performance dissolves into multiplicities and unpredictable choral dimensions, hinging on radical contingency. It makes this artistic form unreproducible on any conventional stage. Its compositional process is transductive, not controlled, hierarchical, or unified.

This multi-player online game is not a game of chance (pure aleatory process) but reflects the potential of a new art form—telepresence—to fuse a narratological frame with a mathematical model of nonlinear causality. *Flying Birdman* is ludic and allegorical, rather than driven by the action rhythms of a video game machine. The transductive ecology of networked performance manifests scientifically derived notions of complexity and emergence, demonstrating how feedback in self-organized, recursive organisms elicits change. But how is change narrativized, represented, beyond the action-reaction circuits, and how do we make sense of the ungraspable gaps between cause and effect, the delays of illusion in what we experience as "action"?

In the performance, we can never become immersed completely in the illusion that our bodies are elsewhere; we remain aware of our being in a separate physical environment. We see our projected arms, shoulders, and faces appear in another site, and since the telematic image has a variable delay, our telepresenced bodies will always try to catch up with us. We act in a strange feedback-loop; sometimes we seem to leave our likenesses in the mirror displacements, and the reflections are still peering out after their owners have stopped acting, except that now the video images might do something the actor had not done before. The ground on which she walked has become the sky, a river, a boat. Head pushed forward, her tongue seemed to lick the dew off a leaf, but now the leaf has morphed into the window frame of a cell, its bars dissecting the light. Little glitches also happen in the network transmission. Our bodies freeze, break up, then recompose, or our partners on the other side have changed our colors, inverted us, or multiplied us into a polyp with many arms. As we gain facility with the interface, we can play with the distanced body images and probe the more sinister mirror displacements in the processing of our (image) movements, enjoy the thrill of the confusion of senses, and savor the natural precariousness of temporary networks with their lags, interruptions, and collapses. Everything evolves through adaptation.

Telepresence challenges interaction. We must find the particular qualities of the interaction experience, and negotiate cultural and technical differences. Cross-cultural communication becomes the litmus test of networked performance, as it cannot be assumed that translocal performers, separated by continents, play with the same real-time application design. Our Brazilian partners worked on a different scale, different speed, different hardware and software (iVisit), and a different aesthetic. Bia Medeiros, Carla Rocha, and their team Corpos Informáticos in Brasília and São Paulo are a literary performance group, not dancers/actors. In our dialogue during *Flying Birdman* (and several other networked performances that happened since then) we used a mixed aesthetic form (webcams, chat) not reliant on full-screen spatialized projection and high frame rates. In their case, small webcams and keyboards became actor-instruments. They played with the spiral through their improvisational writing-commentaries and the micro-mirroring of visual leitmotifs which they captured and recomposed through their webcams. The screen became a fluid, pulsating tissue of many action windows, windows without bars, opening and closing. Internet audience involvement is greater if the software platform is more easily accessible and no studio required. On iVisit everyone can enter the virtual "room" and take part in the performance, send and receive. As we develop new digital scripts for such multiplayer online game performances, we need to devise more easily accessible navigational methods to incorporate online visitors as active participants who want to play with the interface, enter the story. Only then can one argue that the ethos of such collaborative play offers creative, political alternatives to the social Darwinism of most action games.[12]

NOTES

I acknowledge the contributions of the Nottingham team members and thank the collaborative culture of the ADaPT team affiliates, especially the Arizona State University Department of Dance and former and current associates of the Environments and DAP labs.

[1] Mick Grierson, "Noisescape: An Interactive 3D Audiovisual Multi-User Composition Environment," in *Die Welt als virtuelles Environment*, edited by Johannes Birringer, Thomas Dumke, and Klaus Nicolai, Dresden: TMA, 2007, 160–68. For the sake of simplicity, I will refer throughout to video or computer games without dwelling on historical and technical differences between video games played on a console using a video monitor or games played on personal computers (or arcade games installed in public spaces requiring payment).

[2] Sampling and modification, hacking into game consoles and appropriations of game engines to create machine cinema ("machinima") are emergent hybrid forms through which the aesthetics and the technology of video games are adopted and subverted, as it was seen in music and hip hop culture as well over the past decades. The close links between game cultures, club cultures, DJing and VJing are also noticeable. In a broad sense, Paul D. Miller (DJ Spooky) sees such derivations and remixes as part of the general "rhythms" of sampled culture. In DJ Spooky's own mix tape, *Riddim Warfare* (1998), he samples and manipulates sounds from Atari games and fuses them with a range of other cultural references. For an excellent introduction to games research, see Marinka Copier/Joost Raessens's anthology *Level Up: Digital Games Research Conference*, Utrecht: Diagra/University of Utrecht, 2003, published after the inaugural conference of the Digital Games Research Association (DiGRA).

[3] Examples include the work of Merce Cunningham, Bill T. Jones, Wayne McGregor, Company in Space, Troika Ranch, Trisha Brown, Yacov Sharir, Philippe Decouflé, Isabelle Choinière, Carol Brown, Christian Ziegler, Nik Haffner, Sarah Rubidge, Kirk Woolford, Thecla Schiphorst, and others.

[4] Cf. Andrew Darley, *Visual Digital Culture: Surface Play and Spectacle in New Media Genres*, London: Routledge, 2000, 30. But see James Newman, *Videogames*, London: Routledge, 2004, especially his comments on non-contiguity in videogame space.

[5] Ruth Gibson and Bruno Martelli's creative output over the past ten years has had a pioneering role in digital art/performance. Their Website (<www.igloo.org. uk>) is in itself an interactive installation allowing the visitor to move through

expanding terrains (small thumbnail images become larger photographs, movies, or animations) and mirror displacements—*Star Wars* becomes *WarStars*, *The Empire Strikes Back* becomes *BackStrikesEmpire*; Merce Cunningham's *Summerspace* and *Winterbranch* beckon from afar as natural landscapes, the cycle of seasons, metaphorical birds, pixilated creatures, optical illusions and mythical allegories greet the viewer in igloo's *Summerbranch*, *WinterSpace*, *Cuckoo*, and *Viking Shoppers*. Toys for children, an "emoticon gallery," and "wiggly worms" for a chill out screen-saver are also on offer. Coding language joins hands with choreographies of the body, 2-D and 3-D computer graphic media flow into and out live performance, tool systems abound yet are explored to humorous and entirely surprising ends. In *3Ascii Ladies* (1997), red, green, and blue versions of a "character" from *WindowsNinetyEight* (1996) are created by an ASCII camera and used for a looped projection: what is left from the earlier filmic work are kinetic-numeric (body)shapes consisting of computer code. For *dotdotdot* (2002), igloo uses motion-capture, Web tools, animation, games engine technology and custom built software, combined with sound and live movement, to generate a series of animated dancers with which the viewer can interact on line. Igloo's modified Quake-engine allows POV movement and flying through space in *SwanQuake* (2007), its newly released game environment.

[6] Jesper Juul, "The Game, the Player, the World: Looking for a Heart of Gameness," in Copier/Raessens, 35.

[7] Newman, *Videogames*, 16–17.

[8] The Association of Dance and Performance Telematics (ADaPT) was founded in 1999 linking sites in Tempe (Arizona), Columbus (Ohio), Salt Lake City (Utah), Madison (Wisconsin), Irvine (California), then expanding to include Brasília and São Paulo (Brazil), Detroit (Michigan), Nottingham (UK), Amsterdam (The Netherlands) and Tokyo (Japan). Website: <http://dance.asu.edu./adapt/>. For other analyses of our telepresence game, see Josephine Dorado, "Artistic Statement," in *Connected! Live Art*, edited by Sher Doruff, Amsterdam: Waag Society, 2005, 112–15, and Maria Beatriz de Medeiros, *Corpos Informáticos: Arte, Corpo, Tecnologia*, Brasilia: FAC, 2006, 55–58.

[9] Mark Coniglio (Troika Ranch) wrote two interactive programs, Interactor and Isadora, which map data input to control various media outputs (<http://www.troikatronix.com/>). The other main interactive software used is Max/MSP/Jitter. Jitter is plugged into Max/MSP and comprises a set of 135 video, matrix, and 3-D graphics objects for the Max graphical programming environment, extending the functionality of Max/MSP in a flexible way to generate and manipulate matrix data—any data that can be expressed in rows and columns, such as video and still images, 3D geometry,

but also text, spreadsheet data, particle systems, voxels, or audio. Software like Jitter, similar to Supercollider and other VJing software, is vital to anyone working with real-time video processing, custom effects, 2D/3D graphics, audio/visual interaction, data visualisation, and analysis.

[10] Having studied with Deborah Hay, I don't recall any cameras ever being used in her workshops, but her practice and conscious attention to movement at a cellular level, in heightened awareness of others as the subject of one's experience, have been very influential on my thinking about telepresence. See her "Performance as Practice" (2001): <http://www.deborahhay.com/journal.html>.

[11] The Mexican theatre company Teatro de Ciertos Habitantes created an extraordinary live recital and "interpretation" of a subtitled movie in *El Automóvil Gris*, for which they recuperated the long forgotten Japanese benshi tradition of voicing film subtitles but modified it. Their live translation of the film mediates the story through voice over, multilingual fake dubbing, musical soundtracks, amplified audio effects, and partly manipulated and recoded visual footage (with new subtitles and animated graphics on their DVD remastering of the film), highlighting the complex virtuality of such live montage. See my review of *El Automóvil Gris* in *Theatre Journal* 56, 3 (2004): 479–80. For a description of hypertextual poetics, see Bill Seaman, "Recombinant Poetics: Emergent Explorations of Digital Video in Virtual Space," in *New Screen Media/Cinema/Art/Narrative*, edited by Martin Rieser and Andrea Zapp, London: BFI, 2002, 237–55, and Medeiros, *Corpos Informáticos*. For a provocative theory of translocal composition with the KeyWorx multi-user media platform, see Sher Doruff, "The Translocal Event and the Polyrhythmic Diagram," PhD dissertation, University of the Arts, London, 2006. A study of pedagogical techniques for networked performance and the formation on online communities is offered by Sita Popat, *Invisible Connections: dance, choreography and internet communities*, London: Routledge, 2006.

[12] Although focused on performance practice, this chapter implies viewing the Internet as a political sphere of communicative forms and collaborative transcultural action directed against the administration of intensified homogenization, exploitation, and surveillance under late capitalism. The command and control logic of many shooter games offer a perversely sinister allegory of the militant side of this regime. The bottom-up philosophy and cooperative ethos discussed in my examples of networked performance point to an admittedly utopian trust in the Internet as an anarchic medium or arena of "countergaming" open to critical, ecosophical, and poetic uses which contradict the Spectacle, and thus the reproduction of existing structures of passive and isolated spectatorship.

IV.

ARTIFICIAL
INTELLIGENCE

▼▲ Thinking Images: A Conversation with Paul Kaiser & Marc Downie

A series of manifestos and books—including "Why the future doesn't need us" (Bill Joy), "The Second Coming" (David Gelernter), and *The Age of Spiritual Machines: When Computers Exceed Human Intelligence* (Ray Kurzweil)—appeared at the turn of the century, first in print and then in a technology forum on the Web (<www.edge.org>), creating an ominous backdrop to the second international CROSS FAIR exhibition-conference held at the newly opened Choreographisches Zentrum in Essen, Germany.[1] The theme of the event, "The Intelligent Stage," seemed to address theatre and dance practitioners. Yet it turned out that most of the invited guests in fact don't practice on theatre stages but belong to the growing international network of digital artists, software designers, and robotics engineers who show their work at electronic arts or new media centers, in specially de-signed Virtual Reality caves, on screens, the Internet, or public spaces. With-in a period of a few years, the concept of an "intelligent stage" designed as an infra-networked laboratory-theatre for interactive performance already seemed outdated. The Intelligent Stage at Arizona State University, which I visited in 1999, was a black box studio set up with an array of hardware and software, video cameras, artificial perception systems, and synthesizers for MIDI interfaces allowing physical action to be translated into sound, music or video projection in real-time. At MIT's Media Lab and Artificial Intelligence Lab, similar concepts had also been drawn up and tested. But Roy Ascott, CROSS FAIR's keynote speaker, proposed to look ahead to "moist media"—constituted by the convergence of dry digital media and wet biological systems. The creative use of telecommunications and the re-structuring of consciousness are primary, Ascott belives. "Intelligent stage" is a space in which one addresses questions such as:

1. what is it to be human in the post-biological culture, and what is it to have mind and body distributed in cyberspace?

2. how might artists deal with the responsibility of redefining nature and life itself?

3. what might be the consequences for the arts of the convergence of computers, biology and nanotechnology?

Ascott emphasized two main distinguishing features of an intelligent stage: first, its location and effect in cyberspace and in distribution across the Net. Second, its role as a space for modeling new structures and behaviors, both human and artificial, that follow the impact of new technologies and the globalization of culture. The converted Zeche Zollverein, a former coal mine, was a perfect setting for these provocations which, in effect, deal with the transition of an industrial art form, based on technique, hierarchical structures of labor/production, and classical attributes of choreography, composition, and execution traditionally associated with the stage, to the digital era. It was in this setting that I saw Paul Kaiser's and Shelley Eshkar's *Ghostcatching* installation for the first time. A conventional physical and aesthetic understanding of performance is challenged by works such as *Ghostcatching* which present a new form of "writing," one might say, a performance writing constructed through motion-capture and digital processing. The resulting digital performance bespeaks a rich artistic imagination and intelligence, but hardly in the sense of Bill Joy's and Ray Kurzweil's scenario of a posthuman condition in which computer software exceeds human thinking. Yet an open debate on what is meant by intelligence was lacking at CROSS FAIR, which was peculiar since the conceptual boundaries of humanly embodied intelligence, artificial intelligence and artifical life were addressed, if sometimes obliquely, by some of the artists. For a moment, however, let us entertain the idea that the most powerful twenty-first-century technologies—robotics, AI, genetic engineering, and nanotechnology—operate according to the law of accelerating returns and intensify the progression of self-replicating cybernetic systems. How will the image of human nature or the human body be modified by computerized systems? How will images behave? How do humans and machines constantly modify one another? How do machines learn from their environment, and what does it matter for the "consciousness" or "intelligence" of performance?

Paul Kaiser and Marc Downie are two of the most prominent artists currently working in the field of digital creation. Together with Shelley Eshkar, they formed a collaborative team in 2001, operating under the name the

OpenEnded Group. Though the three largely work together, they sometimes work in pairs, create solo artworks, and pursue collaborative projects with others, including key collaborators from a range of arts and science fields (architects, composers, electrical engineers, programmers).

Paul Kaiser's background is in experimental filmmaking; throughout the 1980s he taught students with severe learning disabilities, with whom he collaborated on making multimedia depictions of their own minds. From this work, he derived the key ideas—*mental space* and *drawing as performance*—which became points of departure for the digital artworks he has been making since the mid-90s, including his path-breaking motion-captured performance collaborations with Merce Cunningham (*BIPED*), Bill T. Jones (*Ghostcatching*), and Trisha Brown (*how long does the subject linger on the edge of the volume ...*). *Visionary of Theater* was created as a multimedia documentary on the early theatre work of Robert Wilson, further elaborating "drawing as performance" and offering a video primer of movement on the stage. More recently, a series of public art works and installations (*Pedestrian*, *Trace*) shifted attention to everyday movements of pedestrians and of children by projecting trompe-l'oeil figures and miniature urban landscapes directly onto city sidewalks. *Recovered Light* was a massive "virtual X-ray" projection created for York Minster, UK, while *Enlightenment* and *Breath*, commissioned by Lincoln Center for the Mostly Mozart Festivals (2006, 2007), are considered to be the highest-resolution live digital artworks ever created. They investigate, visualize, and reconstruct the deeper musical structures of Mozart by means of artificial intelligence and real-time graphics.

Marc Downie brings a scientific background to the OpenEnded Group, with an MSci in physics from the University of Cambridge and a PhD from MIT's Media Lab based on artificial intelligence research. His complex algorithmic systems are inspired by natural systems and a critique of prevalent digital tools and techniques. His interactive installations, compositions, and projections have advanced the fields of interactive music, machine learning, and computer graphics. At the MIT Media Lab, he collaborated extensively with engineers on the development of projects such as *(void *)*, presented at SIGGRAPH in 2000, *AlphaWolf* (ars electronica, 2002), *Dobie* (SIGGRAPH 2002), and *Jeux Deux* (2006). His solo works include the series *Musical Creatures* (2000–3), which has been exhibited internationally.

This conversation was conducted via Internet in the spring of 2007.

▲▼

BIRRINGER: Paul, you participated in the 2006 Monaco Dance Forum where you and your collaborators recreated *how long does the subject linger on the edge of the volume ...* (2005) with Trisha Brown's dance company. At the festival, you also showed *22*, a collaboration with Bill T. Jones that had emerged from the same artistic research begun several years earlier. I take it, from having seen some of your previous work, that you think of yourself as an image maker. Do you see *how long does the subject linger on the edge of the volume ...* and *22* as live performance works that present a new kind of image art?

KAISER: Yes, we had the strong sense of opening a new door, especially with *how long....* In that particular piece, we were able to push the door open pretty wide. So how is this a new kind of image? Well, to begin with, the artwork doesn't consist of a skein of pre-made pictures that are triggered "interactively" in the course of the performance. No, it works very differently from that. It has its own autonomy, thanks to the artificial intelligence that Marc Downie has endowed it with. Its imagery comes as it pictures things to itself, trying to make sense of what it sees onstage in real-time as the dance unfolds. Of course, it doesn't proceed from a completely blank slate any more than a newborn baby does. Instead it draws upon a series of structures and intentions that we've given to it, which in combination sometimes bring to mind simple living "creatures," to use Marc's term.

For example, the piece opens up with a triangle creature, whose intention is to move from stage right to stage left. It does so by hitching rides on points in the motion-captured dancers' bodies, guessing which ones are moving in the right direction. Thus it extends a line out to a likely point, and is then tugged that way if it's guessed correctly. Of course, sometimes its hunch is wrong, and it has to relinquish its grip on that point and await the next opportunity. In such a case, that line is left as a trace, and thus the whole image as it progresses is simultaneously a history of its attempts.

This touches on a new element of picturing-making: memory. Not only does our artwork work with a sense of present and of future—by perceiving in real-time what is occurring on stage and guessing what might happen next—but it also works with its memory of the past. Often its images come from its attempting to work out correspondences between past and present configurations on stage. Of course, this is all very well and good on technical grounds, as computer science if you will. But our feeling is that the work should stand or fall on artistic grounds. It's up to the audience whether the quality of our line is exquisite or not, or whether their experience of time as it unfolds in the performance is somehow new and unexpected.

BIRRINGER: The images generated during the performance, in real-time, have a memory as part of their behavior, as well as the power of anticipation. These are not properties we generally associate with the photographic or filmic notion of the image. How are we to understand the idea of such "creatures" in a theatre work? Are you suggesting that there is a new dimension of "artificial life" acting upon the performance?

KAISER: Yes, I think this work does push our notion of what imagery can be. Even "live" imagery of the kind normally seen on stage or in installations reacts only to the present moment (unless of course it's actually being driven by preset external cues). But Marc's creation of live "creatures" does give our imagery the ability both to remember and to form expectations. And it's crucial to bear in mind that each such creature's memories and expectations are its own—that is, unlike each other's and, more to the point, unlike our own. But the question to ask is: why are artificial memory and anticipation so important? To answer this, let's see why our own abilities to remember to form expectations are so crucial to our experience of the world.

As we observe any event, our perception of it derives not simply from the present moment itself, but rather how it stands in contrast to what we think led up to it and where we suspect it might be headed. In a complex event, like that of a great performance, such memories and expectations are never fixed, but are set in constant play as we continually readjust our perceptions and understanding. That's precisely what we want our imagery to do. Each creature works within its own limits to make sense of the world in just this way. And as I said before it pictures its understanding, and it's this process of picturing that becomes the live image.

BIRRINGER: Do you see the creatures as abstract figurations or as having a narrative dimension?

KAISER: The creatures are capable of being either abstract or figurative, and also of having an explicit narrative dimension. To my mind, we humans tend to interpret almost any sequence of events as cause and effect and therefore as narrative, so even a fairly abstract creature automatically suggests a story in much the way an inkblot does. The triangle creature I described above, for example, has a clear goal (to move across the stage)—which we immediately interpret as its desire. And we soon make out its strategy (to link its points to those of the dancers moving in the same direction), which we interpret as some sort of narrative interconnection. One crucial aspect of this is that we see the virtual creature's effort—its mistakes and its misunderstandings, as well as its eventual success—which again adds to its being curiously life-like.

BIRRINGER: Are the creatures' behaviors generated in real-time from the actions on stage, or are they picturing something different, something of their own?

KAISER: The software always looks directly at what is happening on stage and then creates its imagery in response to its understanding of what it perceives. Of course, the picture it forms is idiosyncratic—in part because a given creature attends to just one kind of pattern on stage, rather than to the aggregate of patterns that we in the audience are following. But because it attends so closely to that pattern, it often reveals relationships that we don't notice.

BIRRINGER: How do you and Marc understand the relationship of computing and artificial intelligence to the theatre, to choreography and movement, since here the "images" are neither film nor visualization or illustration. The creatures do have a geometric form, in my mind, animated forms, shapes, architectures. They are non-anthropomorphic, but as you suggest the audience might "read" a narrative into their behavior, humanize it. On the other hand, what intelligence do the creatures have? Do they observe motion, do they respond to the motor sensory—action observation, as the neurophysiologists might call it—or can they respond to choreographic content? Emotions, affect? What is the relationship between movement animation and consciousness/cognition?

DOWNIE: "Artificial intelligence" informs our work in a number of ways, ranging from the mundane to the exquisite, from the general to the specific. To see this you can begin with an extremely broad definition of what "AI" is. Most simply put, this is the field dedicated to getting computers to do "the right thing," by themselves, in situations where programmatic descriptions, of the kind that computers generally require, of what that "right thing" is are inaccessible to us. Stated this way, AI clearly ought to be central to almost any digital artist practice—as soon as, that is, they go beyond the commercially conventional ways of making images and music. What it is that we are wanting out of the computer—the images, the relationships–cannot be programmed in a forward or a forethought-out way. Firstly, many of the "algorithms" are in fact just too complex. Too many values to tune, too many layered decisions, renders conventional engineering impossible. Secondly, and more importantly, our "specifications" for the computer programs—what it is we want the images and relationships to do—will only be discovered as we begin to glimpse them. Thus we seek solutions that allow us to work with computers rather than merely on them. AI, as described this way, is still incredibly broad (and from both a programming and an artistic standpoint rather uselessly broad) but this should at least suggest that AI is not an arbitrary posture, that we introduce it not for its own sake, but rather because the field offers potential solutions to problems that many artists face.

That said, we are focused on a particular class of AI problems and solutions—described variously as "agent-based," "creature-like" or even "reactive"—that emphasizes the computer as an embodied agent. That is, one that is deeply coupled to its environment such that its actions on its environment—mediated by the physical constraints of some "body"—must be carefully produced and its perceptions of its environment—mediated by its all too limited sensory apparatus—must be carefully maintained. Such AI is also often where the most interesting integrative machine learning work occurs, and there learning takes the place of extensive human level domain-specific knowledge (think: birds rather than chess players). And it also makes perfect sense given our preference for images that move between abstraction and figuration to be near a field with a concern for virtual animated bodies. Finally, this "style" of AI is usually practiced in a frankly more interactive way by its community. These preferences dominate our choice of techniques—not any need for our creatures to share a neurophysi-ological basis with the dancers, which they resolutely do not, nor do we have any goal for "human level" choreographic intelligence.

Thus, while this explanation should clarify much of the architecture of our imagery for *how long ...*—it is this thinking that our "thinking images" are about—but it's important to realize that our creatures are not robots. Their bodies and their physics are purely imaginary; their sensory apparatus are not sensing the "real world" but sensing the motion-capture data and other agents in view. Their motivation and affect systems are for their regulation not for our narrative. And the problems that they are forced to solve are not given by the natural world: they are also designed by us as we see opportunities in Trisha's choreography.

BIRRINGER: I am not sure how close theatre and dance are to games, let's say, and the "virtual animated bodies" in game environments, if that is what you meant.

DOWNIE: I don't feel qualified to talk about how close theatre or dance is to games, in general, either in the classical sense or in the sense of computer games. However there is a game-like aspect to our forms in two overlapping senses. Firstly, algorithms *are* rules—nothing more. Our agents describe a set of rules that in application will produce the images seen as the artwork. While it's we who come up with the rules initially, once set we tend to quite rigorously follow them to see where they might lead—we play out the game without arguing over the rules. Coming up with a new set of rules is gener-ally preferable to trying to break our previous set. Secondly, our agents of-ten end up participating in games: the opening Triangle agent for *how long ...* has to get from stage right to stage left by hitching a ride on the dancers at key moments. Clearly, neither of these two aspects is in any way unique to our work; there's precedent in every corner of art history, including, of course, the choreographers we have worked with.

There is also a relationship, but not a terribly interesting one, between our work at a technical level, and computer games. Like everybody else in the field we are parasitic to some extent on the consumer-level graphics hardware created for the game industry. Although recently it has become much easier to avoid the common aesthetics of computer games, this has come at the price of it being much harder to get anything on the screen at all. Finally, much of my code for making "abstract" bodies was tested much more rigorously than you'd expect while at the Media Lab—and it still sees use in drawing and controlling much more computer game-like characters and frighteningly "concrete" robots. I can testify that playing between the abstract and the figurative is technically much easier once you have the figurative worked out on a robot.

BIRRINGER: But you speak of more fully interactive practices in the AI community, while I understood Paul to imply that interactivity on stage is not necessarily your goal.

DOWNIE: It is correct to say that "interactivity on stage" was not our goal for *how long*.... Ultimately the choreography is fixed, and the dancers are accurate from evening to evening (to my eye, supernaturally so). There was no sense while we were making the work that the dancers would ultimately interact with the imagery during the performance. Rather *we* were seeking to interact with Trisha Brown's dance, and we took advantage of the three years that we worked on the project to build a set of tools and ideas to allow us to do just that. This difference is crucial and is present throughout our work—our recent work *Enlightenment* is a cluster of ten computers that interact with themselves. And at present Paul and I are making a series of prints: interactively—but obviously they are not interactive prints. It's not that we are uninterested in the problem of interacting with "the public," we just haven't had any good ideas yet.

BIRRINGER: You said that you designed the creatures' "thinking" behavior in response to the choreography, is that correct to say? In terms of such thinking or learning, is sensing the kinematic data a mathematical/geometrical process of regulation (based on the computer's analysis of the tracked points in space), and an "improvisatory" transformation of a particular body model?

DOWNIE: The "thinking" in *how long* ... certainly extends down to the lowest (and most tedious) technical levels of the piece. One of the lessons we quickly learned when we started to work with real-time motion-capture was that we would have to reconstruct most of the motion-capture pipeline ourselves, on our terms. The priorities of the hardware manufacturers are deeply misaligned with ours, emphasizing the quality of data over the quantity of it. Frustrating and time-consuming as this engineering was, it worked out happily: much of the piece evolved from "staging" these increasingly sophisticated algorithms of machine perception, and in particular staging their repeated failures and attempts to compensate. The piece would have been impossible to execute had we simply accepted the manufacturers' "black boxes" as closed to us; and any AI would have found itself in a much-impoverished environment. However, an unwillingness or an inability to understand, reconstruct or even reject the pre-made pieces of technology that populate the digital art world remains the norm.

BIRRINGER: Paul, has the AI approach to physical performance privileged a certain kind of abstract movement or body model and a non-representational creation of geometry? How do you see such computational sensibilities, digital graphics and animated geometries relating to other forms of music or dance theatre, spoken word theatre or installations, in terms of audience participation? Do you foresee a growing use of such graphical environments in performance?

KAISER: Well, if you take a close look at the particular choreographers we're working with here—Merce Cunningham and Trisha Brown—you'll see that that their reliance on abstract diagrams predates ours by several decades! Both Merce and Trisha choreograph by means of such diagrams, creating amazing graphical depictions of such key dance elements as stage geometry, movement trajectories, temporal repetitions, body kinesphere, and so on. Look, for example, at even so early a work as Merce's *Suite by Chance* of 1953, and you'll see him charting the spatial and temporal axes of the work, with no recourse to stage pictures. Trisha makes similar use of drawing, for example in creating her amazing 1975 solo *Locus*, in which she draws a simple cube and a string of letters, which she then uses to set her choreographic requirements. The cube she imagines as being roughly the size of her kinesphere (the space surrounding her body that she can potentially reach). By labeling each vertex of the cube (actually, cuboid) with a letter, she determines the order in which she must hit each point of space with any given part of her body. The resulting solo is of course a well-known tour-de-force, and Trisha's method led directly, I'd say, to Bill Forsythe's more elaborate invisible geometries.

Let me also point out that Trisha elevated this kind of drawing to a formal art practice, exhibiting the works in galleries and museums, so it's not as if she wanted to keep her diagrammatic thinking hidden from view—behind the scenes, so to speak. To the contrary, which is why she took so quickly and enthusiastically to the diagrammatic creatures of our *how long ...* projections. Parenthetically, I'd like to say something that I hope Marc will take up further, which is that in many ways Merce and Trisha were exploring ideas and processes in a manner very much parallel to what was going on simultaneously in computer science. I'm not suggesting that von Neumann and Turing were ever aware of Cunningham and Brown, or vice versa, but I will say this: what a shame! And it's not too late to cross-pollinate their ideas, even if they never had a chance to do so themselves.

However, I don't want to paint us into too tight a corner here. Your question implies that we committed ourselves exclusively to a style of diagrammatic abstraction and so on, which is far from the case. We've worked with equal interest and intensity with representation. Indeed my first encounter with the stage was through Robert Wilson's drawings, the vast majority of which are simple but incredibly effective series of stage scene thumbnails.

More to the point, we were committed to an AI approach to representation in another collaboration done in parallel with *how long ....* This was with Bill T. Jones, in a work entitled *22*. It entailed an identical technical set-up to Trisha's piece, with twenty-four infra-red cameras capturing Bill's movement in real-time, and our software's responding simultaneously not through abstract creatures but through life-like figures (a young boy and a man) that provided a thematic and visual counterpoint to Bill's solo stage presence. I didn't use this example earlier, for the final piece fell well short of our aspirations for it, for complicated reasons having nothing to do with us. From our standpoint, however, the virtual figures of *22* could work just as well as the abstract creatures of *how long ...* in fulfilling this dream of "thinking pictures."

DOWNIE: I could mention that one of the "complicated reasons having nothing to do with us" was that in *22* there was a need for the images to interact as much with the narrative that was being told in performance by Bill T. Jones as with his movement. If the getting a computer to "understand choreography" live is research, getting a computer to "understand narrative" live is simply foolhardy. So foolhardy in fact that we didn't attempt it in our contribution to this piece which, as it was, seemed to begin to sink under the weight of its rather traditional stage-managed cuing. Such short fallings, however, often indicate future opportunities and each of our more recent pieces have increasingly engaged language, and computational responses to it. This has led us, again, far away from the terrain of *how long ... or 22.*

BIRRINGER: It's interesting that you mention the choreographers' and Robert Wilson's drawings. I tend to think that Wilson's scenography and directing have a computational, almost mathematical-abstract quality, but of course he also works with the figure. Perhaps the terms figurative and non-representational are no longer helpful in this context of complex systems, digital or AI. But given your interest in animation, graphic visual art, and the kind of complexities afforded by an agent-based aesthetics as well as your fascination with disequilibrium, could you speak a little about your work not directly intended for the theatre but for galleries and public spaces? What are the aesthetic differences between the public projections, the gallery works and the collaborative performance works?

KAISER: I'm afraid I don't agree with you on the first point, Johannes. I'd say, actually, that Robert Wilson's scenography and directing are more *mechanical* than computational. It's certainly no secret that much of his staging is a revival of the sophisticated proscenium mechanics of the nineteenth century, repurposed for avant-garde spectacle. In any case, from what I've seen, he mostly works by drawing scenes from a stage perspective rather than diagramming relationships and movements more abstractly the way Merce, Trisha, and Bill Forsythe tend to do.

But to address the main part of your question, it's mainly an issue of context, which of course has aesthetic implications. The great thing about the stage is the way it frames not only the *space* of the artwork, but also the *time* of it. In our hectic day and age, it's quite a wonderful throwback to an earlier age where people more often gave things their undivided attention. Certainly that's rarely the case for museum exhibits, much less for public art, so the pieces you make for those settings need to allow for random access, as it were—people come and go much more randomly in such settings, and the artwork has to withstand, address, or overcome that somehow. For public artworks, you also have to imagine some of the viewers encountering the piece repeatedly over the days of its installation, which again is a very different kind of viewing experience. We try to make works that can disclose themselves in different ways depending on the depth and the frequency of their exposure.

DOWNIE: The parallels between Merce, Trisha, Bill Forsythe's, and others' practices and digital art, at least as it could be practiced, are quite striking. If you pardon the language: these choreographers are producing algorithms that are executed on their dancers, observing the unforeseeable results of the computation, making adjustments, and iterating; culling the potential of their algorithmic ideas; carefully pruning the possibilities they create; constantly negotiating the constraints of human performance, perception and their interfaces with the abstract-computational. Of course, there are often wonderfully talented dancers that perform these computations, and we just have our keyboards and our stupid computers—but those problems are separate, they are *just* technical. After enough work, enough engineering, you strive to find yourself in a position very similar to that of a choreographer and their dancers. I've complained for a long time now that digital art, as a field that refuses to grow up and understand its history, or that there is a history, has generally ignored the possibility that there may be a useful prehistory in the performing arts.

BIRRINGER: Paul, do the projected animations you installed in public places reflect an aspect of image work that you have always been interested in? What has happened in your thinking and practice since your earlier collaborations with Bill T. Jones and Merce Cunningham?

KAISER: The simplest answer to your question is that I started out as a filmmaker and I never gave up my desire for the kind of cinematic experience that large projections allow. It was obvious that I'd never sneak any of my work into the local multiplex cinema, so I found different spaces—a huge scrim at the State Theater or a broad expanse of sidewalk at Rockefeller Center. But there are important differences between the public works and the dance works. The first has to do with framing and audience. You realize when you step into the world of dance how distant it is from the everyday world, even despite various valiant efforts to break down that divide. But I came to realize, as I've said many times before, that the only people who go see modern dance are the people who go see modern dance. Very few outsiders stumble into it—"stumbling in" becoming exactly what public art allows.

Most of the audience encountering *Pedestrian* on the street in Harlem or in a bus station in Seoul or on a market square in Bruges do so completely by accident, unexpectedly having to make sense of an artwork whose context does not automatically supply all the answers as a gallery or museum or stage context invariably does. But the other impetus behind some of the public artworks was a desire to get away from dance movement itself, which has never fascinated me so much as the movements I see through my window on the street below or from a bench in a playground when I take my daughters there. To me, children playing tag on a field or pedestrians maneuvering through a busy intersection in midtown are supreme feats of choreography, but choreography without a choreographer. Absolutely fascinating. Which is not to say that my perceptions of such everyday movements and patterns were not sharpened tremendously by our work with Merce and Bill T. and Trisha.

BIRRINGER: With your interest in more mundane, pedestrian, and nonexpert movement, are you going through your Judson phase?

KAISER: Well, it's an interesting parallel, and I sometimes wish we could have worked with Trisha when she herself was still in that phase. But the answer still is no, for two reasons. First, when a self-conscious adult performer does ordinary movement on stage, well, the movement is no longer ordinary. Certainly it doesn't feel so to any audience member, which for us is the crucial part. So Judson movements are really not the same either physically or psychologically or spiritually as playground movements, and the latter interest us much more.

But second, when I was about twenty years old—back around 1979—I was already fascinated by pedestrian movement, and made an experimental film in Super 8 called *Colorblind* that took as its subject people crossing a single intersection on West End Avenue. In those days, of course, I knew nothing about postmodern dance. In any case I couldn't advance that interest any further for two decades, not only because the right tools didn't exist, but also because I didn't have the right collaborators (after all, Shelley was nine years old at the time, and Marc was two!).

BIRRINGER: How has OpenEnded Group evolved: are you three now a production and research company?

KAISER. The OpenEnded Group is more of a collective than a company—there is no leader, for example, and we make all our decisions unanimously. Research is part of art-making, and art-making part of research. The secret to great collaboration, I learned, is to work with people much smarter than I am. I met Shelley Eshkar in the mid-90s through his former teacher, Robert Breer, one of my filmmaking heroes, and it was immediately apparent that he was incredibly gifted. It was he who solved the problem of making a convincing "hand-drawn space" in 3-D, and he who designed the hand-drawn bodies that made *Ghostcatching* and *BIPED* what they were. We've been working together now for almost twelve years and are essentially telepathic.

Marc Downie came in an arranged marriage, really, for a piece that the MIT Media Lab commissioned from us—our abstract portrait of Merce Cunningham, *Loops*, which was based on our motion-capture of Merce's hand dances. When we first sat down with Marc over coffee, he nodded quietly at every preposterous goal we stated, and a couple of weeks later, had us shaping the piece in real-time in front of his screen at MIT. You have no idea how revolutionary that was! What had taken us overnight to render before, Marc was now drawing to the screen instantaneously. Independently, he had been pursuing some of the same hand-drawn, non-photorealistic goals that we had, most notably in a series called *Musical Creatures*, so it was a natural fit. I also realized he was smartest person I'd ever met, so I helped steer him out of academia. The three of us have been working together ever since.

BIRRINGER: In a recent symposium at the 2007 Cyberarts Festival in Boston, I raised the question why there are so few substantive technological performance works or innovative dance works which use computer augmentation. The works that have had an impact we can count on one hand, why do you think this is so? If there are so few works, perhaps we cannot even speak of impact, in a cultural sense?

KAISER: The most obvious reason is expense. Practically speaking, dance budgets are small, and even set-up times tend to be very short. Talking to lighting designers, for example, I learned that they have far less time to design on stage for dance than they do for plays, for example—and far less than for operas. But a much more important reason has to do with method and approach, for the tools commonly used in interactive work (Max/MSP and Jitter, for example) largely lead to terrible results. They seem to promote the shallowest and the easiest kinds of thinking, and it's no surprise that no masterpieces seem to have emerged from there! I'm no tools determinist, and it's certainly conceivable to create a great artwork with poor tools, but they certainly don't help. But Marc, who devoted part of his thesis to this question, can answer it better than I.

DOWNIE: Perhaps I am a "tools determinist": I just take a unusually broad definition of "tool," one that is expanded to include all of the ideas one uses to arrive at the artwork itself. And I believe that while pleasant surprises can happen, you generally end up in a place that bears the marks of how you got there. The separation of digital tool and formal idea is artificial and convenient only if you are in the unfortunate position of having to purchase your tools from strangers. It's worth studying the tools used for digital art as forms: not just from the perspective of what they can do (and how fast they can do it) but what ideas they embody and privilege or exclude and prevent. There are then two scandals: firstly, that there aren't a tremendous number of tools available today; and secondly they are all the same! Max/MSP/Jitter and its brethren embody nothing more than a set of ideas firmly worked out in the mid-80s which themselves were constructed to be parallel to the ideas embodied by the analog synthesizers of the 50s, which in turn were simply inherited from the physics of electrical engineering.

Outside the digital art world, nobody takes these ideas about interaction and programming seriously: not the artworld, not computer science, not philosophy, not even physics. The third scandal is, of course, that nobody seems to care and digital art becomes increasingly un-interdisciplinary as it becomes un-serious to these fields. My response is two-fold: to make sure that I can take responsibility for any digital tool I use, usually by making it or remaking it; and soon, to make our tools freely available. The goal of our upcoming "Open Source" release is not to skew the hegemony in our direction, but simply to disrupt it and make artists begin to question what many have simply "received" up until this point.

BIRRINGER: Do you think interactivity or interaction design in live performance on stage is limiting or artistically uninteresting? What forms of interactive art do you feel has had a significant artistic impact or corresponds to the increasing interactive design in the culture at large, as in communications, games, etc.?

DOWNIE: It's impossible to rule anything out, but I suspect that on stage "interaction design" is a bad place to start from and a bad place to end up. And as for the influence of interactive art I find that it has had almost no effect on computers let alone culture at large. Digital artists continue to have no effect on Apple's next operating system, Adobe's next image editing tool, Microsoft's next word processor, Google's next start up purchase, W3C's next Web standard, etc. (This makes the idea that artists are content to simply wait for better tools all the more appalling.)

BIRRINGER: What is computer augmentation of performance? What did the designers of the "intelligent stage" at Arizona State University have in mind with the architectures of interactive, networked spaces? If universities are investing in such laboratories, why are arts organizations not following suit? BAM stopped supporting media arts, Dance Theatre Workshop discontinued its digital fellowship program. Is the support for digital art mostly going to be found in visual arts organizations?

KAISER: If I were more politic, I would sidestep this question, but what the hell—as you know, I tend to speak my mind. And in this case I do speak from experience, since I was one of the three artists chosen for the short-lived BAM digital installation program, and since we have worked at Arizona State and in several other university projects as well. You'll remember, Johannes, that you and I first met when you were teaching at Ohio State University, where the Dance department was attempting to collaborate with the Computer Graphics department in a motion-capture studio. As is inevitably the case, the problem comes down to money. Universities and corporations have it; artists and art organizations do not. Let's look at universities first. Big universities are not only committed to advanced research, but many also have very large performing arts centers that are a crucial mainstay for contemporary American dance. I'm thinking of the Zellerbach stage in Berkeley, the Krannert Center in Illinois, the Hancher stage in Iowa, and quite a few others. These places are not only venues for dance, they also commission new works: a fantastic thing.

On paper, then, it makes sense that universities should go even further by supporting advances in digital art and performance, not only because they can tap into many sources of funding that are (unfairly!) out of the reach of artists, but also—and more appropriately—because they have the physical facilities (equipment, labs, stages) to host the development and the staging of complex projects. Universities even have, potentially, many scientific and artistic collaborators who could contribute to such work.

Why then has our experience been largely one of failure and exasperation? And, even worse, why do we harbor suspicions of fraudulence? The sad story is that universities tend to make lofty pronouncements, especially to funders, but fall terribly short in execution. Even worse, when they fail, they don't acknowledge their failure, but simply explain it away as the necessary consequence of experimentation and research, part of what they inevitably call the "process"—a word I've come to detest. I think we need to get back to good old-fashioned "results" instead. The embarrassing fact is that such failures often come in areas of basic competence, not advanced research. University engineers, for example, simply won't know how to operate their expensive optical motion-capture equipment. When we were in long, repeated residence with Trisha Brown at Arizona State, they kept failing to capture any data whatsoever—heartbreakingly, at times. We persuaded Trisha to don the motion-capture costume and to perform her *Locus* solo for posterity, only to learn much later on, and with no accompanying apology, that the data had never been acquired. With little skill in matters of simple competence, was it any surprise that the loftier research goals were rarely met? Of course, you'd never know this from the press releases and status reports streaming forth; and meanwhile those hundreds of thousands of dollars had already dried up in the academic sands.

Well, enough of this. If I sound bitter, that's because I am, but I'll spare you the excruciating details. Despite this terrible experience, I would like to believe that universities could support real research in the arts, but only if they really confront their previous failures in the field. And I would add that it was an art school, Cooper Union, that gave Shelley and me crucial support in working with Bill T. Jones on *Ghostcatching* very early on.

As for corporate support, that is more unabashedly about money or at least value: the value to companies being promotional. Indeed, funds usually come directly from marketing departments, not from any charitable corporate offshoot. Sometimes such support is very simple: in the mid- to late-90s, for example, Compaq supported our work because we were using what were then their advanced NT workstations, and they could boast about that at the National Broadcasters convention and at SIGGRAPH. The most pervasive, and the most pernicious, support for the performing arts has long come from Phillip Morris, the tobacco company—blood money, really, with politically correct artists and art groups putting themselves through all kinds of odd contortions to justify that backing. My opposition to Phillip Morris got me in trouble at the Whitney, where a group show I was in found much-needed but tainted support from them. I protested publicly, and also paid the actual costs of installation myself.

BIRRINGER: I think it's remarkable that you have worked on some of the most crucial artistic performance collaborations over the past decade, especially if your initial background was in film. You mentioned BAM's digital installation program: why did BAM not encourage more of the kind of work you were producing?

KAISER: Again, I think it comes down to simple economics. The Brooklyn Academy initiative was with Lucent, which owns Bell Labs. Both BAM and Lucent wanted to associate themselves with the glory days of the 1960s, of the E.A.T. collaborations (Rauschenberg, Breer, Trisha Brown, et al, working with engineers like Billy Klüver). But there was a key difference: originally, all that was done informally rather than institutionally, with the artists and engineers pairing up on their own. Bottom-up versus top-down. In the later case, Lucent provided money and some equipment, and artists and engineers met in a kind of rapid dating game to see who could mate successfully. The actual results were pretty good—for example, Ben Rubin and Mark Hansen worked together seamlessly to create *Listening Post*, a wonderful installation that did indeed draw on Bell Labs research meaningfully.

For my part, perhaps in reaction to the top-down institutional nature of the whole process—and perhaps perversely—I created an intensely personal work entitled *Trace*. Several research projects I saw at Bell Labs were about new technologies of surveillance, which took me back to my childhood as a diplomat's son in Eastern Europe, where we were constantly shadowed and bugged. *Trace* was about the "self-surveillance" that sort of self-consciousness led me to. But the upshot was that Lucent's share prices tanked shortly thereafter, and when that support went away, so did BAM's. In any case, it was always clear that BAM's heart was in performance, understandably enough. And they still had Phillip Morris to fund it.

DOWNIE: To tie these last two questions together I think it might be useful to ponder the overlap and differences between artists, engineers, and scientists—speaking as an artist who has pretended to be a scientist and an engineer at times. The E.A.T. collaborations are in some ways the canonical bottom-up meetings of artists with engineers. Despite having often irreconcilably different sets of tastes, engineers and artists share a dedication to actually making things, a pride in the things that they make and an understanding that they judge, and are judged on, the things that they end up making. This alignment of perspectives can be tremendously exciting when it happens, and it's possible for everybody to ensure that they are getting back something from the collaboration. But collaborations inside a university are often formulated completely as science-art collaborations; certainly our most recent university experience was ultimately funded by the NSF. Academic science has as uneasy a relationship with engineering as it has with art. And since nobody can independently replicate, say, a motion-recognition system built for Trisha Brown's movement, the junior science faculty and graduate students involved in such collaborations are left scrambling for the limited value that they can extract from the relationship in ways that are often independent of the resulting artwork. Artists then respond by defending the integrity of their process and the artifacts that they are going to be left with. In such pathological collaborations the only uncertainty is just how long it will be before everybody starts bolting for the exits.

Despite an abundance of interdisciplinary ventures by American universities, only a handful will accept artifacts (and even fewer, performances) as part of the tenure or advanced degrees processes for their "science" halves. No wonder then that dot coms were a better bet than the academy. Until this changes, interdisciplinary research is not being done by institutions except by accident or resistance.

BIRRINGER: Yes, I have similar experiences, but in the UK there is some effort made now to fuse the funding for sciences and humanities in so-called sci-art projects. More interesting is the bottom-up model and the many small research networks that I see growing across the world. Can we go back one step: Paul, what made you work on a project involving theatre director Bob Wilson? What kind of exhibition did you create of Wilson's works and drawings? Were you interested in his early long-durational or outdoor work, or his particular interest in working with autistic adolescents?

KAISER: A long story, but I'll shorten it. My start in multimedia was in working with severely learning disabled children, whom I taught for ten years in the 1980s. Well, "whom I taught"—and who taught me. What I learned from them, primarily, was how to collaborate, for in creative classes I soon learned to give up instructing in favor of open-ended exploring. And when Apple's HyperCard program was released on the Macintosh in the mid-90s, we used its multimedia tools to carry on those collaborations on this new frontier. That's in fact when I came up with guiding principles like "drawing as performance" that carried through to many later artworks— and which proved to be one of the keys to my work with Wilson.

Fast forward to 1993 or so, when Wilson's foundation was thinking about a digital archive. A friend told them of my work, thinking of the parallel: Bob Wilson had also started out by working with handicapped and "special needs" kids, two of whom directly inspired the first two—and to my mind most impressive—phases of his work. And then, too, there was the central practice of drawing, with Bob creating all of his work not verbally but visually, in the never-ceasing activity of his thumbnail sketching. So just as with the children I'd taught, my goal was to capture the act of Bob's drawing, as it happened—to put it back into the time of its performance, which eventually I did. Working with Babette Mangolte, I filmed him drawing and narrating his recollections of such pivotal works as *Deafman Glance*, *KA MOUNTAIN*, and *Einstein on the Beach*, and used the resulting video as a guide to dissect the resulting drawings in Photoshop. I could then tie this drawn performance to the video, films, photographs, maquettes, etc., that I found in the archive, which allowed me to reconstruct works otherwise lost to time.

That was just one of several methods I used in making the piece, *Visionary of Theater*. In it, I was at pains to put Bob's best foot forward, to make the best possible case for his early work, and in particular to reveal the extraordinarily collaborative nature of it—*true* collaboration with the likes of Christopher Knowles, Cindy Lubar, Andy deGroat, and so many others. Though the piece was exhibited widely, among other things in a show of

Bob's drawings that I co-curated with Brooke Hodge of Harvard's Graduate School of Design, it was only this year that it finally reached its intended form of CD-ROM—and has now—belatedly, and on teetering, outdated technical underpinnings—entered the collection of the Performing Arts Library at Lincoln Center.

So, yes, I put Wilson's work in the best possible light but all the while I was reacting against it and its kind. Too long a philosophical point to go into here, but I can't omit the fact that I'm deeply troubled by the severing of causality and of history that you find in Wilson and his forbearers (Cage, for instance) and their many followers who crowd the field of digital art. This objection relates to our critique of arbitrariness, the same critique Marc makes of the arbitrary "mapping" techniques embedded in the digital tools like Max/MSP. I think that dream logic, random juxtaposition, asynchronicity, and so on, have become easy evasions of hard thinking. The proof, perhaps, is the degree to which they've been gleefully adopted by mass media—advertising, video games, music videos, and so on. A welter of disconnects.

BIRRINGER: After *Pedestrian* and, later, *Playground*, Paul, you have now been commissioned to create public works in England (York Minster). Are you becoming interested in very large scale work or are these projection works logical continuations of your image-making for the theatre?

KAISER: Well, all the world's a stage, right? So, yes, we've been very interested in expanding the possibilities of public art, and in particular of making permanent works. In the United States at least, "public" is a slightly misleading term, for increasingly our public spaces are in fact "public/private." Bookstores replace libraries; malls replace public squares; and even civic spaces are often partly private, having been underwritten by companies or supported through advertising. Take Times Square, for example: how public is it, really?

So one question when trying to make vast and permanent public art projects is how to work in that odd seam between civic and corporate structures. We've had two tantalizingly close prospects, though neither worked out in the end. One, which I can't discuss in any detail, was to put a single networked artwork in possibly hundreds of stores throughout the country. That would have been a fascinating encounter! But the other one, entitled *Horizon*, was actually commissioned and announced, so I can describe it fully. Atlanta Airport was adding a new international terminal, for which the city's percent-for-the-arts set-aside ensured a pretty fair budget—for our project, three million dollars. We were going to build a long LED display (280 by 30 feet) with intelligent imagery generated interactively and in real-time.

Shelley created an elaborate storyboard for the piece, one of which illustrates our basic idea best—"airport as dollhouse." Here the idea was to invert the sense of scale, by creating large virtual children who play with elements of the airport as if they were parts of a dollhouse. And so there were children's hands propelling airplanes down the runway, and their fingers becoming air bridges for disembarking passengers, passing them from one hand to the next. Here Shelley was inspired by the way in which children sometimes play by passing ladybugs back and forth—carefully, delicately, but with an immense sense of power.

The idea was to reframe the airport experience, which in our post 9/11 world is a particularly unpleasant one. So for example as a passenger you're always aware of being under constant surveillance, with surveillance cameras constantly monitored to detect terrorist activities. *Horizon* would also have such cameras, but for completely benign means: to look at the weather, to study patterns of people's movement, and above all to *play*. So for example Shelley had another storyboard of children playing in Atlanta's Olympic fountains, which might be called up by the AI when it started to rain outside—we'd celebrate the wet weather rather than bemoan it. Or the camera might allow the virtual children to spot people browsing among the displays of a newsstand, and then play hide-and-seek with them there. Or as dusk came on, it would bring down the night in our virtual world as well.

The key was to make a piece that never repeated, continually engaging not only the frequent business travelers who pass through that Atlanta hub regularly, but also of course the airport workers who would have to live with the piece. It's in this context that the idea of "thinking images" plays so crucial and so practical a role. I hate to harp on money and the lack of it, but again this project was indefinitely suspended not because of our budget but rather because of enormous cost overruns on the architectural and engineering design of the overall terminal building. A comedy of errors, which has since devolved into a tangle of legal suits and counter-suits between the city and its various contractors. We've stayed well clear of that mess.

BIRRINGER: What a shame, your description is very vivid and I'd have loved to visit a playful airport, for a change. How do you see the current artistic culture in its gradual embrace of new media technologies? What social or aesthetic aspects do you value, and how do you think about "digital culture"? Why is theatre in the U.S. a relatively minor art form today which has barely developed new ideas or techniques, whereas so much current discourse on performance process, becoming, hybridity and interactive digital media tends to be progressive and also increasingly politically aware of the challenges we face in the biotechnological era?

KAISER. Hmm, I'm loath to prognosticate on too broad a scale here. We work *within* our culture, and so while we definitely respond to the sorts of shifts and concerns you outline in your question, we certainly haven't risen to any elevated, Olympian position from which to assess them as seers. But perhaps I can say a little bit about digital culture and what we make of it as artists. It's a commonplace that the Internet, especially as mediated by Google, has changed the context and the reach of information. Search is now a nearly instantaneous procedure, with tremendously wide scope, and it has become the quintessential mode of thought for our era—the first recourse for nearly everyone, that first step we all take almost automatically. And it's not just Internet search that's so important—DNA sequencing, for example, works essentially the same way.

So we've been interested in applying techniques of search in our own works. Which is not to say that we make so-called "Web art" which uses— and often tries to subvert—the various protocols of the Internet for various postmodernist reasons. Instead, we bring search algorithms into our work itself. We're fascinated by this newfound ability to consider millions of possibilities and contingencies that are well beyond what the naked mind can address by itself. And so, for example, for *Enlightenment* Marc wrote code that could analyze the twenty-five-second coda to Mozart's last symphony and detect on its own not only the five themes of its invertible counterpoint, but also trace back related thematic material through the whole of the 4th movement. Similarly for the public artwork, *Breath*, we perform other sorts of searches: for example, revealing essential semantic threads running through the entire Book of Psalms.

Now if search represents an advance in our culture, I must also point to a sore point of decline. We're often struck by how contemporary culture seems to be heading towards increasingly low resolution—the voice quality on your cell phone is far worse than on your grandparents' old landline; the image quality on your iPod video or YouTube feed is mud compared to the 35 or 70mm films they enjoyed in cinemas; the language of e-mail and chat is impoverished by contrast to that of their old-fashioned letter writing. Attention itself is increasingly low res, as I said earlier: the world seems designed for distraction.

So to this, as artists, we oppose ourselves, rather than just going with the cultural flow, so to speak. Visually, we insist on high-resolution projections and displays: there's no reason why artists should have to accept the fuzzy interlacing of DVDs, for example. For a while now, we've said that we want digital resolution to feel like that of paper—and as a logical conclusion, two of our current projects will be printed rather than projected. We're making lines so fine that we can't even see them on our screens, but only when they emerge from our printer. But this is not some sort of retreat into tried-and-true old-fashioned art-making (the persistence of painting as an art form astonishes me): we're printing texts and imagery for projects that you could never have done by hand. If art advances, it does so unpredictably and not quite in lock-step with the culture at large.

NOTES

[1] "CROSS FAIR 2000: The Intelligent Stage" took place November 9–12, 2000, and was curated by Söke Dinkla and Stefan Hilterhaus for the Choreographic Center North-Rhine Westphalia in Essen. Roy Ascott's keynote address, "The Moist Scenario," is quoted with permission of the author. The exhibition and colloquium brought together numerous media artists, designers and choreographers to debate the implications of the "Intelligent Stage." Paul Kaiser (whose company was then called Riverbed) exhibited the *Ghostcatching* installation. Steina Vasulka, Michael Saup and Louis-Philippe Demers addressed technologies as independent, intelligent systems, and Jeffrey Shaw presented an overview of the innovative interactive installations created at the Zentrum für Kunst und Medientechnologie (ZKM) in Karlsruhe. Shaw spoke of immersive and interactive interface environments and referred to Nottingham University's Mixed Reality Lab where experiments with "MASSIVE," a multi-user distributed virtual reality system, helped the British ensemble Blast Theory to develop *Desert Rain*. The project was completed during their residency at the ZKM. Choreographers like William Forsythe went there to create a CD-ROM project (*Improvisation Technologies*) that required extensive digital video studio and computer processing facilities. With interface design by Volker Kuchelmeister and Christian Ziegler, *Improvisation Technologies* features a hypertextual content of over sixty video chapters showing lecture demonstrations in which Forsythe demonstrates the essential principles of his improvisation techniques. A solo by Forsythe, and other dance sequences performed by Frankfurt Ballet members, can be called up as further illustrations. As Ziegler pointed out at Cross Fair, the "intelligent stage" need not be understood as a physical location, such as the studio designed at Arizona State University. It could as well refer to the specific nature of an interface design or platform on a CD-ROM or the Internet. For Ziegler, the CD-ROM is a "knowledge-reference system." For further information on Paul Kaiser, Marc Downie, and Shelley Eshkar's collective work, see: <http://www.openendedgroup.com/>.

BIOTECHNOLOGIES

Cybernetics and Rhythms

By the end of the last century, it was apparent that the impact of media and digital technologies on the performing and fine arts proffered some of the irreversible evolutions the late Nam June Paik had already antici-pated in the 1960s. As Paik envisioned the electronic superhighway and, for example in *Global Groove* (1973), pioneered many of the techniques of morphing and collaging moving images that are the common language of digital multimedia today, he not only helped to engineer new tools, such as the Paik-Abe Synthesizer, but insistently probed the instrumentalities and properties of a medium. *Magnet TV* strikes us today as a microscopic scan of the cathode ray, exposing the interior flesh and the arteries of electric energy. In the exhibition "Cybernetics Art and Music" at the New School for Social Research (1965), Paik's experiments with electronic signals and feedbacks anticipated the infra-sound and image manipulations so pertinent to the digital culture of the re-mix described in Paul D. Miller's (DJ Spooky) audio recordings and his recent book, *Rhythm Science*.

What's surprising about DJ Spooky's tracks is that they mix music also with early modernist writers or Dada artists (James Joyce, Gertrude Stein, Kurt Schwitters), and his recent video installation *ReBirth of a Nation* pro-vocatively combines D.W. Griffith with other "found objects" from history. The "science" he thinks of is a methodology of cultural engineering on an aesthetic level of sampling and re-recording poignant enough to crystallize dialectical images, constructive moments of re-cognition, in the manner in which Walter Benjamin thought of modern technology's complex reorga-nization of the visual. Though less fraught with the ethical quandaries en-countered in the debates on genetic engineering, the "rhythms" in question are deeply connected to inquiries into cultural knowledge and cognition, and the DJ's "science" is a filtering of sounds, beats, movements, and tor-sions amidst a raving biopolitics of information-processing systems. The DJ works with the mobile, performative aura of tracks and iPods, channeling the listener's rage against the machine.

My concern throughout this book has not been with styles of re-mixing and recombination as a phenomenon of the digital media or a superficial reflection of science in art (sci-art, scientific representation), but with the underlying ecology of the interrelations between performance and computer science/engineering. I have referred to various models of organization, derived from the sciences and the mathematical machine driving today's microcomputing revolution, largely reflecting a rhythmic progression of representational technologies applied by artists to structure our sensorial apprehension of the world. Such structuring in performance always implies physical techniques, and I tried to illuminate how such techniques have become interactional/interface techniques. They are also always techniques of "ordering" data material, relationships, and operative control parameters. Cybernetics offered explanations of phenomena in terms of information flows and feedback loops in mechanical and biological systems. Its influence on composition and the aesthetic concern with the regulation of a system (homeostasis) has expanded, while computer models of information processing and Artificial Intelligence merged with experimental studies in physics, molecular biology, and neuroscience.

Most programmers, whose role in today's digital performance composition needs to be emphasized since so much of the interactive work described here relies on code and software systems, have a firm grounding in physics and mathematics, and I have not addressed this ground properly as I cannot lay claims to developing or interpreting technical theory. Composer Joel Ryan once said in a workshop that innovation in digital music has resulted in an explosion of detail (in the technical parameters), which generally eludes our capability to give it musical character. He was referring to the multiplication of operative parameters in the complex new machines of sound synthesis, but warned that Fourier synthesis and constantly increasing computational power can generate hundreds or thousands of numbers a second, yet even a well developed technical theory gives little insight into its musical applications and how sound and music, whatever its 2-D or multidimensional models, are perceived and imagined. Ryan's concern was with the possible "visualizations" or visual geometries of the imagination, but his caution also addresses, I believe, the role of data dissipation in general. There is a constantly growing amount of information generated by what

Vannevar Bush in the mid-twentieth century referred to as the "universal machine," but the databases are in a constant process as well, potentially linked, potentially distributed and also transformed, lost. DJ Spooky's "rhythm science" is an artistic concept of such frail instability, reminiscent of Benjamin's constellation of passages (the apparitional commodities he examined in *Passagen-Werk*).

Technically speaking, the constellation means that the growing amount of knowledge (just think of today's Google search engines and what they provide) makes it necessary to have tools that quantitatively and qualitatively collect and distribute data material to be presented through interfaces. It also means that digitally created art or performance selects and orders "knowledge" (discussed here primarily as sensorial-social processes) through various generative or randomly chosen interactional scenarios. Multiple tracks, combined in DJ Spooky's mix-tapes, arrange images of sound in motion—the storage systems themselves are experienced in motion and no longer as a static library. All aesthetic forms today are potentially hybrid and in fluctuating associative constellations: a "text" or a "work" is emerging out of permutations and cannot easily be tracked back. This is the principle of digital variability. In many of the performances, prototypes, and installations I have discussed, the emergent and the virtual—in the aesthetic sense of the compositional arrangements—connote a space full of information that must be activated and experienced by the performer or the user. Thecla Schiphorst therefore proposes a "circuit training" for performers, developing strategies and techniques of paying attention to the fluctuations between hardware, software, interaction design and somatic practices, i.e., between physical or software engineering and perceptual processes through which the living body-mind constructs knowledge. She suggests that such methods of embodiment destabilize and soften "previous boundary conditions, problematizing technical processes (body, code, method). In order to design our circuits, living as they do alongside the electromagnetic energy of the body, traditional electrical engineering employs techniques that 'retrofit' our selves. Are we retrofitting our bodies into our technologies, or reverse-engineering the self to map the 'shortening circuit'? Is there a radical reinvention of engineering that can create a longer exhale in the design lifecycle?"[1] What Schiphorst expresses so eloquently here raises questions about the arts as partners (retro-engineers?) in scientific research and tool-invention. It also invites us to ponder the kinds of work processes necessary for sustained experiments in the epistemological laboratory that can yield new art works, new inventions, and new knowledge.

The dynamic model of generative data has implied a focus on performance process, not always on "results" as Paul Kaiser demands. Rather than interpreting a theatrical play (e.g., Michael Frayn's *Copenhagen*) or choreography (Rambert Dance Co's *Constant Speed*) thematizing modern mathematics—or evoking a scientific hypothesis through a particular abstract compositional aesthetic (e.g., Robert Wilson's *Einstein on the Beach*)—my choice in this book has been to ask how performance uses an instrument of analysis or generates a conceptual system to analyze the organization and structure of the system, its metabolism, and its boundary. Regarding dance, for example, it is indicative that choreographers like Marie-Claude Poulin (kondition pluriel) and Alejandro Ahmed (director of the Brazilian company Cena 11) speak of research into "behaviors" and the body's modes of reorganization and adaptation. Rather than inventing movement phrases, Ahmed's work deeply probes physical conditions for the reorganization of the body, for example in the company's extensive work on patterns of falling (involving gravity, weight, muscular strength, pressure, etc.), and specific instances in which changes emerge in states of stillness and movement.

Addressing this research at the 2006 IN TRANSIT festival in Berlin, dramaturge Fabiana Britto used analogies with quantum theory to emphasize the dancers' attention to probabilities of interconnection between the patterns. The world premiere of *pequenas frestas de ficção sobre realidade insistente* (Small Fissures of Fiction in a Stubborn Reality) in Berlin was a stunning manifestation of Grupo Cena 11's systematic research on unpredictable patterns of bodily resistance to, and hyperextension of, physical limits. The physical work was combined with uncanny robotic and animal intrusions into a performance continuously refracted through digital projections of the dancers' facial expressions captured by small moving cameras. At one paradoxical moment, a large German shepherd dog jumped forward and appeared to rest atop Ahmed's shoulders, supremely calm and composed, with Ahmed frozen in place while Leticia Lamela forced Adilso Machado to carry her weight standing on his back, pushing, tearing, and pulling him with ropes attached to his upper body. As we experienced Machado's increasingly exhausted motion across the space, we also gradually realized that the performers were not using dance techniques but were short-circuiting two contrasting physical phase-states (freeze and acceleration), manipulating the time/interval between physical perceptions which bifurcate under the emotional stress we endure. In our sense-percep-tional processing of this scene we were pushed to the cusp of two mutually exclusive states that, at any point, could change or, if the dog attacked, result in a dangerous crisis. The scene was already a virtual crisis, as no one in the audience (I cannot speak for Cena 11) could have predicted how the dog would behave as it processed the precarious action that happened on the other side of the stage. The animal, it turned out, was not perturbed by the human behavior of a woman riding a man.

Engineering and Theatre

The "small fissures of fiction" opening up in a stubborn empirical reality are dissonances, splittings of the psychic organization of sensory perception. The small fissures can also be thought of as disorientations or disruptions of cultural and scientific *ordering systems*. Do such disorientations not arise when noise infects the predilection to control experience, when regimes appear to be mixed up and identities crossed? Disequilibrium (in thermody-namic terms) resembles the hybrid disunity of the techno-human-animal, the "unnatural" phenomena that are to be expected when organisms and systems with different characteristics are combined. In biology, the com-plexity of hybrids is not valued negatively; on the contrary, mutations of identity result in hybrids that are more efficient and less prone to hereditary diseases. In regard to technical systems and materials science, hybridization is also a measure of increased efficiency achieved through the combination of different technical materials and energies. For example, in new transma-terials production, efficacy as well as attractiveness are judged according to the quality of transformative or intelligent characteristics of recombinant materials which are highly flexible, modular, and can undergo metamor-phosis based on environmental stimuli (e.g., in thermochromic wall paper or breathing kinetic surfaces that change color or pattern in response to temperature).[2]

The issue of control and its destabilization has been a constant through-out this book, but an emphasis on technological innovation and perfor-mance can hardly overlook the fact that a mechanistic and regulatory world view underlies the contemporary, late modernist programs, whether scientific or aesthetic. Control remains central to contemporary technolo-gies, as it was in earlier scientific experiments we learnt in school (Skinner's behaviorist stimulus/response model). Control theory in the twenty-first century looks at programming algorithms and other techniques (often on a microscopic scale) needed for controlling dynamic systems, yet earlier notions of (self)governing systems, for example in Piaget's theory of early child (sensorimotor) development, already deduced "instinctive" servomechanisms from species behavior, such as wanting/finding pleasure in needing to "be the cause." If the pleasure of being the cause is an animal pleasure, the inventors of the field of cybernetics studied various kinds of controllers in animals and machines to come to the conclusion that a positive feedback loop is vital for automated systems and just about anything (mechanical, digital, or biological) that processes information, reacts to information, and changes or can be changed to more efficiently accomplish the first two tasks.

Referring back to the experimental era of the 60s ("Performance and Engineering"), I tried to pinpoint 9 *Evenings: Theater and Engineering* as a significant precursor to current art and technology productions and to the many hybrid performances and installations created by technical collaboration that, if we follow the cybernetic thought model, is built upon efficiency. One is almost tempted to deduce that the effect of efficiency is an aesthetic principle for performance that is grounded in engineering, even if illusionist media try to disguise the machinery. Cybernetics has undergone its own cycle of re-evaluations, but like modern physics and biology it overshadows twentieth-century artistic avant-gardes in its enormous significance, having begun as an interdisciplinary study connecting the fields of control systems, electrical network theory, mechanical engineering, logic modeling, evolutionary biology, and neuroscience (in the 1940s), and now being revitalized again—through research in AI and machine-biological interfaces—for more complex systems of control and emergent behavior (including related fields such as game theory, the analysis of group interaction, systems of feedback in evolution, and transmaterials). It has been argued that successful pedagogy in technical education introduces the "thrill" of control early on, instructing the young engineer in the correct spin of the electron, much as a theatre director would instill the proper acting techniques, precise cuing systems and the functions of stagecraft, scenography, and lighting to the actors. It must not be forgotten that stage technologies are hereditary crafts in the world of performance, and anyone who has ever attended the Prague Quadrennial in theatre scenography cannot but be moved by the extraordinary exactitude, skill, and imagination displayed in the countless designs for scenic space, costumes, lighting, and stage architecture.

This is perhaps a good moment to demystify some the thrill I felt when writing that Robert Rauschenberg, Billy Klüver, and the large co-laboratory that produced the twenty performances for 9 *Evenings* in 1966 provided a fascinating historical model of research experimentation between scientists and artists. While the peer-to-peer model remains path breaking, its aesthetic success had already been questioned back then. The documentary evidence of the event, recently exhibited at the MIT List Visual Arts Center, is even more revealing if one takes a closer look at the engineering side.[3]

It is telling, for example, that many early commentators deplore both theatrical and technological failures. Lucy Lippard dryly notes that no theatre professionals were actually involved who might have given the artists a hand in "directing" such a complex show, or warning them of the unmanageable scale of the building. Yet rarely ever do critics address the many technical details sorted out by the engineers who supplied John Cage with an array of live feeds and frequency modulators or built the remote control devices and paddle-operated lights for Rauschenberg's hotwired racket match (*Open Score*), not to speak of the infrared camera equipment that at that time was held as classified material for U.S. military research and was commercially unavailable, and thus had to be imported by Larry Heilos. The TEEM (Theater Electronic Environmental Module), designed as a central control panel to operate all the remote functions, was composed of more than 250 elements including decoders, encoders, power amplifiers, power relays, tone control units, FM receivers, FM transmitters, photocells, speakers, program drums, preamplifiers, Speaker Distribution Matrix, Proportional Control System, and a specially developed wireless system that set up a "networked" environment in the Armory. Such a wireless system, using transmitters and FM receptors, was novel at the time and, most likely, untested by the artists who envisioned interactive performances with new materials (such as the electrodes worn by Alex Hay which transmitted muscle activity, heart beat, eye movement, and brain waves into sound) and "physical things," as Steve Paxton called the enormous plastic inflatable tunnels made out of polyethylene. There was no guarantee that anything would work, as Billy Klüver and Herb Schneider reported, since most of the engineers had trouble understanding the artists' visions, and a practical method of translation had to be found. Schneider's engineering diagrams, depicted in the original program for *9 Evenings* for each individual performance system and superimposed as one composite diagrammatic image on the cover, served the role of technical drawings—"black boxes" explaining the electrical circuits and overall system architecture of each piece.

A study of the technical drawings and other archival material reveals that the "black boxes" were of critical importance for finding a common ground between engineers and artists. Schneider drew them five weeks before the opening and also commented, in later interviews, on the importance of setting up the control center (TEEM) and getting additional specialized equipment from Bell Labs and AMP Inc., allowing for the construction of a computer-like command center that connected all the electrical instruments. Schneider was pleased with the collaborative ethos that evolved amongst engineers and artists, noting that TEEM and the AMP equipment functioned like a proto-computer, demonstrating to the artists the fundamental principles and logic of computer science: programming, data storing, shifts between one media form and another, random logic, combinatories, and the wired and wireless system architecture.[4] The overarching framework of TEEM also allowed for the flexible insertion of specific devices, such as Robert Kieronski's Vochrome and various other objects built for David Tudor's *Bandoneon ! (a combine)*, and it is noticeable that Billy Klüver envisioned Tudor turning the entire cavernous Armory into a musical instrument for immersive acoustic experience. More precisely, Tudor must have been thinking of an excitable, dynamic system for interaction performance (between sound channels and eletronic modulators). In his program notes with engineer Fred Waldhauer, he suggests

> *Bandoneon !*, (bandoneon factorial), is a combine incorporating programmed audio circuits, moving loudspeakers, tv images and lighting, instrumentally excited. The instrument, a bandoneon, will create signals which are simultaneously used as material for differentiated audio spectrums (achieved through modulation means, and special loudspeaker construction), for the production of visual images, devised by Lowell Cross, for the activation of programming devices controlling the audio visual environment, devised by Bob Kieronski ("Vochrome," and programmed patch-board) and Fred Waldhauer (Proportional Control). *Bandoneon !* uses no composing means; when activated it composes itself out of its own composite instrumental nature.[5]

In spite of the carefully engineered patch-boards and controllers, this extraordinary "self-composing" system with its multiple microphones and loudspeakers not only struggled with the Armory's extended reverberation time and ambient noise, but when "played" by Tudor became literally uncontrollable. When activated, its many evolving sonic and visual conditions, continuously affected by feedback, reverb, and signal processing, made the performance totality categorically unstable, and while Tudor, Cage, or Paxton no doubt welcomed this insurgent behavior of the effects of systems devised for *Bandoneon !*, *Variations VII*, and *Physical Things*, other artists may have been more baffled (Lippard calls it "cheated") by delays and technical failures. There were many technical glitches, and most ironically, TEEM did not work at all during the first night of Rauschenberg's *Open Score*, forcing the engineers to manually unpatch all the lights which were to go out during the electrified raquet game (without anyone in the audience noticing the difference to the second night, when TEEM worked perfectly).

In Yvonne Rainer's case, her collaboration with Per Biorn called for "two separate but parallel (simultaneous) continuities and two separate (but equal) control systems." Though Rainer was discomforted by the remote control machinery, her instructions for minimalist, task-oriented activities (conveyed to performers via walkie-talkie) joined TEEM's randomly selected film and sound clips in a manner which appears symptomatic for the overall engineering effort of *9 Evenings*. There was congruence between conceptual ideas and the technical possibilities made available by engineering, even if the resultant work was theatrically disappointing. Or, in theatre terms, a misunderstanding.

Surely the visual artists and Judson dancers involved had no interest in making theatre. Most radical avant-garde conventions already established at the time (after Happening, Judson, Fluxus, and Minimalism) embraced chance and indeterminacy, abstraction, matter of fact, task-oriented behavior, anti-spectacle, participation. Despite its misleading reference to "theatre," *9 Evenings* meant twenty different interactional performances, each work engineered in a particular way to centralize and—paradoxically—decentralize at the same time the instruments and the orchestra (actors, chorus, objects, devices), the actions and the effects within the large matrix of performative possibilities. While some of the works may have indeed collapsed under the scale of the site, the advance hype, and the surface of effects (Lippard argues that the most technologically complex pieces were the dullest), the paradox of a controlled environment generating simultaneous, equivalent processes (emergent, dissociated, acausal) is still a major techno-aesthetic problem today, forty years later. Alex Hay, collaborating with Schneider, Kieronski, Tudor (and Paxton and Rauschenberg as performers), pushed the performance medium to the same limits we still clearly see today in interactive sensor-driven performance at the beginning of the twenty-first century. The biofeedback apparatus worn by Hay simultaneously emphasized the body's materiality as well as its abstraction. The body's interior workings, invisible, were translated into productive representational effects (aural and visual), while other, exterior actions were carried out methodically: one hundred six-foot squares of cloth which Hay had laid out in a modular pattern were "retrieved in a correct arithmetic progression and placed centrally."

As I will point out further below, behind this idea of translation lies an engineering and computational understanding that processes are translatable into each other since they share an equivalence of information, materials, or time. The inner organic rhythms were here conjoined with the external "natural" movement of a formally coherent action, even if the action appeared non-sensical. Hay's description of his work's unrelated, simultaneous processes is purely syntactical: they are *equal in time*. Yet he locates the organic body (his own) in the spatial center, whereas Paxton's *Physical Things*—together with Cage's second performance of *Variations VII* the only audience-participatory piece—performs a similar syntactic maneuver: the transparent, plastic inflatable tubes seem to play with inside and outside, confusing the textures of plastic and skin. The visitors entered into a translucent intestine-like space, a resonating "blurred" architecture:

> Wading throughout the warrens of Steve Paxton and engineer Dick Wolff's *Physical Things*, the *9 Evenings* audience was also made to confront ruptures in interactivity and transmission. Spectators palpated the tunnels' translucent plastic skin, then entered a magnetic potlatch of sound picked up on handheld receivers. Bodily sensation and receiving process overlaid each other. Like *Variations VII*, *Physical Things* mapped not only the space of the Armory but the commercial airwaves that girded it. During the first night, the work also entailed infamously long delays. The transmission to the modified transistor radios was weak, resulting in less aural incident than intended. As one critic complained,

"There was nothing to throb over." Yet Paxton himself opposed such climactic thrills. Rather, the work was to unfurl in a slow series of haptic discoveries.... The intrusion of dead air and delay enhanced this halting process, as the synaesthetic turned to an awareness of mediated reception. Unlike the brassy showmanship of much kinetic art, these works inhabited a space of fissures and temporal lags. It was in this sense that Klüver explicitly positioned 9 *Evenings* against the immediacy of "flashing lights and psychedelic effects."[6]

The haptic discoveries point to the biophysical imagination underlying these installations. Both *Grass Field* and *Physical Things* conjured images of metabolisms and electromagnetic energy systems. These early interactional performances were modeling complexity, and they understood organisms to be complex control systems that are vulnerable to perturbations.

Human-Computer Interfaces

Let's examine at a few contemporary areas where scientific observation and experimentation overlap with performance to the extent that they take varying bodies, living beings, or physiological/cognitive processes as the medium of inquiry. In the UK, for example, the Engineering and Physical Sciences Research Council supports PLAN (Pervasive and Locative Arts Network—Enhancing Mobile and Wireless Technologies for Culture and Creativity), a network of computer scientists and artists interested in developing mobile and interactive media that are directly embedded into the world around performers or "creative users." Performance groups such as Blast Theory, igloo, or Active Ingredient have explored the boundaries of pervasive media using innovative locative games played on mobile phones in outdoor locations or deploying avatars in redesigned computer game worlds. Scripts, the textual term we once used in the theatre for written dialogue and stage directions, here become programming code, and neural networks the metaphor for algorithms, which define the functional behaviors, *actes sans paroles*, of the actors involved in such transductive telecommunicational scenarios. In many cases these functional behaviors have to do with motion/gesture. When Steve Benford, director of Mixed Reality Lab and scientist-collaborator on Blast Theory's roaming urban performances, speaks of system input and expressive latitude, he is referring to design strategies for HCI. He classifies "public interfaces" according to the extent to which movements and gestures, i.e., a performer's manipulations of an interface and their resulting effects, are hidden, partially revealed, fully revealed or even amplified for spectators.

Such taxonomies of an interaction system, which tend to apply to performances in everyday life, also have implications for artistic design decision and the iterative stages of prototyping now increasingly prevalent in interactive art processes that involve wearable computing (e.g., sensors or conductive fibers in intelligent garment design), biofeedback, and the programming or orchestration of responsive environments.[8] Computer scientists borrow the musical term "orchestration" from Brenda Laurel's writings, *Computers as Theatre* (1993), an earlier attempt at explaining interactive experiences in terms of the methods in which actors and technical crew monitor and intervene in ongoing interactions in order to subtly shape an unfolding experience. In regard to museums and the digital curating of new media artworks, such orchestration can also involve participatory strategies designed to manage visitor flow or interactive behavior of the spectators. The museum, in this case, is analyzed as a system of visitability, attention management, flow, etc. But this is also a response to changes in art production itself. A recent conference at the Tate Modern focused on immaterial systems and asked how curating can respond to new forms of self-organizing and self-replicating systems, databases, programming, Net art, software art, and generative media. If the language of the debates echoed systems theory and neurobiology, it seemed quite intentionally so (<http://www.kurator.org/>). The scientific approach, I suggest, was owed to the recognition that the idea of the "system" is crucial in this context in that it not only refers to the physical site of curatorial production, the computer and the network, but also to the technical and conceptual properties of what constitutes the curatorial object and the "operating system" of art. What new models of curatorial practice are required to take account of shared, distributed, and collaborative objects and processes? Has the museum started to apply the molecular gaze and recognize work derived from scientific epistemologies?

Gestures, Real-time Capture, Animation

Another significant change we see today in interaction design for performance is the care given to the subtleties and nuances of gestural quality. Troika Ranch recently performed their new piece *16 (R)evolutions* almost as an allegory of this development of gestural control and refinement of motion tracking within the programming environment they have created (combining tracking camera, their own custom-built Isadora software, infrared lighting). Rather than deploying a high-end multi-camera motion-capture system for real-time graphic animation, as it was used in Trisha Brown's *how long does the subject linger on the edge of the volume…*, Mark Coniglio designed a small, inexpensive system for Troika Ranch that can easily travel, combining Isadora with a motion-capture software (EyesWeb) created by Italian scientists at Antonio Camurri's Laboratorio di Informatica Musicale (InfoMus Lab) at Genoa.[7] After a period of research and consultation with Camurri, Coniglio began using EyesWeb, a software that takes a single camera to track the silhouette of the performer, superimposing a twelve-point skeleton onto the silhouette (head, shoulders, elbows, wrists, top of pelvis, knees and ankles). EyesWeb sends information about the pathway of each of these points to Isadora where the information is analyzed and converted to dynamic graphic animation. Again, it is tempting to call this a process of translation or performance writing, as I had discussed it referring to Cloud Gate and Shen Wei Dance Arts ("Between Mapping and Artificial Intelligence"). The dancer onstage moves and activates the graphic shapes and their relations in a projected timespace that is also a computational environment: the movement-action directly results in animated images. The points in space, recognized each second almost as in Etienne-Jules Marey's or Eadweard Muybridge's chronophotography a hundred years ago, are here transformed instantly in real-time. They generate a trail of successive movements in fluid continuity, which form a calligraphic momemtum and a Gestalt, a digital *anime*.

As I suggested in "Between Mapping and Artificial Intelligence," at this historical point in the development of machine learning and computational analysis used in motion studies, interactivity is no longer merely focused on direct mapping of gesture (gesture to sound, gesture to video) but on the creation of complex "action paintings," metaphasial calligraphies or mitotic gestures translated into image-flows. In the late 1990s, we saw the beginnings of such work in Merce Cunningham's and Bill T. Jones's collaboration with Shelley Eshkar/Paul Kaiser. *Biped* and *Ghostcatching* were milestones on this research path. Interestingly, Eshkar, Kaiser and OpenEnded Group have now become more interested in pedestrian movement rather than interactive virtuosity. A public projection piece such as *Pedestrian* is a typical example of artistic work dedicated to system exploration: the street walkers' actions are ordinary, but after longer observation, the patterns they form begin to seem oddly coordinated, as if unfolding in some hidden story or deriving from a set of unknown principles. The "capture" is not a choreographic composition, it is an attempt to observe daily action-behavior. One could argue this is a bioscientific epistemology used for artistic ends. In the case of Troika Ranch's work, the mathematical procedure is identical: the Isadora software (and its movie-input camera) tracks motion and analyzes the bodily data. The software functions as a measuring tool or tool of observation. Depending on the values, filters, and modifiers assigned to the data, the program analyzes slight changes in the motion gesture—observing the "living state" or properties of such movement (four categories: straight, curved, lateral, complex). Recognizing change of direction, speed, dynamics, and velocity of movement within these categories, the program then renders the media output in real-time, and we can perceive the three-dimensional dance and the projected 3-D worlds of colors and shapes. Using musical and biological analogies here, one could argue that the software program observes "tonal" or cytokinetic properties of human movement.

Another level of critical analysis would then have to be applied to the particular choices the artist-designers make for the visualization of the data. Numerous researchers in the hard sciences, including molecular biologists working on cellular dynamics and chemical transformations, are currently preoccupied with visualization technologies, and here an exchange of knowledge between fields of observation appears relevant, even if aesthetic or socio-political questions about the meaning and affect of gestures may address different concerns from those of the cell biologist. What is important to point out, however, is that creative research on motion behavior derives from a shared scientific understanding working with systems to analyze, recognize, learn, perceive, model, or follow movement with the computer. Frédéric Bevilacqua, a scientist at IRCAM's Real Time Musical Interactions Lab in Paris, has directed "gesture follower" research since 2003, with the aim of establishing methods for computing high-level parameters of movements similar to the ones used by choreographers in creation and performance (e.g., notions of movement quality, expressiveness, and meaning). Bevilacqua's mathematical, motion-capture-based investigation, which also involved collaboration with dancemakers Myriam Gourfink and Bertha Bermudez, the Amsterdam-based group Emio Greco | PC, programmer Chris Ziegler, and neuroscientist Corinne Jola, relies on the concept of a "learning phase," during which movement phrases are recorded and then processed by the computer.

The extracted features reveal parameters that are re-introduced into the system as a recognition schema. The schema is then applied in real-time to movement phrases as they are performed again, and Bevilacqua argues that the gesture follower induces the possibility of creating a score, which can be annotated. This procedure of recognition/following enables the information to be extracted from the motion-capture data in direct correlation to examples given by the performer. A highly systematic approach, which also involves partitioning movement to break down gestures into smaller components in order to learn something about the whole, such gesture analysis is therefore dependent on the information contained in the examples chosen in the learning phase. In this sense, the procedure sets up a "context-dependent analysis." Such a system can undoubtedly facilitate a closer understanding between the choreographer's and the programmer's perception of the process, since it introduces observations of the performer as information at key points directly into the digital tracking/analysis loop.[8]

In scientific terms, we are here looking at inscription devices, ways in which we construct categories for observation. The computer, for example, cannot "feel" the gesture in the way in which the human audience will sense the weight or import of a particular movement behavior and movement quality of expression. Coniglio, who wrote the Isadora software, admits that he wouldn't know himself where a gesture begins and ends. The software reacts to properties of the motion and is set to modify the gestalt of the image we see projected continuously (color changes, change in size, one can also rotate the planes and effect a more three-dimensional and topsy-turvy feeling of the images). The images themselves can have various tactile characteristics connected to the "gestural-ness" of drawing and painting (sinewy) or the more architectural look of geometric, polygonal shapes. In one scene of *16 (R)evolutions*, a meshwork of lines (vertical and horizontal) appears all over the floor and back projection which is pulsating and constantly moving/growing/decreasing/turning/evolving (rendered through particle systems programming). In another, a meshwork of more densified criss-crossed lines and architectural gestalts gain polyphonic complexity in motion, and in rotations that defy Euclidian space. Choreographer Dawn Stoppiello suggests that such current explorations in motion tracking and visualization (along with granular sound synthesis) emphasize highly subtle manipulations of visual and aural propagations, correlated to new concepts of dynamic systems or semi-chaotic systems whose philosophical and scientific thought-models are derived from research in biology, a-life, computer science, and the cognitive sciences (Maturana/Varela, Prigogine/Stengers, Kauffman, Iberall, and others). No longer based on notational systems (Labanotation) but on computational analysis and mathematics, "description of movement" is rendered as image-movement. Yet the fuzzy logic in the chaotic state of the system reminds us how difficult it is to speak of a digital aesthetics. The digital medium itself is indifferent to movement poetics or authorship.

Robotics and Tissue Cultures

Interaction designers, in other words, now reflect on what could be called the psychology of spontaneous, intuitive, unpredictable, or patterned behavior in "traversable interfaces" that allow fluid transitions between spectating and performing. The difference to earlier studies of role-play by social anthropologists (Victor Turner, Ernest Goffman) lies in the fact that performance is here always understood to take place in relationship to system-design which often encloses performer and interface within a physically traversable projected display or immersive environment. In the case of performers such as Stelarc or Marcel.li Antúnez Roca who work with robotics, the language of object manipulation (actuators) also enters the scene, creating a fascinating and complex re-orientation of our anthropomorphic assumptions about performance and agency.

When the performer is tethered to the interface, as it has been the case in numerous performances by Stelarc (e.g., *Fractal Flesh*, 1995–98, or more recently, *Exoskeleton*, a pneumatically powered six-legged walking machine actuated by arm gestures), the effects of an interface act directly upon the performer. In extreme cases the system is actively and perhaps autonomously controlling the performer's body. In *Fractal Flesh*, Stelarc and his engineering partners developed a touch-screen interfaced Muscle Stimulation System, enabling remote access, actuation, and choreography of the body through a series of electrical impulses, triggered by spectators. In *Requiem*, Antúnez hangs in an exo-skeleton that is capable of executing most of the movements of the human body. The robotic engine reacts to spectators by optical sensors, which activate the machine, and registers the random movements. In performance, Antúnez becomes a marionette whose movements are imposed by the spectators. Research in robotic performance has found fascinating manifestations in such works and others by Louis-Philippe Demers, Bill Vorn, Simon Penny, Eduardo Kac, etc., and the engineering focus on the nature of the robot's behavior (autonomous, semi-autonomous, responsive, interactive, organic, adaptable, telepresential, etc.) again points to qualities of a work residing in the manner in which machinic embodiment is capable of specific responses to differing stimuli in the environment. Collaborations between Louis-Philippe Demers's robots and dancers have yielded two remarkable new works, *Devolution* (Australian Dance Theatre) and *kubic's cube* (Ventura Dance Company), the latter more radical as the robot is the only mover in the interactive choreography. Demers's twelve-foot robotic aluminium sculpture hangs from the ceiling; it moves according to the construction of its limbs, and performs to the music and sound installation of Francisco López. Ventura programmed the robot as a cubist kinetic sculpture, an instrument of rhythmic movement. The visitors can walk freely around the robot in the installation space, and the effect of Ventura's programming makes static positions and coincidental interactive movement patterns produce the illusion that the robot is alive.

The London-based Arts Catalyst organization, fulfilling a similar role to E.A.T.'s in advocating research that connects the arts and sciences, has been particularly interested in aspects of such machinic embodiment which illuminate and critique the manipulation of living systems from an informed practical perspective. The practical components of their recent Biotech Art and Wetware workshops (featuring, for example, Portuguese bio-artist Marta de Menezes and the Australian bio-researchers Oron Catts and Ionat Zurr of SymbioticA) included DNA extraction and fingerprinting, genetic engineering, selective breeding, plant and animal tissue cultures, and basic tissue engineering techniques. The relevance of the robotic imagination to such bio art practices becomes clearer if we look at how the notion of "living artworks" drives spatial, sculptural and kinetic experimentation through engineering/software programming on the one hand, and transgenic plants, animals, and tissue cultures through the manipulation of biological organisms on the other. Both strategies center on biotechnological procedures as a medium of expression, and the trajectory from body art to working with living cells or skin cultures is evident particularly in performative exhibitions that establish interrelationships between modifications of bio materials at small levels (cells, proteins, genes) and their economic, political, legal, and philosophical framework conditions. While there is growing interest among philosophers (e.g., Giorgio Agamben, Alphonso Lingis) to debate the political and economic definitions of being human/being animal, of life/consumable meat, and thus to call into question the differentiations among species, the notorious "biotech" projects of the CAE (Critical Art Ensemble) have drawn attention to the molecular research of corporations and their genetic modifications of plants and food. CAE, whose member Steve Kurtz was arrested on suspicion of bioterrorism in 2004, refers to their contestational biology as a form of reverse-engineering operating at the intersections between the "performativities of science and theatre" (<www.critical-art.net>). When the provocative critical elements are foregrounded and even spectacularized, as in Kac's glowing rabbit, SymbioticA's semi-living "Worry-Dolls," or Stelarc's recent effort to use tissue culture to grow a surgically constructed "Extra Ear" on his left arm, the scientific knowledge produced is much less convincing.

But why are audiences fascinated and disturbed by tissue culture projects? The misunderstanding, by the authorities, of the uses to which the biological materials and laboratory equipment found in Kurtz's home were put, of course can be seen as a symptom of the changing relationship between science, art, and politics, in an international context of war and terrorism with fundamentalist features, and in the context of very sensitive ethical controversies about the Human Genome Project and evolution/creationism. On the one hand, the increased presence of science in public discourse can confound the language. Earlier I wrote of "intelligent design" but hardly meant to evoke religion or what Richard Dawkins has called the "god delusion." I was referring to interactivity, and when transgenic art is involved, the issue of responsibility begins to loom large. Who has the right to use genetic engineering techniques to transfer, in Kac's terms, "synthetic genes to an organism or to transfer natural genetic material from one species to another, to create unique living beings"?[9] At a time when the life sciences are enjoying extraordinary public visibility, artists are using biological materials in the most unexpected and unorthodox ways. On the other hand, the very notion of a critical engagement with science and politics, say in the case of Kac's *Genesis* installation or his genetically altered rabbit (*GFP Bunny*), becomes questionable when the artist's theory and practice mimic creation in a literal sense, combining genetic engineering of animal or plant life with telepresence and inviting the "user"—indirectly—to take the risk of further stimulating biological mutations in *E. coli* bacteria.

Kac's interactive installation, *Genesis*, stimulates a remote control enactment of the kind that was unthinkable ten years ago, but it is thinkable now and places the role of the user into a politically complex scenario of having to make ethical choices. Commissioned by ars electronica 1999, Kac's Website tells us, *Genesis* presents a transgenic artwork that "explores the intricate relationship between biology, belief systems, information technology, dialogical interaction, ethics, and the Internet." The main element of the work is an "artist's gene," a synthetic gene created by Kac by translating a sentence from the biblical book of Genesis into Morse Code, and converting the Morse Code into DNA base pairs according to a conversion principle specially developed by the artist for this work. The sentence reads: "Let man have dominion over the fish of the sea, and over the fowl of the air, and over every living thing that moves upon the earth." It was chosen, Kac argues, for what it implies about the dubious notion of divinely sanctioned humanity's supremacy over nature. The *Genesis* gene was incorporated into bacteria, which were shown in the gallery. Online participants could turn on an ultraviolet light in the gallery, causing real, biological mutations in the bacteria. This changed the biblical sentence in the bacteria. The ability to change the sentence, Kac claims, is a symbolic gesture, implying that we don't accept its meaning in the form we inherited it, and that new meanings emerge as we seek to change it.

The promise of such "symbolic gestures" has been all too tempting to a growing number of artists who, since 1999, have also gone into science laboratories and examined the tools, for example cell culture techniques and observational methods, with sophisticated research equipment such as electron and light microscopes, to produce high-quality images of cells in culture or experiment with cell growth and mobility. A workshop at Lancaster University ("Bio-Remediation between Art and Science: Art, Science and Institutions") in 2006 and the 2007 Subtle Technologies Festival in Toronto ("Art—Body—Medicine") looked carefully at this development and the material artefacts associated with the life sciences, as well as the transgenic "work" moving across institutional boundaries that might be said to separate the laboratory, the art gallery, and the museum. While Kac claimed, after "creating" the green glowing rabbit named Alba in 2000, that he has been investigating the new ecology of fluorescent creatures evolving worldwide and meant to emphasize, at the core of such work, a commitment to respect, nurture, and love the life thus created, it is difficult to separate the media attention Alba received from questions of benefit, namely whether biomolecular science is served here or whether artistic gestures add to the critical conversation between science and culture.

Oron Catts, who directed a workshop on tissue engineering and bio-art for "Art—Body—Medicine" (<http://www.subtletechnologies.com/>), has questioned the ways in which artistic work that focuses on technologies such as the GeneChip courts the risk of endorsing genetic reductionism and determinism, especially when handled in a purely formalist fashion. He understands his own work to advance a more ephemeral understanding of life insofar as the very act of touching the artefacts he produces results in their death. This peculiar proposition, I think, reflects back on the practices of genetic engineering and how they have been appropriated by artists like Kac who focus on the use of the mundane green fluorescent protein marking to produce the "GFP Bunny"—engineering for aesthetic, rather than scientific, purposes. Some critics even question whether Alba can really be considered an example of the intersection of art and recent developments in the life sciences, insofar as the fluorescence of the "GFP Bunny" is an effect of photographic, rather than genetic, techniques. Others might question the extent to which genetic engineering can be said to be any more ethical when mobilized for scientific rather than artistic purposes. At the Lancaster workshop, Maureen McNeil called for greater attention to the ways in which the artefacts emerging from contemporary developments in the life sciences, especially the gene, acquire aesthetic value, at the expense of questions of political economy. McNeil encouraged us to ponder the role of the Wellcome Trust or governmental research foundations in policing either scientists' or artists' representations of new experiments in the life sciences to draw boundaries between "legitimate" and "illegitimate" images.

It is the borderline that has always been at the core of the political, ethical, and cultural debates on humans, animals, monsters, and hybrids. Robotics and transgenic art, in this sense, politicize the vexing questions of the production of life in the laboratory, scientific and artistic. Challenging the borders of biology and aesthetics, such works conceptually produce a much needed philosophical space of reflection on societal discourses about reproduction and the environment, the discomforts of biocybernetics and—given today's paranoid climate of suspicion—the politics of security. Creative experiments in transgenic art, wet biology art or tissue culture are necessarily parasitic, but in their public installations they can spell out the fundamental technical determinant of the new century, involving the spectators as an interactor required to confront specific concerns of safety or care taking. Biocybernetic reproduction—if it confuses the distinctions between humanity, animal species, dynamics systems, cultures, and other parallel universes (extraterrestrial, mythical, supernatural)—raises a specific metaphysical dilemma for the interactor who cares not to remain a disengaged spectator or consumer. How do you use your perceptions *in vivo* or *in vitro*, in the virtual real, in a reality in which structures of life, biological existence, intelligence, or consciousness are unintelligible without the help of extra sense-machines (those of science, mathematics)? How do you use protocols of care, safety and responsibility to "living art production"? Chaotically speaking, is not such hybrid reality the condition of an impossibility of setting up boundaries, perimeters, and limits, presuming that everything crossbreeds, entangles, merges, and penetrates everything else? Is *Genesis* a sophisticated game, displaying one Judeo-Christian engine and mythical machine of nature while also breeding another engine, displaying the malleable structure of biological coding? This is the digital world in which we play our games; for what is the digital if not a powerful technique of hybridization, contamination, and dissemination?

Habitats

We can conjecture that performance of science here delves into its biomedical tradition: it manufactures or contrives experimental variations on the evolution of the human, testing the limits of the body or what we know of it, rehearsing an unimaginable condition which also can be considered a predictable adaptation once a corporeal and cognitive challenge is posited. How do we move on planet Mars? Scientists at the NASA Haughton-Mars Project on Devon Island (Canada) are testing it (<www.marsonearth.org>). Olympus donates the epifluorescence miscroscope for endolithic microbiological analysis. Carnegie Mellon's Robotics Institute provides the "Hyperion" rover for autonomous traversing of the imagined Mars. Coincidentally, the New York based Builders Association, in their new multimedia production *Invisible Cities*, collaborate with the developers of Mobile Augmented Reality Systems (MARS) at Columbia University to develop a special interface for the performance, which involves Brooklyn teenagers of color in the creation, design, and development of a game that critically comments on virtual racism. "Invisible Cities," the Builders Association's homepage claims, refer to the imaginary cities of the future and of the past, and to cities within cities. MARS, appropriately, combines mobile computing and augmented reality, in which 3-D displays are used to overlay a synthesized world on top of the real world. Increasingly small computing devices, linked by wireless networks, are used while roaming the real world, but in the end, we are told, "content from workshops with the teens will be transferred to the MARS software along with texture-mapped models of performance event locations in lower Manhattan." The teens won't return to the hood, it seems, but will be biometrically "mapped," and thus undergo the image surveillance and compositing techniques already strikingly employed in *Alladeen* and *SUPER VISION*. The Builders seek to combine a "modeling software with the MARS interface that would take a photo of the participant and merge averaged ethnic and racial characteristics of a typical NYC native in 2105 with the participant's existing facial features. The new composite image will become an avatar representing the participant's game persona" (<www.thebuildersassociation.org>). This, admittedly, sounds rather more alienating to me than the fun-loving scientist crew on Devon Island, whose chief physicist Stephen Braham is a space networking specialist as well as a cunning Buster Keaton-like metteur-en-scène of "arctic survival demos." The physicist, in this case, is indeed playing games with the media attention the Mars testing ground received.

And how would we adapt to living under water? Australian diver/performance artist Sarah Jane Pell will test it in a performance at the Roundhouse, London, where she plans to spend a week submerged in a human-scale aqueous bioreactor connected to a satellite of semi living aquanauts in self-contained mini biospheres. Her project, SUBCULTURE, proposes to test duty of care issues in difficult habitats as well as our understanding of such "medium" states or systems ("actual," "symbolic," "symbiotic," and "simulated" and/or "real" systems) by investigating the various relationships between subject/object, inside/outside, host/body, and entity/non-entity through strategies of cognition and communication applicable across multiple living systems and new media practice. Her exploration activity, partly administered by SymbioticA, will be webcast live on the Net. When I last met her, she had received a six-month training residency at the NASA Ames Research Center, not the customary place to go for a performer, but deeply meaningful to her pursuit of scientific and medical questions. Collaborating with Dr. Sheryl Bishop (University of Texas Medical Branch) who is NASA's clinical psychologist and the head of the Life Sciences Faculty at the International Space University where Pell had studied, the young performer can take the opportunity to propose some unconventional and creative applications of technology and biomonitoring of crews (including herself) in extreme environment conditions. SUBCULTURE, which Pell lovingly refers to as her "Hydromedusa" project, currently involves a series of tests accessing new possibilities for future bio-mapping, monitoring, feedback, and human performance behavior integration. On a technical level, it also involves getting all the technologies water-proofed. But her scientifically creative endeavor now applies neuro-gaming devices to use real-time neurological response (linked with the vestibular function) in order to measure propulsion, movement, behavior and expression, both underwater and onscreen.

Brain Dance

How have performances contributed to our knowledge of the mind, of cognitive states? The significance of movement for human development surely was never in doubt. In evolutionary terms, we gathered from Charles Darwin and Stanley Kubrick, dance is as vital for the survival of the species and its expressions in ritual, social, and theatrical contexts as it is for the evolution of the Hollywood film industry. Movie images encapsulate popular stereotypes and icons, revealing the roles of gender, race, fashion, economic, and political force. There are movies playing in our minds all the time—images of objects, images of spatial organization, motor processes, memory, body maps, etc. In science fiction we can step into the brain room and switch off the automated technology when it becomes too threatening. In reality, it has proven to be more difficult to grasp how the brain inside the human organism engenders mental patterns—*how it moves*, in other words.

The Cartesian idea of a disembodied mind had an enduring impact on the philosophical history of reason in Western culture, on our thinking about thinking and the rational instruments of human behavior. Philosophical, artistic, and religious speculation on the mind has shaped our notions of consciousness, ethics, and the human condition. The neural processes of the brain, which had attracted Professor Hans Berger's curiosity when he invented the EEG (electroencephalography) in a neuropsychiatric clinic in Jena (1929), were not a common subject for the humanities and the arts. I first encountered brain waves in a dance workshop at Hellerau (2000), when a neuroscientist attached electrodes to my head and made an EEG spectral analysis of my brain activity while dancing, using a measuring software that allowed the frequencies to be processed as real-time data for sound generation. To my disappointment, the music of my brain was not as good as I would have liked it to be. Today, such "biofeedback applications" are commercially available—you can buy them on the Internet and digitally record, store, process, and work with brainwaves using a computer to "create displays, sounds, or other effects" (<http://www.futurehealth. org/brainmas.htm>). These recordings, however, explain very little about why someone is unable to lift a leg or move a hand, for example when the connections between the thalamus, the basal ganglia, and the motor cortex are damaged.

Explaining behavior and the mechanisms of life has been the domain of the sciences. Remarkably, the mind was in fact neglected in Western biology and medicine, as medical research focussed on the physiology and pathology of the body proper, developing ever more specialized areas of internal medicine. Neurology as the study of brain diseases developed relatively late in the course of the last century. Eventually, over the past few decades, a growing interest in the nervous system and the mind has led to the current wave of research in the "embodied mind" and the "neural self" (Antonio Damasio).

But how did the "neural self" and the "dancing brain" meet? As Corinne Jola (Institute of Cognitive Neuroscience, London) and Fred Mast (Zentrum für Neurowissenschaft Zürich) suggest, experimental dance science has only recently become possible through interdisciplinary university programs, while research in dance previously "focused mainly on philosophical, historical, and aesthetical questions as well as on physical problems such as frequent injuries in dance. Much less is known about the mental processes associated with dance."[10]

Similarly, the use of performing arts to study the brain doesn't have a long history. When you ask researchers in the sciences, they'll say that it's a very competitive field and easier to get funding for hardcore science that yields findings useful to industry and the medical health sectors. Why would governments spend money on dance research when neurological study can discover improvements for patients suffering from trauma, epilepsy, or Parkinson's Disease. Scientists need to publish results or gain patents that are considered significant contributions to knowledge in their fields, rather than offering a service (and some scientific visualizations) to the arts, as it has been very superficially proposed in recent trends to promote neuroaesthetics.

Warren Neidich's symposium at London's Goldsmiths College (<http://www.artbrain.org/>) in 2005 claimed that artists have begun to investigate the brain, neuroaesthetics being a dynamic process through which questions of neuroscience are made "ready-mades." Concepts such as sensation, perception, memory and, recently, networks, plasticity and sampling incite artistic experimentation. While this may be true, neuroaesthetics again strikes me as parasitic and, like my experience at Hellerau, quite banal. It's easy today to use biofeedback devices and body scans to generate visual images or sound for performance, as it was done in Otmar Gendera's and Dieter Heitkamp's *BrainDance* project (2004), Jennifer Monson's *BirdBrainDance* (2005), MorrisonDance's *Inside* (2005), or numerous other performances reaching back to the 1990s when Diane Gromola (with Yacov Sharir) explored virtual reality and immersive design using manipulated "objective" MRI data of her body to "move inside" them. Gromola's *Dancing with the Virtual Dervish* may have been a stunning experience, but it would not have yielded the knowledge that Jola/Mast, Beatriz Calvo-Merino, Annette Hartmann, Catherine Stevens, Phil Barnard, Steven Brown, Frédéric Bevilacqua, Scott deLahunta and other scientists and performance scholars today are thinking of when they initiate collaborative research to investigate brain activity in the mirror system (mirror neurons) during action observation or compare brain activation during execution and observation of specific motor skills.

When choreographer Wayne McGregor (Random Dance Company), along with Scott deLahunta, received science funding to work with experimental psychologists at the Cambridge University Department of Neuroscience, the "Choreography and Cognition" project (<www.choreocog.net>) opened up a new platform for dance studies and cognitive science—not because McGregor later composed *AtaXia* and based it on his research experience, but because dancers and neuroscientists worked together over an extended period of time exchanging hypotheses and methodologies.

A ground was thus prepared for testing representations of kinematic properties, looking at the tools of research and the framework of observation, questioning the notion of "mental images" (the movie in your head while you dance may not only be visual but involve various complex somatosensory contributions to spatial cognition, coordination, proprioceptive processing, etc.). Perhaps even questioning the transactions of knowledge, namely what exactly is considered of value or significance as a professional outcome within different communities of practice. Similarly, William Forsythe and Ivar Hagendoorn convened an international symposium on "Dance and the Brain" (Frankfurt 2004), which revealed the extent to which neuroscientific investigation, for example of the motor repertoire and the recognition of possible or impossible movement, is based on *neuroimaging technologies* (PET, fMRI) which historically seem to evolve alongside very sophisticated digital tools and scanning/capturing techniques choreographers recently began to use for sensory "measuring" of action and qualities of gesture.

The shared tools and technologies of observation are one common platform for productive transactions between scientific, artistic, and educational communities. Mental training (often cited in regard to sports), health issues, and cultural assumptions about bodymind and mental maps of bodies provide ample ground for research, and current neurobiological interest in emotions and feelings, similar to psychoacoustic research in music, offers provocative questions about representation. At the 2004 Monaco Dance Forum, a team of dance and media artists, acoustic and technology experts, as well as psychologists specialized in kinesiology studied such neuroanatomical representation by testing how interactive technologies give a high degree of fidelity to registering positions, speed, direction, and intensity of small and big movements. Armando Menicacci, director of the Médiadanse Lab in Paris, was able to demonstrate the significance of "pre-movements" in the abdominal musculature, which cannot be perceived by the naked eye. The recent software developments, deLahunta noted, make it possible to work with a high resolution of data and to trace sound, light/image, and even haptics effects which allow the instantaneous recording in the field of the consciousness of the movement.

This is an exemplary avenue of shared study which promises the more sustained *rencontres entre le monde de l'art et la recherche scientifique* envisioned by the 2005 science lab at the Grenoble Festival des Imagi-naires. It involves collaboration on a global level, as was demonstrated at the recent Digital Cultures Lab (<www.digitalcultures.org>) when Rachel Zuanon (Brazil) spoke about her cross-cultural research in "Co-evolution-ary Interfaces: the communication among brain, computer and body that dances." Jayachandran Palazhy (India) presented his extraordinary *Nagari-ka* DVD—an integrated information system on Indian Physical Traditions which delves deeply into the subjects' extended consciousness and memory of dance forms. Palazhy is not a scientist explaining the neural basis of Bharatanatyam, as Steven Brown tried to do in his experiment with tango dancers in Texas. But the master teachers in his DVD explain eloquently (and demonstrate) what happens in the form and how they know the feel-ing of what happens. Brown's PET scan provides objective, comparative data; the Indian masters tell comparative stories of dancing practiced almost over their entire lives. The objectives of each project are different, yet the methods, stimuli, and tasks demonstrated by the dancers indicate shared possibilities for dance and science collaborative research. The study of men-tal imaging for the execution of complex, polyrhythmic movement (e.g., in African, Latin, and Indian dance) or the analysis of specific motor skills to enhance execution seems of obvious relevance to dancers. The reciprocities between dance or music improvisation and cellular movement, now increas-ingly recognized in the study of dynamic, self-organizing systems, suggest the kind of inquiries into time consciousness (temporality, sequencing) and the physical biology of flow that were anticipated in Kenneth King's writings on dancing perception—the scanning of detail and pattern recognition.[11]

A wide area of investigation has opened up that links the cognitive and social science field with the arts, as was again demonstrated impressively at a recent conference at Brunel University's Center for Cognition and Neu-roimaging. More than twenty scholars discussed cutting edge research in the field and drew especially on motion analysis and psychoacoustic data relevant to the study of brain activity and models of emotion, motives, and affective states (dispositional tendencies) and the overall architecture of im-portant emotions typically found in human beings, though possibly not in all other animals, such as humiliation, excited anticipation, infatuation, the thrill of discovery, despair, etc. Not surprisingly, several scholars ad-dressed the issue of control and the question of how emotions can be con-sidered as emergent properties of the complex control systems comprising the entire cognitive apparatus rather than being mediated by separate structures. Emergent states were referred to as "perturbances," and this concept indeed was one of the guiding compositional research questions in Random Dance Co's *AtaXia*.

When I interviewed McGregor, he replied that during a first phase he went to the labs where the neuroscientists normally observe the "movement of the brain" under controlled conditions. "But it's hard to dance with electrodes attached to the head," I suggested. "Yes, this phase was really more about finding alternative modes of looking, analysis and questioning through the eyes of the scientists." Later in 2003, when the cognitive scientists and experimental psychologists came to McGregor's studio, they first tried to explore the interface between mind and body in a non-verbal manner. McGregor asked himself whether they could collaborate without words, looking for synergies in their mutual ways of thinking about creativity and cognition, movement control and coordination.

"So are there parallel interests," I asked, "or do the scientists observe different things?" McGregor's enthusiastic responses indicated that he enjoyed the interest that scientists have recently shown the performing arts. "There may be different frames of reference, in clinical and experimental psychology or in a dance studio, but we share a common interest in how the brain carries out movement, how digital systems show data from neurological processes, how we experience the relations between imagined and real movement." Of course, he added, "as highly trained dancers we tend not to think of the non-virtuosic, or the break-downs, in the way a neuropsychologist may work with deficits or traumata. In clinical contexts the scientists collect data that help to deal with sensorimotor or cognitive deficits. But there are overlaps, in the way in which we explore mental spaces or look at reactive and predictive control of movement. In dance we need practical information to move, to exercise our kinaesthetic intelligence, our excess of kinetic potential."

I became curious, imagining McGregor and the dancers going through their rehearsal processes being watched silently by neuroscientists. Those processes are familiar to an increasing number of dancers and children in Europe attending his workshops or benefiting from Random's much-praised educational outreach program "System R" (aimed at young people in school and community projects). In 2001 McGregor also participated in the "Tanz und Neue Medien" workshop at the Choreographische Zentrum NRW (see "Trackback 2: Algorithms, Dance, and Technology"), where he taught working with animation and telematics as techniques to "extend the body." The workshop students were given small tasks to solve, a method of generating movement material that is quite common. What confused the students was McGregor pushing them to use physical and digital images for movement, which completely undermined their familiar body images. He enjoys finding forms in which the live body on a real stage behaves as if it were virtually "unnatural."

Is it a matter of what problems one asks the performers to solve? "How did *AtaXia* emerge from working with the scientists?", I inquired, noticing that in the "Choreography and Cognition" project McGregor responded to the neuroscientists' interest in the *perturbance* of normal patterns of perception and motion control. "Yes, rehearsing *AtaXia* focused on the disorganization of the body, discoordination, and loss of control. It was strange, we had started to work with this notion of 'loss' when one day a woman walked into our studio who suffers from *ataxia*, a brain condition which causes severe loss of coordination, and she told us how she experiences this condition. For example, there are times when she cannot remember how to walk down a staircase, but she told us incredibly vivid images that she dreams about movement. Her condition also relates to how older people may not be able to walk anymore without help."

In the rehearsals, McGregor began to introduce "perturbations"—disruptions and interferences into movement coordination—which became the creative strategy for the choreographic design of *AtaXia*. The dancers were given conflicting instructions or dual tasks; they performed with eyes closed or using different parts of their body with different speeds. Playing tricks with mind and memory. I tell McGregor that I found it hard to watch the performance when I first saw it. For once, the excessively loud and pounding minimalist music score by Michael Gordon drove me nearly insane, it kept me on edge all the time and made it hard to concentrate. McGregor laughed, "Well, of course we try to enhance the ambivalence or sensory confusion our audience feels when watching the piece. Body and senses are an integral part of understanding the world, but how do you perceive when the information in the brain is scrambled?" Harsh neon lighting, randomly programmed and constantly changing, created a nervous environment. *AtaXia* is not easy to watch: the extraordinary dancers, whose technical capabilities remind me of Forsythe's former Frankfurt Ballet, show such precisely articulate control of movement in the opening solos that it comes as a shock—

registered as a slow awakening in my drowned-out inner ears—to see them gradually flailing, needing to rely on the support from other dancers, as they slink down to the floor, tumble out of control. A film screen descends, halfway through the piece, and an extremely fast sequence of distorted abstract images and sentence fragments flies by, as if the brain's synapses were firing aimlessly and furiously. The film is like an homage to Kubrick's *Space Odyssey*, the brain shooting into a black hole while our heads are twitching. In the third part of the dance, perspex sheets are lowered: now the dancers are behind surfaces that further distort their bodies and movement. *AtaXia* blurs, and our consciousness cannot recover from it.

"At this point," McGregor suggests when I told him how the work left me emotionally detached, "you may experience the complete depletion of attention in the body. We use the sound and the doubling of distorted body images to aggressively affect your ability to watch in a particular way." But, I protest, is this not a highly technical formalism that keeps me disengaged? McGregor believes it's the opposite, his perturbations are visceral and cut to the bones, since there is no harmony (between movement and music) but I am watching a multiplicitly broken choreography against the turbulences of the visual and acoustic environment. I suffer depletion, quite literally.[12]

The Singing Detective

Cynthia Hopkins's multimedia operetta, *Accidental Nostalgia*, may not reflect the laboratory-based approach to art and science, but she and her band Gloria Deluxe exquisitely remind us of the theatrical power of a charged performance that claims its introspections into the mind, in song and visuals, as a poetic journey filled with superb ironies. These are journeys exceeding computational analysis. The qualities of her gestures are infused with dark humor and the ambiguous smile of the cabaret chanteuse, making us ponder how to interpret the inflections of her voice, the musical arrangements, and the perplexing micro-video vignettes, created right there on the stage by her media designers and co-performers, Jim Findlay and Jeff Sugg, who use a small spy camera to great effect, for example in the scene where Hopkins's character returns home to Georgia to go to the house where she thinks she might have killed her father. On a miniature set, stage right, Hopkins steps into the "street" that leads to the "door" of the "house"—dramatic real-time video shots created inside a little puppet theatre box.

On the surface, *Accidental Nostalgia* takes off as a research lecture into memory processes, amnesia, and the after-effects of incestuous abuse. Medical slides depict the struggle over the possibility of blocking out and later retrieving repressed memories of traumatic events. But then Hopkins performs her journey through amnesia, surreal rememberings, self-observation, speculation, and dreams, and the scientific imagination is translated into the artistic. She ends up transforming herself, undressing/redressing as her mother/herself in Morocco, now partly veiled and beginning a life reborn as a daughter whose disappeared father's confession finally reaches her via a video letter, brilliantly staged for us. The reading of a testimony performed by the father in front of the camera is simultaneously performed, adopted, and ironically subverted by the daughter. At its most imaginative, such performance is like opera, a heightened concentration of many perspectives, rhythms, voices, and polyphonic energies, sustained for hours. In *Accidental Nostalgia*, the science of the brain is refracted as continuous transfers between film, dance, music, and computer-assisted montage—live digital art at its best, reviving narrative traditions. My nostalgia for opera is growing stronger now, after all these years of having written on technology and media. The Robert Wilson "template" ("Deafman Glance and Molecular Gaze") remains a model for polyphonic scenography on the proscenium stage, whereas many of the other templates I have discussed here depart from the stage and enter into the newly emerging interactive real-time environments.

I hope it's not paradoxical to invoke opera against the real-time environments, but mindful of a continuous effort to observe how digital performance can distill and exceed the laboratory experiments and incomplete prototypes, and—like Monteverdi's *Orfeo* and *L'incoronazione di Poppea* marking the beginnings of modern opera—come into its own or, rather, into its own complex interactions. When Poppea sings about lust and ambition, is she, like Hopkins in *Accidental Nostalgia*, not singing about a body's mind performing with someone else's programming? This body, Stelarc would argue, has become a host for remote and multiple agents. In the performance ethos of the scientific era, such organisms are being reengineered in all the terrains of our digital cultures.

NOTES

[1] Thecla Schiphorst, "Soft, Softer and Softly: [whispering] between the lines," in *aRt&D: Artistic Research and Development*, edited by Joke Brouwer, Arjen Mulder, Anne Nigten, Laura Martz, Rotterdam: V2_Publishing/NAi Publishers, 2005, 169. Her epistemological method refers to the design construction of the wearables for her interactive installation *whisper*, shown at the Respond Interchange festival in Cambridge, 2003 and at SIGGRAPH, Los Angeles, 2005.

[2] Blaine Brownell, *Transmaterial: A catalog of materials that redefine our physical environment*, New York: Princeton Architectural Press, 2006, 7–10.

[3] The MIT List Visual Arts Center offered its 2006 exhibition *9 evenings reconsidered: art, theatre, and engineering, 1966* as a critical homage to the original event, featuring the records of 1966 to focus on a ground breaking link in the history of performance, art, and technology. The excellent catalogue of the exhibition was edited by curator Catherine Morris. When looking back to Rauschenberg's "open score" for the tennis match or to Alex Hay's abstract formal, mathematical patterns in *Grass Field*, it is tempting to think of The Wooster Group's *To You, The Birdie!* ("Interactive Systems") and the widening spectrum of performance obsessions with game play (and their Duchampian roots in science and engineering).

[4] See Clarisse Bardiot, "The Diagrams of *9 Evenings*," in *9 evenings reconsidered: art, theatre, and engineering, 1966*, 44–53, and the interview with Herb Schneider, ibid., 55–63, which includes all the technical drawings.

[5] Quoted from the original program, transcribed in *9 evenings reconsidered*, 17–18. Tudor wanted to push the work toward "total oscillation," suggesting that "a performer activating interacting media will instigate an unscannable environment." Cf. David Tudor, "*Bandoneon !* Pre- and Post-Operative Note," 1973, quoted in Michelle Kuo, "*9 evenings* in reverse," 42. See also Lucy Lippard, "Total Theatre?" in *9 evenings reconsidered*, 65–73.

[6] Kuo, "*9 evenings* in reverse," 33.

[7] Mark Coniglio and Dawn Stoppiello presented the technical aspects of their collaborations at the Digital Cultures Lab: <www.digitalcultures.org>. Their use of EyesWeb is also described at: <http://www.troikaranch.org/16revs/technology.html>. For research in real-time analysis of expressive gesture, see for example: *Gesture-Based Communication in Human-Computer Interaction*, edited by Antonio Camurri and Gualtiero Volpe, Berlin: Springer Verlag, 2004.

[8] Scott deLahunta and Frédéric Bevilacqua, "Sharing descriptions of movement," *International Journal of Performance Arts and Digital Media*, 3,1 (2007): 2–16.

⁹ Eduardo Kac, "Transgenic Art": <http://www.ekac.org/transgenic.html>; originally published in *Leonardo Electronic Almanac*, 6, 11 (December 1998).

¹⁰ Corinne Jola and Fred W. Mast, "Mental Imagery Processes in Dance," in *Tanz im Kopf/Dance and Cognition*, 2005, 211–32.

¹¹ Kenneth King, *Writing in Motion: Body—Language—Technology*, Middletown, CT: Wesleyan University Press, 2003. Steven Brown, in a scientific lecture on "Brain Imaging Technology and the Performing Arts" at the *Performing Art Performing Science Conference* (Simon Fraser University, June 16–18, 2005), argued that the incorporation of brain imaging technology into dance is still in the realm of the fanciful at present, as the incorporation of brain data obtained from the imaged person would depend on portable technologies rather than metabolic techniques such as fMRI (functional magnetic resonance imaging). See also: Steven Brown, Michael J. Martinez, and Lawrence M. Parsons, "The Neural Basis of Human Dance," *Cerebral Cortex*, 16 (2006): 1157–1167.

¹² The full interview with Wayne McGregor appeared in *ballettanz* 8–9 (2005), 18–21.

▼▲ Conclusion:
Bio-Art & Interactors

Pointing to the many convergences of performance, technology and science, this book has reached a difficult border line where the production of "cultures," in the sense in which bio-art approaches the design of new functions of biological organisms to manufacture artificial life, has moved beyond the human performer to processes of *embodiment* that are not represented by "body artists" but mediated as organic presences, *in vivo* and *in vitro*, so to speak. Bio-artists like Kac, Zaretsky, or Catts and Zurr (SymbioticA) perform tissue engineering or culture and grow life forms to compose concretions/presences that seem to fall outside the symbolic space of art. Yet their artistic reframing of bio-scientific methods refocusses cultural reception of critical issues of the *bios* and the ethical-political debates on DNA, which is a biological and informatic compound, and surely an ideological artefact itself. In intermingling art and the living they inevitably "perform" conceptual work directed at audiences whose interactive complicity, multisensorial affection, and critical sensibility are provoked. Such work is heterotopic, in the sense in which Foucault speaks of heterotopias as sites that contest the real and open up other, virtual spaces. If it is claimed here as part of the emerging digital aesthetics, it is because bio-art makes a bold foray into the circulation of biological metaphors, using unconventional artistic metaverses to reflect on real life and address our beliefs in the presence of life, our understanding of DNA. One could say such art uses extreme engineering (just as synthetic genomics does), presencing the un-presentable by rewiring animated biochemical processes—as "scientific processes"—into an unsettling dialectical relationship to our own presence. On the side of the receiver (can one speak of "user" here?), this creates uncomfortable emotional and ethical tensions, as if one had stepped onto the secret or hidden/forbidden ground of living matter.

Inevitably, there are mediating technologies and contextualizing epistemological discourses involved in a-life installations, needed to postulate the complex and often non-visual organic processes of the molecular biochemical agents. And those are aligned with the coding and interactive principles examined throughout these chapters in which I asked how performance has been affected by emergent techniques that bring with them a need to grapple with scientific engines, methods, concepts, and languages of knowledge. Bio-art does not evacuate representation but compensates for the nearly incomprehensible complexity of science, of cellular biochemistry in league with quantum theories, by proposing artistic figuration.

Researchers in fields ranging from computer engineering to medicine and the life sciences also rely on figuration, on digital imaging, and draw inspiration from the mutual interpenetration of the organic and the technical. Their work is dedicated to scientific discovery and follows the protocols of scientific research.

But at the 2007 Subtle Technologies conference, Jennifer Willet and Sean Bailey of BIOTEKNICA (Concordia University) postulated a future where biotechnological protocols produce designer organisms based on consumer demand, displaying a variety of virtual and laboratory based artefacts focusing on irrational and grotesque incarnations of the biotechnological body. Their work turned out to be modeled on the Teratoma, a cancerous growth containing multiple tissues like hair, skin, and vascular systems. Preposterous as this may seem, scientists are in fact interested in the Teratoma as an instance of spontaneous cloning and a source of stem cells, while the BIOTEKNICA project sets up a "quasi-cinema"—as Hélio Oiticica might have called it—of transdisciplinary bio-art, seeking to challenge the public with contradictions within these technologies once we fully realize that contemporary science produces shifting conceptions of the body as a biotechnological resource. Rooted perceptions of the classification of living beings change, and so do the subjects of technologically mediated and augmented life.

Performance, I have tried to argue, confronts this subject especially in and through the mediating and tethering techniques, and the psychosensory discourses of the current era of interactive and networked art. It is an art, as the curious names chosen for projects or companies indicate (kondition pluriel, SymbioticA, NOX, Asymptote), that performs the unstable and indeterminate metabolisms emerging from technogenesis, here defined primarily as the mutual interpenetration of the organic and the technical. But for our notion of what "art" is, the expansion of hardware and software to the current biologically-inspired concepts of "wetware" is ominous insofar as it will be necessary to alter existing notions of the art object altogether once tissue cultures and microorganisms are grown to be engaged in an aesthetic, interactive environment. A whole spectrum of biotechnological methods are appropriated in the name of art. Understandably, Paul Kaiser hesitated at the end of our dialogue ("Thinking Images") to predict how such hybridity in sci-art practices might affect common modes of production and reception in the biocybernetic era, but it appears that the curators at ars electronica, for example, are quite eager to prepare the public for new kinds of performances in scientific contexts for which we may not have any names or explanations yet. Gerfried Stocker, artistic director of ars electronica, already made an effort in this direction in 2000 when he invited the art "farmers" Joe Davis and Katie Egan, who dismissed "new media" as rather old and proposed to look at new developments in molecular biology. Explaining their new instruments with which they will grow molecular artworks, they write:

> In order to maintain a supply of many different organisms Katie Egan and I have learned to maintain a wide variety of wild protist cultures. We call this collection of microbial cultures "the farm." "The farm" now includes many species of ciliates, nematodes, euplotes, rotifers (bdelloids), motile algae and other tiny invertebrates. As we are artists still, with little or no ambition to become scientific taxonomists, many of our organisms are referred to in lab by our own names for them such as "green scudders," "red weirdos," and "scary finbacks." Because many of these organisms originated as "wild" organisms it is possible that some of them have not yet been scientifically classified anyway. We also are fortunate to have available a variety of typical laboratory microorganisms in reasonably pure culture including E. coli, Bacillus, Pseudomonas, and others. The existence of the farm has itself spurred us on to other work. We are for instance now pursuing a microfabrication project that will allow us to "go fishing" for microbes with equipment that is basically analogous to an anglers "rod and reel." We will install both the audio microscope/spectrum analyzer and elements of "the farm" at Linz. The installation will feature a "library" of captured sound and video from a variety of organisms as well as real time examinations of organisms from "the farm" and of organisms we

hope to obtain locally. (<http://www.aec.at/festival2000/texte/ artistic_molecules_2_e.htm>)

Their artist statement for the exhibition at ars electronica at times reads like a humoristic futurist manifesto, without the fascist undertones glimpsed in Marinetti's proclamations of the Synthetic Theatre Manifesto almost a hundred years ago. Interestingly, however, Marinetti spoke of compression and the glorious speed of machine time, while the bio-artists now concern themselves with a very old, slow medium: deoxyribonucleic acid. Their dramaturgy of compression consists of exploring possible interfaces of molecular biology, microbiology, and the arts to generate new "substances."

I don't want to predict the future either, since I have argued throughout that interactive performance has just modestly entered its second generation and finds itself still at the very beginning of a slow evolution. Looking at many examples from performance, dance, installation and architecture, I tried to sketch hybridities and fluid systems in performance media art/design which comprise a crucial domain for experimentation with the conditions of embodied human life in the contemporary technosphere, as philosopher Mark Hansen has argued. He called such experimentation a properly existential task, and I agree that at this moment in history one imagines digital performance to operate beyond the process-oriented art movements of the 60s and 70s. It re-materializes the substances of performance. It reactivates our sensorium precisely with the tools of digital abstraction that extend, translate, amplify, or stimulate the senses.

For what is at stake in the processes catalyzed by digital performance is not the dissociation of the psyche and the senses, but various forms of reintegration, mindful of the cultural, ethical consequences of the inseparability of technology from life itself. A biological mindset is indeed growing in the digital arts, and in my comments on architecture and performance I tried to point out that architectural practice and interactive design, for example, have increasingly embraced scientific models and ideas. Whereas the Modern movement incorporated advances in technology and industry, there were remarkably few attempts to come to terms with the more radical scientific developments of the era, such as relativity or quantum mechanics. But today's designers are increasingly schooled in new developments in science and mathematics, from neuroscience and computation, to complexity theory and embryology. This turn in thinking indicates to me a biological habit of mind which of course challenges all of our ideas of observing, inhabiting, activating, and interacting with the (bio)art object, the object of performance.

The engines of performance making have changed, and some of my forays into the aesthetics and the politics of emergence, complexity, control and real-time networked multi-media collaboration open out to various charged constellations, whether we call them "virtual art," as Frank Popper has proposed, or digital performance. Popper mostly describes the "aesthetic-technological logic" of installation art in his overview of current practices, and he acknowledges that the logic of what he calls virtualism pivots on interactivity, on potentiality and openness exercised by the artists and the users in their reciprocating actions. For performance, some specific prerequisites remain at issue in order to distinguish the use of interactivity in performance throughout the first and second generations. Definitions of these interactive generations will remain subject to change, but I want to end by suggesting that one of the rooted meanings of composition or choreography, namely the production of a completed aesthetic structure that can be enacted through repeated rehearsal, has been poignantly dissolved, and this concerns the professional performer as well as the reciprocating public.

Performance anxiety, in the era of digital performance, has nothing to do anymore with the ephemerality of performance and the question of sustainability through repetition and reproduction, the older matters of legacy and reception. New modes of emergent design and real-time, translocal performance are created which constitute themselves as radically open and interactive systems, organisms, game scenarios, and sensorial propositions. An entire new book could be written on the scientific/aesthetic techniques of "postchoreography," of virtual performances activating cross-sensory associations and experiences that can never be fixed or cued in compositional "writing" that requires absolute precision. The perturbed dancer in Wayne McGregor's Random Dance Co. follows a choreographic proposition, as do William Forsythe's performers who have been trained in the Frankfurt Ballet system of improvisation technologies and immediately know what is meant by "reverse inscription," "room inscription," "u-ing" or "o-ing," and who can adapt instantly to spontaneous cues in the manner imagined by Yvonne Rainer in her use of the remote plotting device in *Carriage Discreteness* (1966). The actors of the Wooster Group or the Builders Association also follow a precise dramaturgy; they are operators of multimediated scenarios, roles, image and sound (re)productions. In *Alladdeen,* the actors literally act out Indian "call operators" whose telecommunicational roleplaying in an American global economy makes them live-edit their voices and their images. As audience members, we watch how the actors (and technicians) manipulate the images of their wishful selves on the projected surfaces of a fully technologized proscenium stage (faces merged with faces of actors from a popular TV series).

But the audience in kondition pluriel's *the puppet(s)* is invited to touch and disturb the performers to an extent which no longer allows the performer to know in advance what will unfold and what is inscribed both physically and digitally within the recursive, dynamic system. In this scenario, as in many instances of interactive installations, performance departs from constructed linearity and becomes submerged in generative, emergent, adaptive processes, transmuted into virtual environments or gaming landscapes. "Thinking images" in intelligent architectures respond to the interactor and learn from movement and gestural behavior, perhaps even from more subtle, emotional expressions. Subtle interface techniques will be required for such interactive presences, when trained and untrained users move together to generate an intimate dialogue via an artificial life system (cf. *Intimate Transactions*). And as I have pointed out, we are increasingly able to study complex phenomena like dance, non-verbal movement and cognition with dynamic systems models and real-time capturing technologies. Performance practices are becoming the subject of scientific research, while artists turn to the sciences and their technical methodologies to explore the expansion of the sensorium. On a very large (and wildly successful) scale, Olafur Eliasson achieved such an expansion through the artificial atmosphere he built in his *Weather Project* at Tate Modern, where the public roamed in the vast envelope of luscious colored light. The experiential, sensorial embodiment leaves passive spectatorship and the central perspective of the theatrical and cinematic apparatus behind. The interactor will move to the foreground of cultural analysis, in the broadest sense, but also in the immediate context of digital art and its manifold interfaces. Iterative design processes and experimental testing of interfaces reveal artists are working within both scientific and artistic frameworks.

This allows me to broadly sketch propositions for an understanding of the roles of the interactor in performance scenarios: 1) on the stage (from the scenographic Wilson template to the Wooster Group's live post-production);

2) in kinaesthetic environments (kondition pluriel; Gretchen Schiller and Susan Kozel's kinesfields); 3) in user-oriented sensory installations (*Olfactorium, Kurort; Intimate Transactions*); and in translocal, networked spaces (Blast Theory, *Telematic Dreaming, Flying Birdman*):

The performers as post-producers

In this scenario, trained actors, dancers, or musicians operate/manipulate the multiple media modules, prerecorded data, and recording devices (audio, video) provided by the metadesign of the composition. They are embedded in the conceptual or programmed architecture, and their acting in such precisely scripted live montage—what Elizabeth LeCompte calls "dancing with technology"—is a form of editing. The enactment of the performance is its post-production.

The performers as interactors

In many of the examples described in this book, it was difficult to adhere to precise professional notions of dancer, actor, singer, musician, instrumentalist, etc., since these assignations are not very meaningful in the context of performances with real-time computational environments. I generally chose to speak of "performers" even if this term now also begins to be diffuse. We need new terminologies for an aesthetic no longer based on scripts, scores, and choreographies. When interactive performance is presented to a viewing public, the interactor engages a real-time system and environment of feedbacks that require specific subtle techniques to generate processes. While the software and hardware design for the environment may be deployed for specific purposes, and thus have a compositional or conceptual dimension, the performance application focuses on a reflexive and adaptive (often quasi-improvisatory) role of experience in the embodiment and articulation of the system's virtualities. The challenges of such virtual performances are particularly evident in situations where the interactor works with sensor interfaces (direct mapping) and wearables (emergent design). Referring to Company in Space, for example, I explained how fascinating it can be to observe an interactor wearing an electromagnetic motion tracking suit (Polhemus) on the torso, thus revealing directly how her movement explorations and expressions affect the virtual world, the avatars, or digital translations which are created and, in turn, affect the behavior of the person whose full bodily experience both drives the interface and self-moves, interlacing her body with the virtual. Intelligent fashion design will make the Polhemus disappear and turn clothing itself interactive.

The audience as interactors

In audience-directed interactive scenarios, the user has an immersive or sensorial experience of an environment in which perceptional/cognitive processes affect embodiment and open up transformative possibilities built into the reactive system that is designed for reciprocating actions. Properly speaking, this is the sphere of emergence in a distributed *chora*, a resonating space which might be experienced as chaotic by untrained interactors but which also allows intuitive and gradual learning processes absorbing the interactor into the ritual of a game or the internal emotional repercussions of the experience. Multi-layered digital installations generally affect a shift of sensory registers from the visual to the aural, proprioceptive and tactile, and therefore the orientations of the interactor, her psychic dispositions toward space, time, and self-organization (codes of behavior), are challenged and prosthetically extended. Interactive behavior has nothing to do anymore with choreography or "dancing with technologies," but enacts synaesthetic processes which constitute the physical involvement, the coupling of organism and virtual environment.

The (multi)players as online community

The collective telematic scenario points to translocal spaces of interactivity where the mutual incorporation of remote sites and actions, with the real-time feedback processes, is complicated by the contingent rhythms of transmission which create a nervous system—a kind of unstable atmosphere. In this atmospheric metabolism, single authorship and the signatures of design and choreography dissolve, as multi-player collaboration with real-time media transmissions is based on fundamental assumptions of distributed, networked content. Aesthetic criteria for "content" have not settled down yet, genres have not been stratified. This is perhaps the most interesting and vexing side of digital performance, since with live online art the question of the "object" is muted, and the "experience" is difficult to locate if processual interaction implies an aesthetics of intuitive relations between relations, between expressions generated by team-play through all available mediums, where the mediums themselves are changed by the expressions. The semantic implications of such a collaborative environment, a digital commons with interactive platforms for multi-players, suggest something else, then. The content of performing "play" in a social laboratory of co-presences grows out of the dynamic and affective (subjective) experience of intersensitivity itself.

The heterotopic presence of such interactive multimodal platforms is a contemporary phenomenon that reaches into countless imagined communities of interest (from game cultures and activist networks to weblogs and YouTube). Once you engage distributed real-time interaction strategies and negotiations for data sharing and processing, you tend to operate in a wholly mediated sphere without established (choreographic) principles of data sharing. There's not one measure of counting, but many exchanged and changing protocols. The studio, the phenomenal place, where some of the action might be generated, recedes from sight. Again, you are left with a beautiful paradox: it is to be assumed that the interface is tactile, kinaesthetic, close to the skin—someone there and someone else over there perform, write, move, touch instruments, create and respond in dialogue. Energies are exchanged and affect the atmospheric conditions in which they are created. And yet performances built on media interaction and data transmission tend to disconnect from physical context and decompose, no documentation able to recover (fully) the distributed interaction. The traces of the synergy resonate in the continuous coming together of human and technical presences, the connecting movement that has become a part of your biological movement.

Index